TOWER OF THE FUTURE

Vol. 3

by Saki Hiwatari

TOWER OF THE FUTURE
CAST OF CHARACTERS

▲ **TAKERU MATSUYUKI:**
AN IMAGINATIVE TEENAGER
WITH A LOT ON HIS MIND.

▲ **ICHIGO SUZUNARI:**
A BRIGHT, ENERGETIC
YOUNG GIRL WHO TAKERU
HAS A CRUSH ON.

◄ **ZEN HOKUOUIN:**
A MYSTERIOUS
KINDERGARTEN-
AGE BOY.

◄ **KENTO
MATSUYUKI:**
TAKERU'S FATHER.

**KIMIE
MATSUYUKI►**
TAKERU'S MOTHER;
SHE DIED IN A CAR
ACCIDENT.

▲ **HYOUJU MAXWELL**
(AKA HYOUJU MATSUYUKI):
TAKERU'S HALF-SISTER.

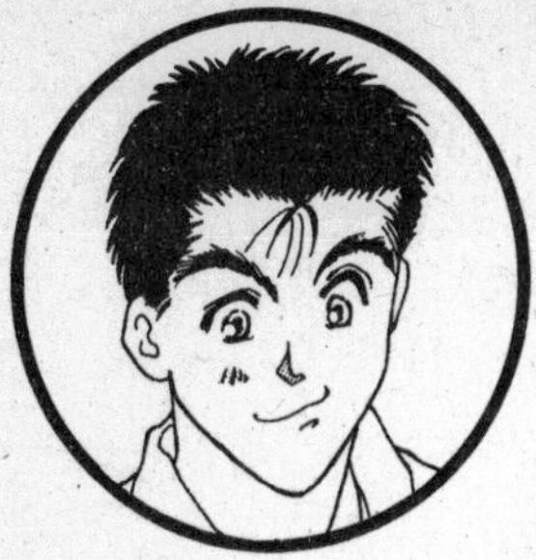

◀ **DAIGO TSUKIKAWA**: TAKERU'S FRIEND SINCE CHILDHOOD. A HAPPY-GO-LUCKY GUY.

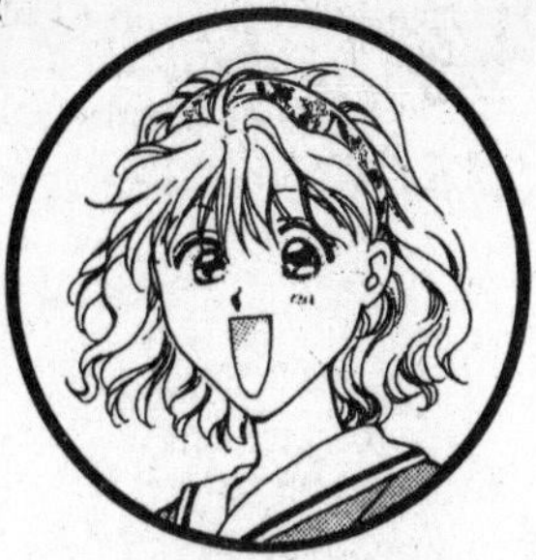

SEIKA NISHIZAWA: ▶ SHE SITS NEXT TO TAKERU AT SCHOOL; SHE'S ALSO ICHIGO'S BEST FRIEND.

▼ **KOUKI NODA**: TAKERU'S CLASSMATE; VERY STRONG-WILLED.

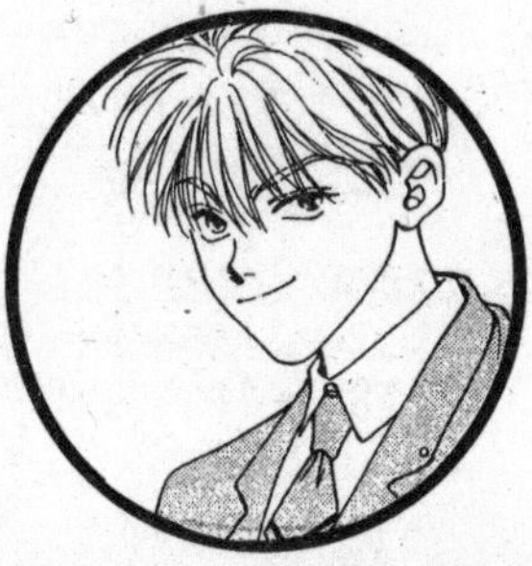

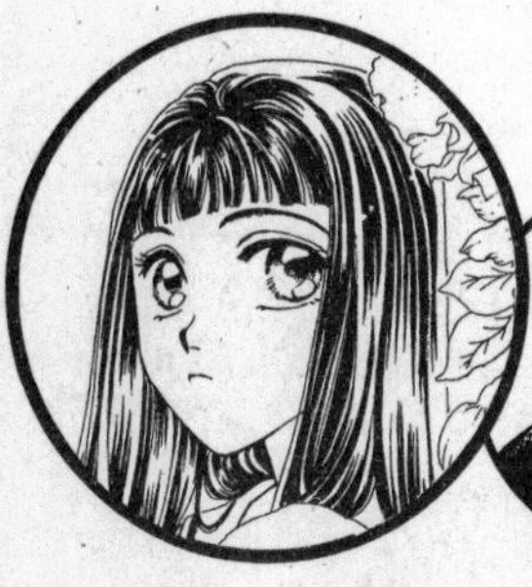

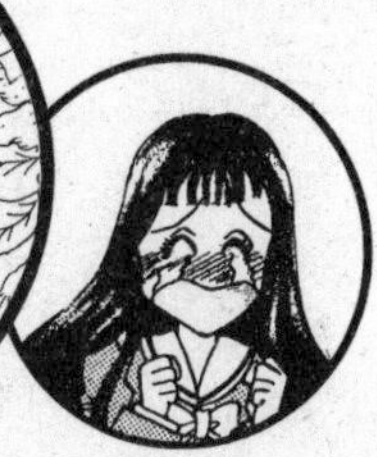

▲ **YORUKO TOUSAWA**: TAKERU'S CLASSMATE AND IS VERY COOL AND BEAUTIFUL.

▲ **MIYA TOUSAWA**: YORUKO'S TWIN SISTER.

While on a tour of Honami High School, middle-schooler Takeru Matsuyuki fell in love at first sight with Ichigo Matsunari, a student from another school.

Takeru's excitement soon turned to tragedy as his mother was in an auto accident and he learned a family secret on her death-bed—that he had a half-sister named Hyouju. After the funeral, Takeru's father wanted to bring Hyouju to Japan to live with them and after an initial fight, Takeru agreed.

Spring comes and Takeru learns he didn't make it into Honami High School. Disappointed, he attends Tennendou High, thinking his true-love isn't even at the same school...until he learns her class is actually right next to his! Then, after school, Takeru gets in an argument with Zen and inadvertently confesses his love to Ichigo...

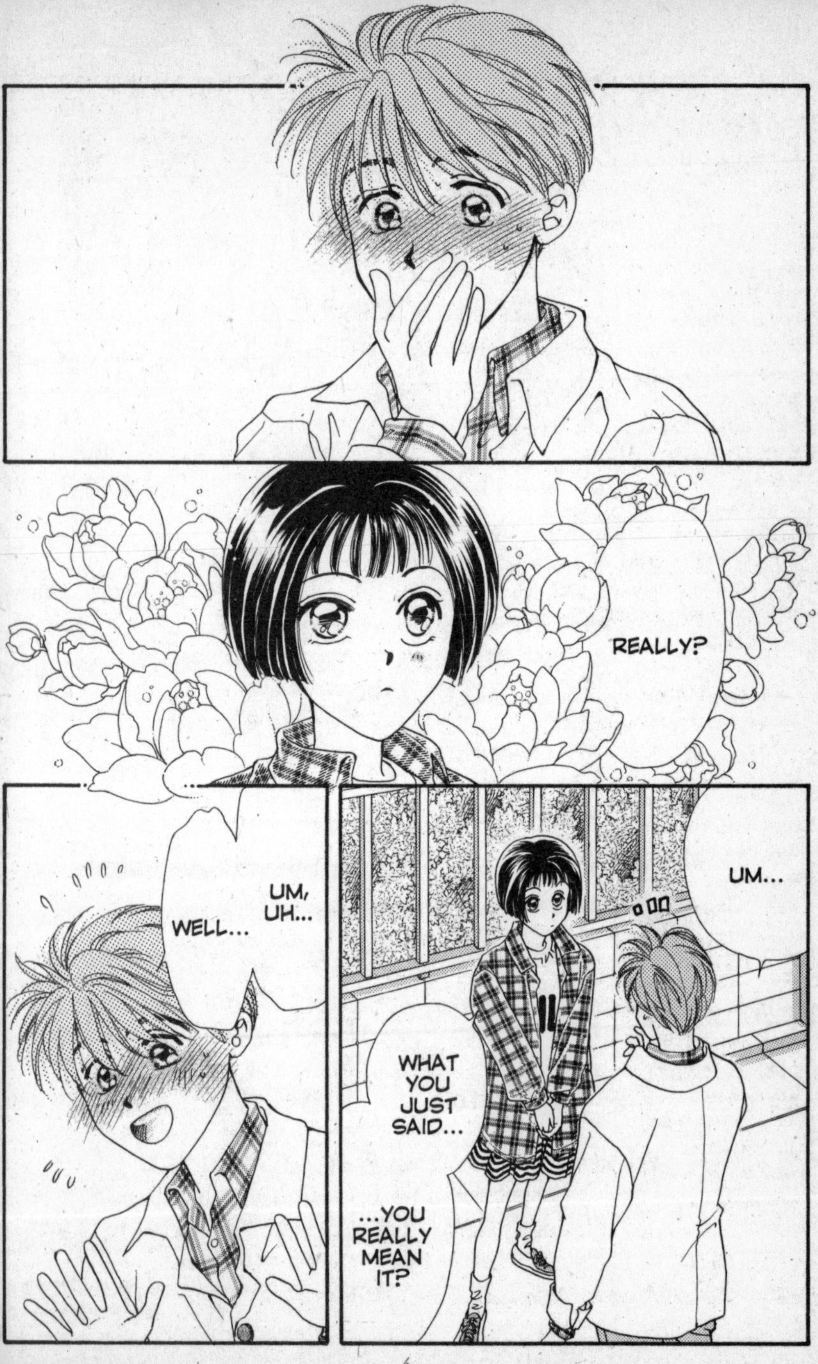
REALLY?
UM...
WHAT YOU JUST SAID...
...YOU REALLY MEAN IT?
UM, UH...
WELL...

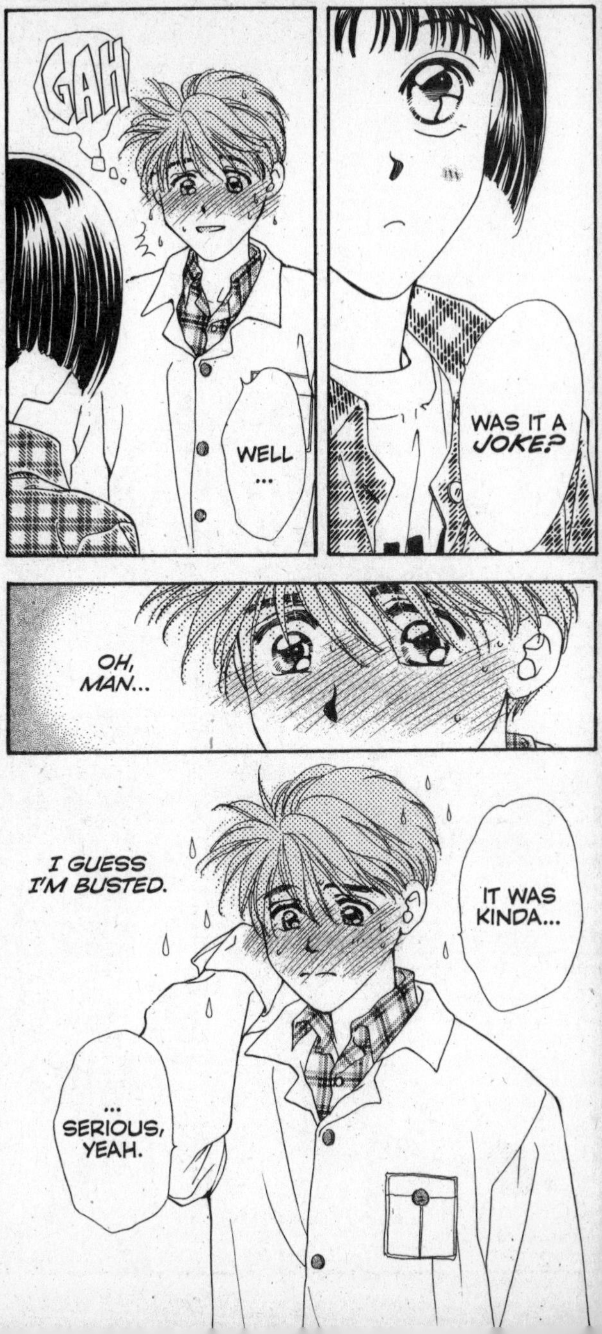
WAS IT A JOKE?
GAH
WELL ...
OH, MAN...
IT WAS KINDA...
I GUESS I'M BUSTED.
... SERIOUS, YEAH.

Sidebar No. 1

Long time no see! Last time, in this little sidebar here, I wrote that I was really enjoying Final Fantasy VI. I got so many letters about that! Final Fantasy VI seems to have a lot of devoted fans! Well, since that installment, I've gone on to play and complete Final Fantasy IV and V as well. I especially liked Final Fantasy V. The characters have a lot of simple emotion. It's easy to relate to them. Man, right here from the beginning, I'm talking about games. If you don't care about videogames, my apologies!! Ahh...there's no use avoiding talking about them. They're too much fun. Everyone who sent me doujinshi, mix tapes, CDs--thank you very much! I'm listening to them everyday!

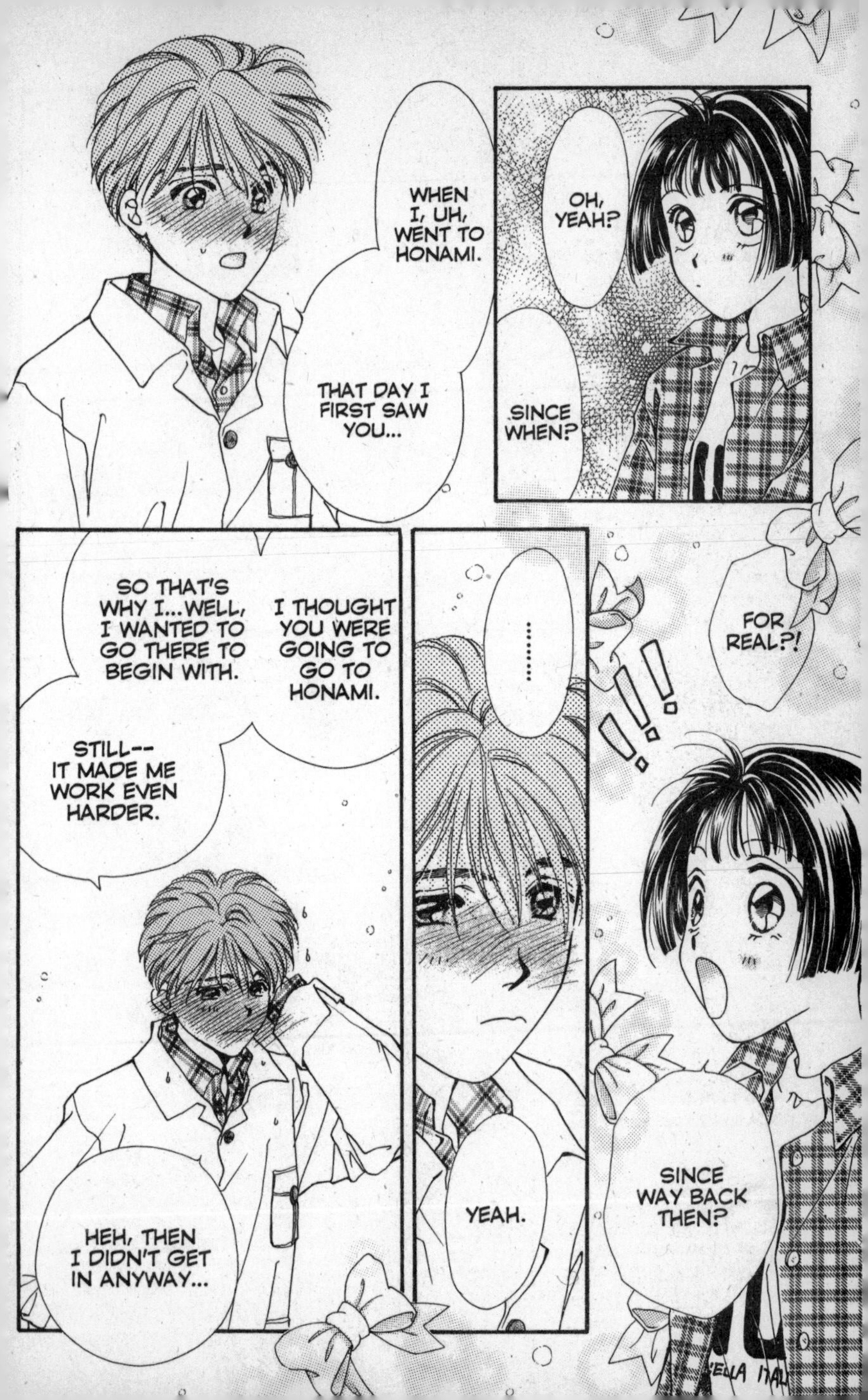
OH, YEAH?
SINCE WHEN?
WHEN I, UH, WENT TO HONAMI.
THAT DAY I FIRST SAW YOU...
FOR REAL?!
!!!
SINCE WAY BACK THEN?
......
YEAH.
I THOUGHT YOU WERE GOING TO GO TO HONAMI.
SO THAT'S WHY I...WELL, I WANTED TO GO THERE TO BEGIN WITH.
STILL-- IT MADE ME WORK EVEN HARDER.
HEH, THEN I DIDN'T GET IN ANYWAY...

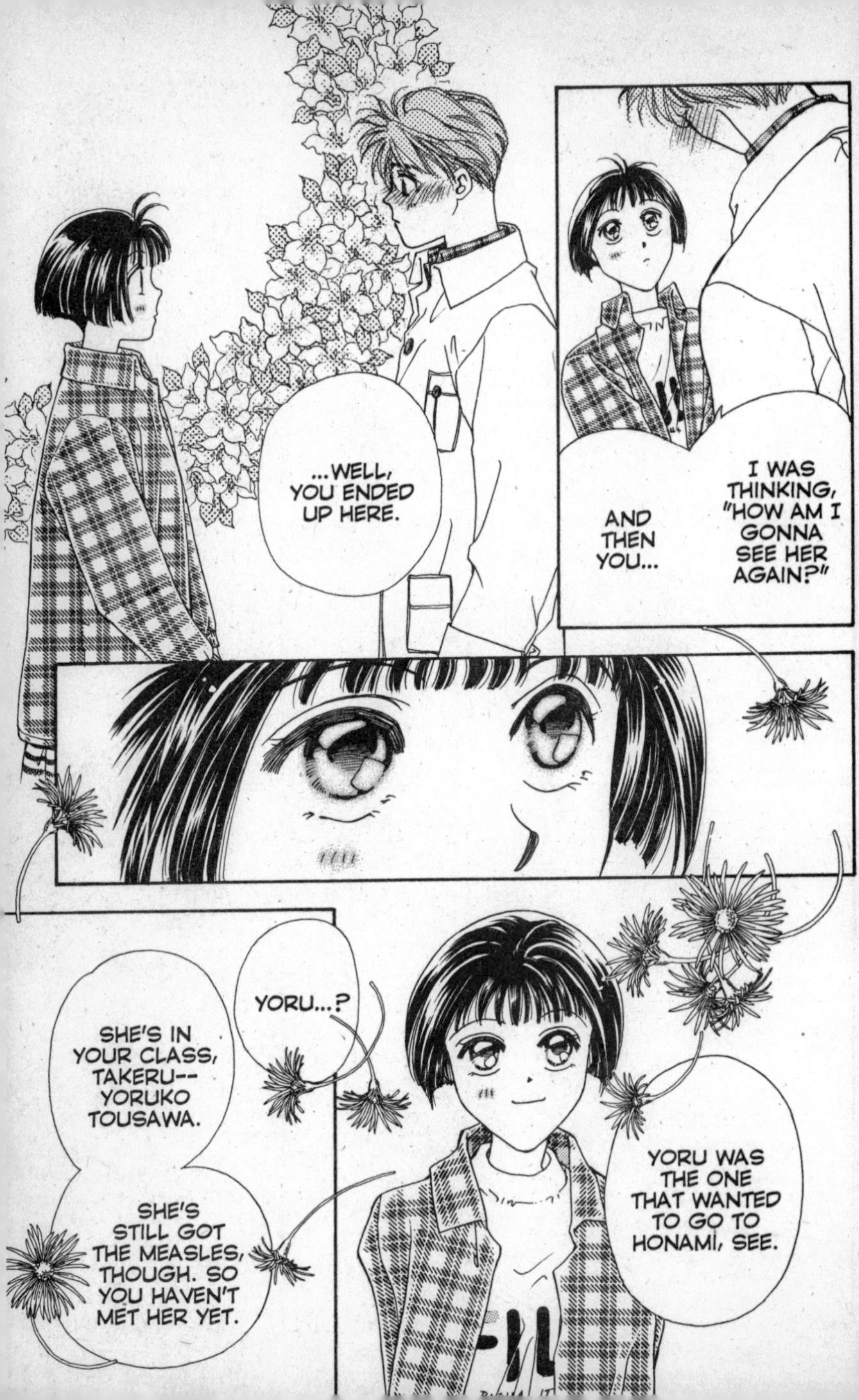
I WAS THINKING, "HOW AM I GONNA SEE HER AGAIN?"
AND THEN YOU...
...WELL, YOU ENDED UP HERE.
YORU WAS THE ONE THAT WANTED TO GO TO HONAMI, SEE.
YORU...?
SHE'S IN YOUR CLASS, TAKERU-- YORUKO TOUSAWA.
SHE'S STILL GOT THE MEASLES, THOUGH. SO YOU HAVEN'T MET HER YET.

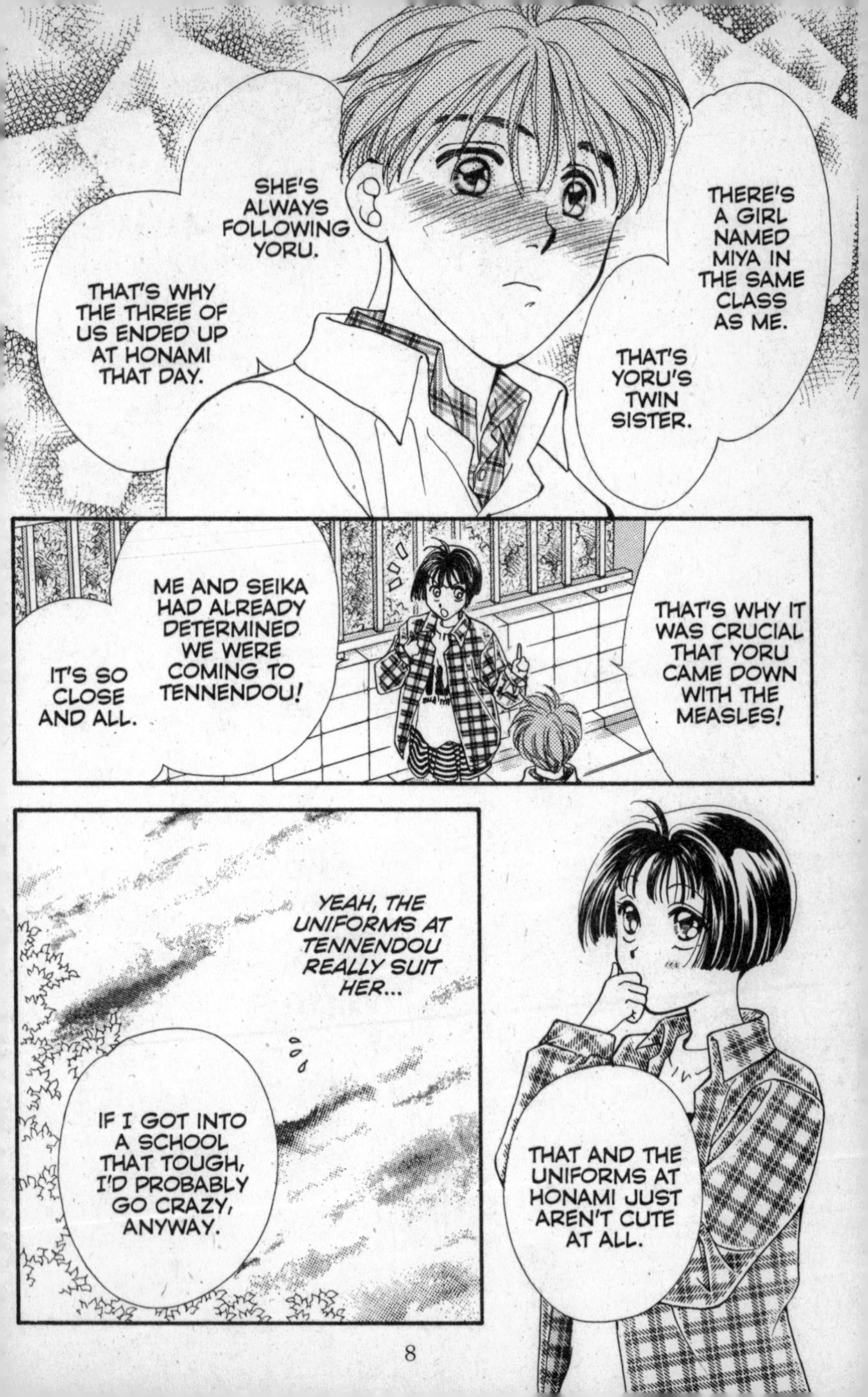
THERE'S A GIRL NAMED MIYA IN THE SAME CLASS AS ME.
THAT'S YORU'S TWIN SISTER.
SHE'S ALWAYS FOLLOWING YORU.
THAT'S WHY THE THREE OF US ENDED UP AT HONAMI THAT DAY.
THAT'S WHY IT WAS CRUCIAL THAT YORU CAME DOWN WITH THE MEASLES!
ME AND SEIKA HAD ALREADY DETERMINED WE WERE COMING TO TENNENDOU!
IT'S SO CLOSE AND ALL.
THAT AND THE UNIFORMS AT HONAMI JUST AREN'T CUTE AT ALL.
YEAH, THE UNIFORMS AT TENNENDOU REALLY SUIT HER...
IF I GOT INTO A SCHOOL THAT TOUGH, I'D PROBABLY GO CRAZY, ANYWAY.

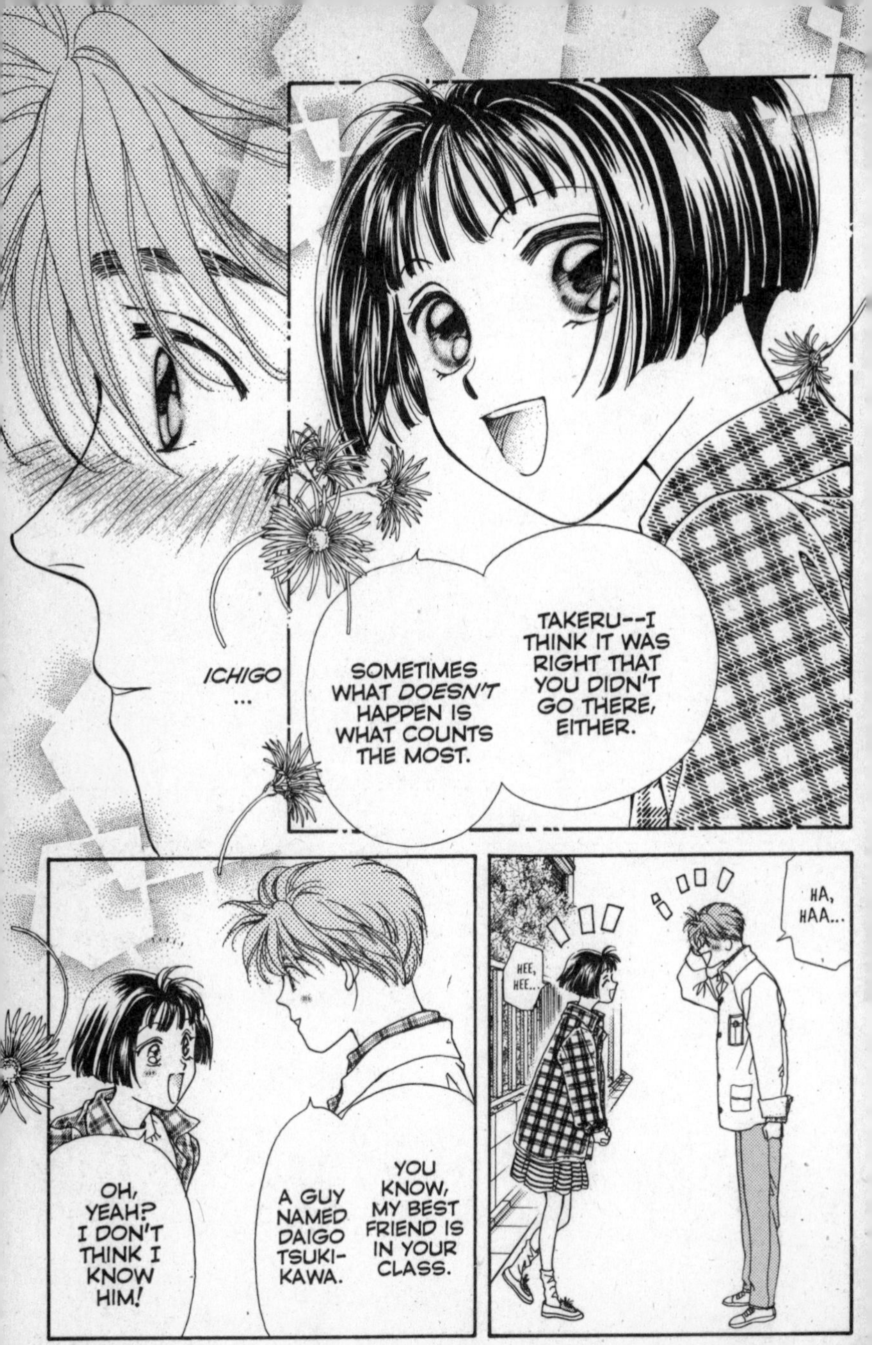
TAKERU--I THINK IT WAS RIGHT THAT YOU DIDN'T GO THERE, EITHER.
SOMETIMES WHAT *DOESN'T* HAPPEN IS WHAT COUNTS THE MOST.
ICHIGO ...
HA, HAA...
HEE, HEE...
YOU KNOW, MY BEST FRIEND IS IN YOUR CLASS.
A GUY NAMED DAIGO TSUKI-KAWA.
OH, YEAH? I DON'T THINK I KNOW HIM!

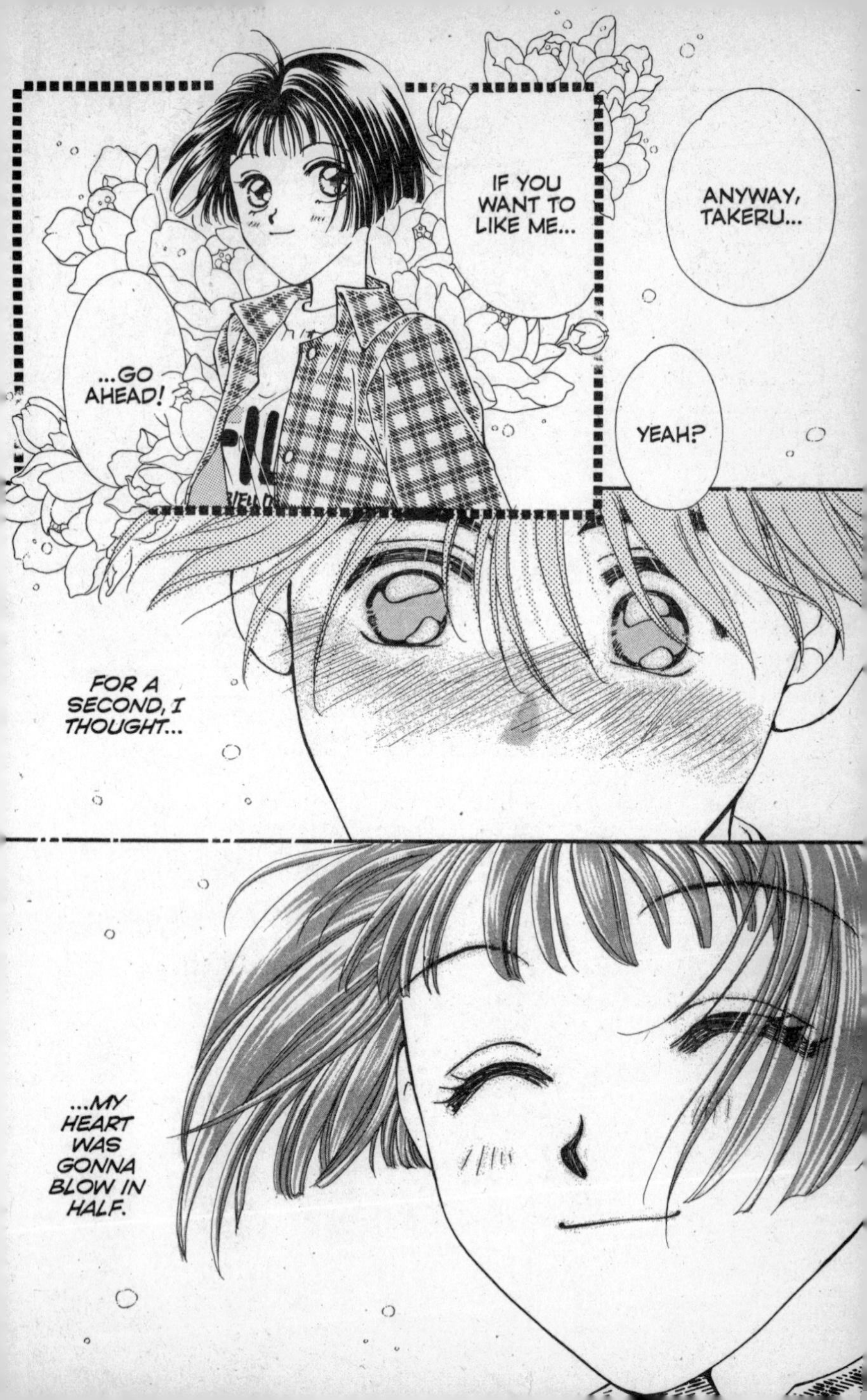
ANYWAY, TAKERU...
YEAH?
IF YOU WANT TO LIKE ME...
...GO AHEAD!
FOR A SECOND, I THOUGHT...
...MY HEART WAS GONNA BLOW IN HALF.

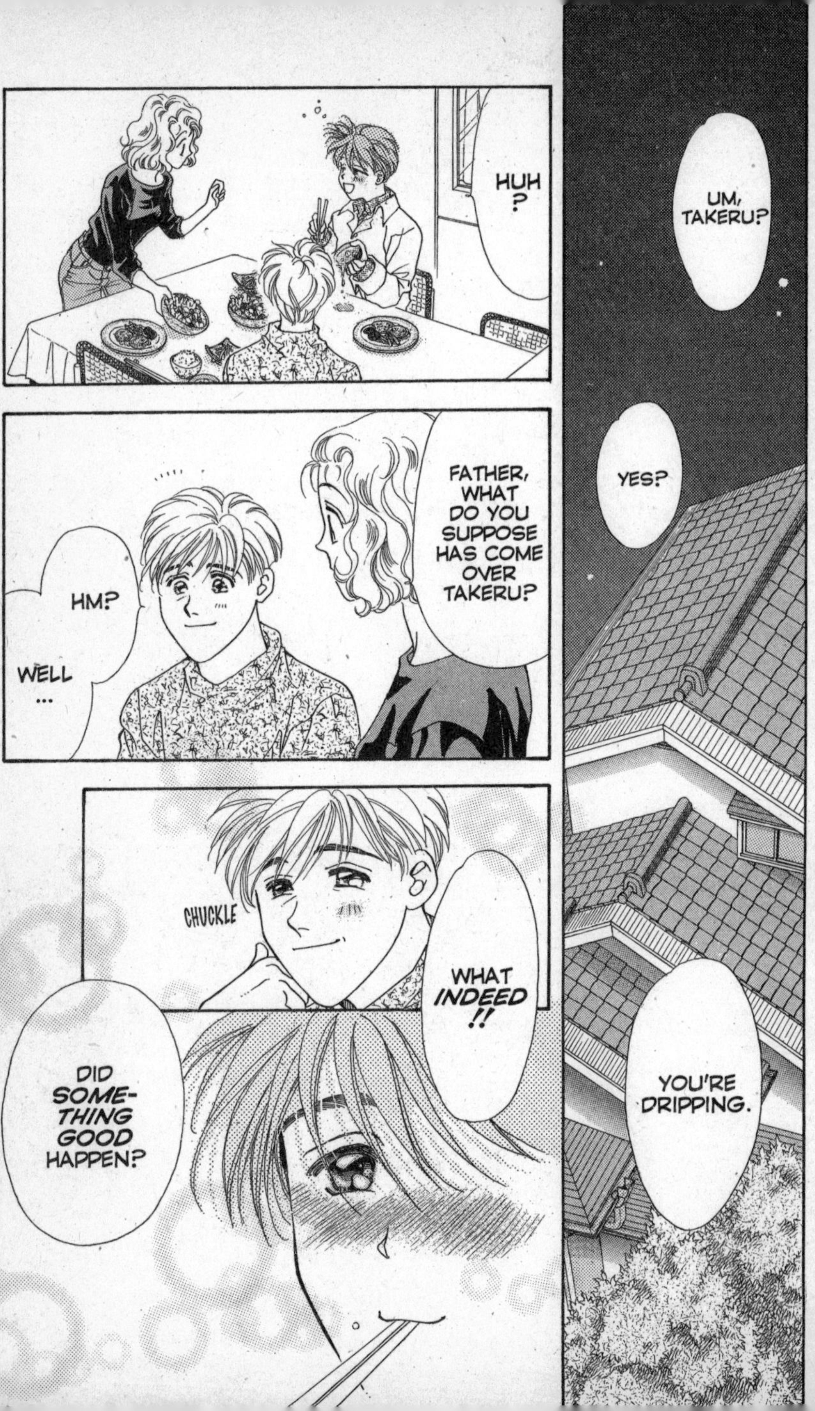
UM, TAKERU?
YES?
YOU'RE DRIPPING.
HUH ?
FATHER, WHAT DO YOU SUPPOSE HAS COME OVER TAKERU?
HM?
WELL ...
WHAT INDEED !!
CHUCKLE
DID SOMETHING GOOD HAPPEN?

BRAVE KNIGHT!
WAS IT FATE...
...THAT WE SHOULD MEET IN SUCH A WAY?
COMMAND
Speak to Ichigo
Cuddle with Ichigo
Hold hands with Ichigo
Investigate Ichigo
Have dinner with Ichigo
Go to an inn with Ichigo
OH, MY GOD!!!

Sidebar No. 2

Anyway!! Final Fantasy V's main character, Butz! I can't think of anyone to play him other than SMAP's Kusanagi-kun. If he were made up to look something like Yoshitaka Amano's original character art, man, girls would go nuts over him. I'm always watching TV dramas while I'm working on my manga, and I really like Kusanagi-kun. Still, there are a lot of other young actors on television these days, and a lot of them are starting to look like Yoshitaka Amano drawings. This is a good thing! I immediately think, "Oh, this guy could play Faris..." or something like that. And then baseball or something comes on and I lose interest. Hmmm...

I don't care
if there's an
ending or not.

I just want to
continue this
journey with
my beloved.

Even until the
end of the world!!

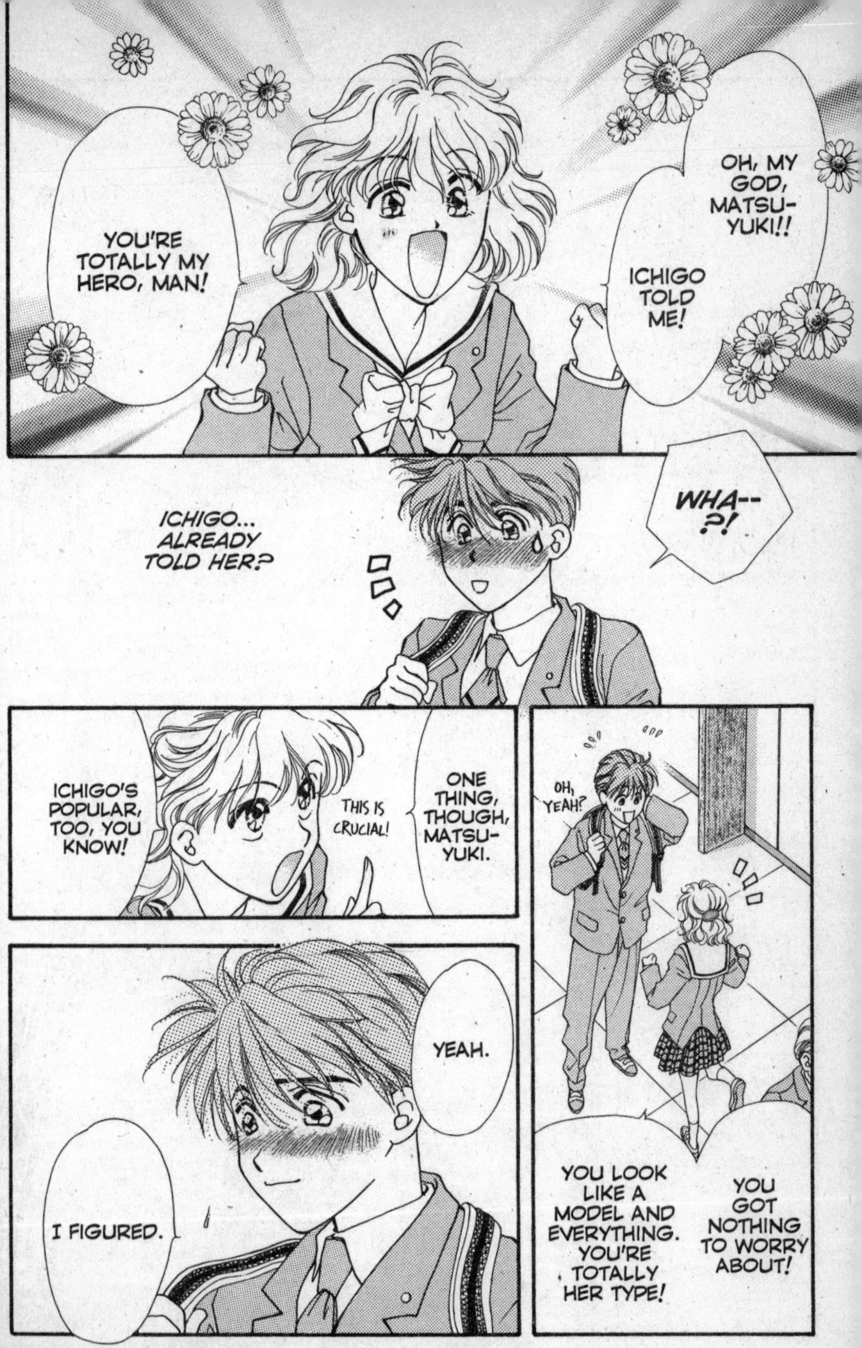
OH, MY GOD, MATSU-YUKI!!
ICHIGO TOLD ME!
YOU'RE TOTALLY MY HERO, MAN!
WHA-- ?!
ICHIGO... ALREADY TOLD HER?
OH, YEAH?
YOU GOT NOTHING TO WORRY ABOUT!
YOU LOOK LIKE A MODEL AND EVERYTHING. YOU'RE TOTALLY HER TYPE!
ONE THING, THOUGH, MATSU-YUKI.
THIS IS CRUCIAL!
ICHIGO'S POPULAR, TOO, YOU KNOW!
YEAH.
I FIGURED.

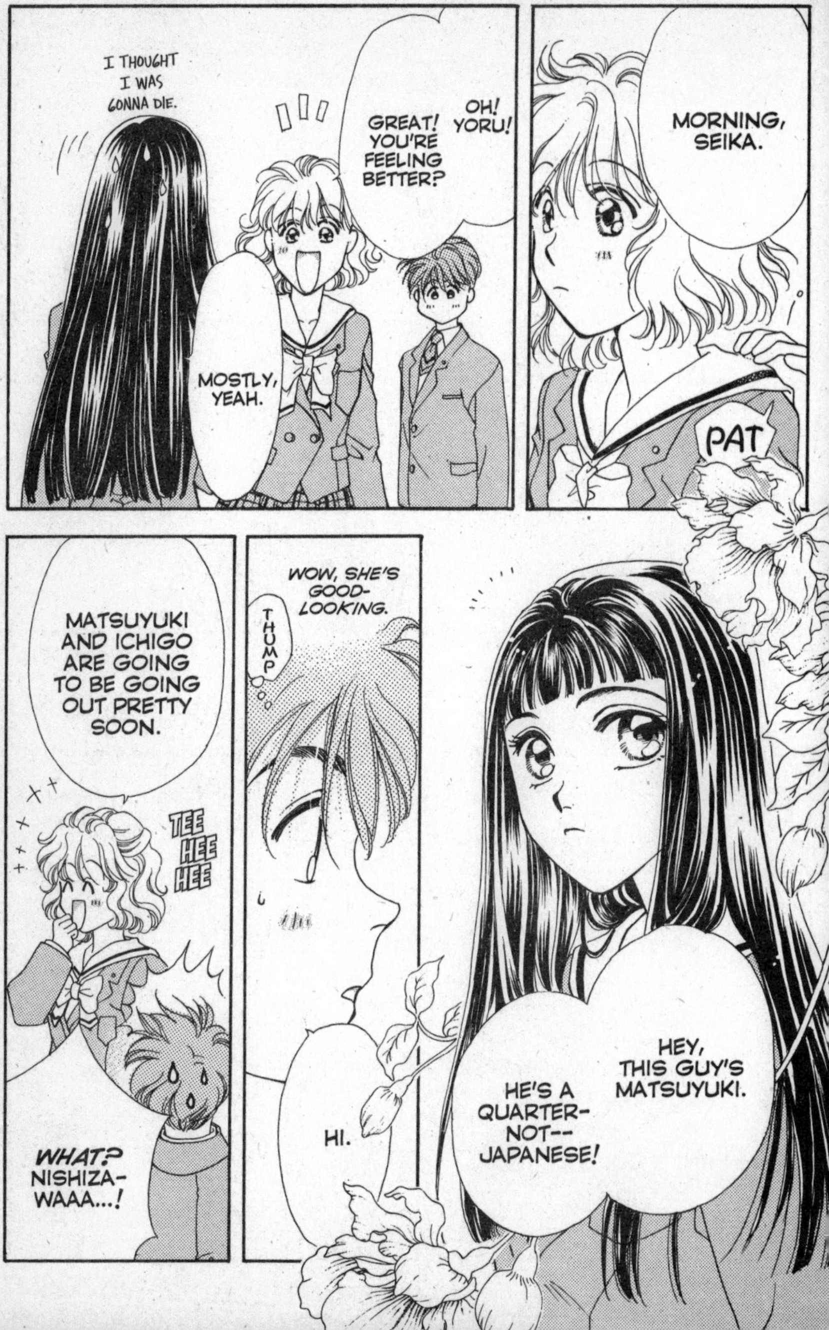
MORNING, SEIKA.
PAT
OH! YORU!
GREAT! YOU'RE FEELING BETTER?
I THOUGHT I WAS GONNA DIE.
MOSTLY, YEAH.
HEY, THIS GUY'S MATSUYUKI.
HE'S A QUARTER-NOT--JAPANESE!
WOW, SHE'S GOOD-LOOKING.
THUMP
HI.
MATSUYUKI AND ICHIGO ARE GOING TO BE GOING OUT PRETTY SOON.
TEE HEE HEE
WHAT? NISHIZA-WAAA...!

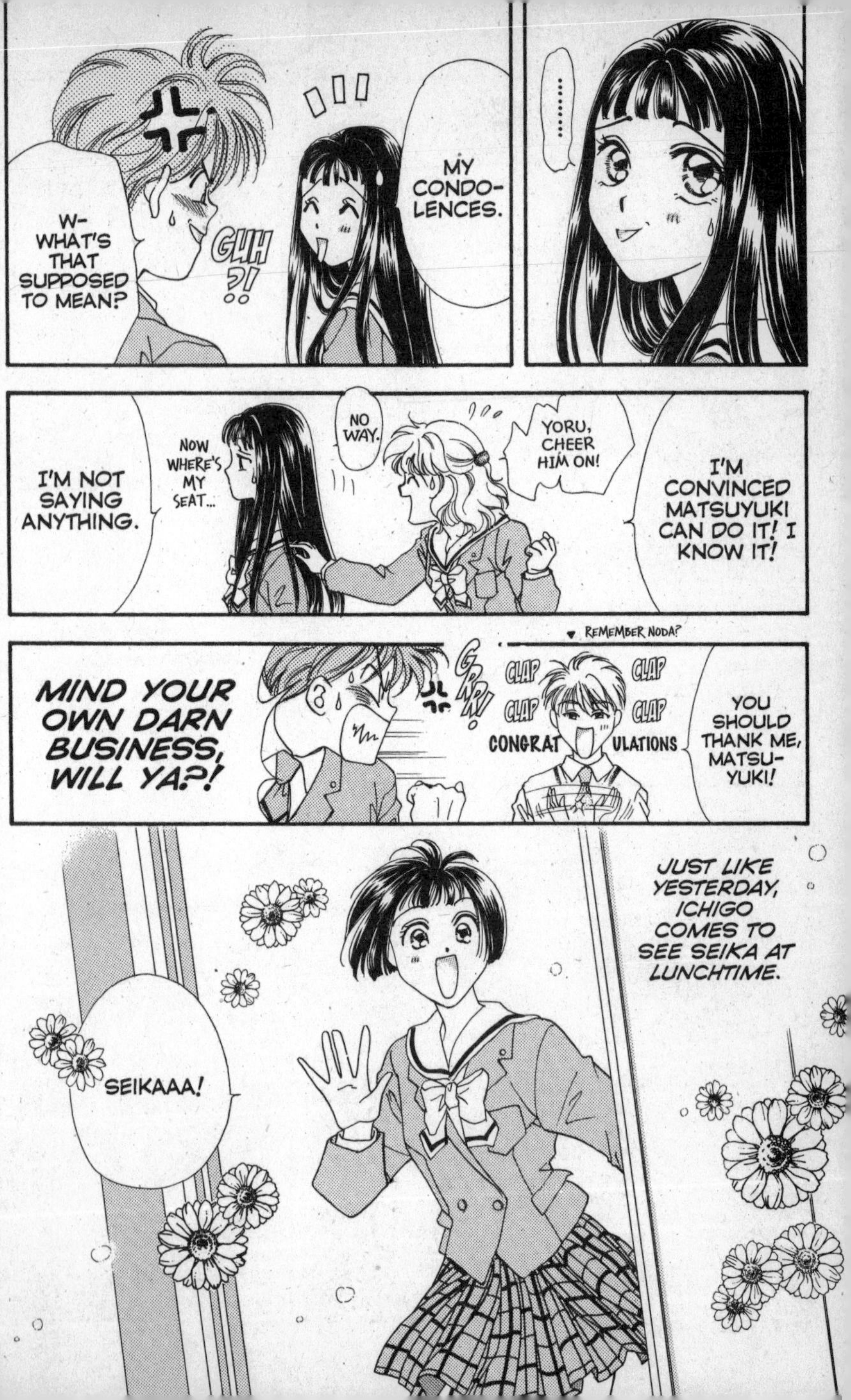
......
MY CONDO-LENCES.
GUH ?!
W-WHAT'S THAT SUPPOSED TO MEAN?
I'M CONVINCED MATSUYUKI CAN DO IT! I KNOW IT!
YORU, CHEER HIM ON!
NO WAY.
NOW WHERE'S MY SEAT...
I'M NOT SAYING ANYTHING.
REMEMBER NODA?
YOU SHOULD THANK ME, MATSUYUKI!
CLAP
CLAP
CLAP
CLAP
CONGRAT ULATIONS
GRR!
MIND YOUR OWN DARN BUSINESS, WILL YA?!
JUST LIKE YESTERDAY, ICHIGO COMES TO SEE SEIKA AT LUNCHTIME.
SEIKAAA!

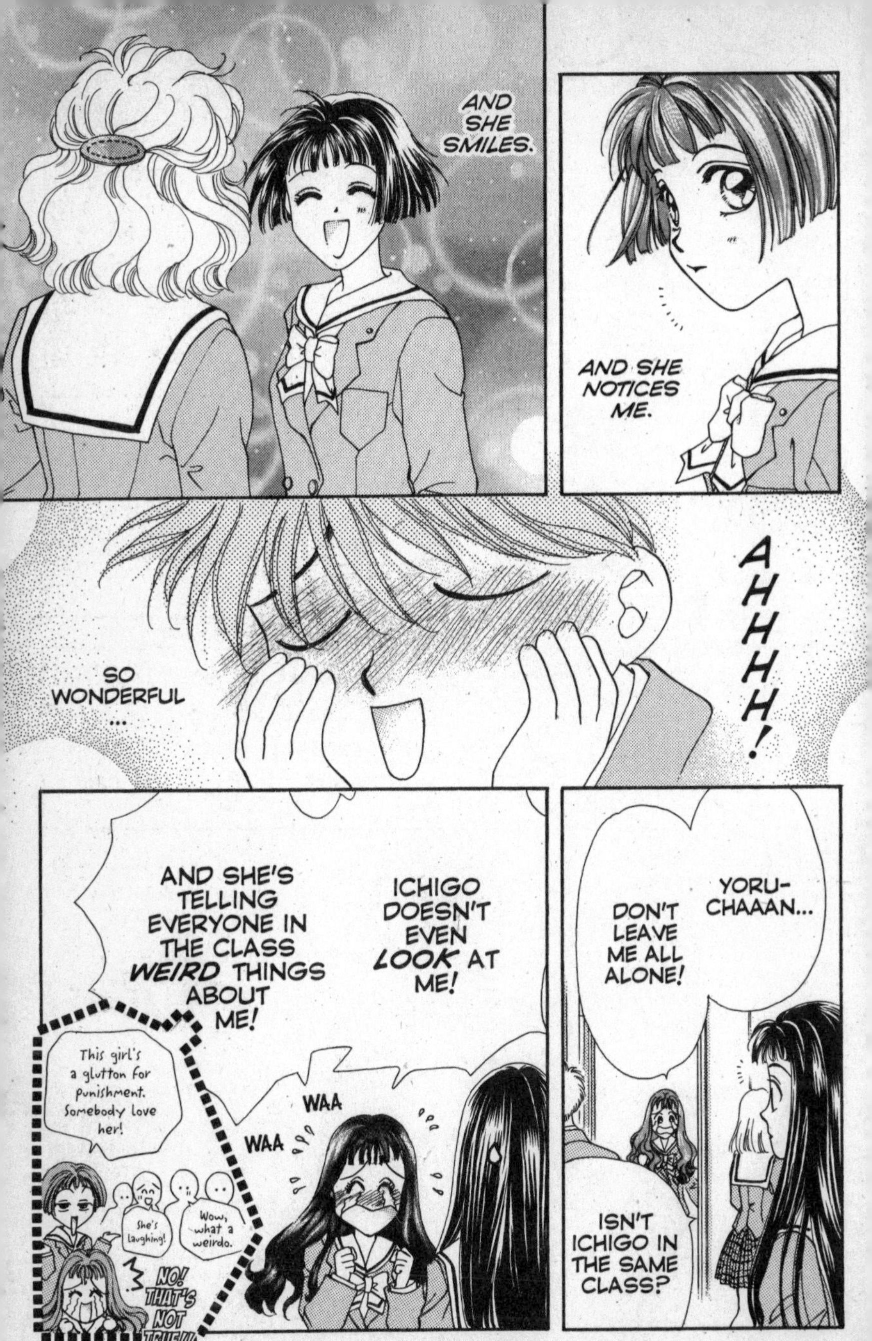
AND SHE NOTICES ME.
AND SHE SMILES.
AHHHHH!
SO WONDERFUL ...
YORU-CHAAAN...
DON'T LEAVE ME ALL ALONE!
ISN'T ICHIGO IN THE SAME CLASS?
ICHIGO DOESN'T EVEN LOOK AT ME!
AND SHE'S TELLING EVERYONE IN THE CLASS WEIRD THINGS ABOUT ME!
WAA
WAA
This girl's a glutton for punishment. Somebody love her!
Wow, what a weirdo.
She's laughing!
NO! THAT'S NOT TRUE!!

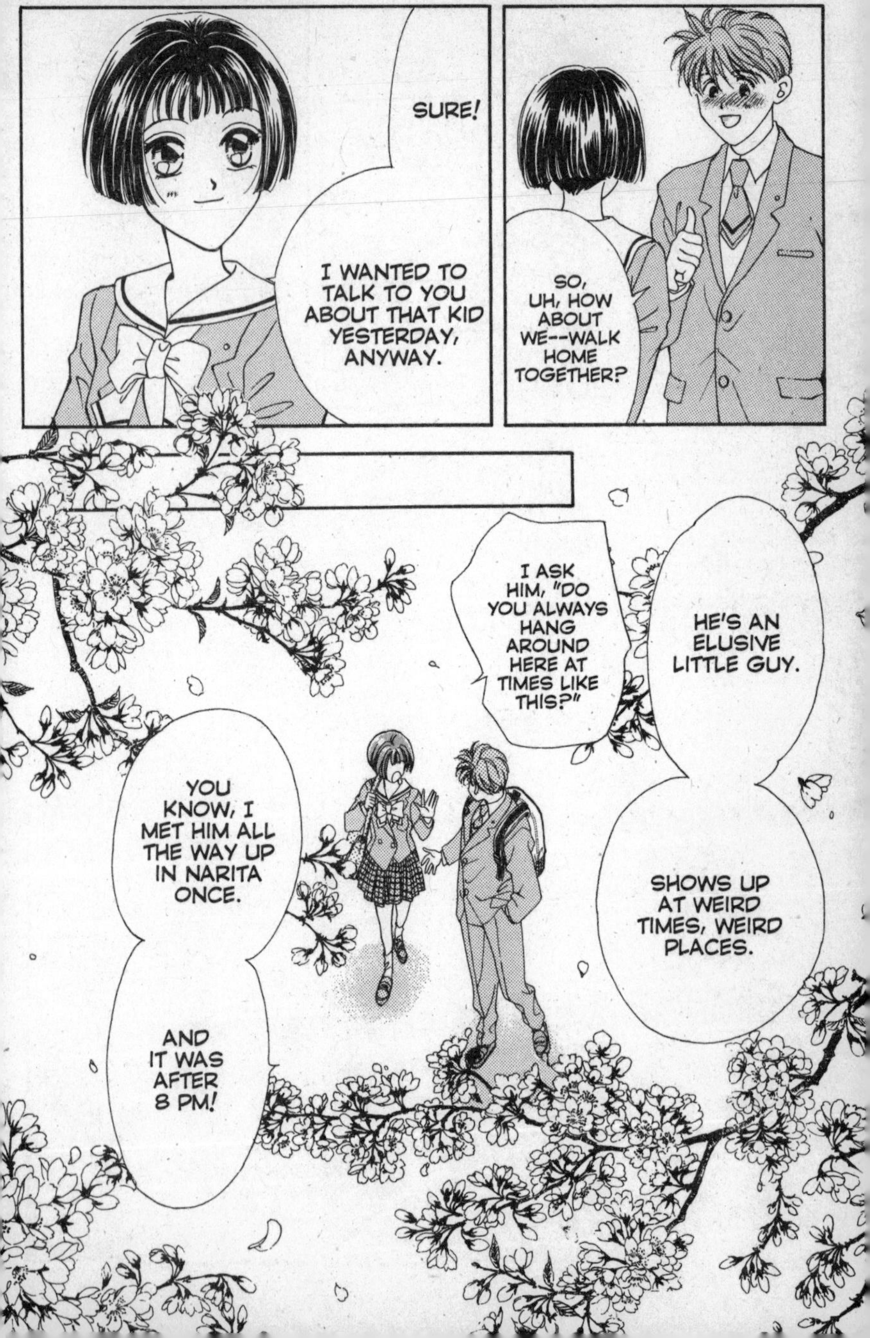
SO, UH, HOW ABOUT WE--WALK HOME TOGETHER?
SURE!
I WANTED TO TALK TO YOU ABOUT THAT KID YESTERDAY, ANYWAY.
HE'S AN ELUSIVE LITTLE GUY.
SHOWS UP AT WEIRD TIMES, WEIRD PLACES.
I ASK HIM, "DO YOU ALWAYS HANG AROUND HERE AT TIMES LIKE THIS?"
YOU KNOW, I MET HIM ALL THE WAY UP IN NARITA ONCE.
AND IT WAS AFTER 8 PM!

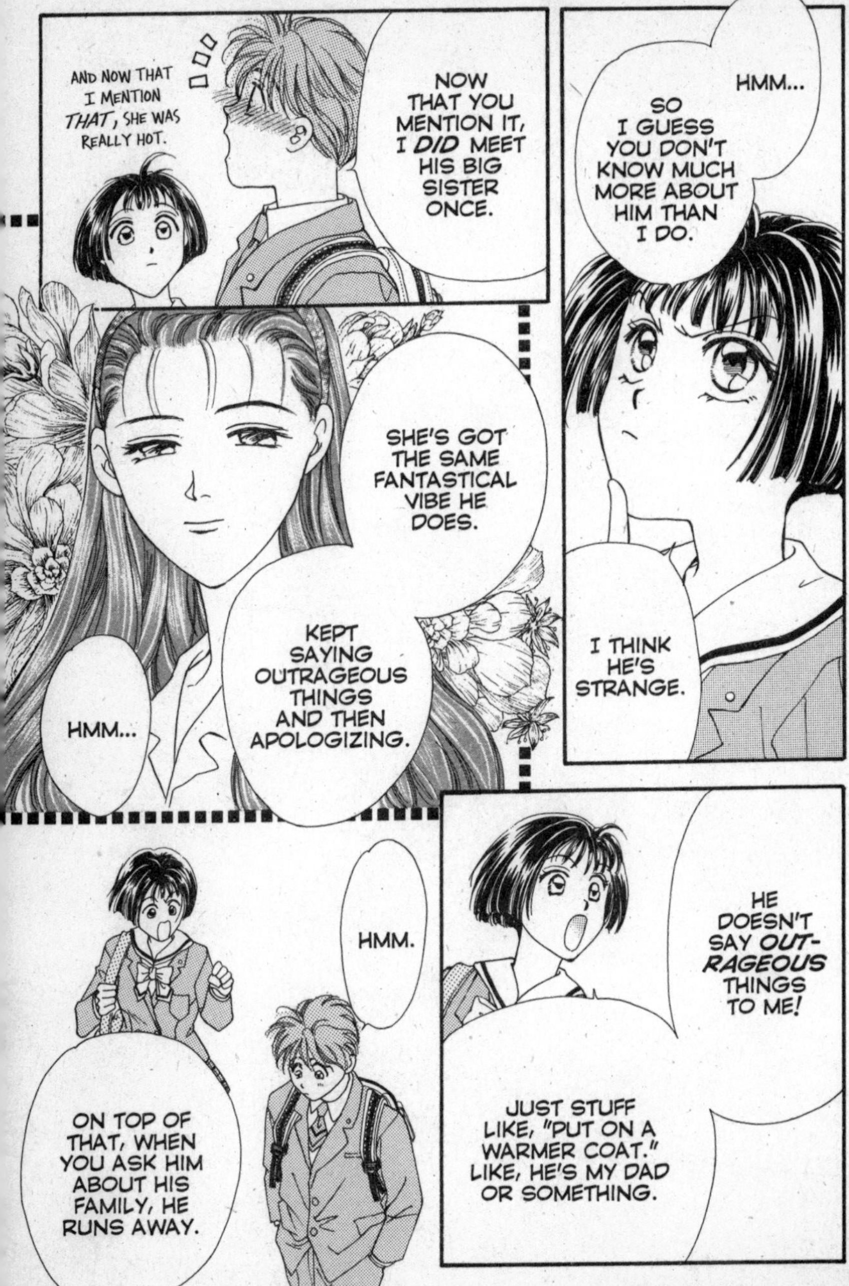
HMM...
SO I GUESS YOU DON'T KNOW MUCH MORE ABOUT HIM THAN I DO.
I THINK HE'S STRANGE.
NOW THAT YOU MENTION IT, I *DID* MEET HIS BIG SISTER ONCE.
AND NOW THAT I MENTION *THAT*, SHE WAS REALLY HOT.
SHE'S GOT THE SAME FANTASTICAL VIBE HE DOES.
KEPT SAYING OUTRAGEOUS THINGS AND THEN APOLOGIZING.
HMM...
HE DOESN'T SAY *OUTRAGEOUS* THINGS TO ME!
JUST STUFF LIKE, "PUT ON A WARMER COAT." LIKE, HE'S MY DAD OR SOMETHING.
HMM.
ON TOP OF THAT, WHEN YOU ASK HIM ABOUT HIS FAMILY, HE RUNS AWAY.

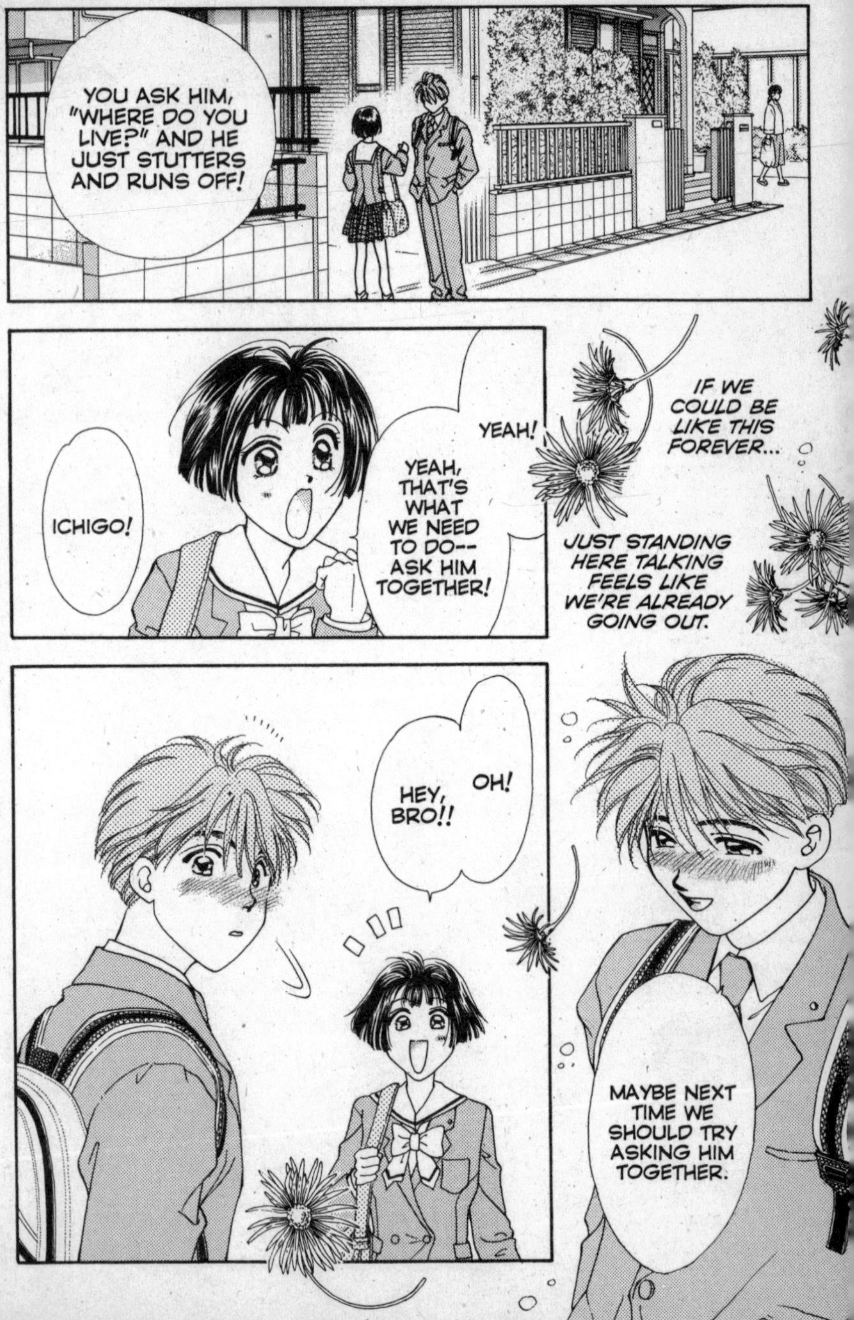
YOU ASK HIM, "WHERE DO YOU LIVE?" AND HE JUST STUTTERS AND RUNS OFF!
IF WE COULD BE LIKE THIS FOREVER...
JUST STANDING HERE TALKING FEELS LIKE WE'RE ALREADY GOING OUT.
YEAH!
YEAH, THAT'S WHAT WE NEED TO DO-- ASK HIM TOGETHER!
ICHIGO!
MAYBE NEXT TIME WE SHOULD TRY ASKING HIM TOGETHER.
OH!
HEY, BRO!!

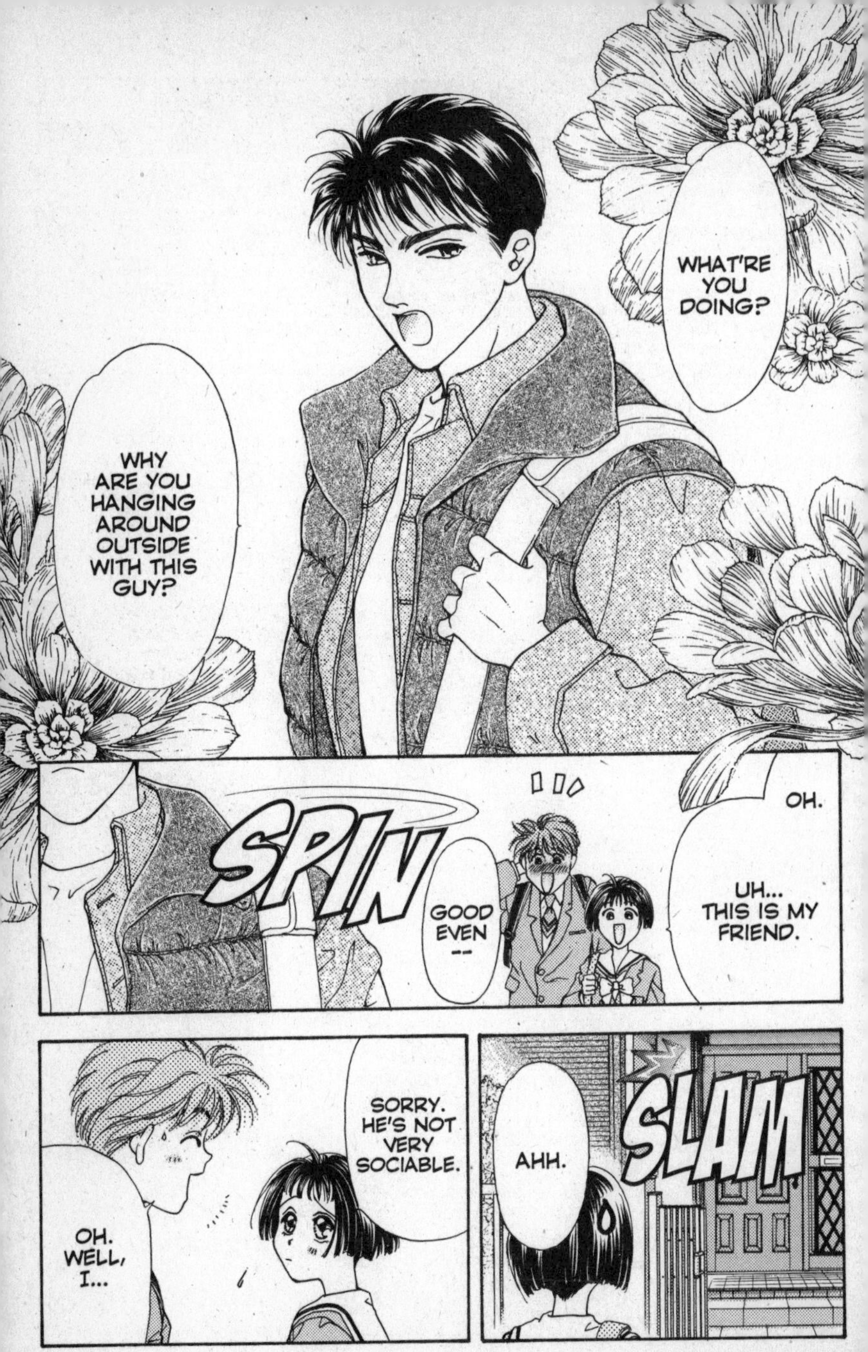
WHAT'RE YOU DOING?
WHY ARE YOU HANGING AROUND OUTSIDE WITH THIS GUY?
OH.
UH... THIS IS MY FRIEND.
GOOD EVEN --
SPIN
SLAM
AHH.
SORRY. HE'S NOT VERY SOCIABLE.
OH. WELL, I...

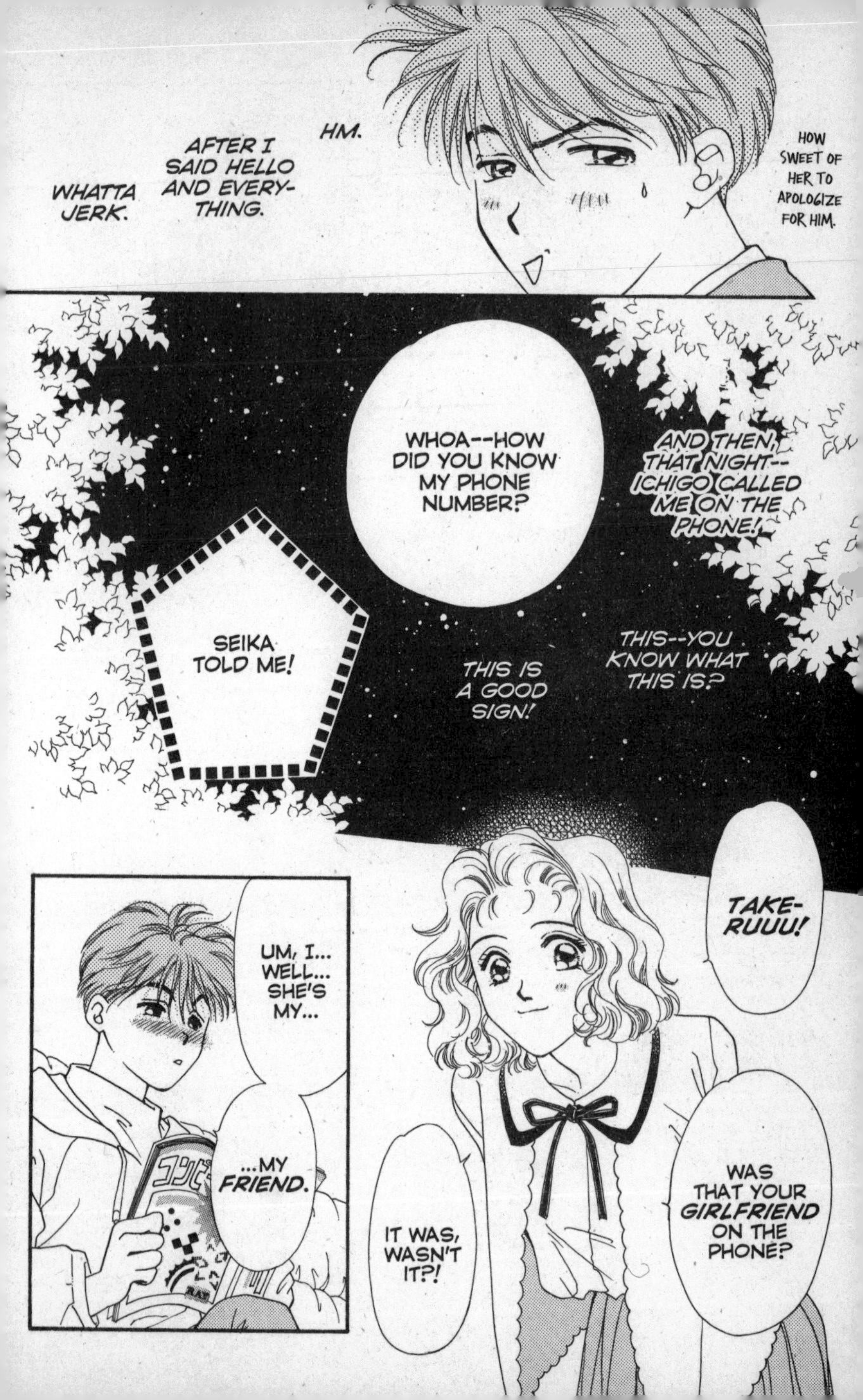
HOW SWEET OF HER TO APOLOGIZE FOR HIM.
HM.
AFTER I SAID HELLO AND EVERY-THING.
WHATTA JERK.
AND THEN, THAT NIGHT-- ICHIGO CALLED ME ON THE PHONE!
WHOA--HOW DID YOU KNOW MY PHONE NUMBER?
THIS--YOU KNOW WHAT THIS IS?
THIS IS A GOOD SIGN!
SEIKA TOLD ME!
TAKE-RUUU!
WAS THAT YOUR *GIRLFRIEND* ON THE PHONE?
IT WAS, WASN'T IT?!
UM, I... WELL... SHE'S MY...
...MY *FRIEND*.

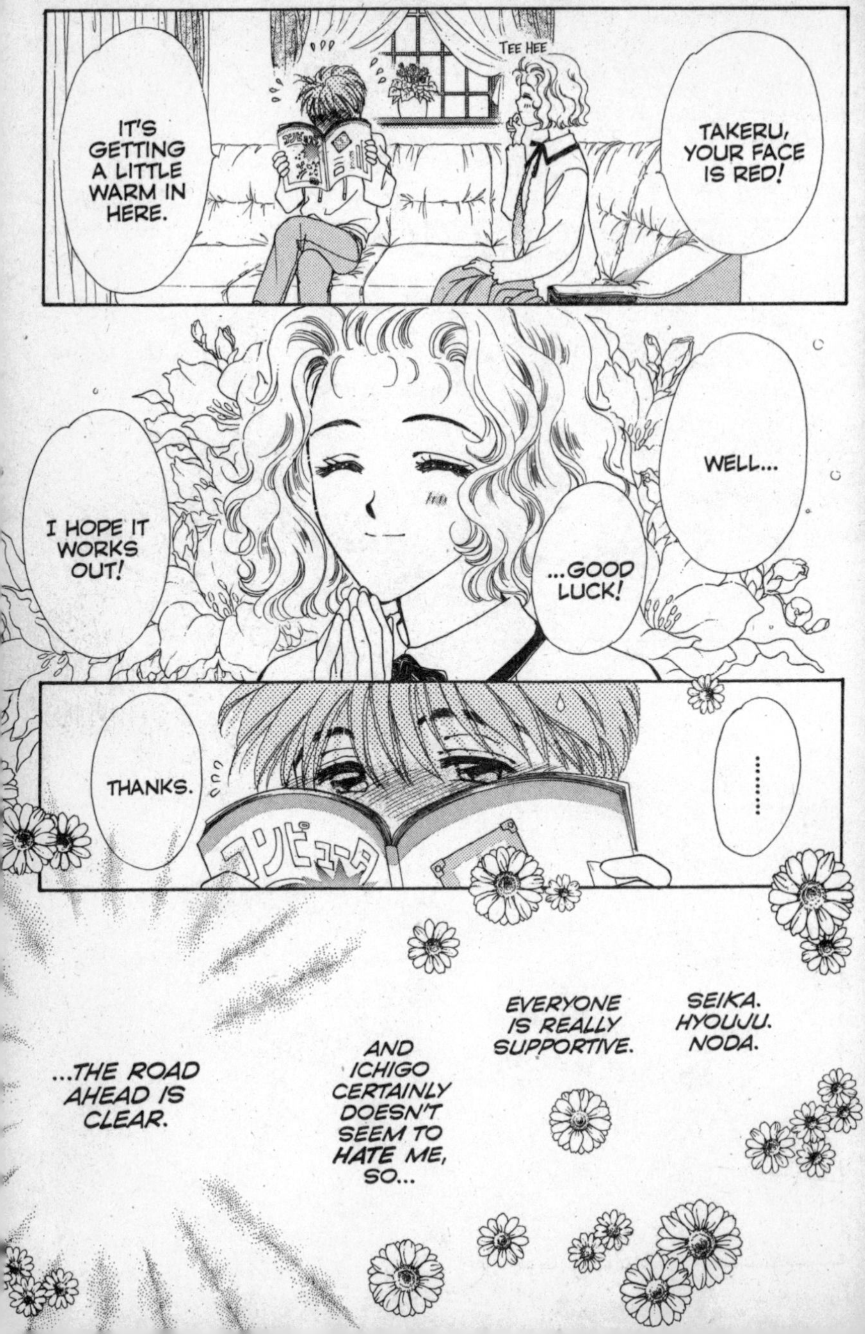
TAKERU, YOUR FACE IS RED!
TEE HEE
IT'S GETTING A LITTLE WARM IN HERE.
WELL...
...GOOD LUCK!
I HOPE IT WORKS OUT!
......
THANKS.
SEIKA. HYOUJU. NODA.
EVERYONE IS REALLY SUPPORTIVE.
AND ICHIGO CERTAINLY DOESN'T SEEM TO HATE ME, SO...
...THE ROAD AHEAD IS CLEAR.

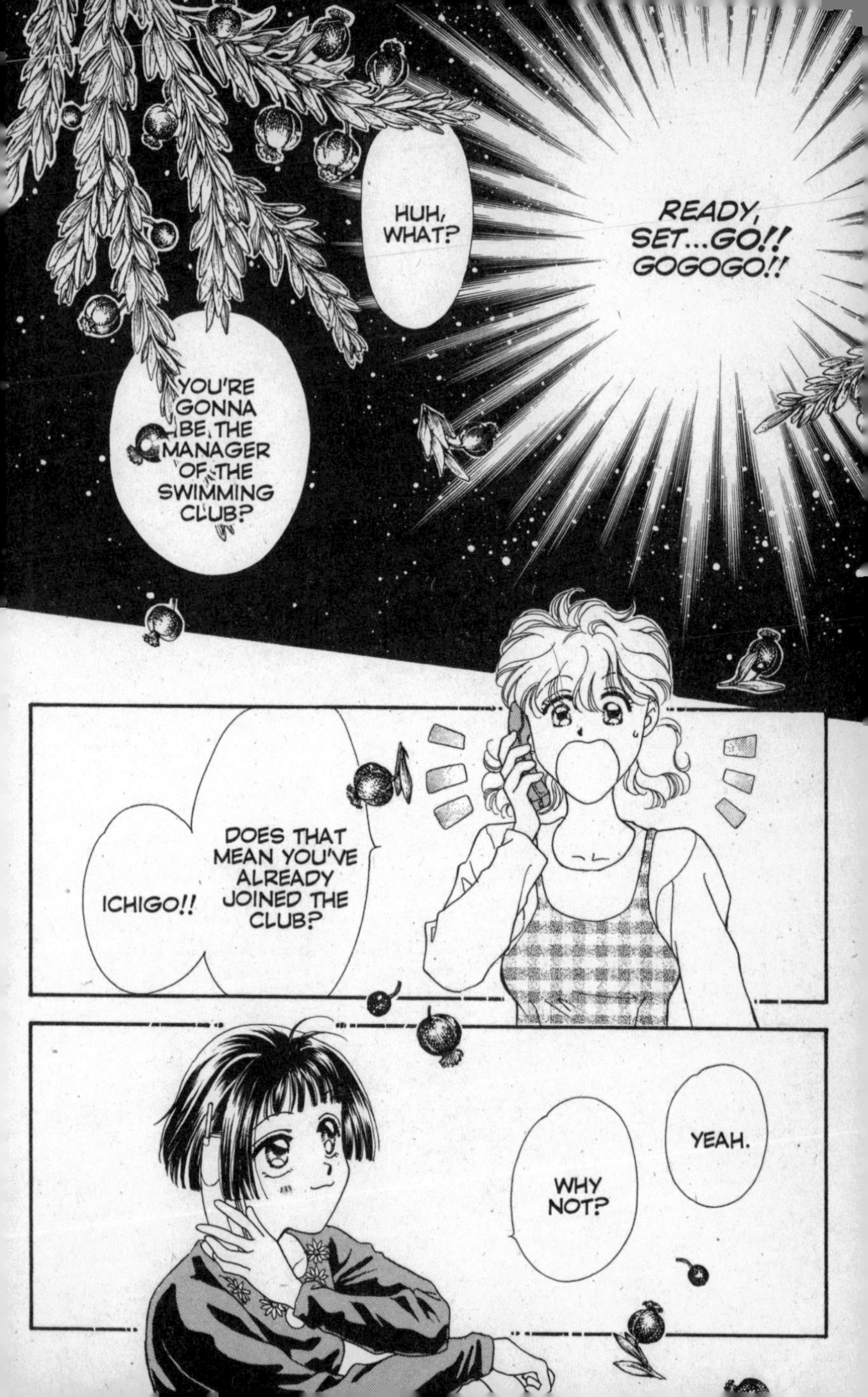
READY, SET...GO!! GOGOGO!!
HUH, WHAT?
YOU'RE GONNA BE THE MANAGER OF THE SWIMMING CLUB?
DOES THAT MEAN YOU'VE ALREADY JOINED THE CLUB?
ICHIGO!!
YEAH.
WHY NOT?

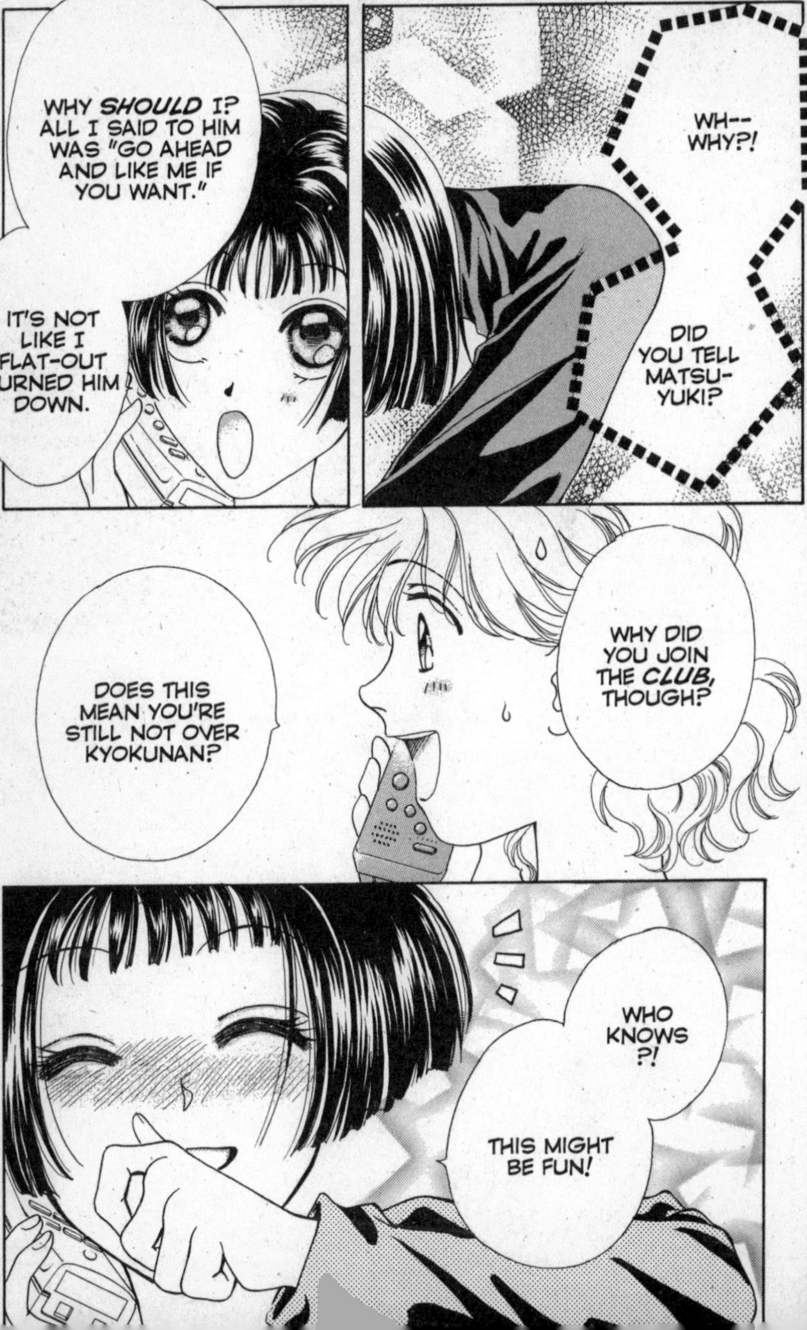
WH-- WHY?!
DID YOU TELL MATSU-YUKI?
WHY SHOULD I? ALL I SAID TO HIM WAS "GO AHEAD AND LIKE ME IF YOU WANT."
IT'S NOT LIKE I FLAT-OUT TURNED HIM DOWN.
WHY DID YOU JOIN THE CLUB, THOUGH?
DOES THIS MEAN YOU'RE STILL NOT OVER KYOKUNAN?
WHO KNOWS?!
THIS MIGHT BE FUN!

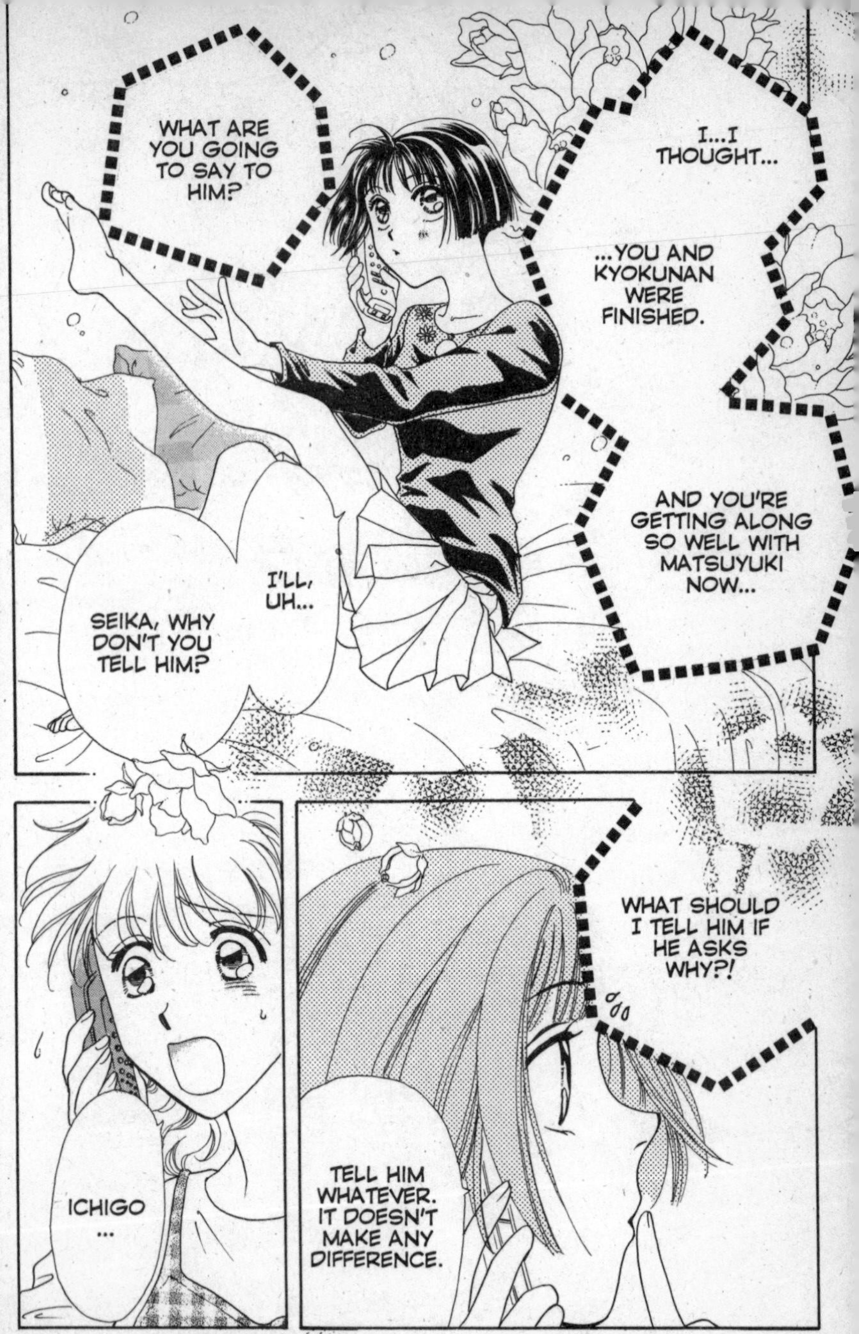
I...I THOUGHT...
...YOU AND KYOKUNAN WERE FINISHED.
AND YOU'RE GETTING ALONG SO WELL WITH MATSUYUKI NOW...
WHAT ARE YOU GOING TO SAY TO HIM?
I'LL, UH...
SEIKA, WHY DON'T YOU TELL HIM?
WHAT SHOULD I TELL HIM IF HE ASKS WHY?!
TELL HIM WHATEVER. IT DOESN'T MAKE ANY DIFFERENCE.
ICHIGO ...

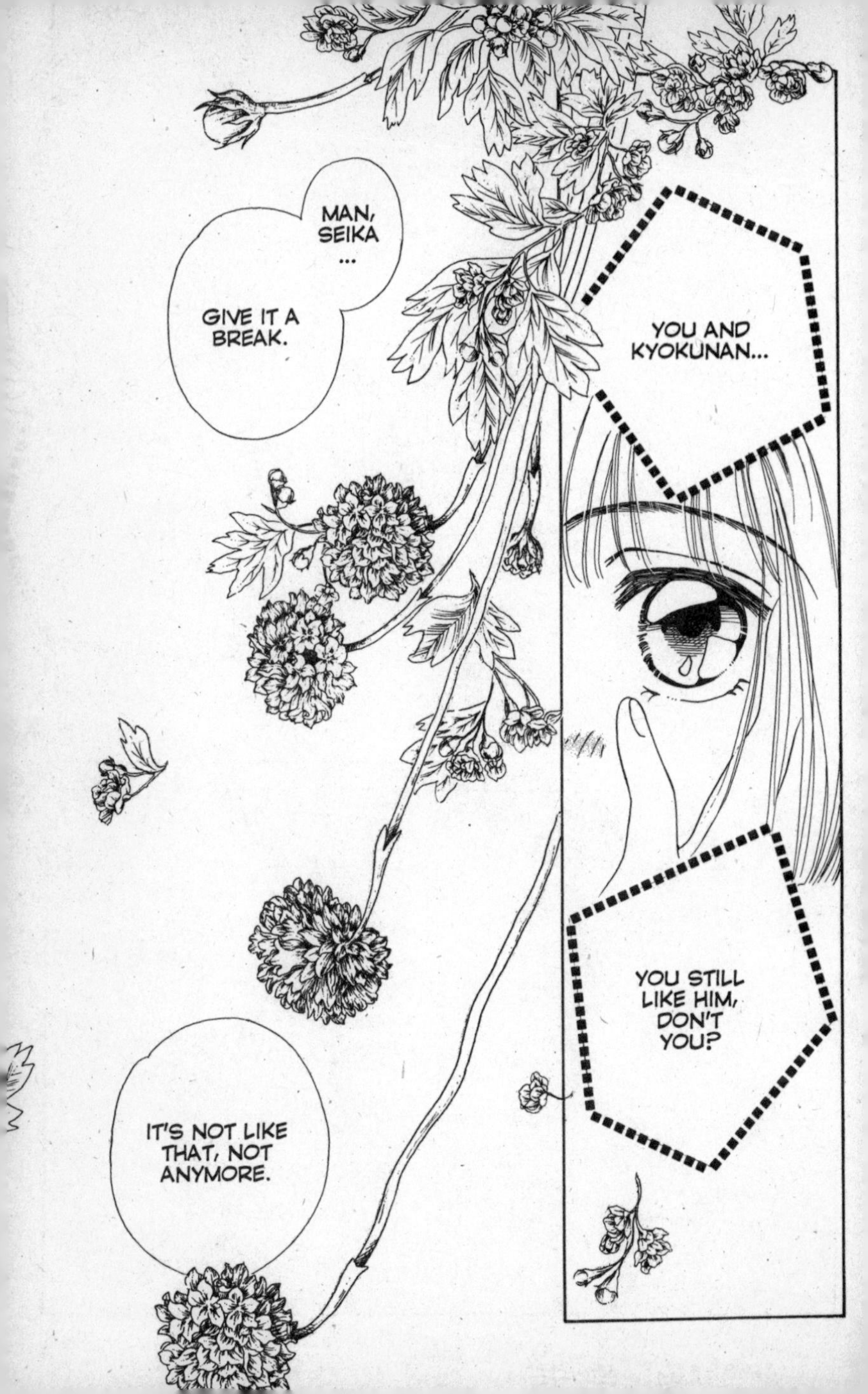
YOU AND KYOKUNAN...
YOU STILL LIKE HIM, DON'T YOU?
MAN, SEIKA ...
GIVE IT A BREAK.
IT'S NOT LIKE THAT, NOT ANYMORE.

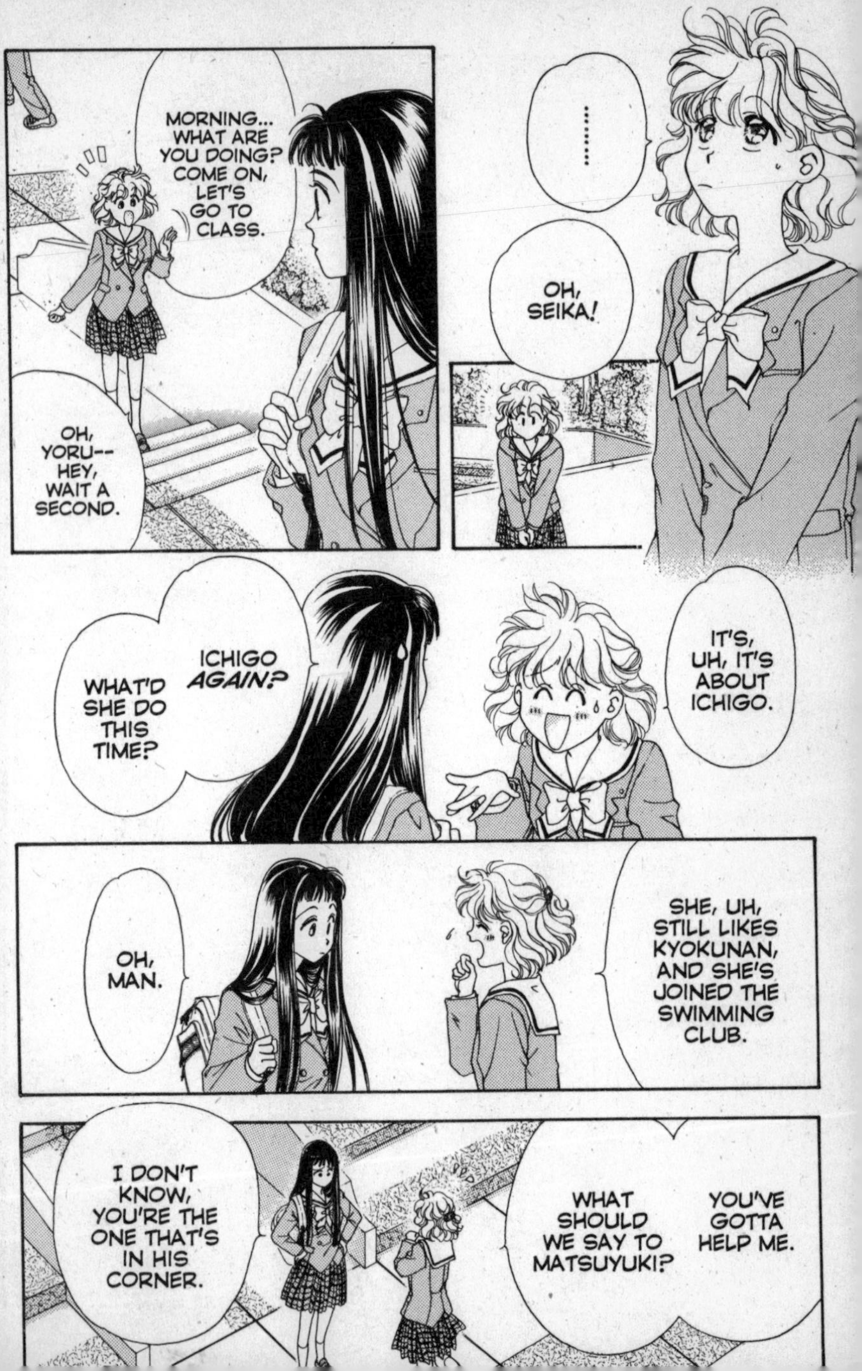
......
OH, SEIKA!
MORNING... WHAT ARE YOU DOING? COME ON, LET'S GO TO CLASS.
OH, YORU-- HEY, WAIT A SECOND.
IT'S, UH, IT'S ABOUT ICHIGO.
ICHIGO *AGAIN?*
WHAT'D SHE DO THIS TIME?
SHE, UH, STILL LIKES KYOKUNAN, AND SHE'S JOINED THE SWIMMING CLUB.
OH, MAN.
YOU'VE GOTTA HELP ME.
WHAT SHOULD WE SAY TO MATSUYUKI?
I DON'T KNOW, YOU'RE THE ONE THAT'S IN HIS CORNER.

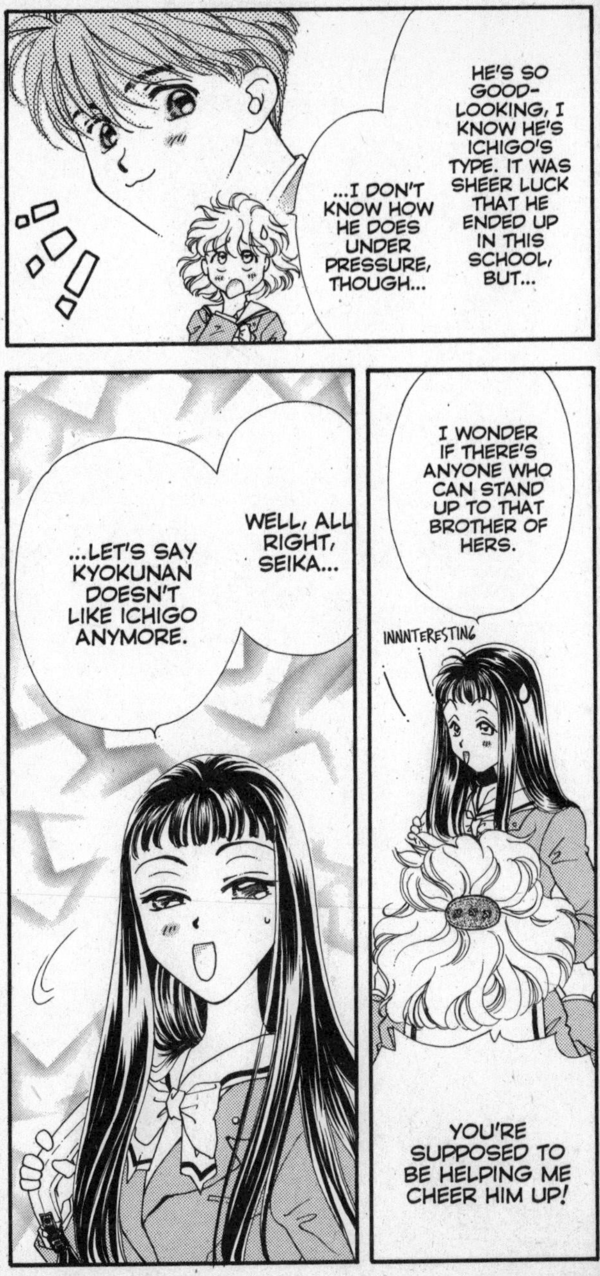
HE'S SO GOOD-LOOKING, I KNOW HE'S ICHIGO'S TYPE. IT WAS SHEER LUCK THAT HE ENDED UP IN THIS SCHOOL, BUT...
...I DON'T KNOW HOW HE DOES UNDER PRESSURE, THOUGH...
I WONDER IF THERE'S ANYONE WHO CAN STAND UP TO THAT BROTHER OF HERS.
INNNTERESTING
YOU'RE SUPPOSED TO BE HELPING ME CHEER HIM UP!
WELL, ALL RIGHT, SEIKA...
...LET'S SAY KYOKUNAN DOESN'T LIKE ICHIGO ANYMORE.

Sidebar No. 3

Actually. The game I've been entranced by the most lately is "Torneko's Mysterious Dungeon." Man, what a game! Have you guys played this? We'll talk about "Angelique" in a minute--first, this. Oh, I can't say it. I can't say it...I've heard a rumor that deeper into the "Even more mysterious dungeon" there's a hot springs and I want to get there. How the heck are all of you people beating this game so easily? You make me jealous. Even though it's so hard, it's still a really good game. I feel like...I don't know, like I could just sit here playing it, finding and opening treasure boxes forever!

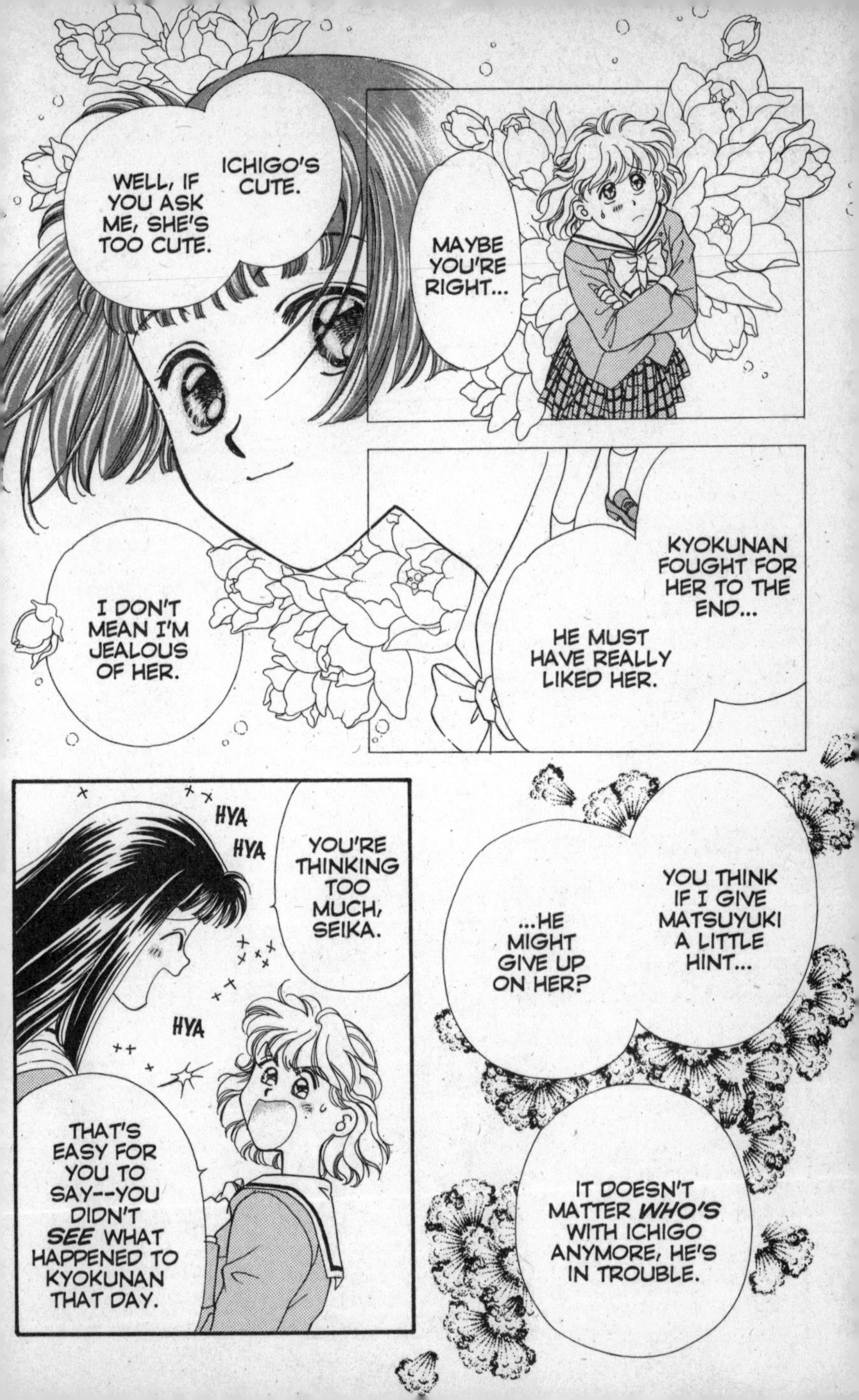
MAYBE YOU'RE RIGHT...
KYOKUNAN FOUGHT FOR HER TO THE END...
HE MUST HAVE REALLY LIKED HER.
ICHIGO'S CUTE.
WELL, IF YOU ASK ME, SHE'S TOO CUTE.
I DON'T MEAN I'M JEALOUS OF HER.
YOU THINK IF I GIVE MATSUYUKI A LITTLE HINT...
...HE MIGHT GIVE UP ON HER?
IT DOESN'T MATTER *WHO'S* WITH ICHIGO ANYMORE, HE'S IN TROUBLE.
YOU'RE THINKING TOO MUCH, SEIKA.
HYA
HYA
HYA
THAT'S EASY FOR YOU TO SAY--YOU DIDN'T *SEE* WHAT HAPPENED TO KYOKUNAN THAT DAY.

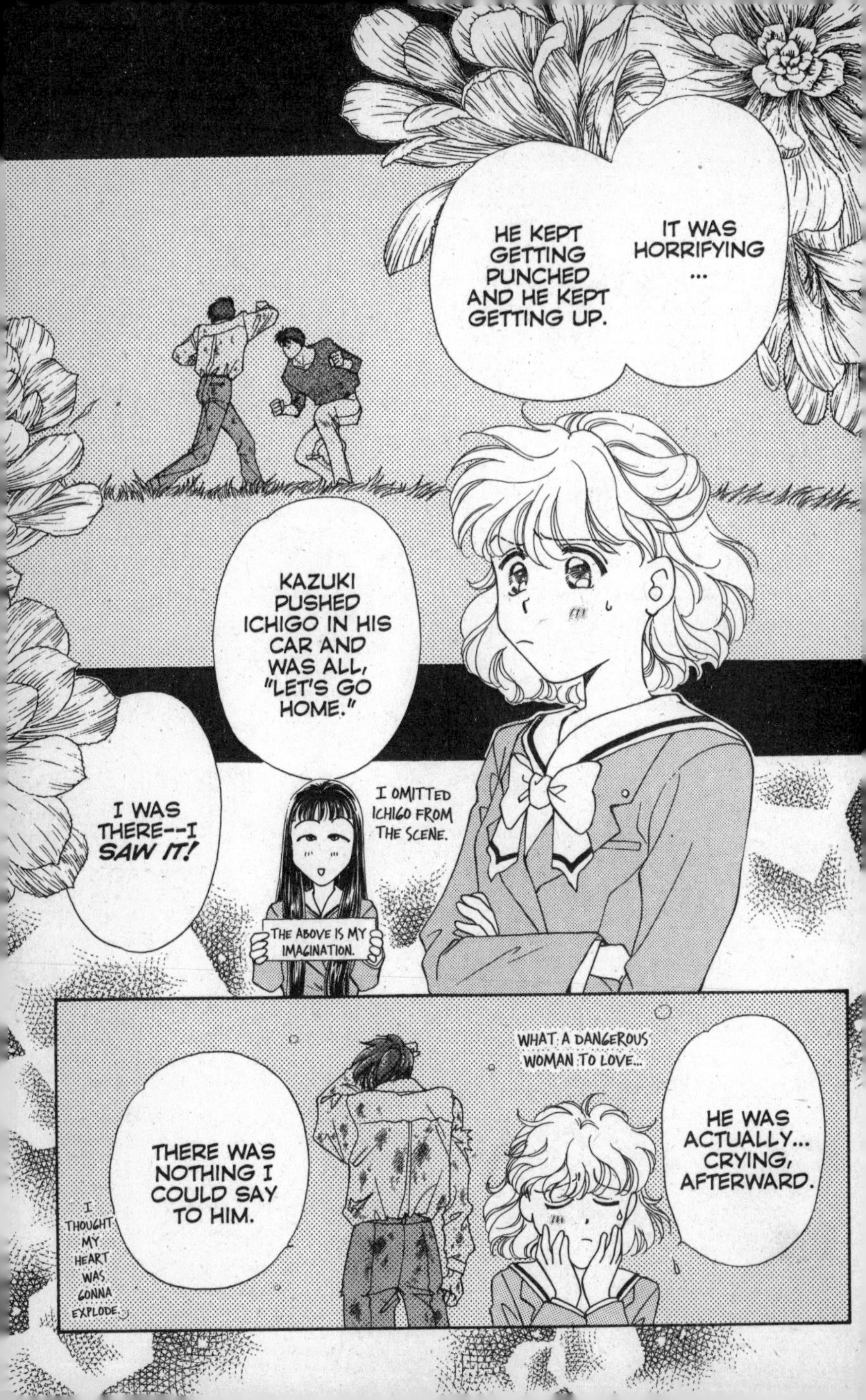
IT WAS HORRIFYING ...
HE KEPT GETTING PUNCHED AND HE KEPT GETTING UP.
KAZUKI PUSHED ICHIGO IN HIS CAR AND WAS ALL, "LET'S GO HOME."
I WAS THERE--I *SAW IT!*
I OMITTED ICHIGO FROM THE SCENE.
THE ABOVE IS MY IMAGINATION.
HE WAS ACTUALLY... CRYING, AFTERWARD.
WHAT A DANGEROUS WOMAN TO LOVE...
THERE WAS NOTHING I COULD SAY TO HIM.
I THOUGHT MY HEART WAS GONNA EXPLODE.

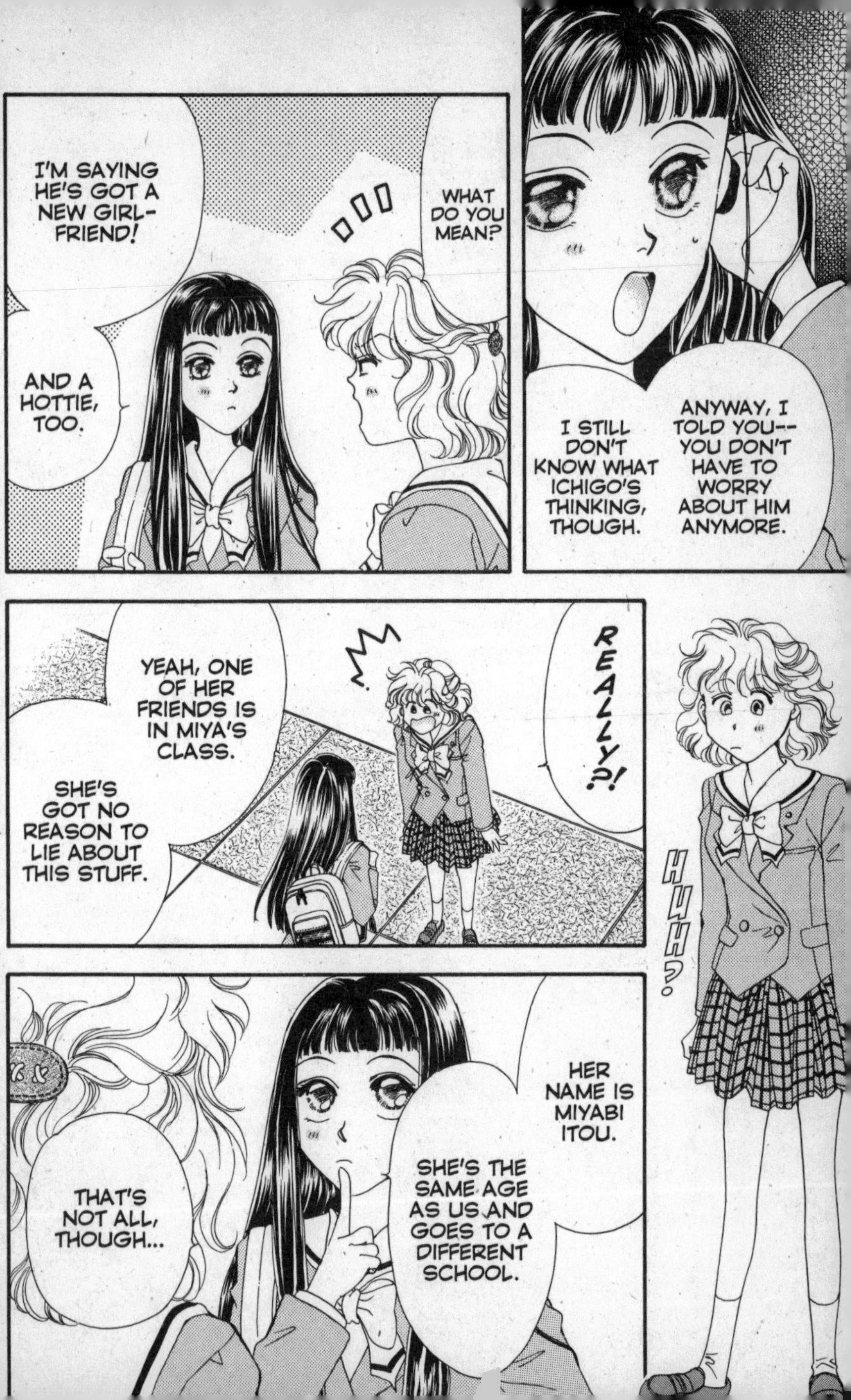
ANYWAY, I TOLD YOU-- YOU DON'T HAVE TO WORRY ABOUT HIM ANYMORE.
I STILL DON'T KNOW WHAT ICHIGO'S THINKING, THOUGH.
WHAT DO YOU MEAN?
I'M SAYING HE'S GOT A NEW GIRL-FRIEND!
AND A HOTTIE, TOO.
HUH?
REALLY?!
YEAH, ONE OF HER FRIENDS IS IN MIYA'S CLASS.
SHE'S GOT NO REASON TO LIE ABOUT THIS STUFF.
HER NAME IS MIYABI ITOU.
SHE'S THE SAME AGE AS US AND GOES TO A DIFFERENT SCHOOL.
THAT'S NOT ALL, THOUGH...

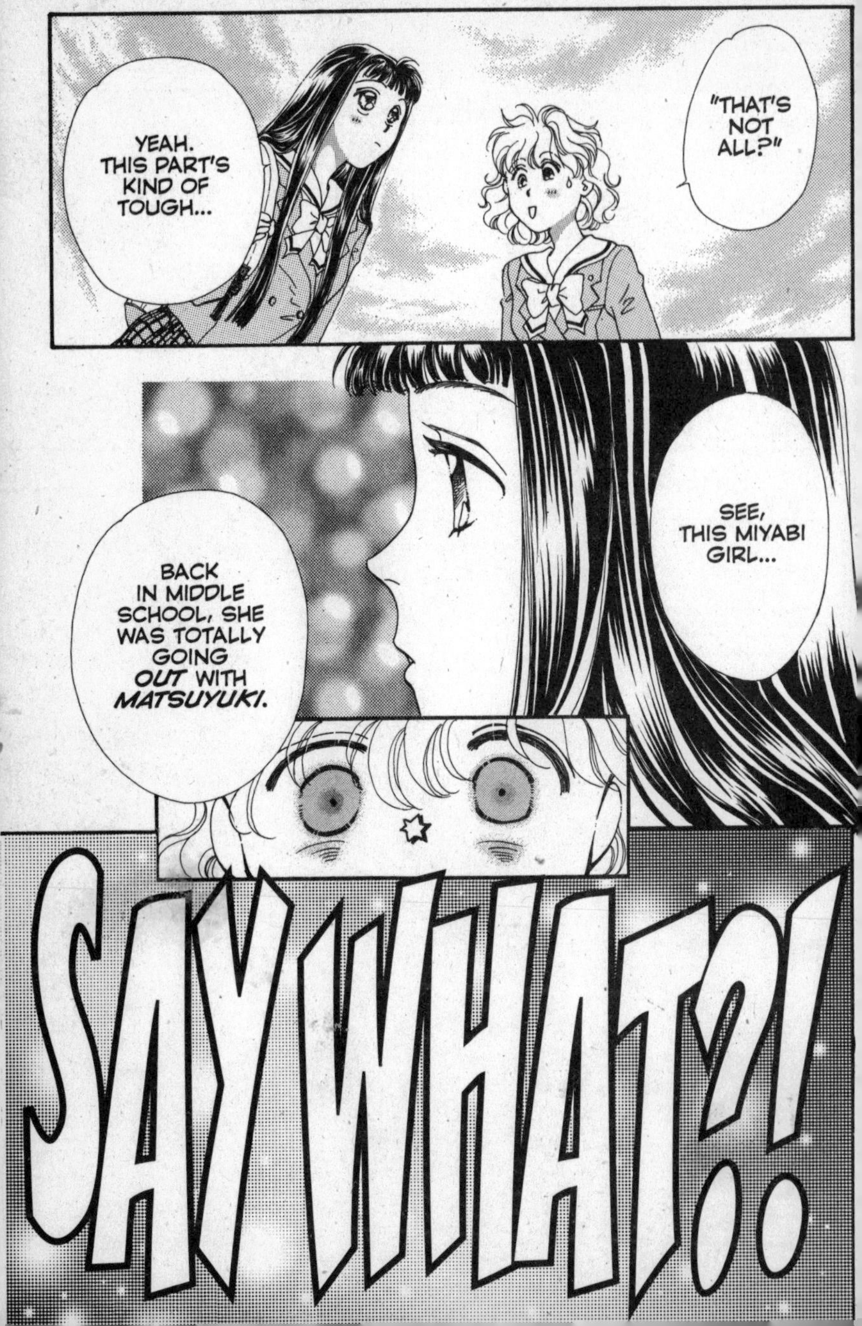
"THAT'S NOT ALL?"
YEAH. THIS PART'S KIND OF TOUGH...
SEE, THIS MIYABI GIRL...
BACK IN MIDDLE SCHOOL, SHE WAS TOTALLY GOING *OUT* WITH *MATSUYUKI*.
SAY WHAT?!

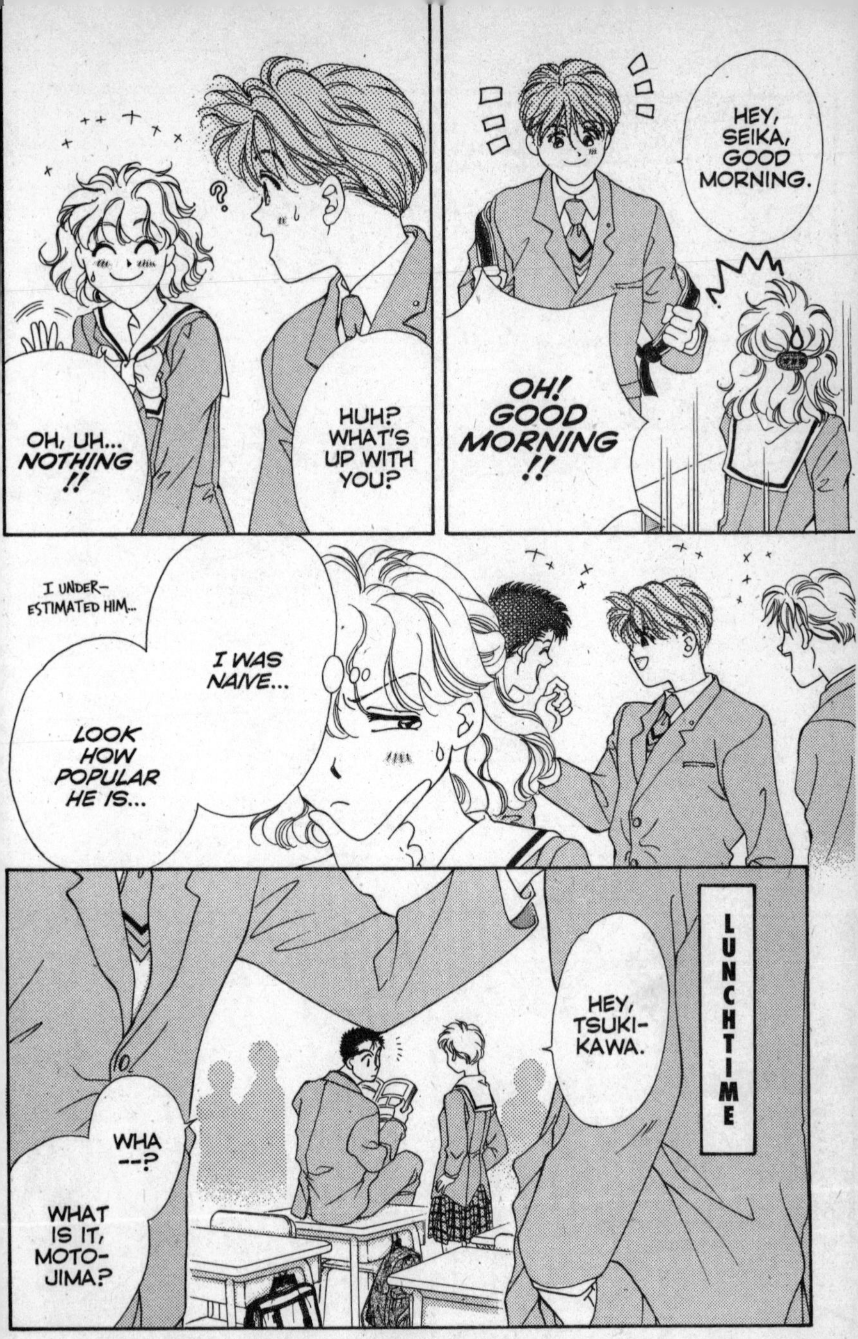
HEY, SEIKA, GOOD MORNING.
OH! GOOD MORNING !!
HUH? WHAT'S UP WITH YOU?
OH, UH... NOTHING !!
I WAS NAIVE...
LOOK HOW POPULAR HE IS...
I UNDER-ESTIMATED HIM...
LUNCHTIME
HEY, TSUKI-KAWA.
WHA --?
WHAT IS IT, MOTO-JIMA?

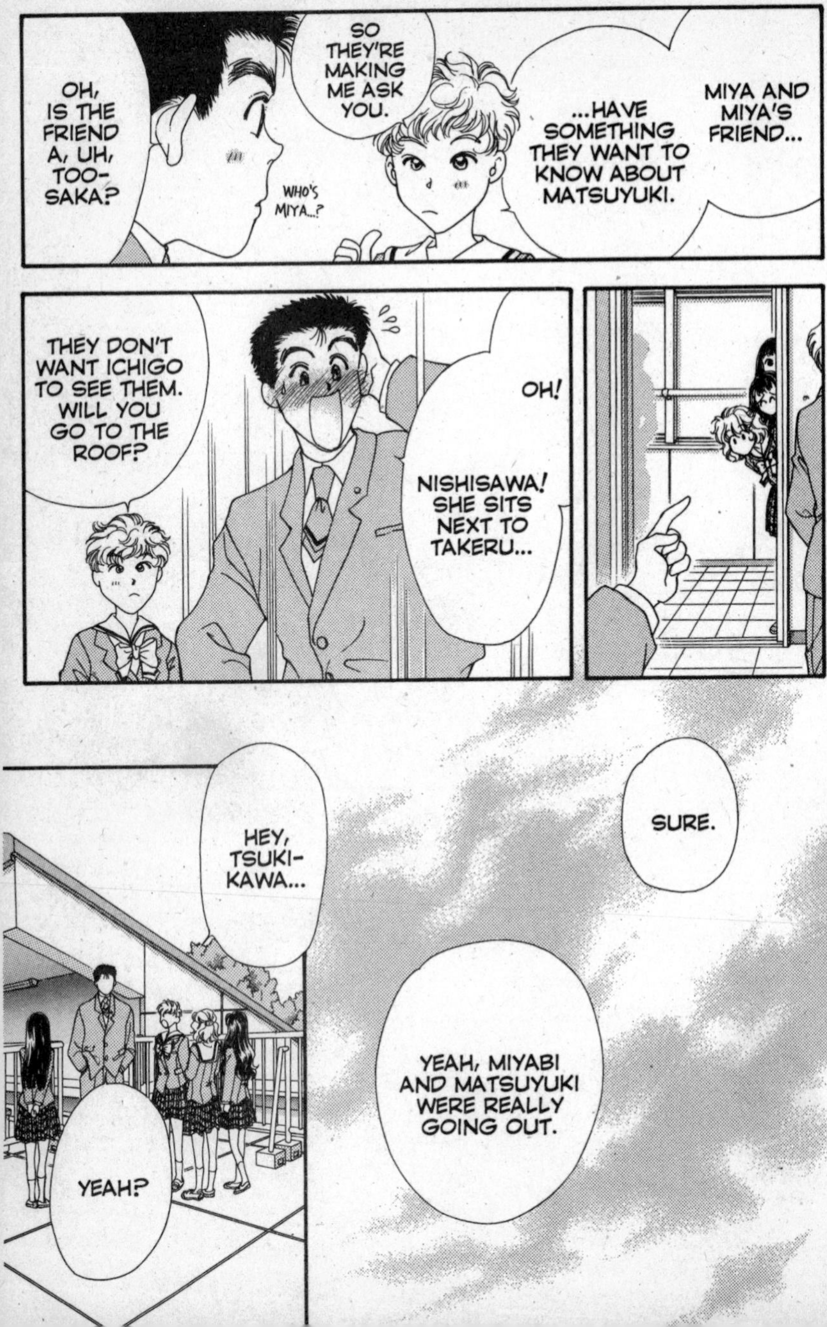
MIYA AND MIYA'S FRIEND...
...HAVE SOMETHING THEY WANT TO KNOW ABOUT MATSUYUKI.
SO THEY'RE MAKING ME ASK YOU.
WHO'S MIYA...?
OH, IS THE FRIEND A, UH, TOO-SAKA?
OH!
NISHISAWA! SHE SITS NEXT TO TAKERU...
THEY DON'T WANT ICHIGO TO SEE THEM. WILL YOU GO TO THE ROOF?
SURE.
HEY, TSUKI-KAWA...
YEAH?
YEAH, MIYABI AND MATSUYUKI WERE REALLY GOING OUT.

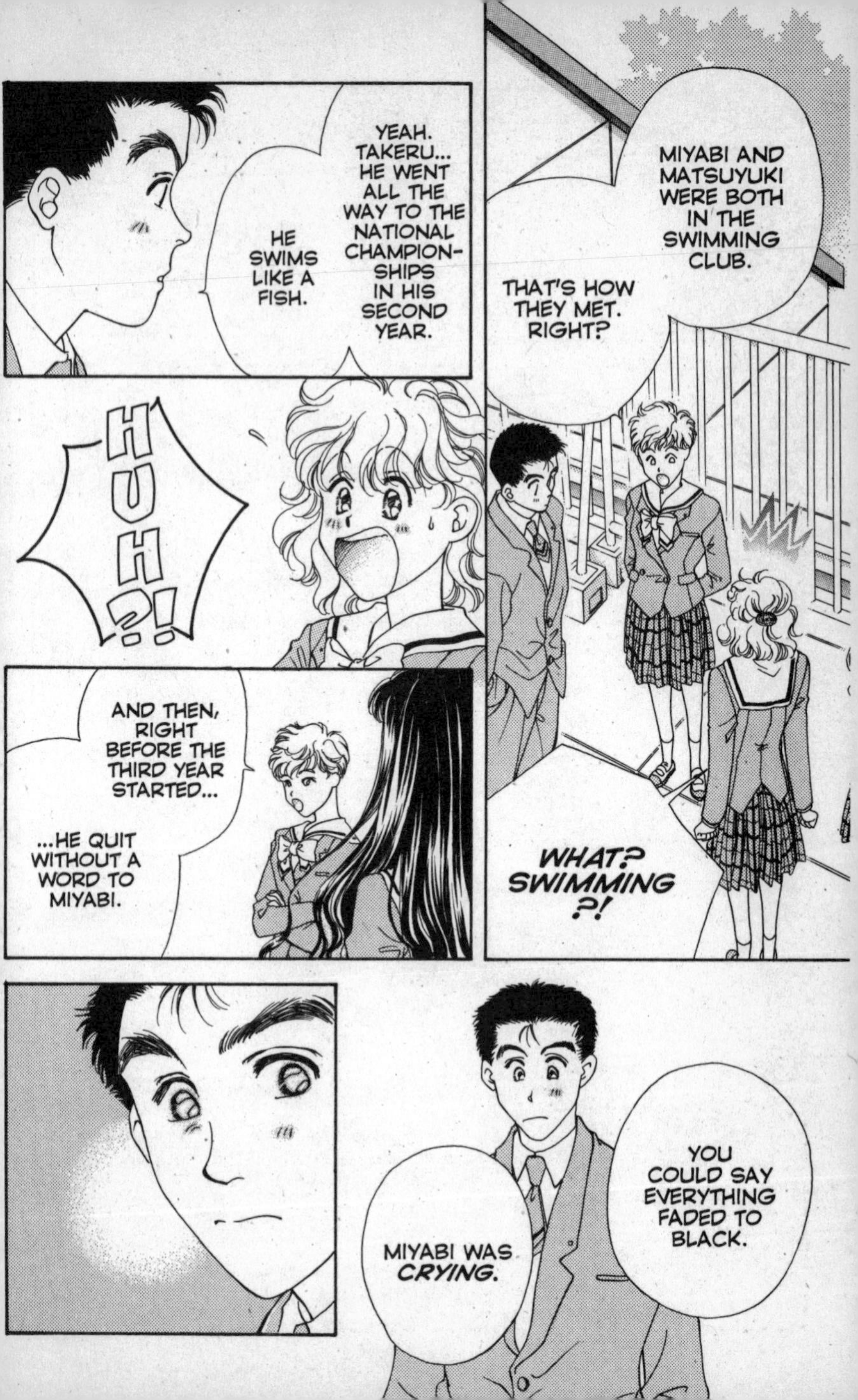
MIYABI AND MATSUYUKI WERE BOTH IN THE SWIMMING CLUB.
THAT'S HOW THEY MET. RIGHT?
WHAT? SWIMMING ?!
YEAH. TAKERU... HE WENT ALL THE WAY TO THE NATIONAL CHAMPION-SHIPS IN HIS SECOND YEAR.
HE SWIMS LIKE A FISH.
HUH?!
AND THEN, RIGHT BEFORE THE THIRD YEAR STARTED...
...HE QUIT WITHOUT A WORD TO MIYABI.
YOU COULD SAY EVERYTHING FADED TO BLACK.
MIYABI WAS *CRYING.*

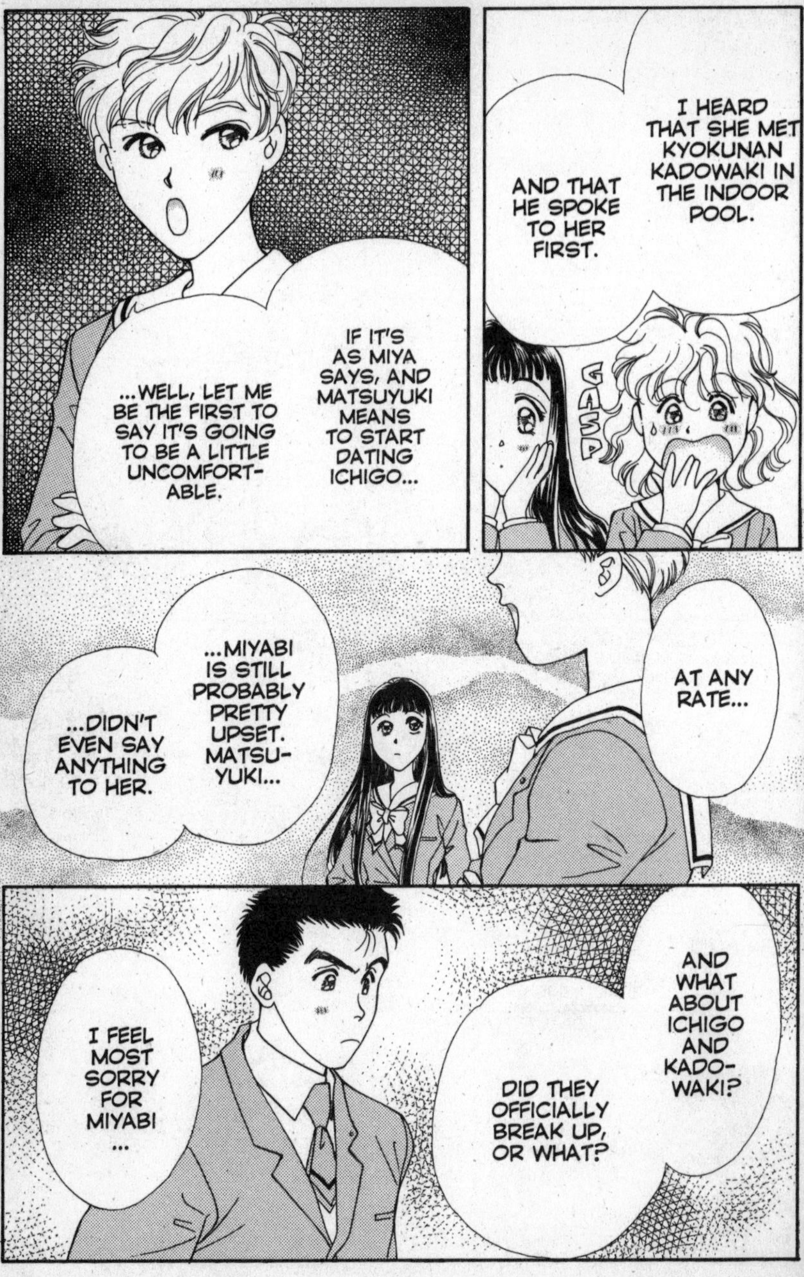
I HEARD THAT SHE MET KYOKUNAN KADOWAKI IN THE INDOOR POOL.
AND THAT HE SPOKE TO HER FIRST.
GASP
IF IT'S AS MIYA SAYS, AND MATSUYUKI MEANS TO START DATING ICHIGO...
...WELL, LET ME BE THE FIRST TO SAY IT'S GOING TO BE A LITTLE UNCOMFORT-ABLE.
AT ANY RATE...
...MIYABI IS STILL PROBABLY PRETTY UPSET. MATSU-YUKI...
...DIDN'T EVEN SAY ANYTHING TO HER.
AND WHAT ABOUT ICHIGO AND KADO-WAKI?
DID THEY OFFICIALLY BREAK UP, OR WHAT?
I FEEL MOST SORRY FOR MIYABI ...

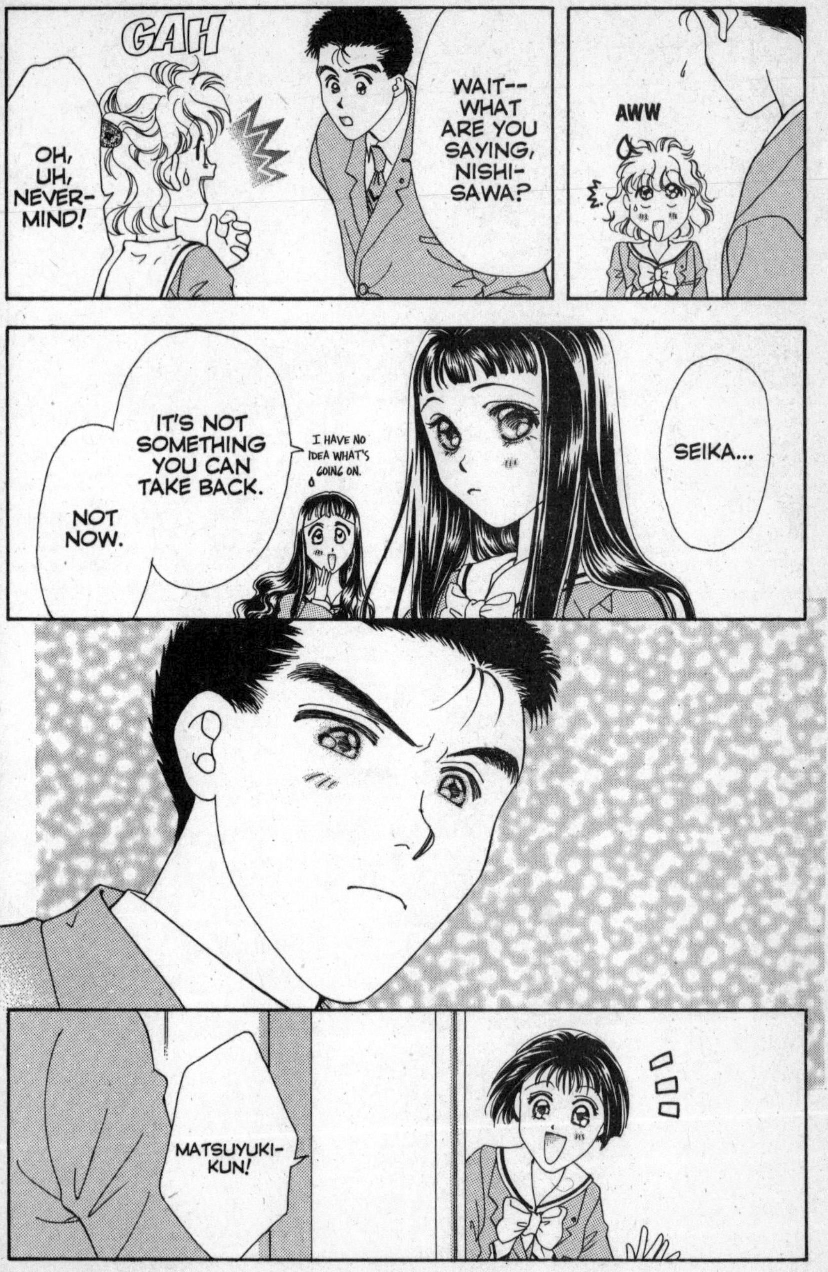
AWW
WAIT-- WHAT ARE YOU SAYING, NISHI-SAWA?
GAH
OH, UH, NEVER-MIND!
SEIKA...
I HAVE NO IDEA WHAT'S GOING ON.
IT'S NOT SOMETHING YOU CAN TAKE BACK.
NOT NOW.
MATSUYUKI-KUN!

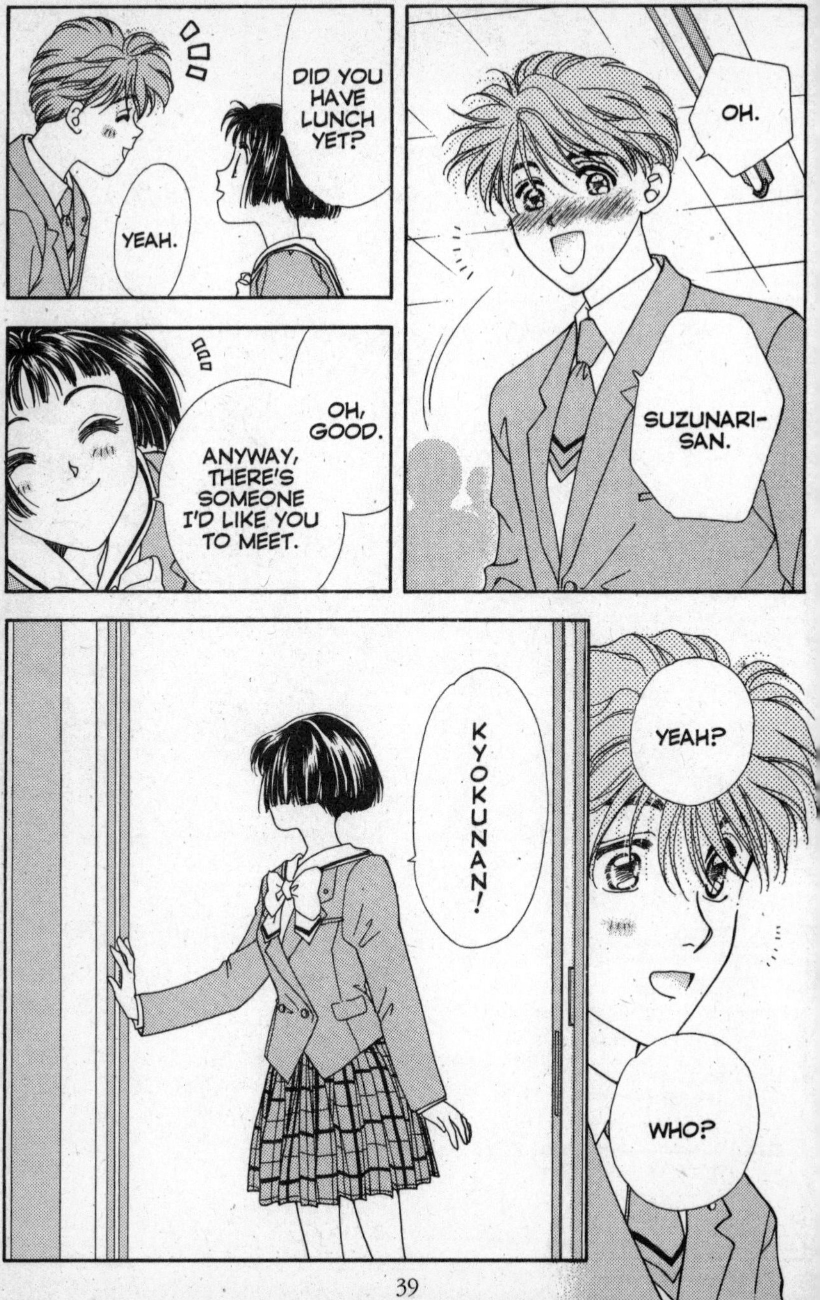
OH.
SUZUNARI-SAN.
DID YOU HAVE LUNCH YET?
YEAH.
OH, GOOD.
ANYWAY, THERE'S SOMEONE I'D LIKE YOU TO MEET.
YEAH?
KYOKUNAN!
WHO?

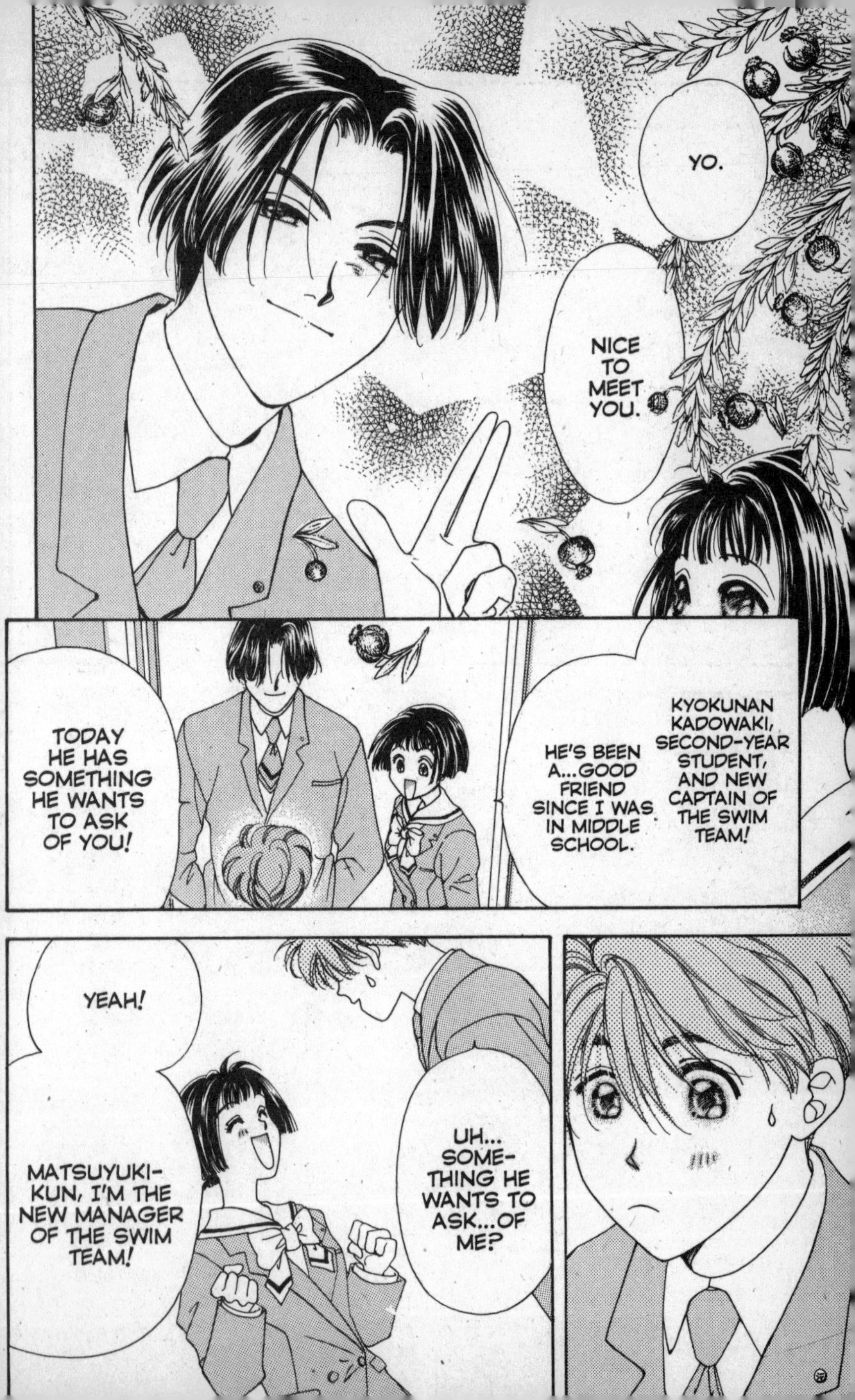
YO.
NICE TO MEET YOU.
KYOKUNAN KADOWAKI, SECOND-YEAR STUDENT, AND NEW CAPTAIN OF THE SWIM TEAM!
HE'S BEEN A...GOOD FRIEND SINCE I WAS IN MIDDLE SCHOOL.
TODAY HE HAS SOMETHING HE WANTS TO ASK OF YOU!
UH... SOME-THING HE WANTS TO ASK...OF ME?
YEAH!
MATSUYUKI-KUN, I'M THE NEW MANAGER OF THE SWIM TEAM!

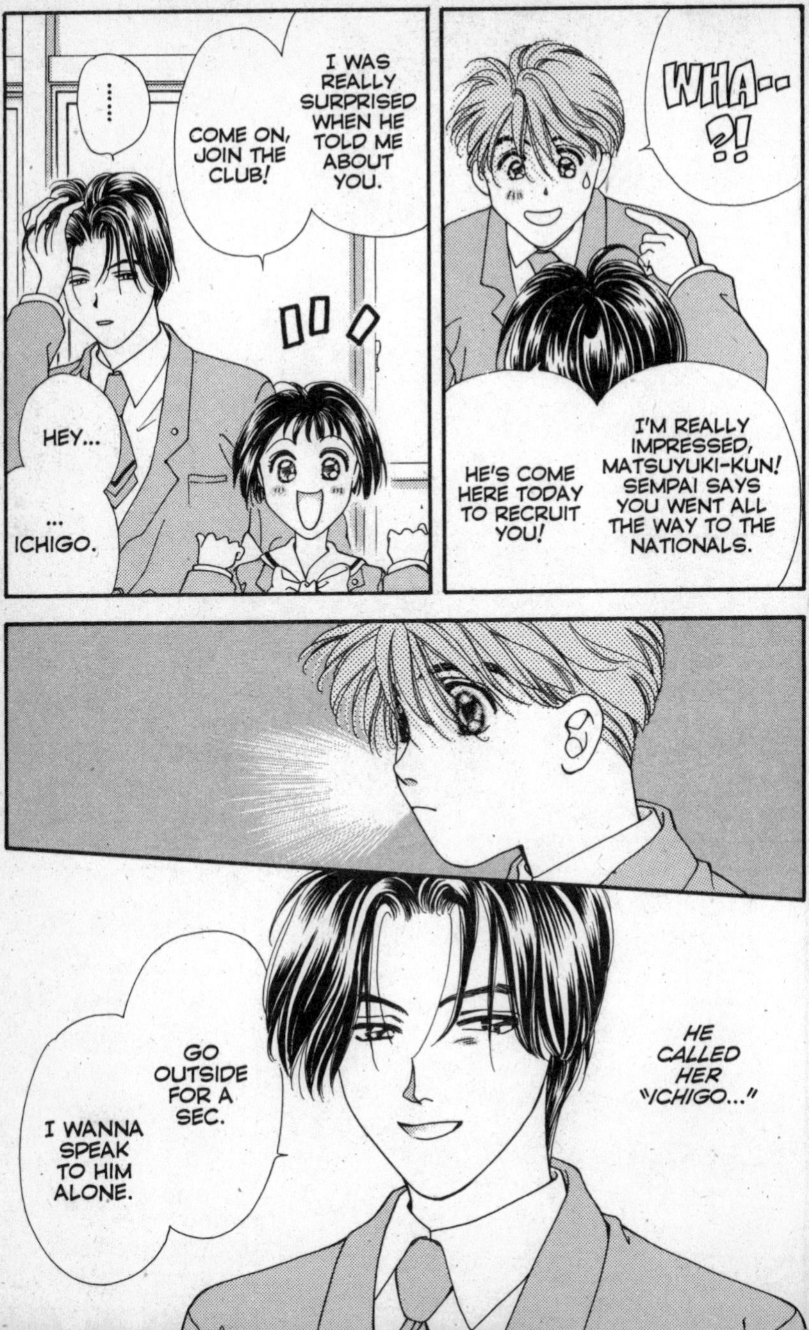
WHA..?!
I'M REALLY IMPRESSED, MATSUYUKI-KUN! SEMPAI SAYS YOU WENT ALL THE WAY TO THE NATIONALS.
HE'S COME HERE TODAY TO RECRUIT YOU!
I WAS REALLY SURPRISED WHEN HE TOLD ME ABOUT YOU.
COME ON, JOIN THE CLUB!
......
HEY...
...ICHIGO.
HE CALLED HER "ICHIGO..."
GO OUTSIDE FOR A SEC.
I WANNA SPEAK TO HIM ALONE.

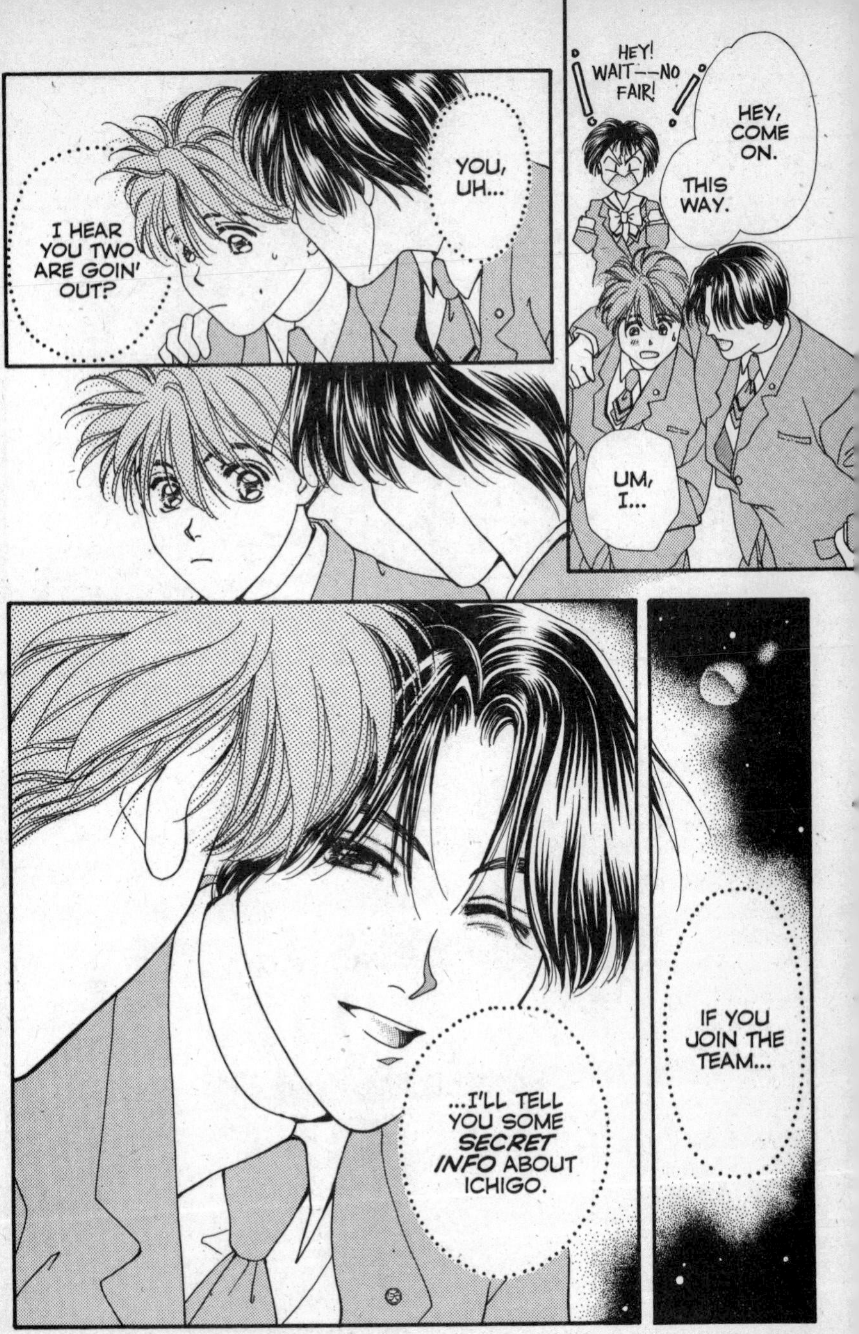
HEY, COME ON. THIS WAY.
HEY! WAIT--NO FAIR!
UM, I...
YOU, UH...
I HEAR YOU TWO ARE GOIN' OUT?
IF YOU JOIN THE TEAM...
...I'LL TELL YOU SOME *SECRET INFO* ABOUT ICHIGO.

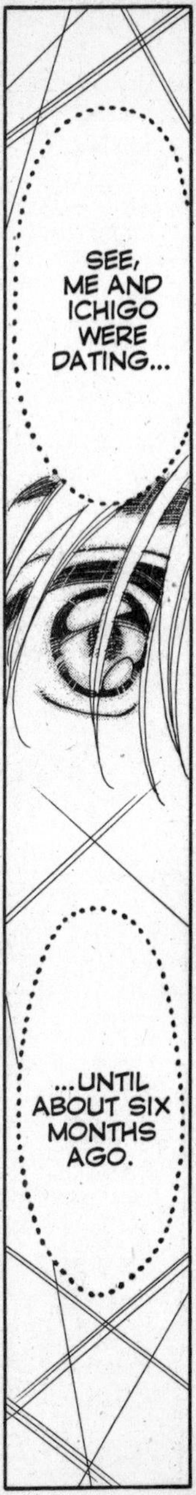
SEE, ME AND ICHIGO WERE DATING...
...UNTIL ABOUT SIX MONTHS AGO.

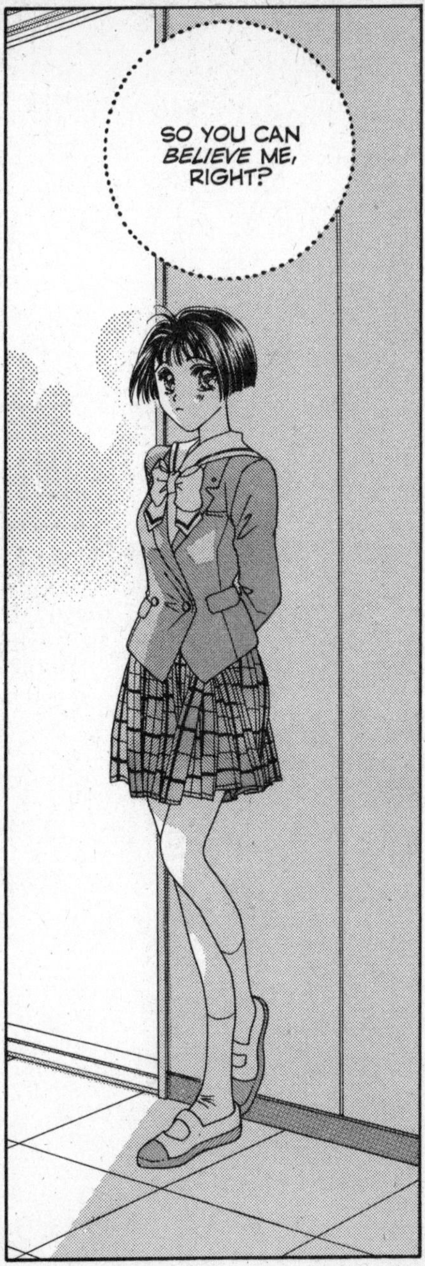
SO YOU CAN *BELIEVE* ME, RIGHT?

Sidebar No. 4

Ahhhh... let's talk, shall we? It happened one day. I was reading letters from all of you fine people, which my publishers had forwarded to me. And there it was, in one of the letters: "I read your coloumn in Tower of the Future Volume 2. I'm a girl who liked games enough to become a writer for a games magazine. There is a game I love very deeply, and I would like to recommend it to you with confidence. That game is called...

"'ANGELIQUE'."

Right then and there...

(to be continued!!)

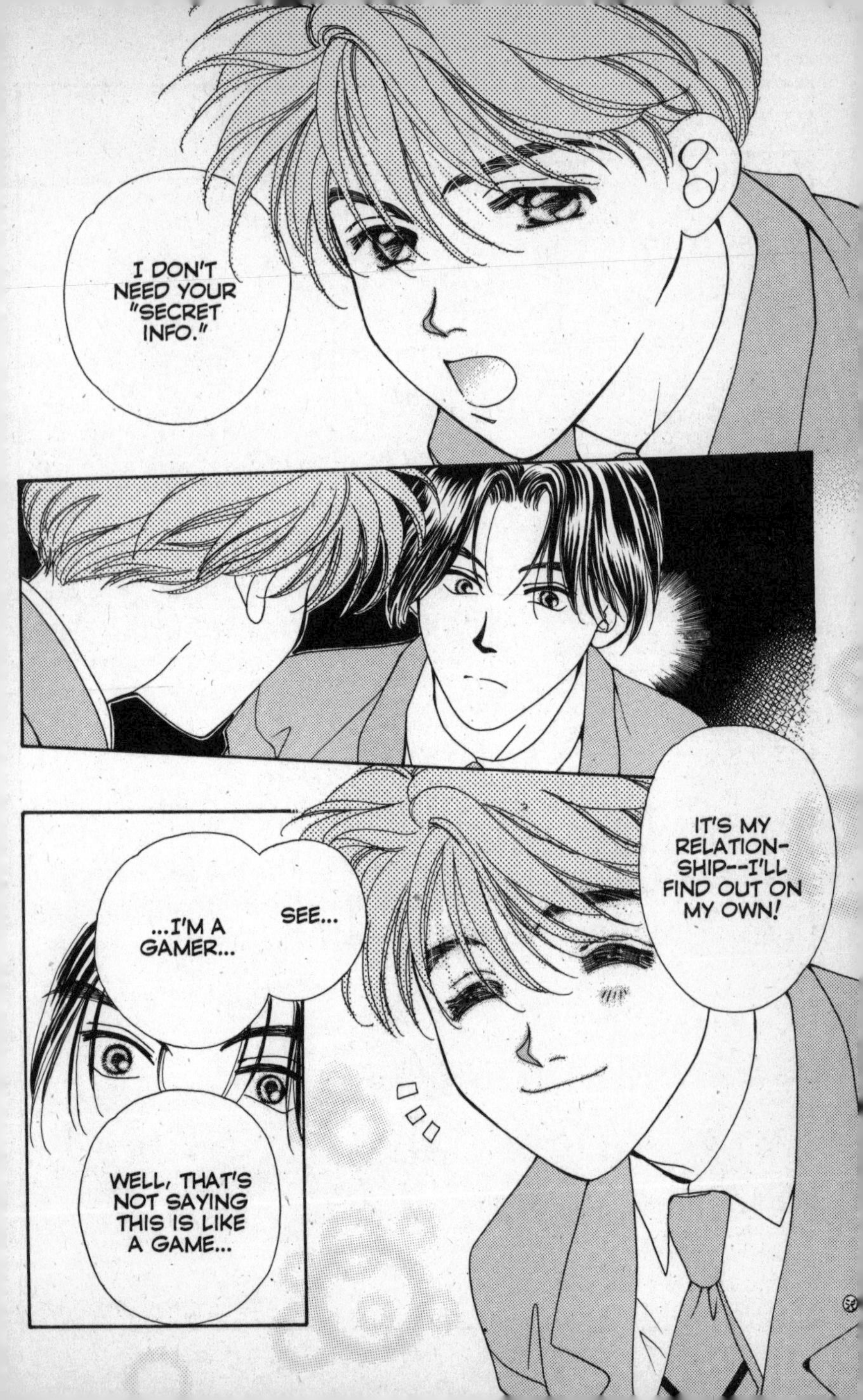
I DON'T NEED YOUR "SECRET INFO."
IT'S MY RELATION-SHIP--I'LL FIND OUT ON MY OWN!
SEE...
...I'M A GAMER...
WELL, THAT'S NOT SAYING THIS IS LIKE A GAME...

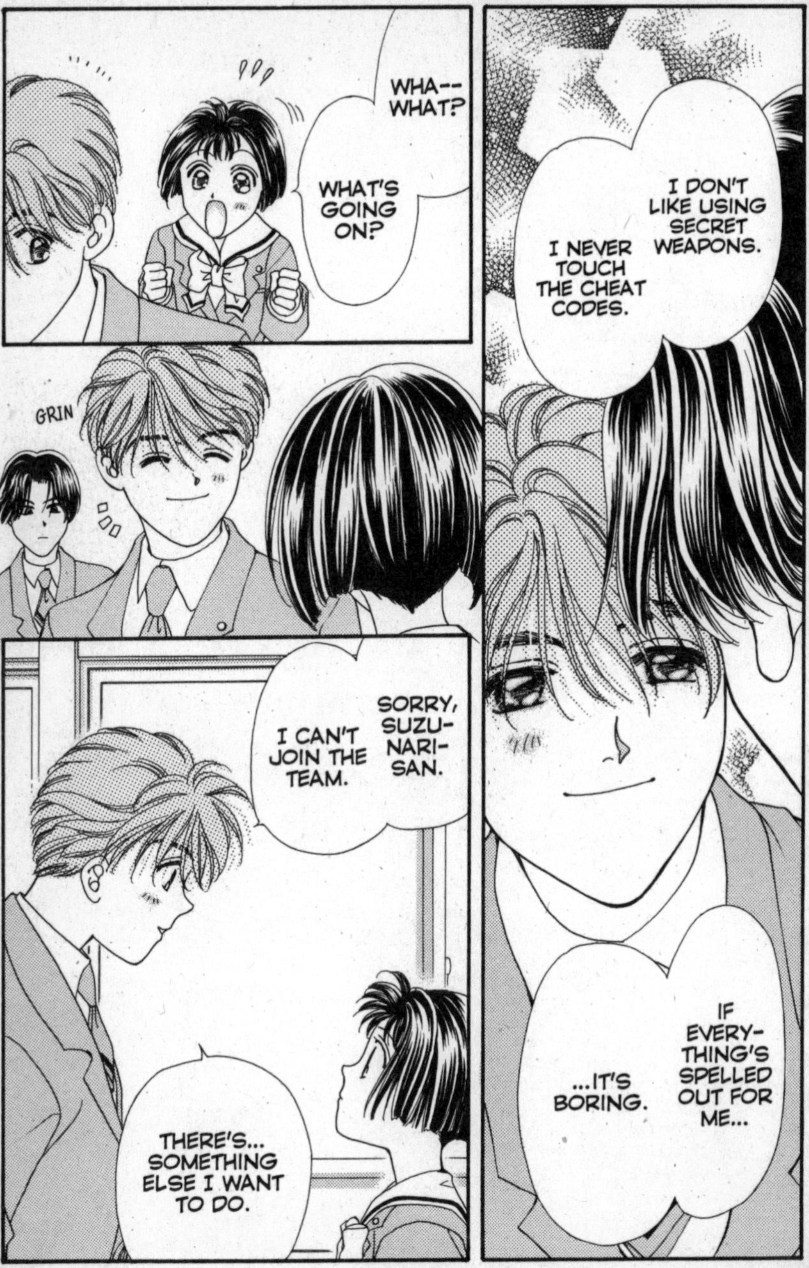
I DON'T LIKE USING SECRET WEAPONS.
I NEVER TOUCH THE CHEAT CODES.
IF EVERY-THING'S SPELLED OUT FOR ME...
...IT'S BORING.
WHA-- WHAT?
WHAT'S GOING ON?
GRIN
SORRY, SUZU-NARI-SAN.
I CAN'T JOIN THE TEAM.
THERE'S... SOMETHING ELSE I WANT TO DO.

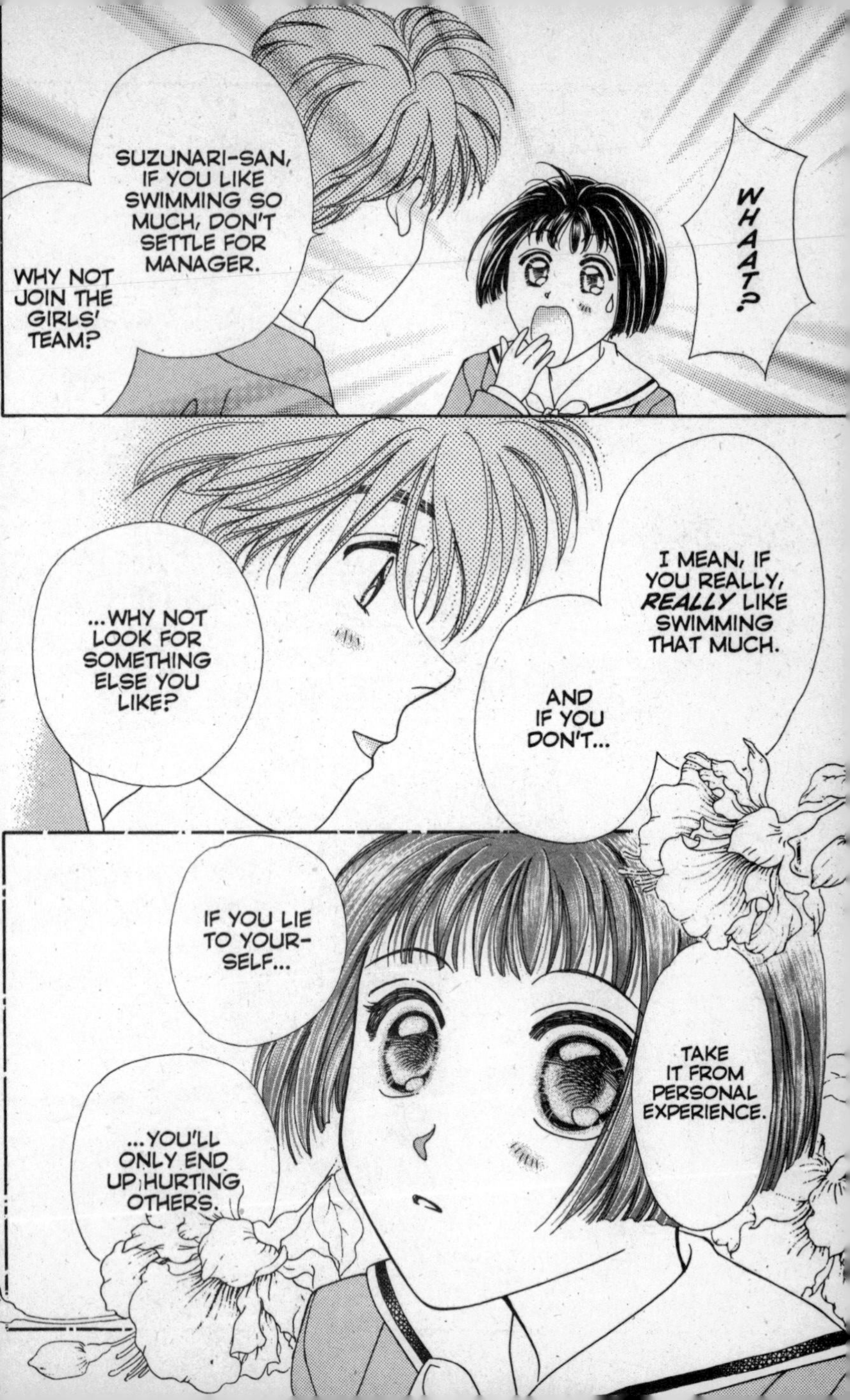
SUZUNARI-SAN, IF YOU LIKE SWIMMING SO MUCH, DON'T SETTLE FOR MANAGER.
WHY NOT JOIN THE GIRLS' TEAM?
WHAAT?
I MEAN, IF YOU REALLY, *REALLY* LIKE SWIMMING THAT MUCH.
AND IF YOU DON'T...
...WHY NOT LOOK FOR SOMETHING ELSE YOU LIKE?
IF YOU LIE TO YOUR-SELF...
...YOU'LL ONLY END UP HURTING OTHERS.
TAKE IT FROM PERSONAL EXPERIENCE.

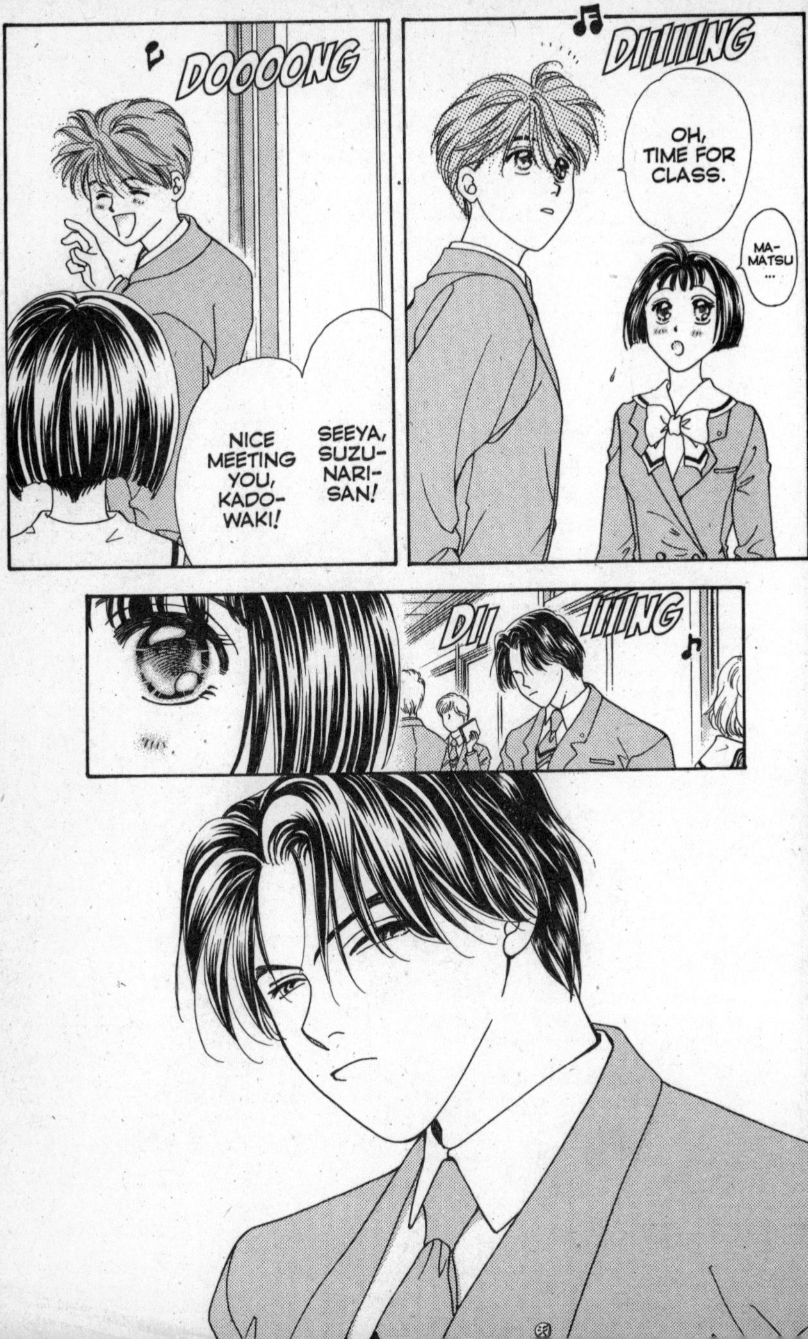
DIIIIING
OH, TIME FOR CLASS.
MA-MATSU...
DOOOONG
SEEYA, SUZUNARI-SAN!
NICE MEETING YOU, KADOWAKI!
DII IIIING

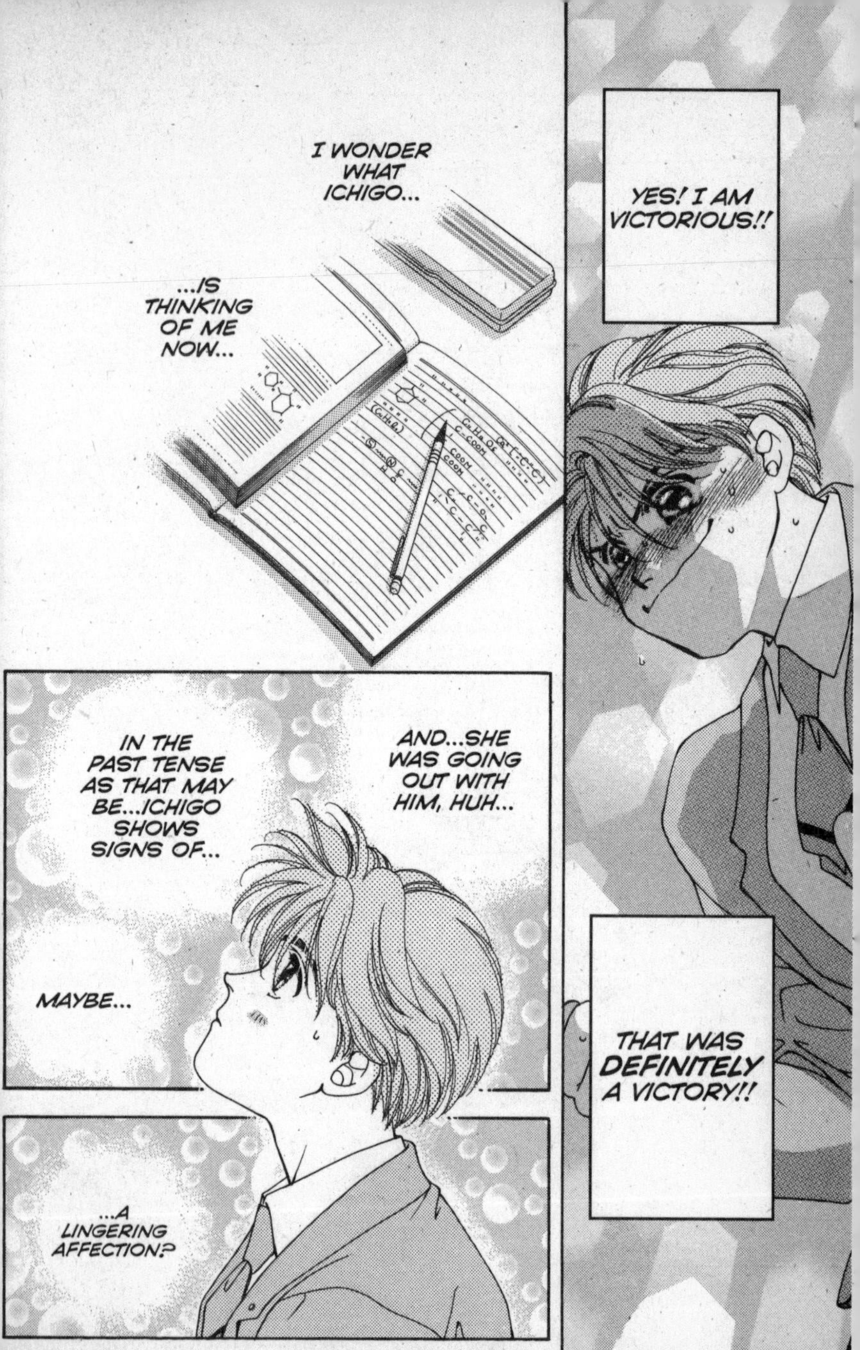
YES! I AM VICTORIOUS!!
THAT WAS DEFINITELY A VICTORY!!
I WONDER WHAT ICHIGO...
...IS THINKING OF ME NOW...
AND...SHE WAS GOING OUT WITH HIM, HUH...
IN THE PAST TENSE AS THAT MAY BE...ICHIGO SHOWS SIGNS OF...
MAYBE...
...A LINGERING AFFECTION?

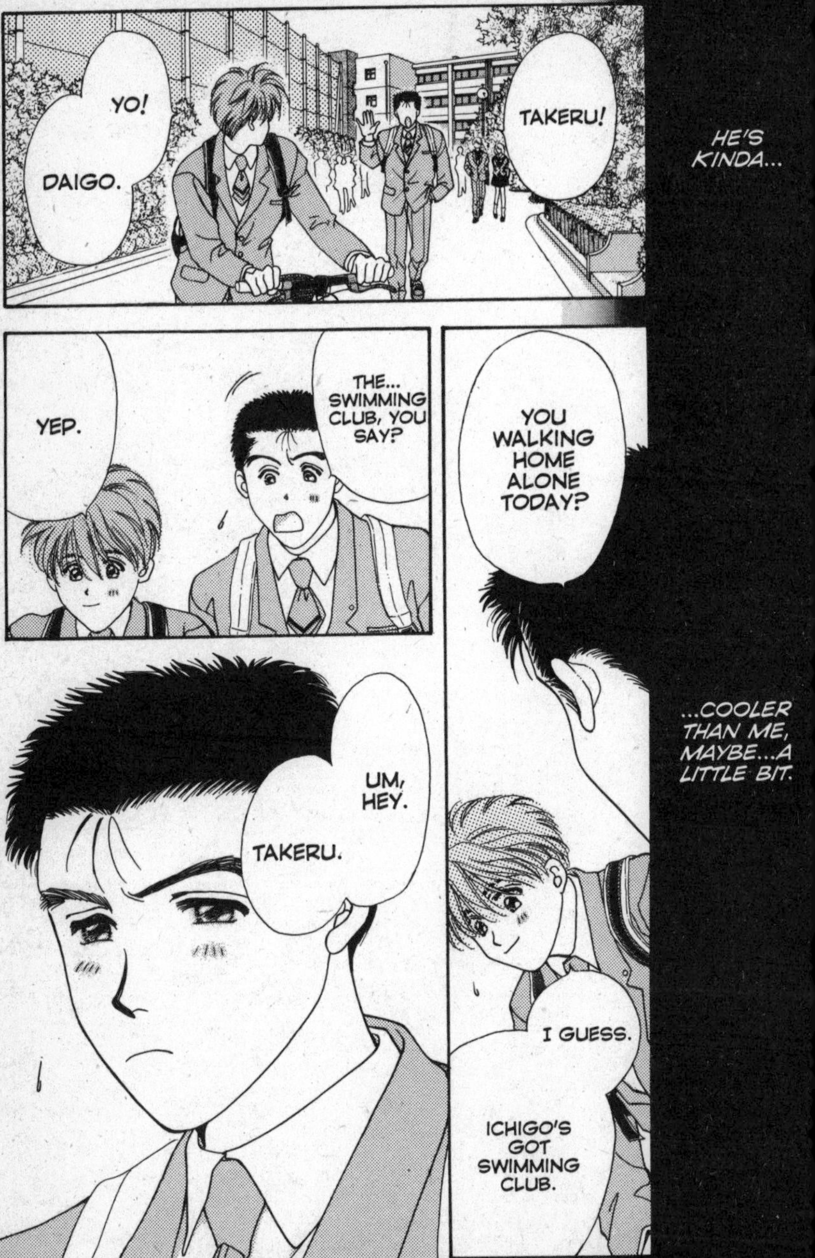
TAKERU!
YO! DAIGO.
HE'S KINDA...
YOU WALKING HOME ALONE TODAY?
I GUESS.
ICHIGO'S GOT SWIMMING CLUB.
...COOLER THAN ME, MAYBE...A LITTLE BIT.
THE... SWIMMING CLUB, YOU SAY?
YEP.
UM, HEY. TAKERU.

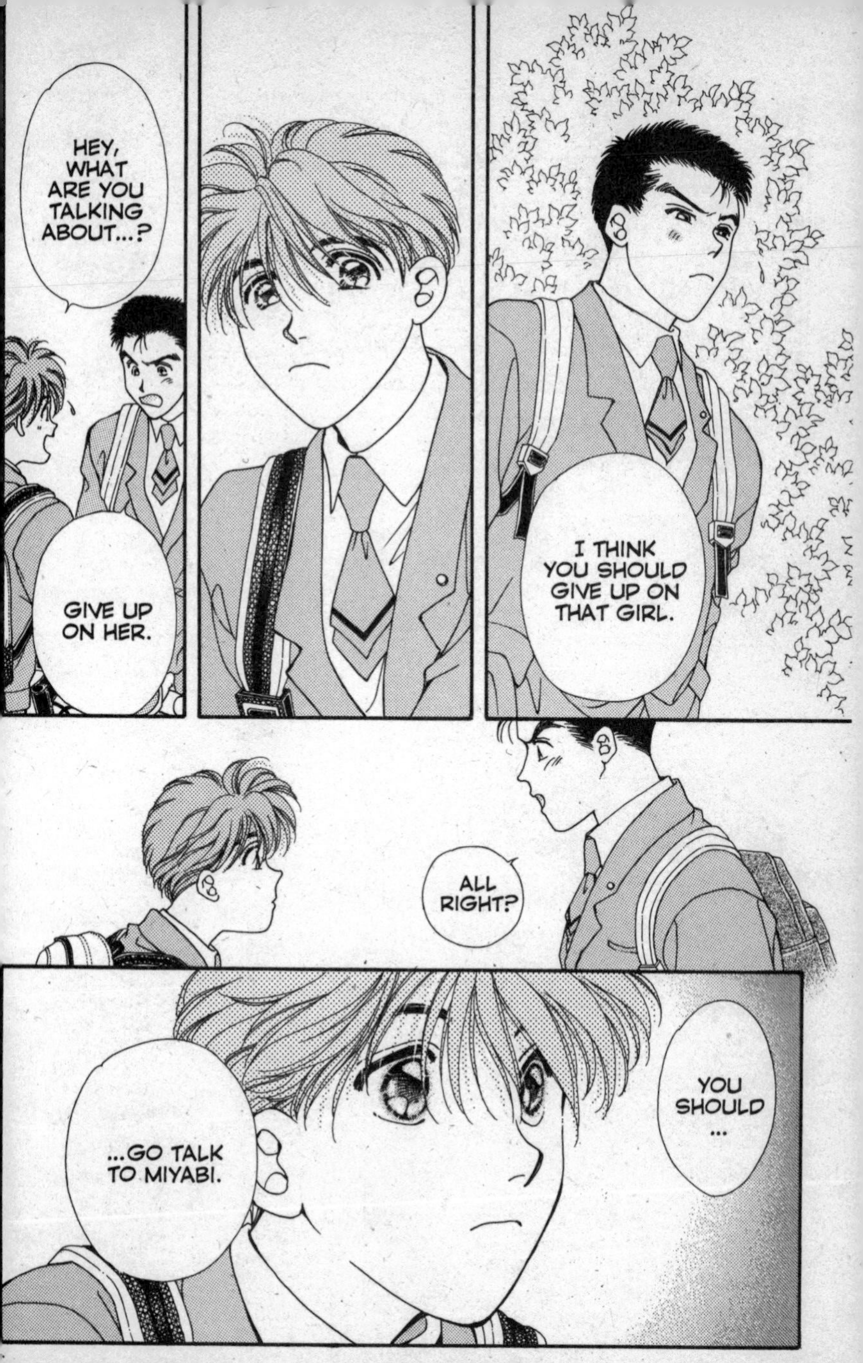
I THINK YOU SHOULD GIVE UP ON THAT GIRL.
HEY, WHAT ARE YOU TALKING ABOUT...?
GIVE UP ON HER.
ALL RIGHT?
YOU SHOULD ...
...GO TALK TO MIYABI.

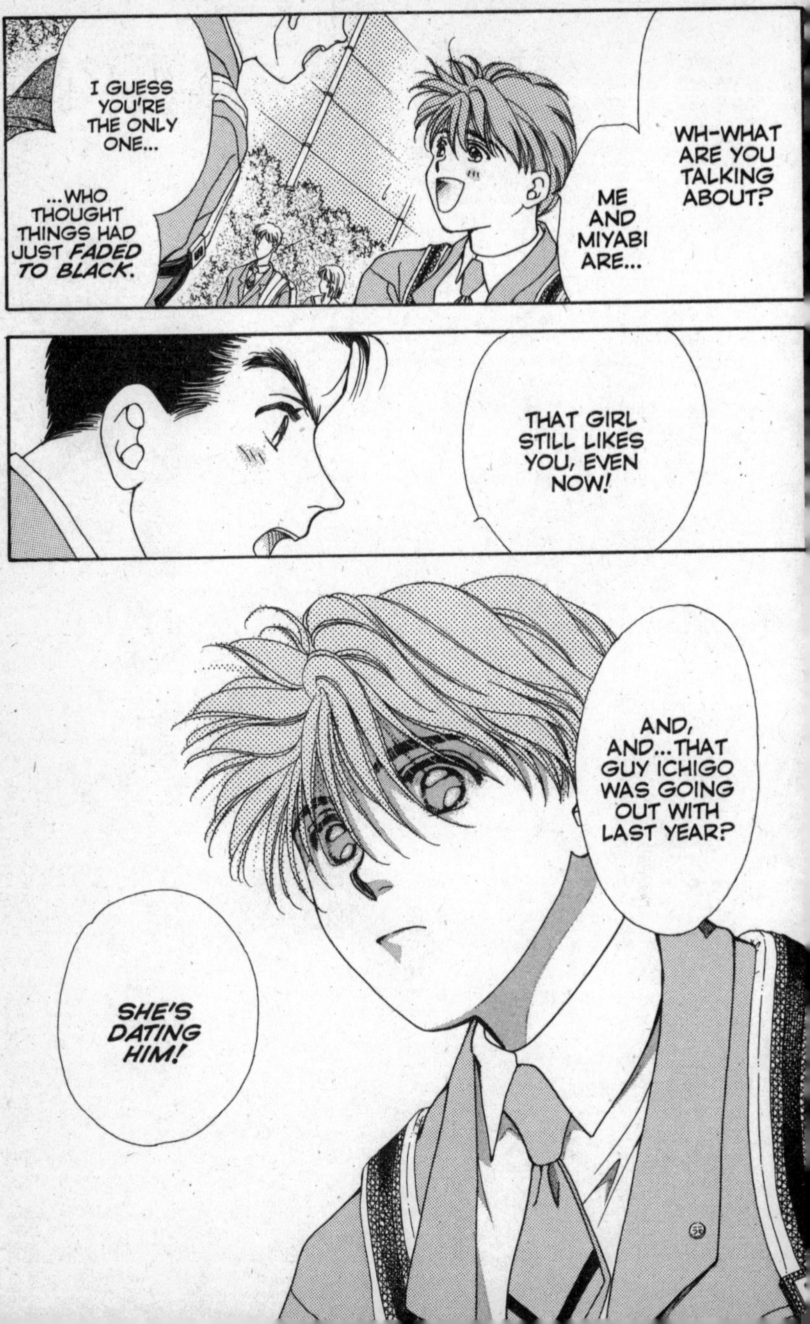
WH-WHAT ARE YOU TALKING ABOUT?
ME AND MIYABI ARE...
I GUESS YOU'RE THE ONLY ONE...
...WHO THOUGHT THINGS HAD JUST *FADED TO BLACK*.
THAT GIRL STILL LIKES YOU, EVEN NOW!
AND, AND...THAT GUY ICHIGO WAS GOING OUT WITH LAST YEAR?
SHE'S DATING HIM!

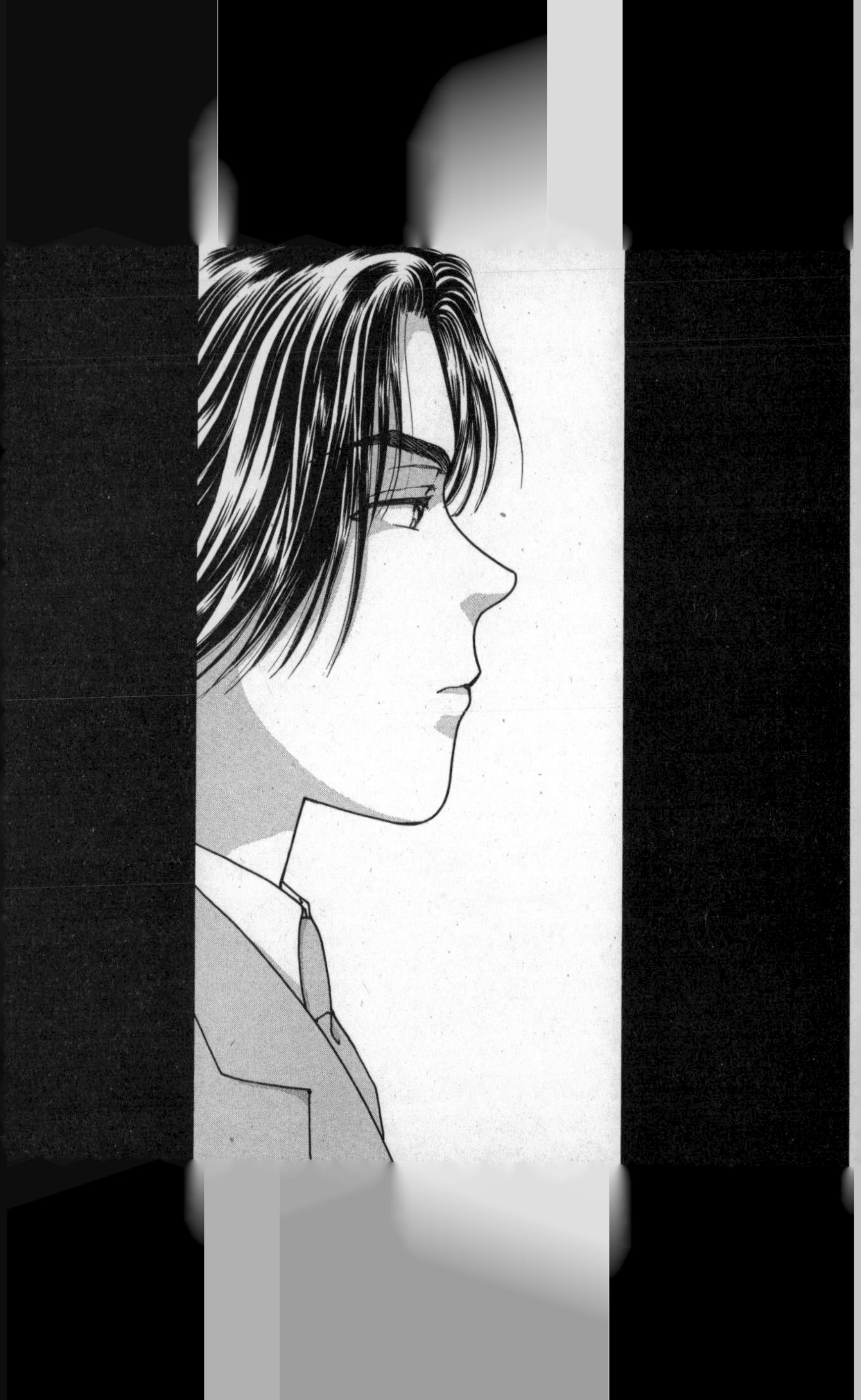

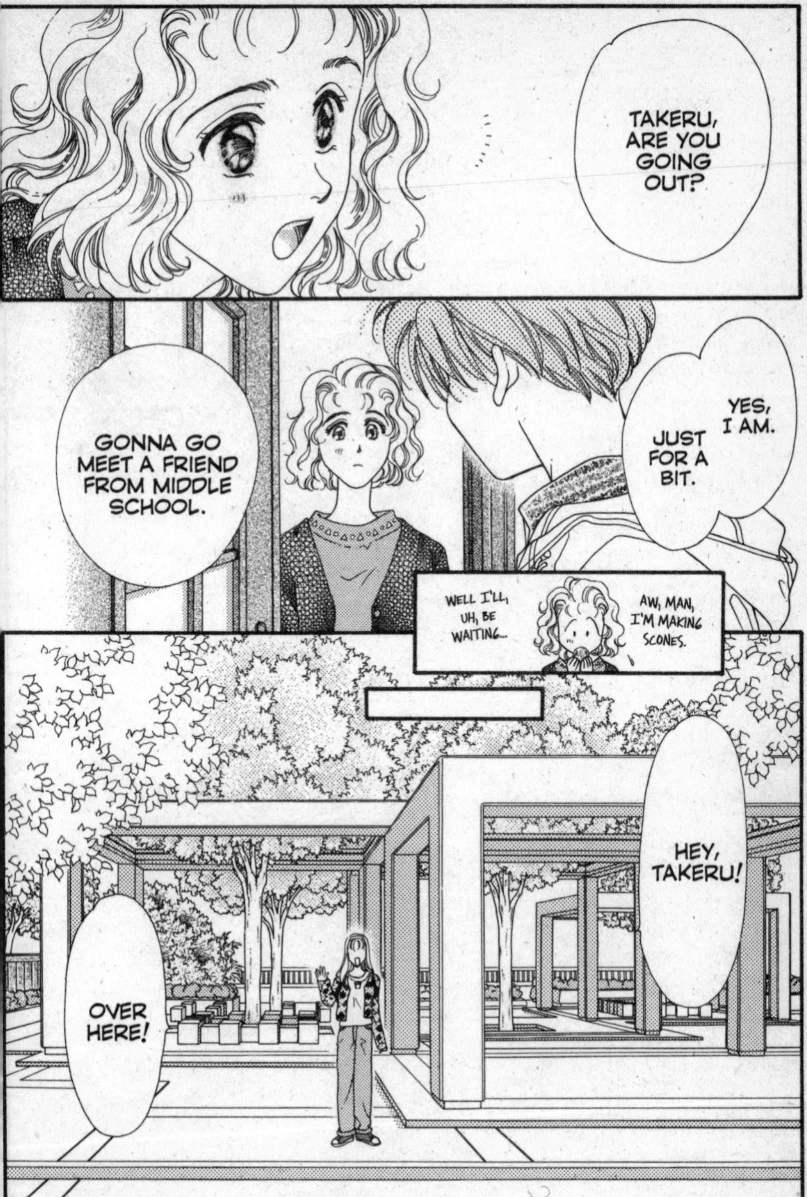
TAKERU, ARE YOU GOING OUT?
YES, I AM.
JUST FOR A BIT.
GONNA GO MEET A FRIEND FROM MIDDLE SCHOOL.
AW, MAN, I'M MAKING SCONES.
WELL I'LL, UH, BE WAITING...
HEY, TAKERU!
OVER HERE!

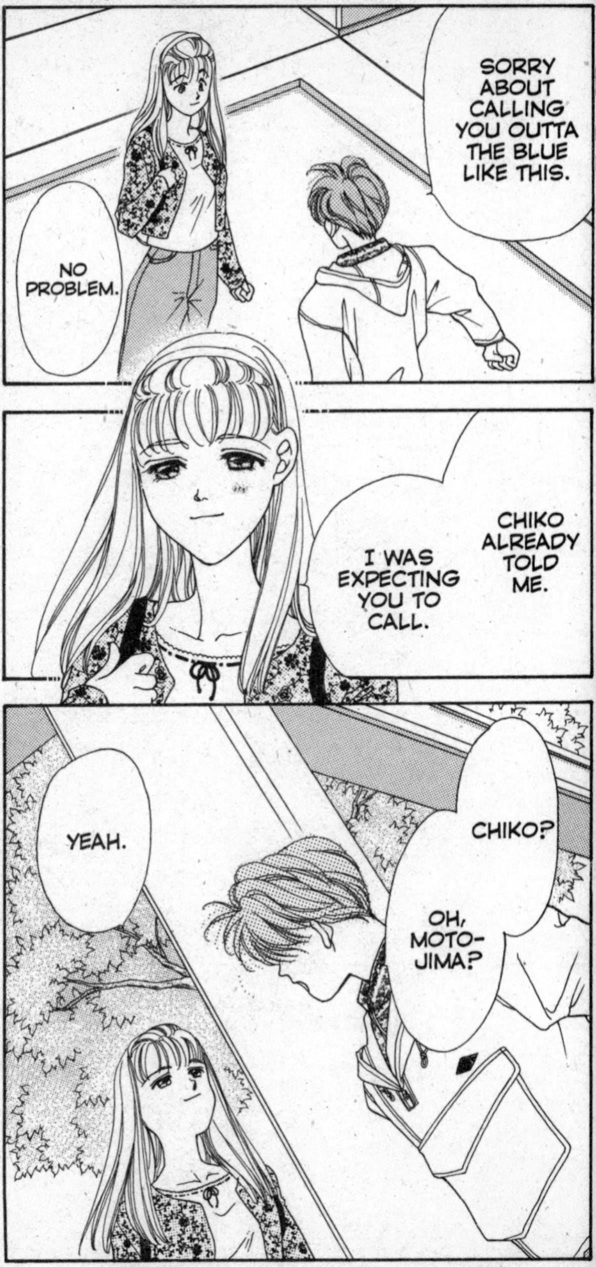
SORRY ABOUT CALLING YOU OUTTA THE BLUE LIKE THIS.
NO PROBLEM.
CHIKO ALREADY TOLD ME.
I WAS EXPECTING YOU TO CALL.
CHIKO?
OH, MOTO-JIMA?
YEAH.

Sidebar No. 5

The way the writer explained it, "Angelique" was a game where you make a bunch of really pretty-boy characters build houses for you. Of course, this interested me greatly, and so when I had some free time I went and hunted it down. I couldn't find it right away--it must have been sold out. I was despairing that I'd never be able to get a hold of it before I had to start working again--and then, there it was. And in the premium boxed set, no less!! Here I was, thinking I'd end up disappointed, and now I have the game! I couldn't even **begin** to tell you how much fun I'm having! Maybe I'll try to, later!

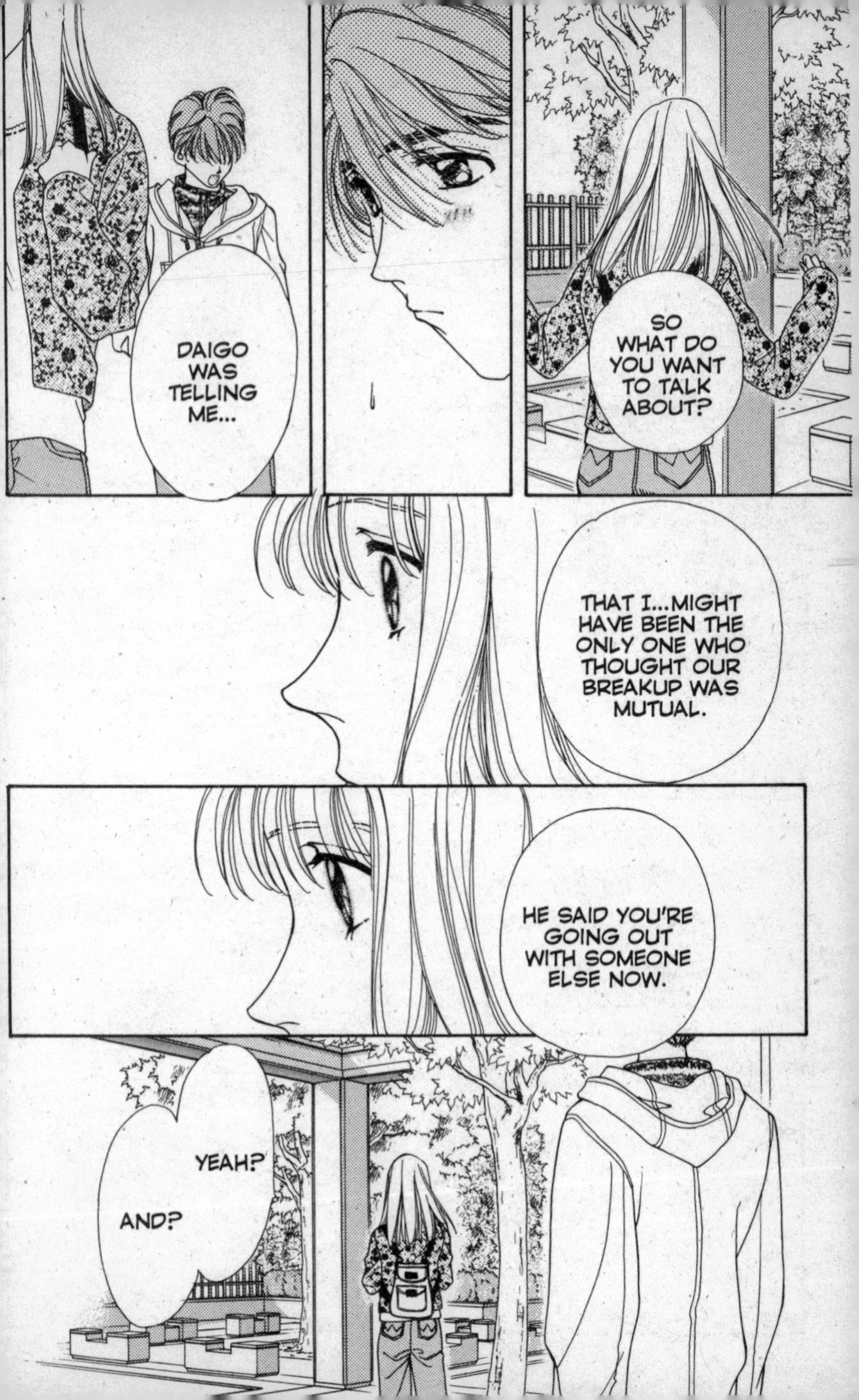
SO WHAT DO YOU WANT TO TALK ABOUT?
DAIGO WAS TELLING ME...
THAT I...MIGHT HAVE BEEN THE ONLY ONE WHO THOUGHT OUR BREAKUP WAS MUTUAL.
HE SAID YOU'RE GOING OUT WITH SOMEONE ELSE NOW.
YEAH? AND?

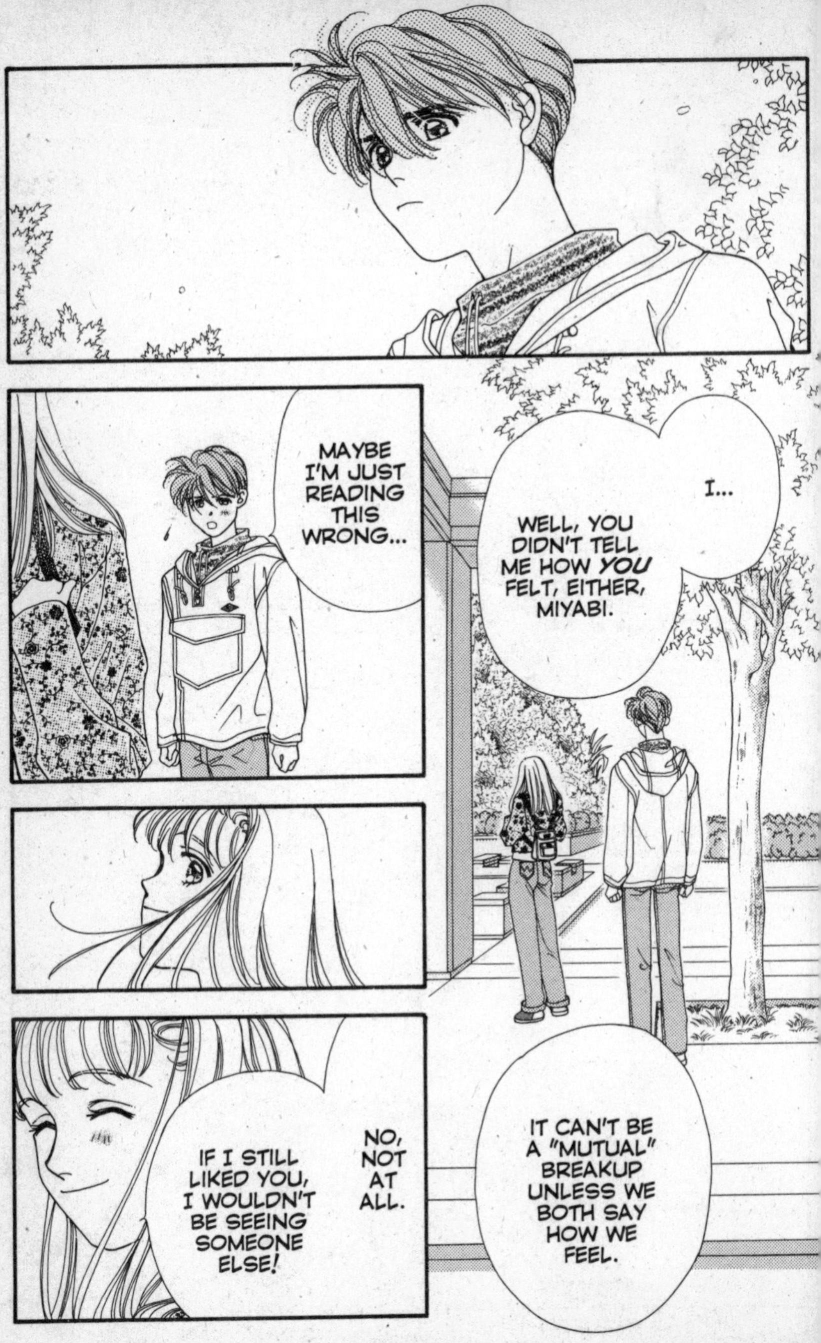
I...
WELL, YOU DIDN'T TELL ME HOW *YOU* FELT, EITHER, MIYABI.
IT CAN'T BE A "MUTUAL" BREAKUP UNLESS WE BOTH SAY HOW WE FEEL.
MAYBE I'M JUST READING THIS WRONG...
NO, NOT AT ALL.
IF I STILL LIKED YOU, I WOULDN'T BE SEEING SOMEONE ELSE!

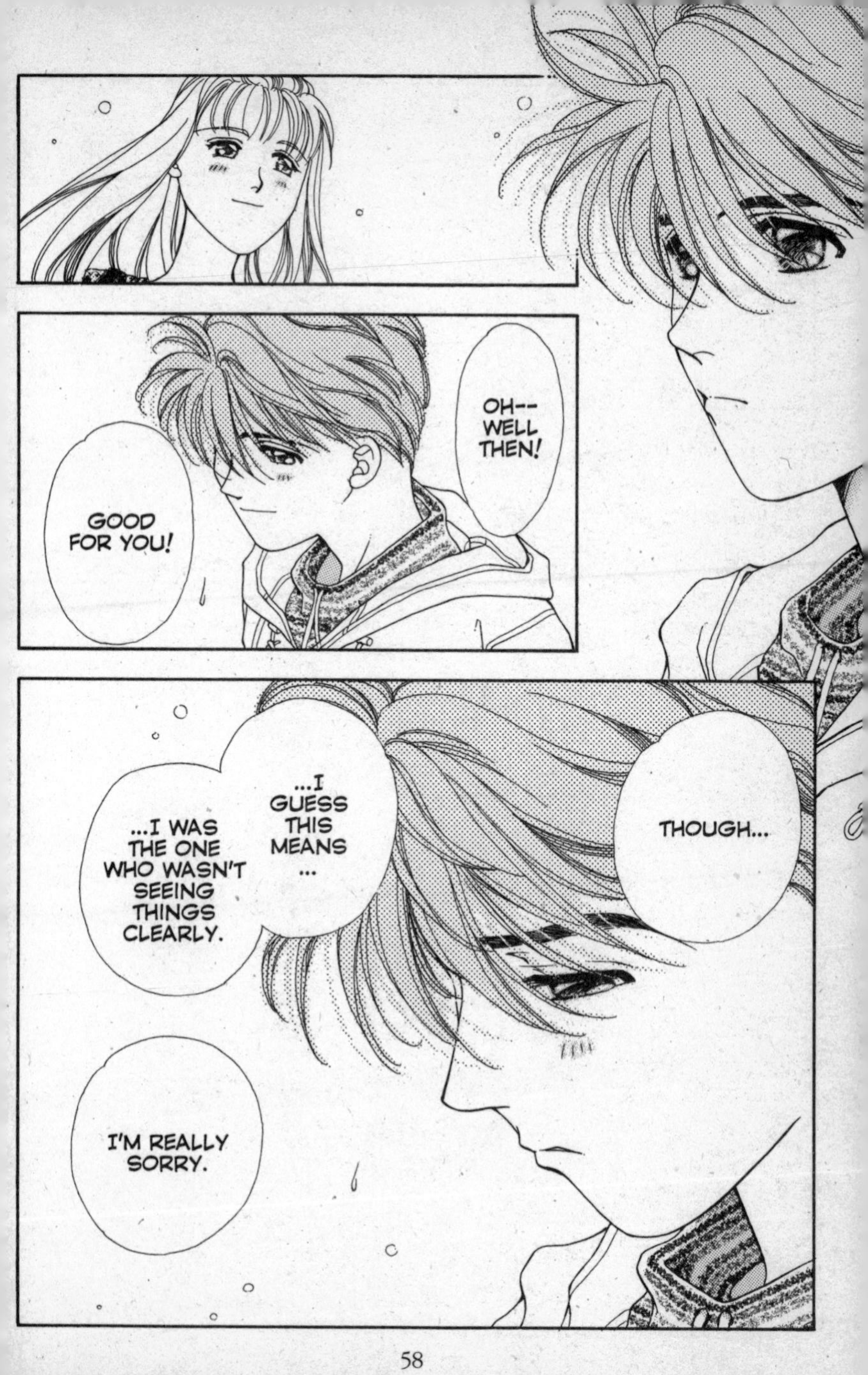
OH-- WELL THEN!
GOOD FOR YOU!
THOUGH...
...I GUESS THIS MEANS ...
...I WAS THE ONE WHO WASN'T SEEING THINGS CLEARLY.
I'M REALLY SORRY.

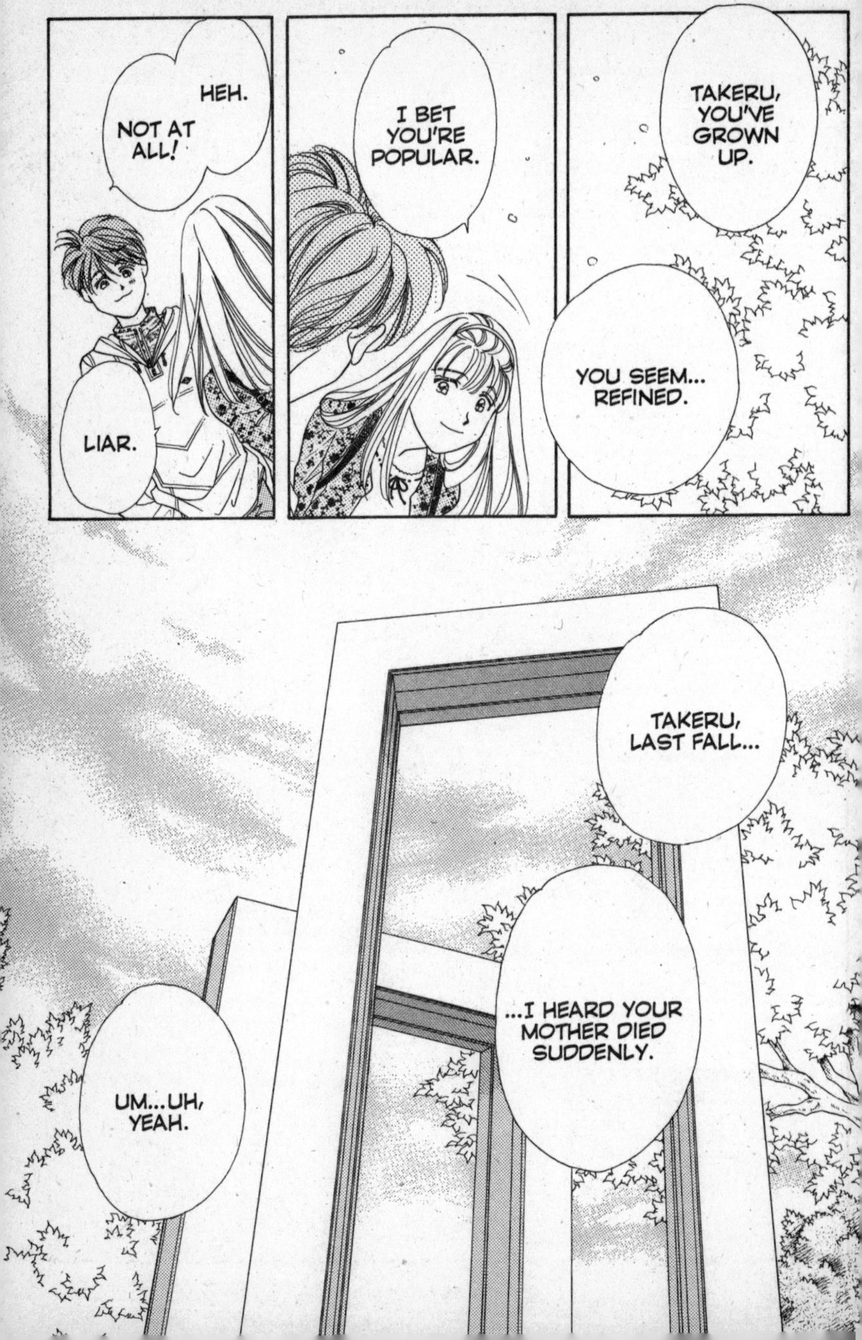
TAKERU, YOU'VE GROWN UP.
YOU SEEM... REFINED.
I BET YOU'RE POPULAR.
HEH. NOT AT ALL!
LIAR.
TAKERU, LAST FALL...
...I HEARD YOUR MOTHER DIED SUDDENLY.
UM...UH, YEAH.

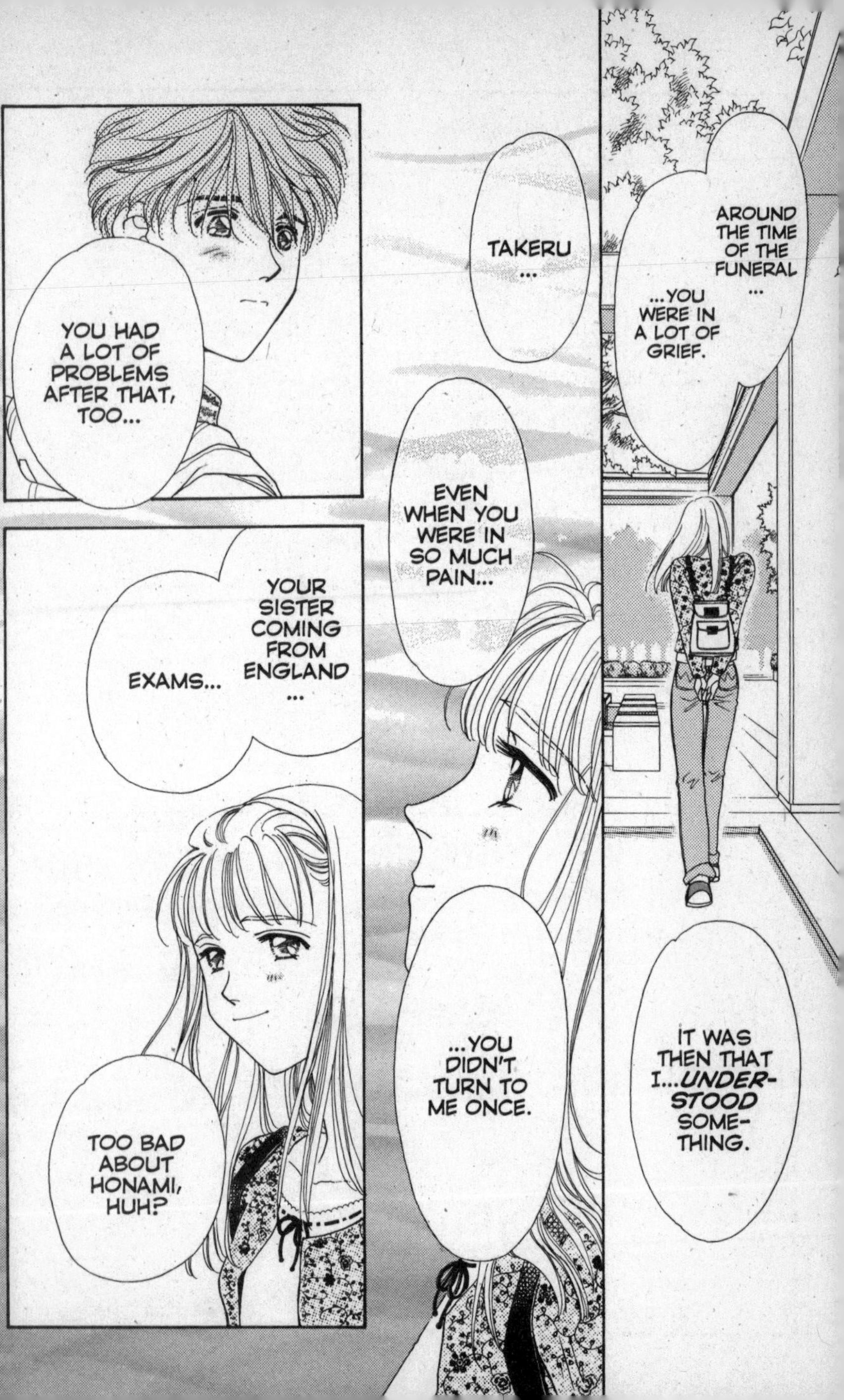
AROUND THE TIME OF THE FUNERAL...
...YOU WERE IN A LOT OF GRIEF.
IT WAS THEN THAT I...*UNDERSTOOD* SOMETHING.
TAKERU...
EVEN WHEN YOU WERE IN SO MUCH PAIN...
...YOU DIDN'T TURN TO ME ONCE.
YOU HAD A LOT OF PROBLEMS AFTER THAT, TOO...
YOUR SISTER COMING FROM ENGLAND...
EXAMS...
TOO BAD ABOUT HONAMI, HUH?

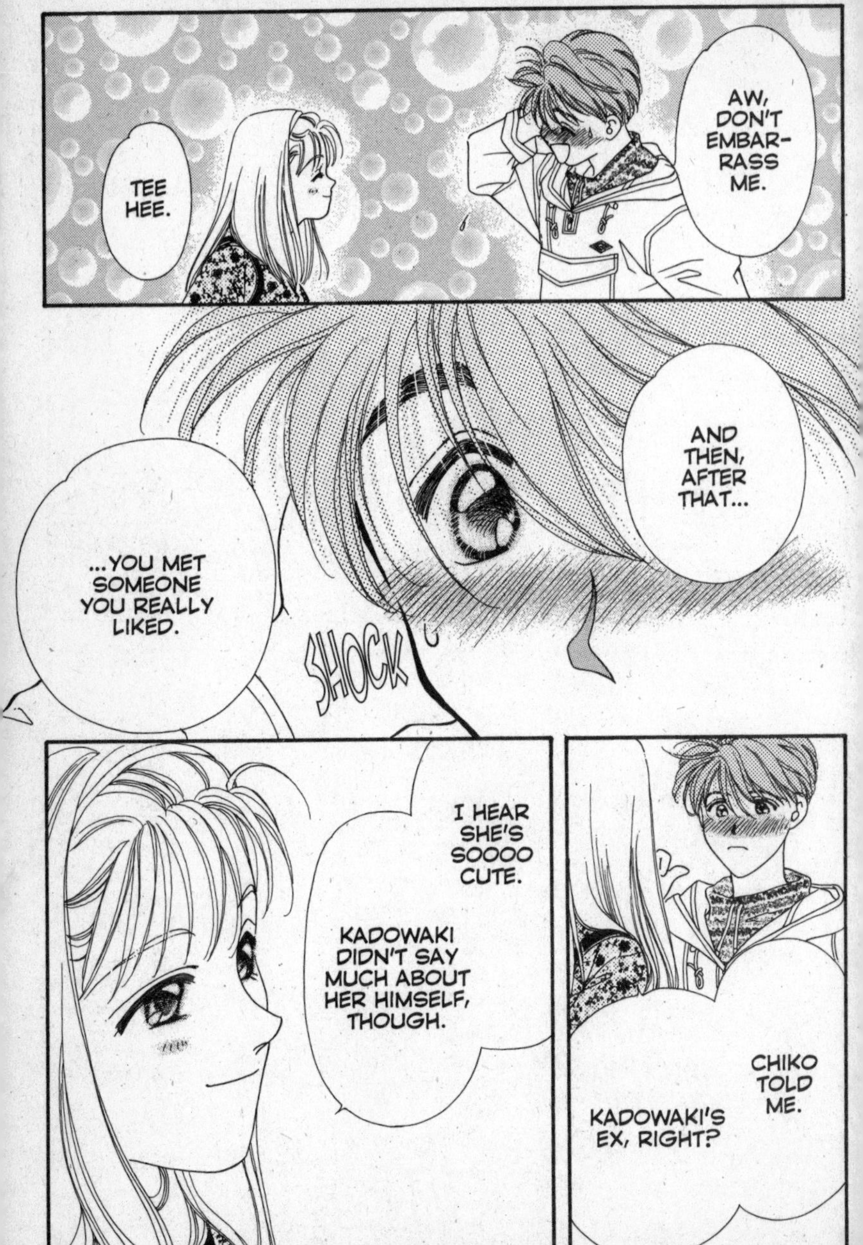
AW, DON'T EMBARRASS ME.
TEE HEE.
AND THEN, AFTER THAT...
SHOCK
...YOU MET SOMEONE YOU REALLY LIKED.
CHIKO TOLD ME.
KADOWAKI'S EX, RIGHT?
I HEAR SHE'S SOOOO CUTE.
KADOWAKI DIDN'T SAY MUCH ABOUT HER HIMSELF, THOUGH.

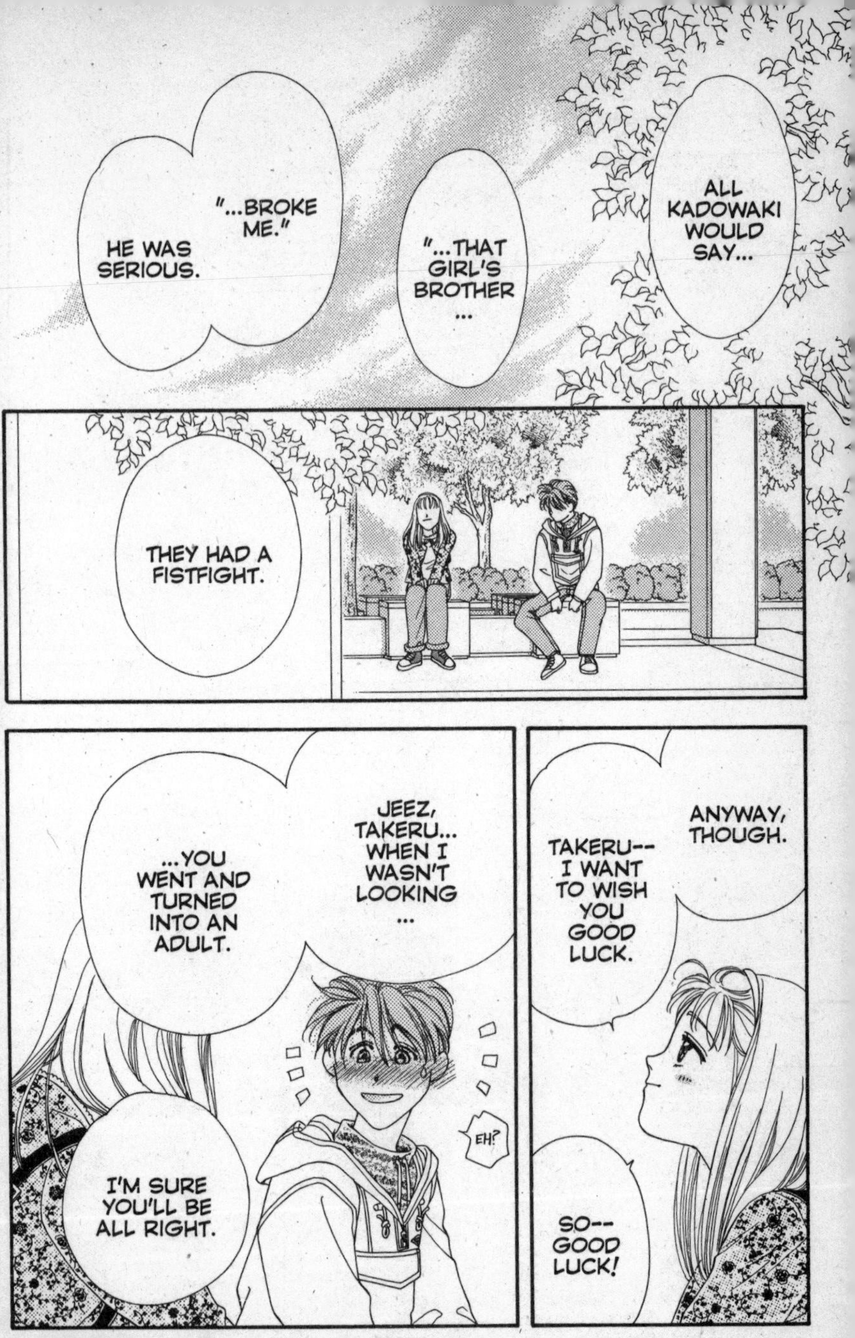
ALL KADOWAKI WOULD SAY...
"...THAT GIRL'S BROTHER ..."
"...BROKE ME."
HE WAS SERIOUS.
THEY HAD A FISTFIGHT.
ANYWAY, THOUGH.
TAKERU-- I WANT TO WISH YOU GOOD LUCK.
SO-- GOOD LUCK!
JEEZ, TAKERU... WHEN I WASN'T LOOKING ...
...YOU WENT AND TURNED INTO AN ADULT.
EH?
I'M SURE YOU'LL BE ALL RIGHT.

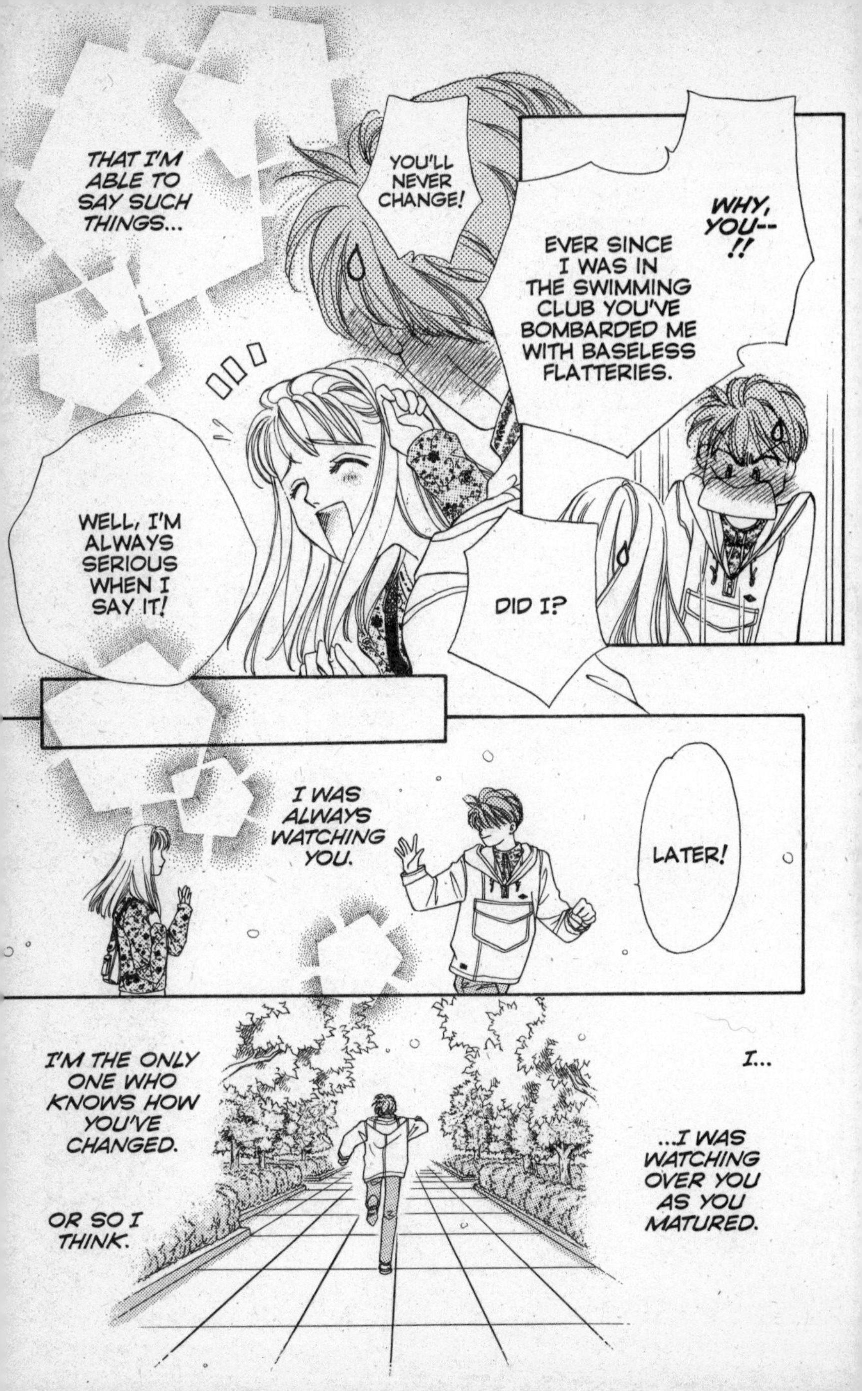
EVER SINCE I WAS IN THE SWIMMING CLUB YOU'VE BOMBARDED ME WITH BASELESS FLATTERIES.
DID I?
WHY, YOU-- !!
YOU'LL NEVER CHANGE!
WELL, I'M ALWAYS SERIOUS WHEN I SAY IT!
THAT I'M ABLE TO SAY SUCH THINGS...
LATER!
I WAS ALWAYS WATCHING YOU.
I...
...I WAS WATCHING OVER YOU AS YOU MATURED.
I'M THE ONLY ONE WHO KNOWS HOW YOU'VE CHANGED.
OR SO I THINK.

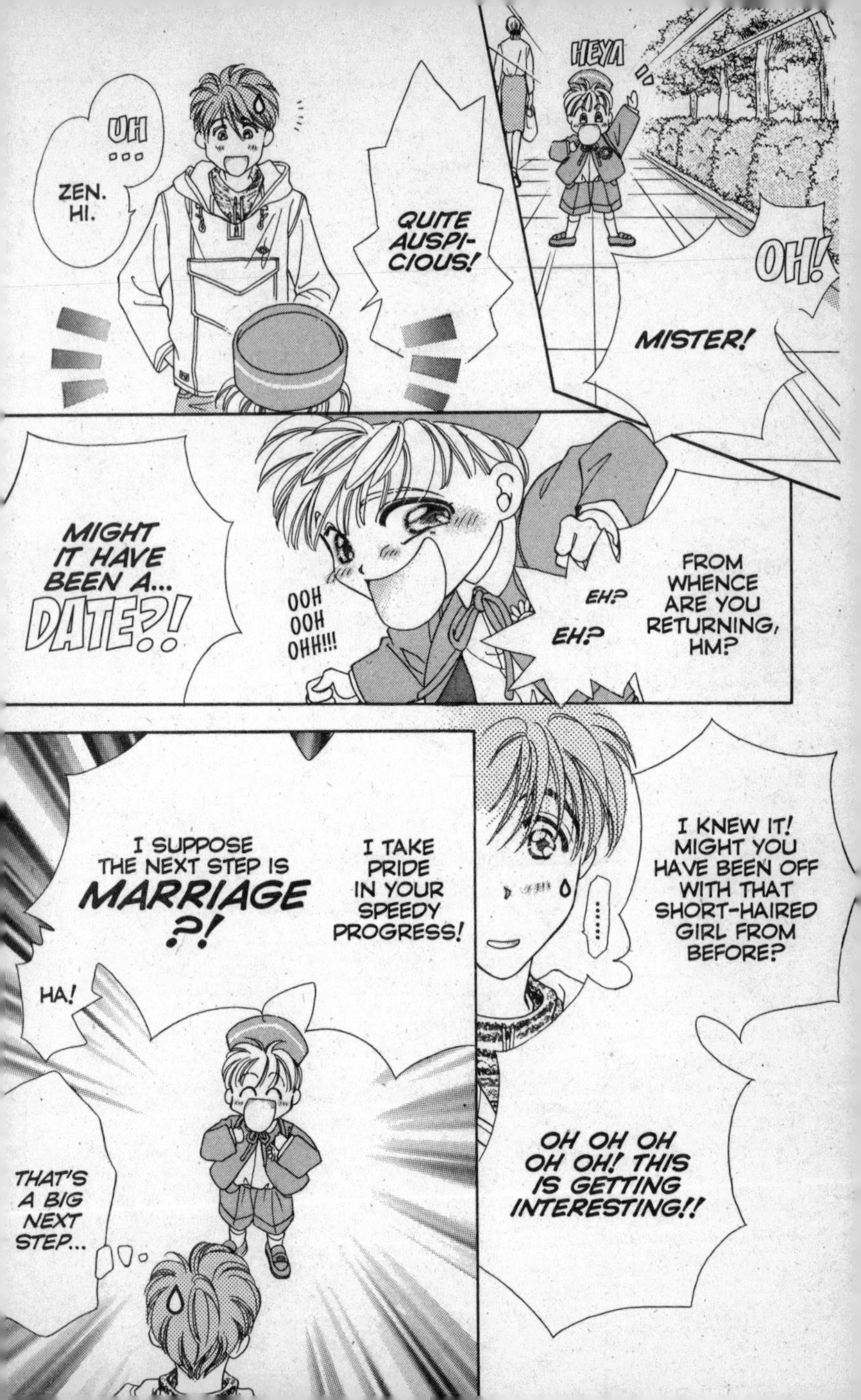
HEYA
OH!
MISTER!
QUITE AUSPICIOUS!
UH... ZEN. HI.
FROM WHENCE ARE YOU RETURNING, HM?
EH?
EH?
OOH OOH OHH!!!
MIGHT IT HAVE BEEN A... DATE?!
I KNEW IT! MIGHT YOU HAVE BEEN OFF WITH THAT SHORT-HAIRED GIRL FROM BEFORE?
......
OH OH OH OH OH! THIS IS GETTING INTERESTING!!
I TAKE PRIDE IN YOUR SPEEDY PROGRESS!
I SUPPOSE THE NEXT STEP IS MARRIAGE?!
HA!
THAT'S A BIG NEXT STEP...

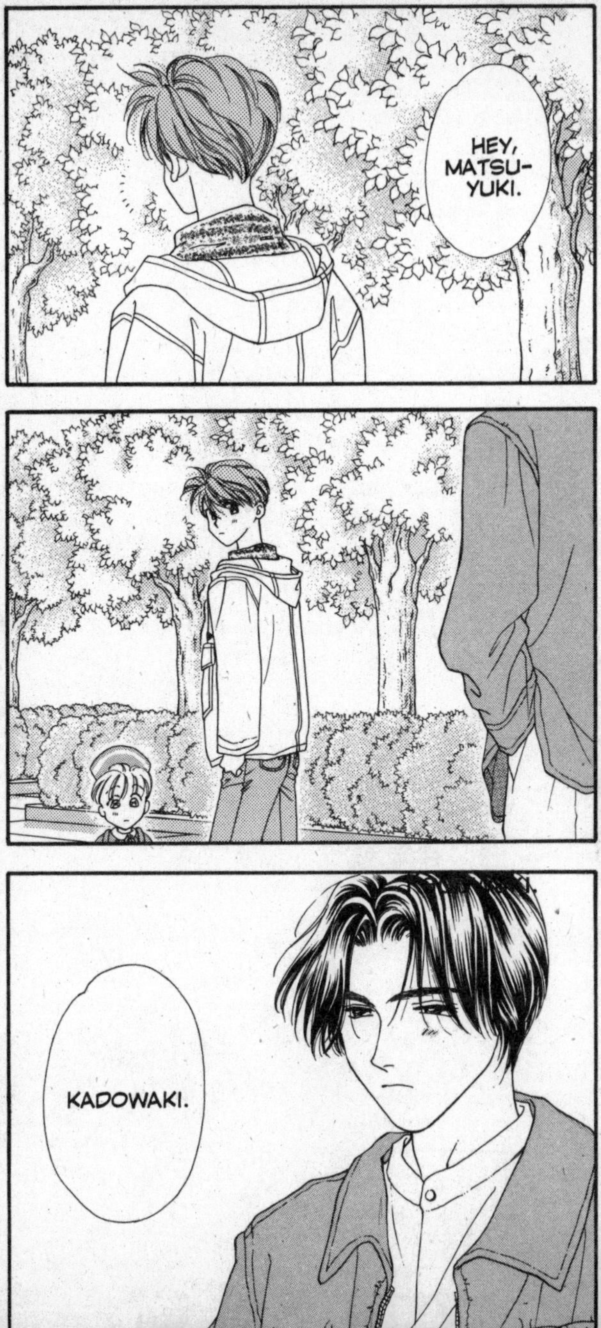
HEY, MATSU-YUKI.
KADOWAKI.

Sidebar No. 6

I am forever in debt to the one who first recommended this game to me. However, the letter is lost; I cannot find it. If you are reading this right now, know that I express to you my sincere thanks. I am enthralled by this game, just like you said I would be. To think I'd become this infatuated with a game about a bunch of guardian angels. "Confession" takes on a whole new meaning with them. I wonder what's going to happen next. I can't believe I found a game I love this much. There's that part where Clavius says "I am...different." And I was like... Wow!!

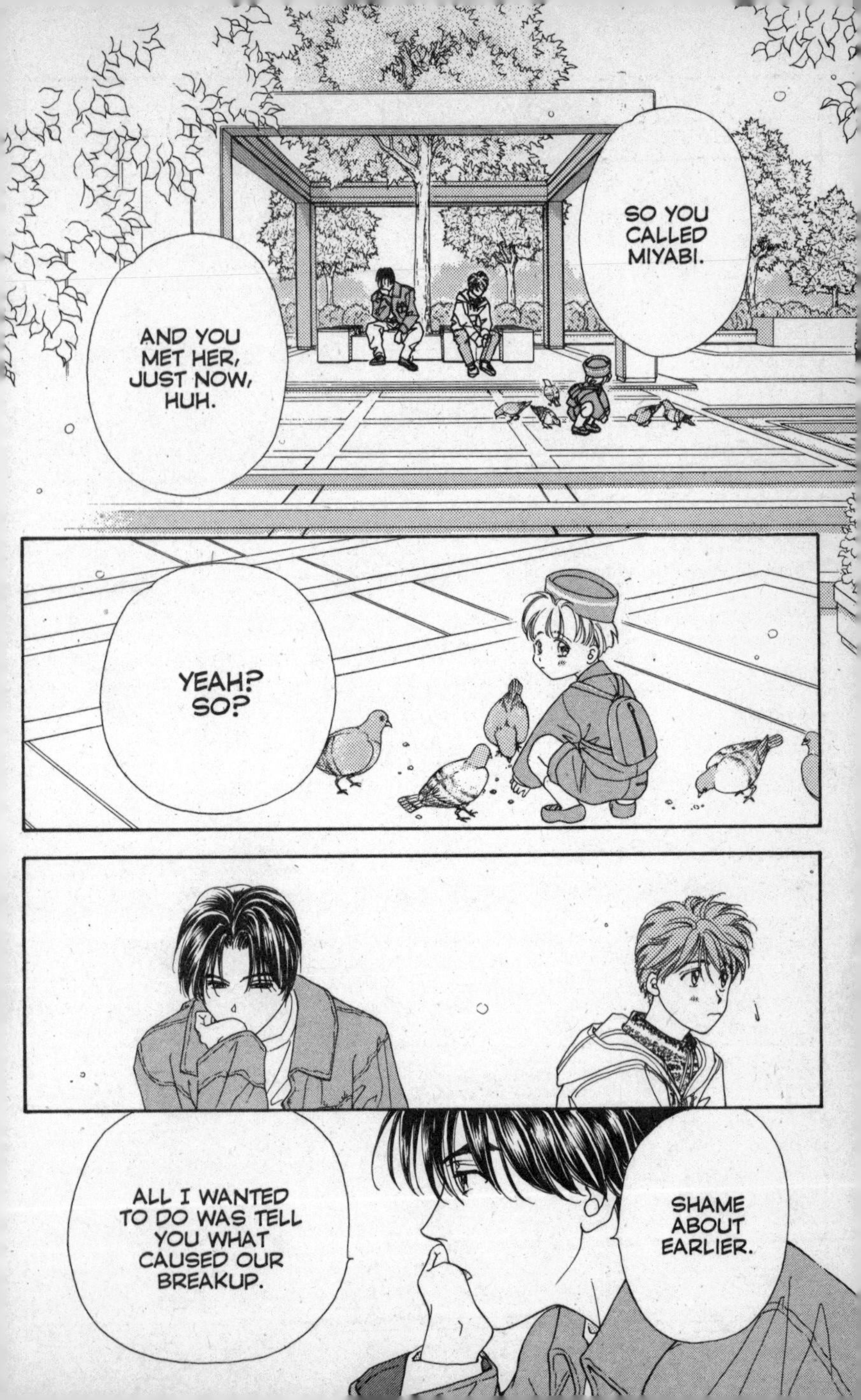
SO YOU CALLED MIYABI.
AND YOU MET HER, JUST NOW, HUH.
YEAH? SO?
SHAME ABOUT EARLIER.
ALL I WANTED TO DO WAS TELL YOU WHAT CAUSED OUR BREAKUP.

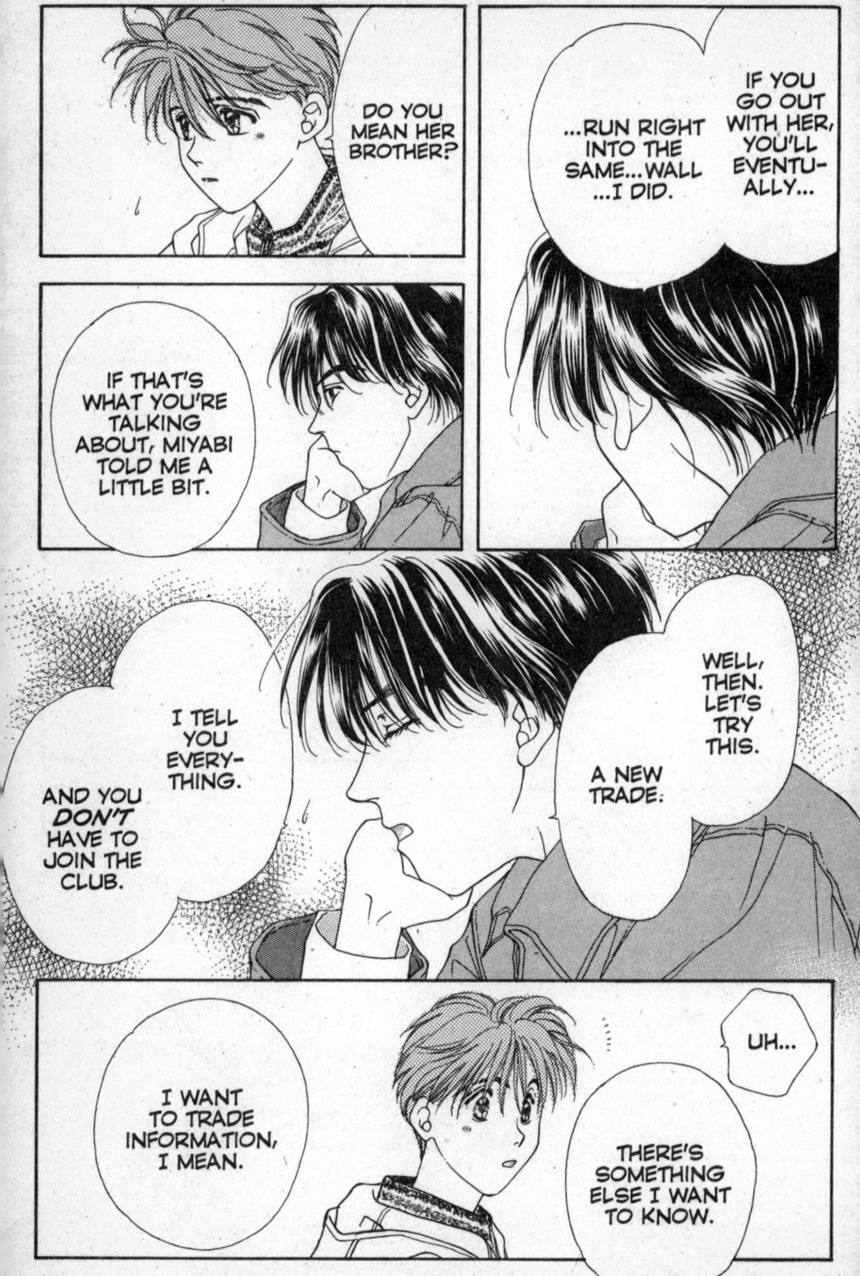
IF YOU GO OUT WITH HER, YOU'LL EVENTU-ALLY...
...RUN RIGHT INTO THE SAME...WALL ...I DID.
DO YOU MEAN HER BROTHER?
IF THAT'S WHAT YOU'RE TALKING ABOUT, MIYABI TOLD ME A LITTLE BIT.
WELL, THEN. LET'S TRY THIS.
A NEW TRADE.
I TELL YOU EVERY-THING.
AND YOU *DON'T* HAVE TO JOIN THE CLUB.
UH...
THERE'S SOMETHING ELSE I WANT TO KNOW.
I WANT TO TRADE INFORMATION, I MEAN.

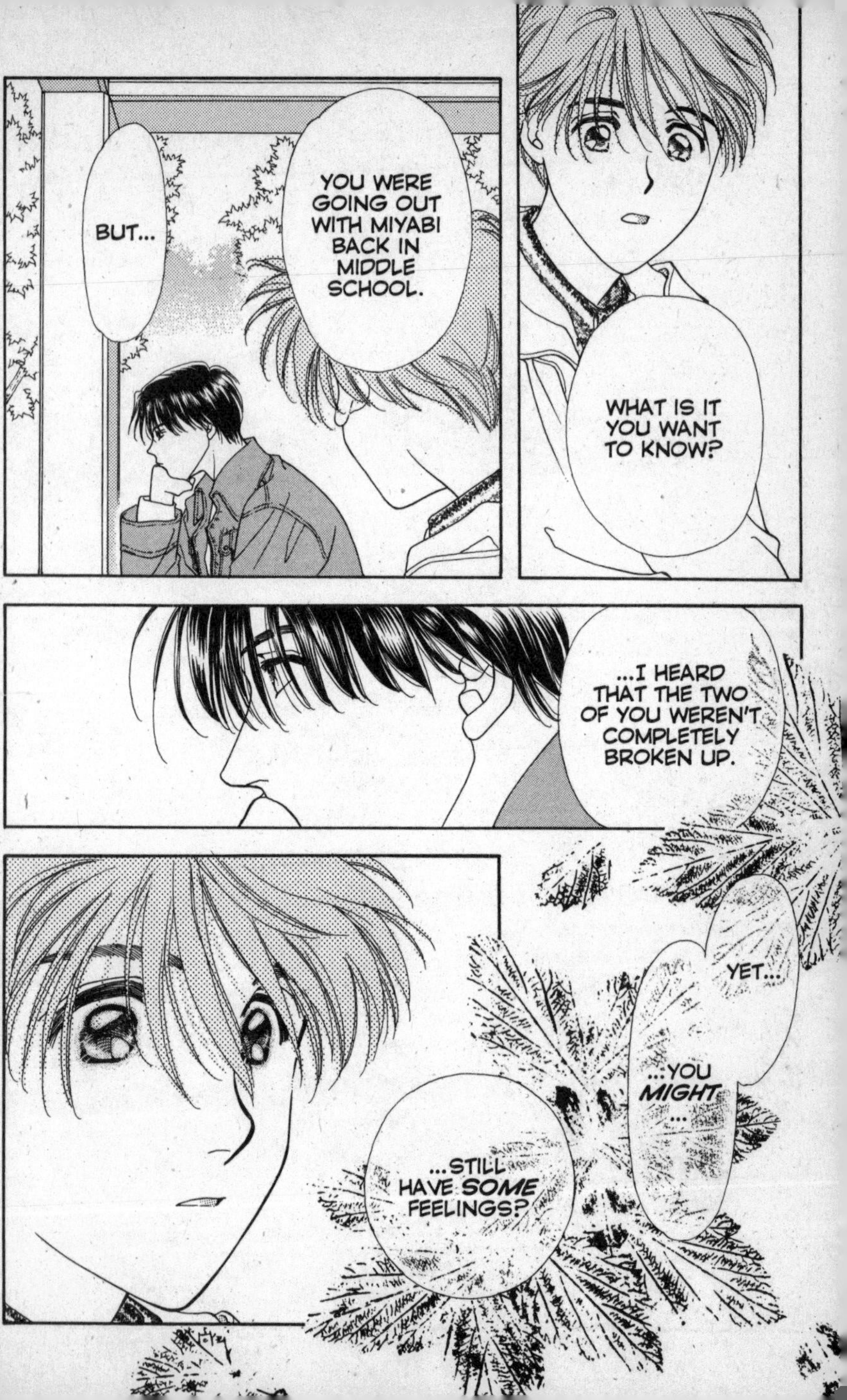
WHAT IS IT YOU WANT TO KNOW?
YOU WERE GOING OUT WITH MIYABI BACK IN MIDDLE SCHOOL.
BUT...
...I HEARD THAT THE TWO OF YOU WEREN'T COMPLETELY BROKEN UP.
YET...
...YOU *MIGHT*...
...STILL HAVE *SOME* FEELINGS?

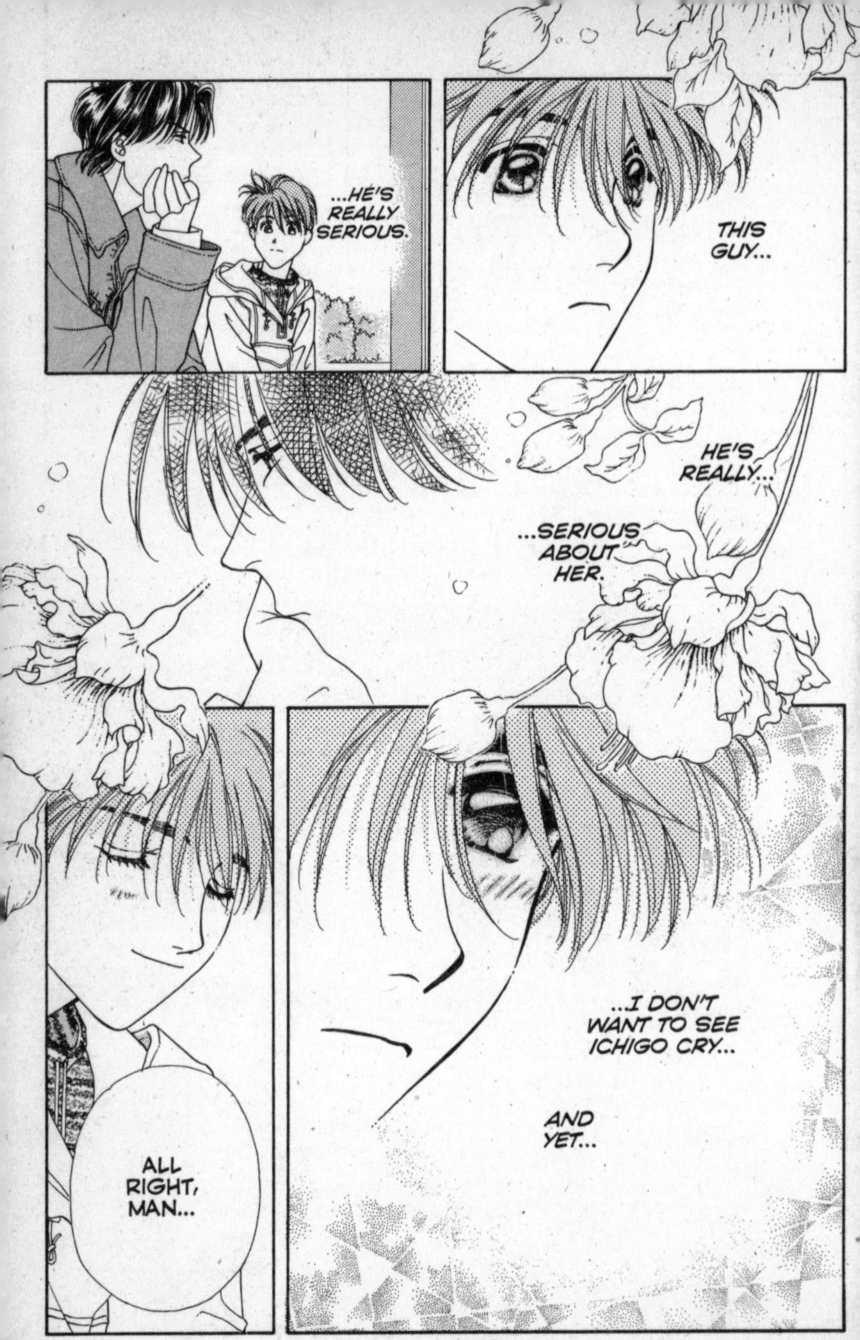
THIS GUY...
...HE'S REALLY SERIOUS.
HE'S REALLY...
...SERIOUS ABOUT HER.
...I DON'T WANT TO SEE ICHIGO CRY...
AND YET...
ALL RIGHT, MAN...

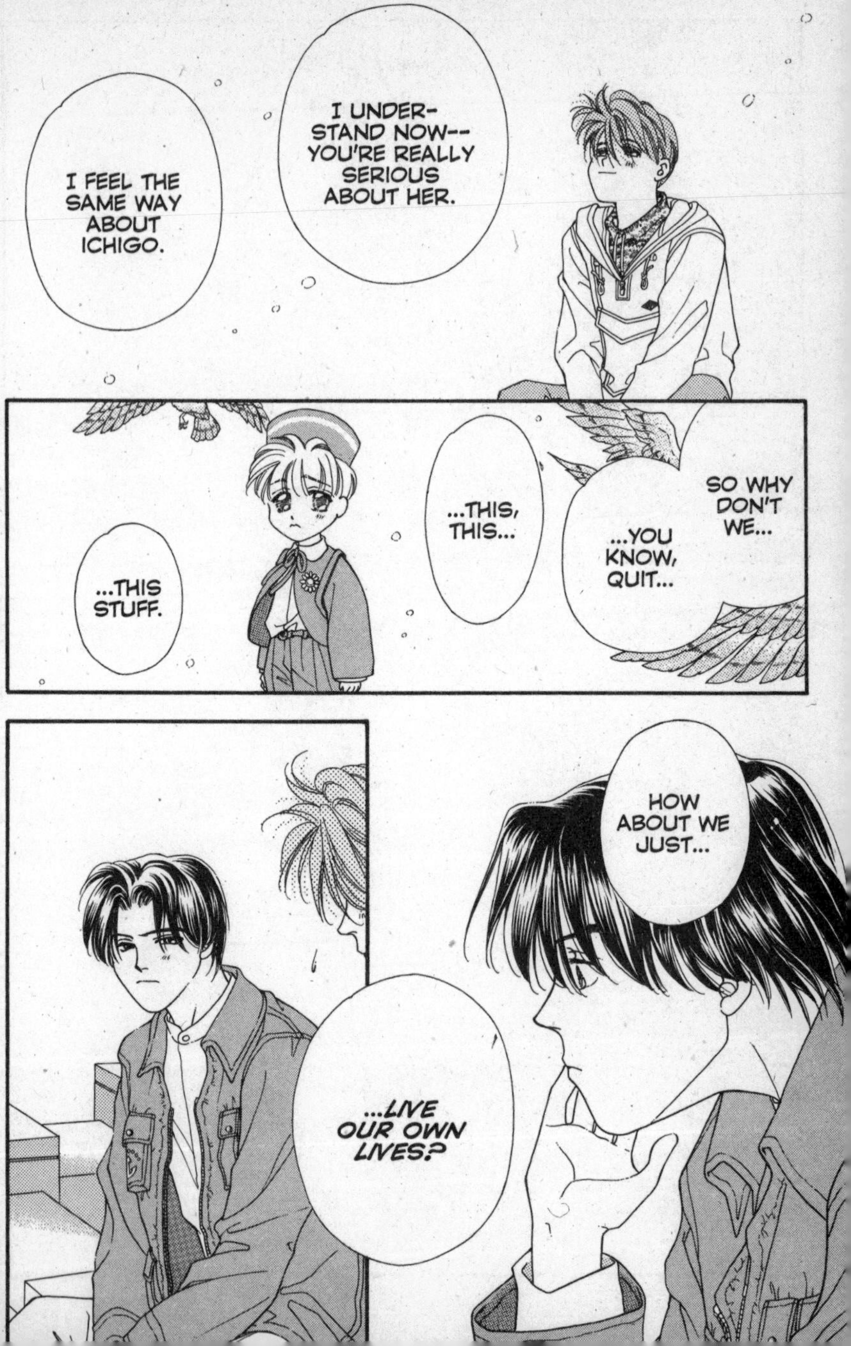
I UNDER-STAND NOW-- YOU'RE REALLY SERIOUS ABOUT HER.
I FEEL THE SAME WAY ABOUT ICHIGO.
SO WHY DON'T WE...
...YOU KNOW, QUIT...
...THIS, THIS...
...THIS STUFF.
HOW ABOUT WE JUST...
...LIVE OUR OWN LIVES?

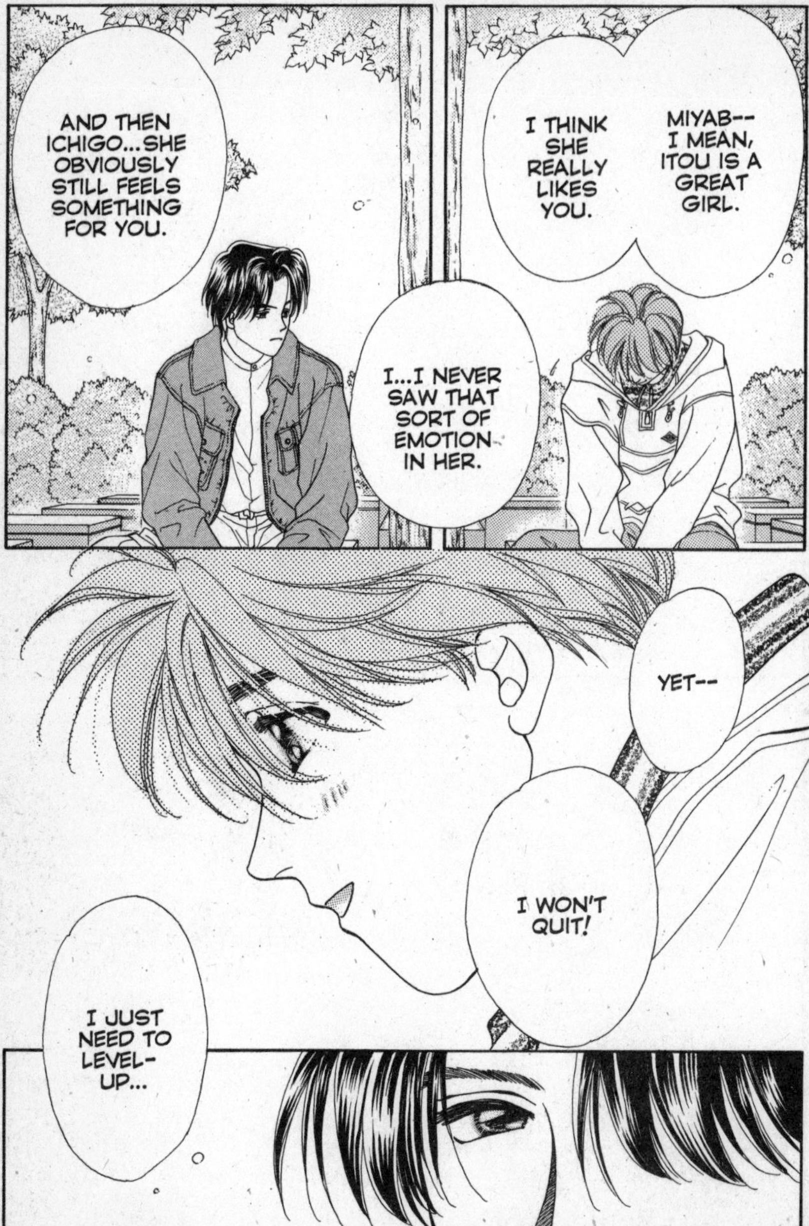
MIYAB-- I MEAN, ITOU IS A GREAT GIRL.
I THINK SHE REALLY LIKES YOU.
AND THEN ICHIGO...SHE OBVIOUSLY STILL FEELS SOMETHING FOR YOU.
I...I NEVER SAW THAT SORT OF EMOTION IN HER.
YET--
I WON'T QUIT!
I JUST NEED TO LEVEL-UP...

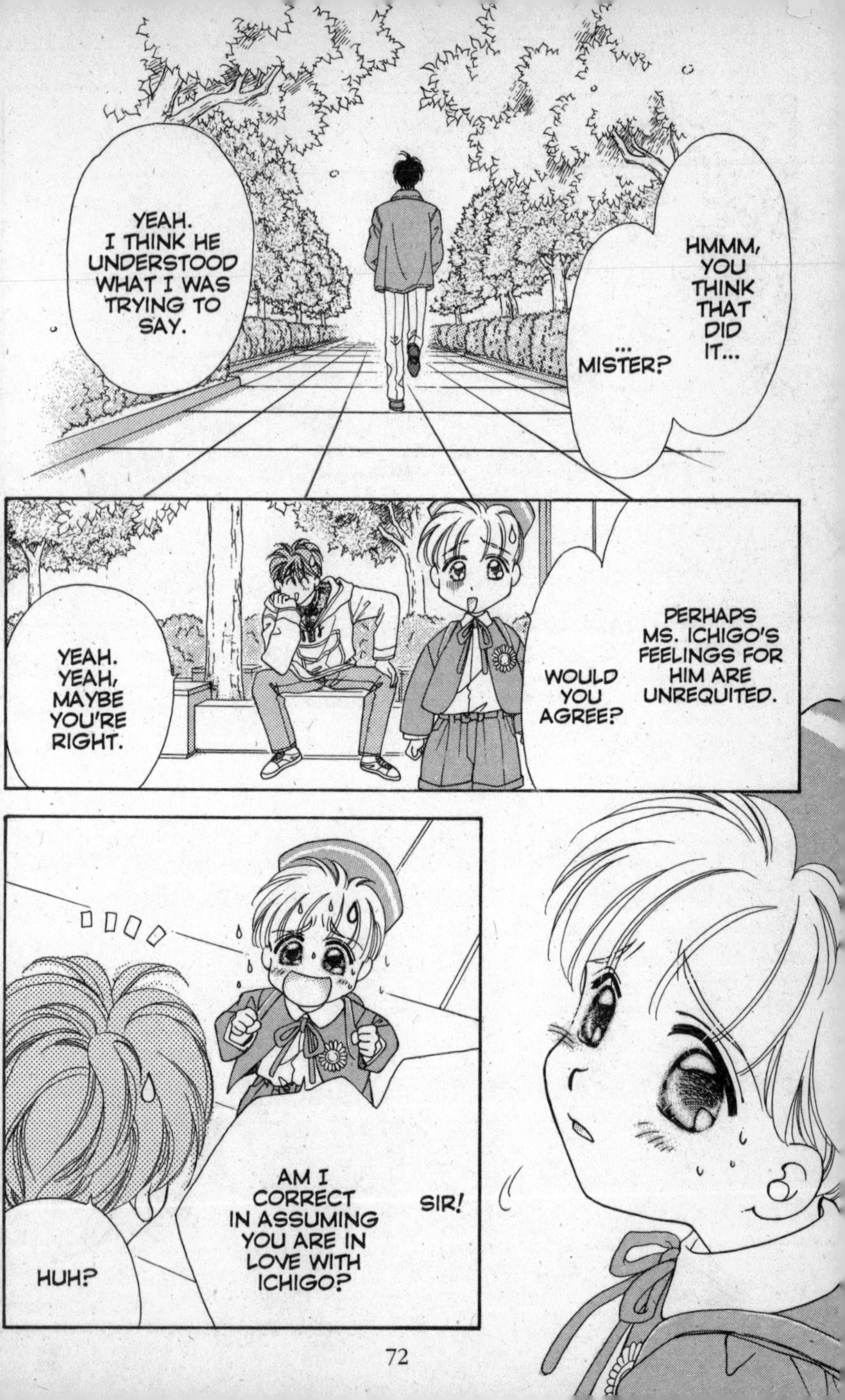
HMMM, YOU THINK THAT DID IT...
...MISTER?
YEAH. I THINK HE UNDERSTOOD WHAT I WAS TRYING TO SAY.
PERHAPS MS. ICHIGO'S FEELINGS FOR HIM ARE UNREQUITED.
WOULD YOU AGREE?
YEAH. YEAH, MAYBE YOU'RE RIGHT.
SIR!
AM I CORRECT IN ASSUMING YOU ARE IN LOVE WITH ICHIGO?
HUH?

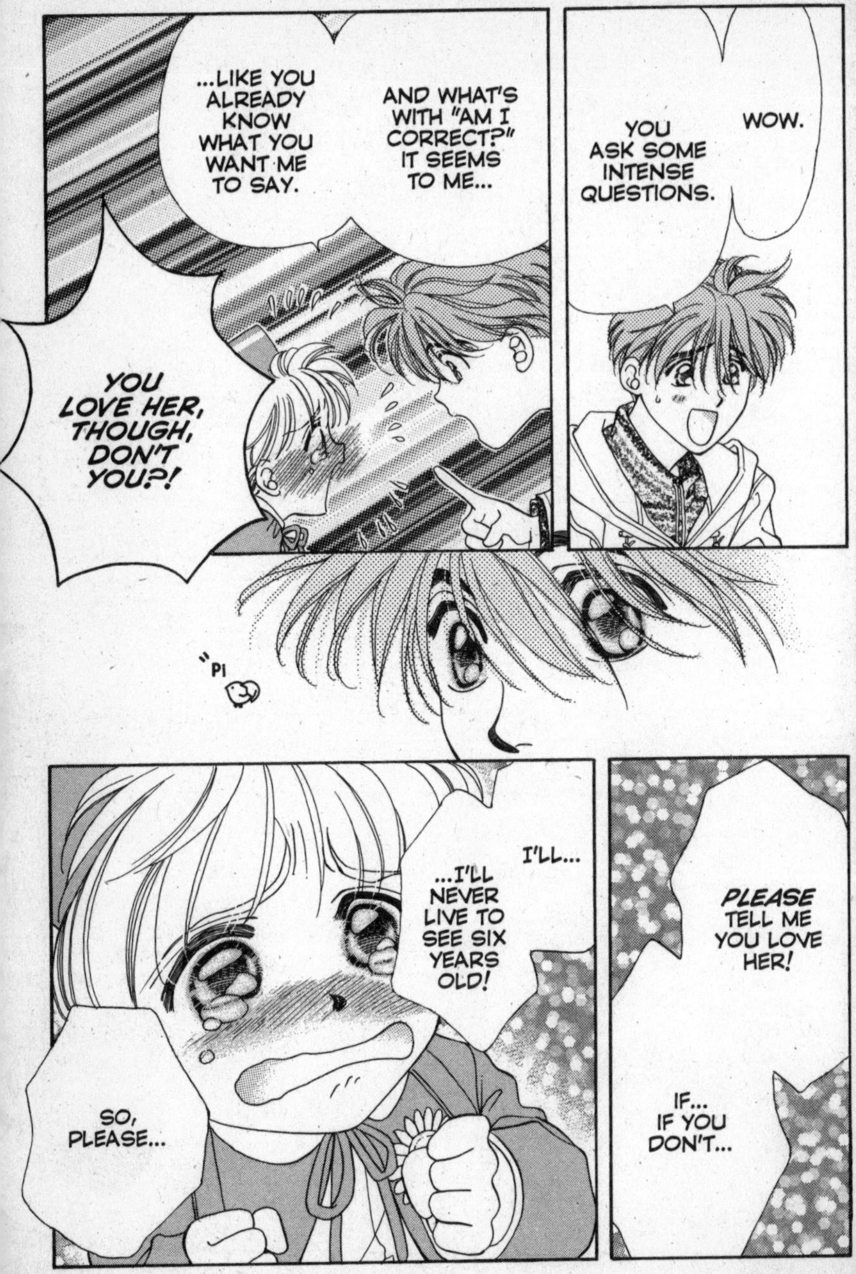
WOW.
YOU ASK SOME INTENSE QUESTIONS.
AND WHAT'S WITH "AM I CORRECT?" IT SEEMS TO ME...
...LIKE YOU ALREADY KNOW WHAT YOU WANT ME TO SAY.
YOU LOVE HER, THOUGH, DON'T YOU?!
PI
PLEASE TELL ME YOU LOVE HER!
IF... IF YOU DON'T...
I'LL...
...I'LL NEVER LIVE TO SEE SIX YEARS OLD!
SO, PLEASE...

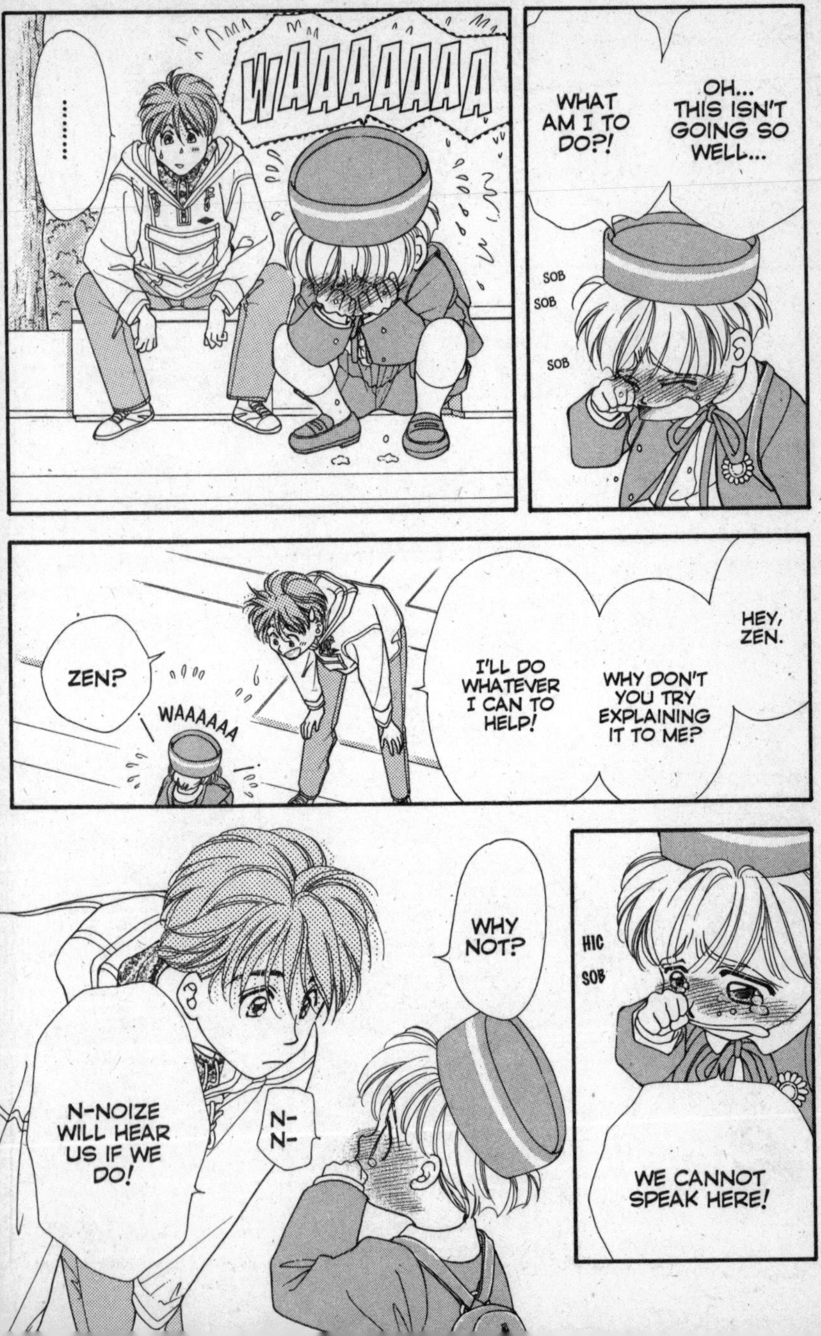
OH... THIS ISN'T GOING SO WELL...
WHAT AM I TO DO?!
SOB
SOB
SOB
WAAAAAAAA
......
HEY, ZEN.
WHY DON'T YOU TRY EXPLAINING IT TO ME?
I'LL DO WHATEVER I CAN TO HELP!
ZEN?
WAAAAAAA
HIC
SOB
WE CANNOT SPEAK HERE!
WHY NOT?
N- N-
N-NOIZE WILL HEAR US IF WE DO!

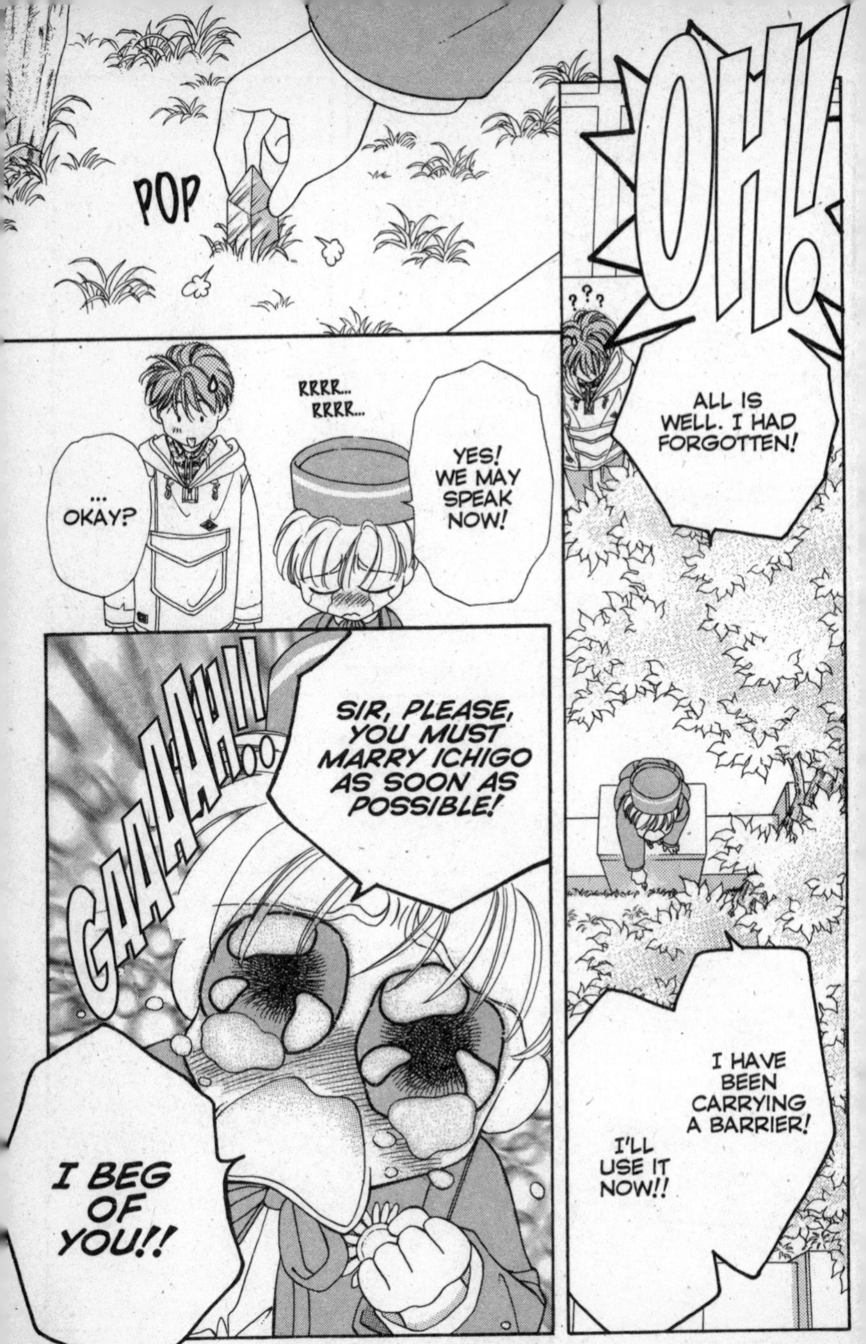
OH!!
? ? ?
ALL IS WELL. I HAD FORGOTTEN!
I HAVE BEEN CARRYING A BARRIER!
I'LL USE IT NOW!!
POP
RRRR... RRRR...
YES! WE MAY SPEAK NOW!
... OKAY?
GAAAHH...
SIR, PLEASE, YOU MUST MARRY ICHIGO AS SOON AS POSSIBLE!
I BEG OF YOU!!

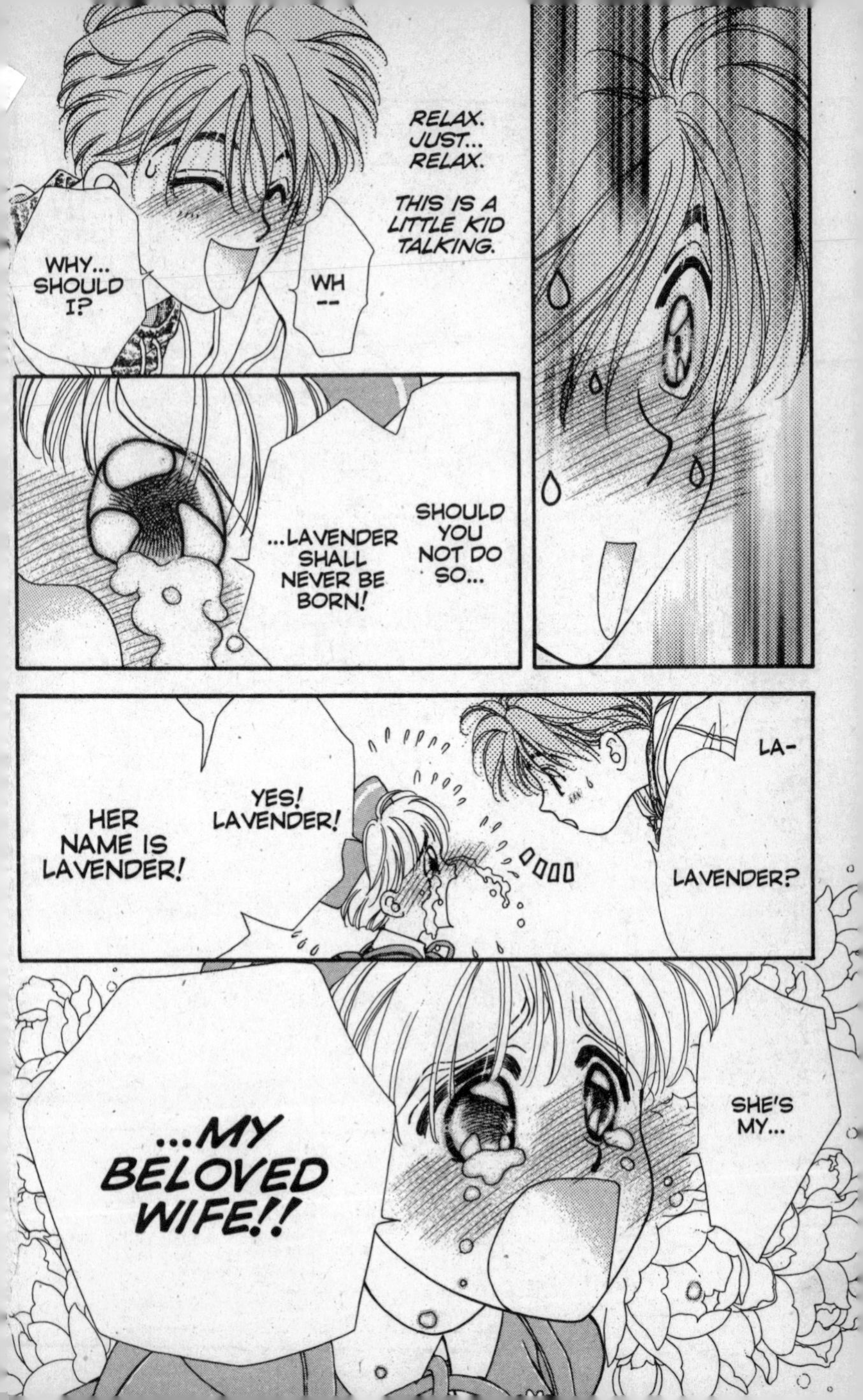
RELAX. JUST... RELAX.
THIS IS A LITTLE KID TALKING.
WH --
WHY... SHOULD I?
SHOULD YOU NOT DO SO...
...LAVENDER SHALL NEVER BE BORN!
LA-
LAVENDER?
YES! LAVENDER!
HER NAME IS LAVENDER!
SHE'S MY...
...MY BELOVED WIFE!!

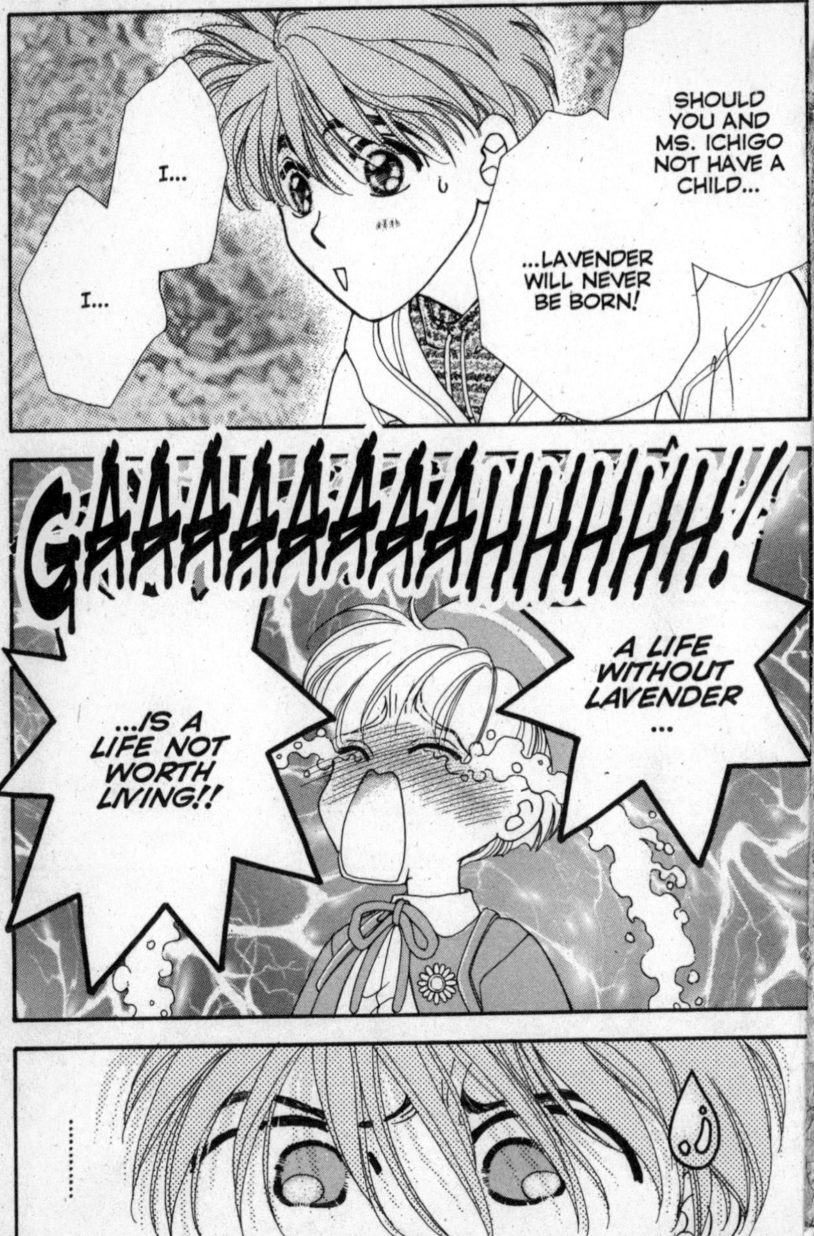

SHOULD YOU AND MS. ICHIGO NOT HAVE A CHILD...
...LAVENDER WILL NEVER BE BORN!
I...
I...
GAAAAAAAAAHHHHHH!!
A LIFE WITHOUT LAVENDER ...
...IS A LIFE NOT WORTH LIVING!!
....

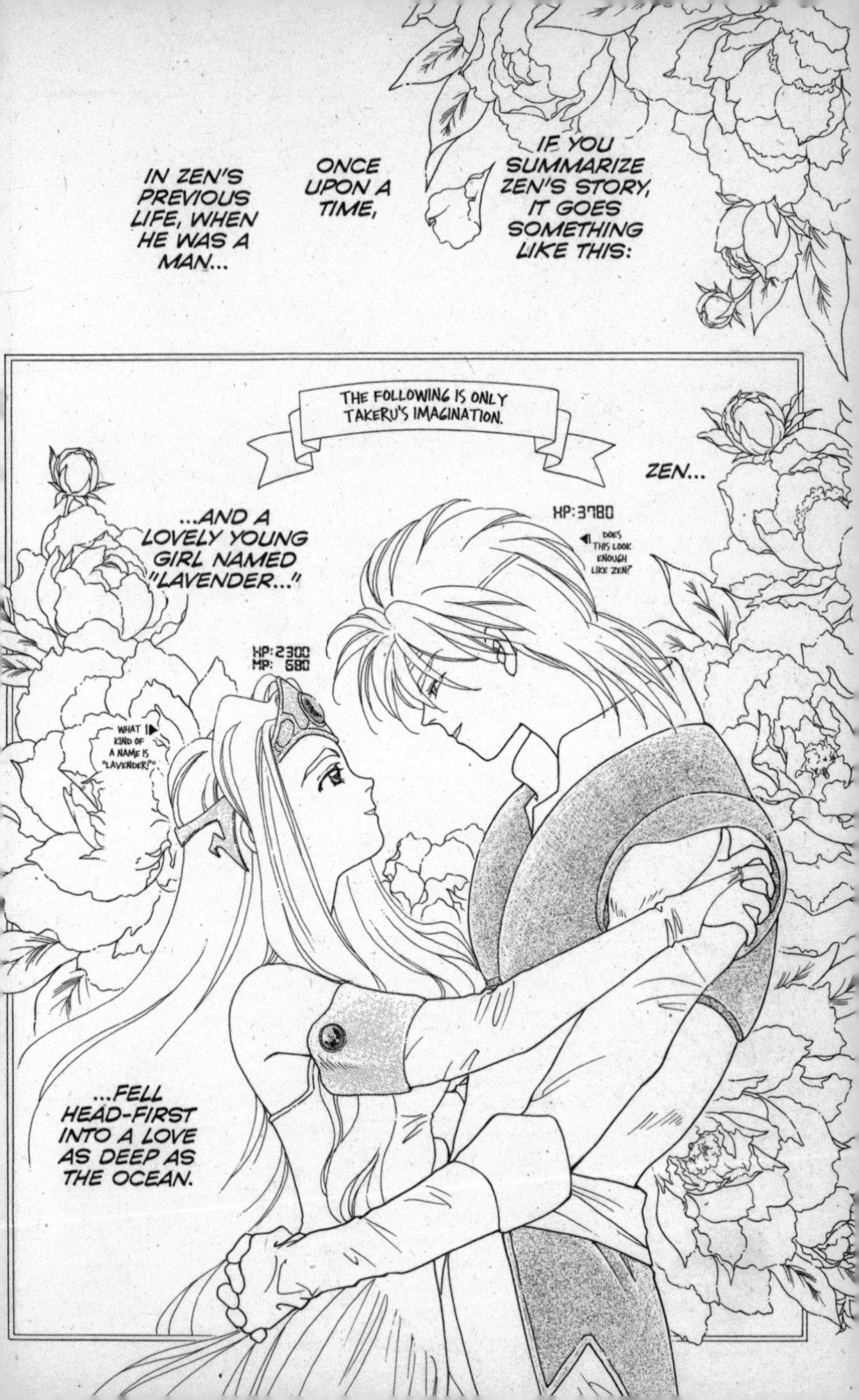
IF YOU SUMMARIZE ZEN'S STORY, IT GOES SOMETHING LIKE THIS:
ONCE UPON A TIME,
IN ZEN'S PREVIOUS LIFE, WHEN HE WAS A MAN...
THE FOLLOWING IS ONLY TAKERU'S IMAGINATION.
ZEN...
HP:3780
DOES THIS LOOK ENOUGH LIKE ZEN?
...AND A LOVELY YOUNG GIRL NAMED "LAVENDER..."
HP:2300 MP: 580
WHAT KIND OF A NAME IS "LAVENDER?"
...FELL HEAD-FIRST INTO A LOVE AS DEEP AS THE OCEAN.

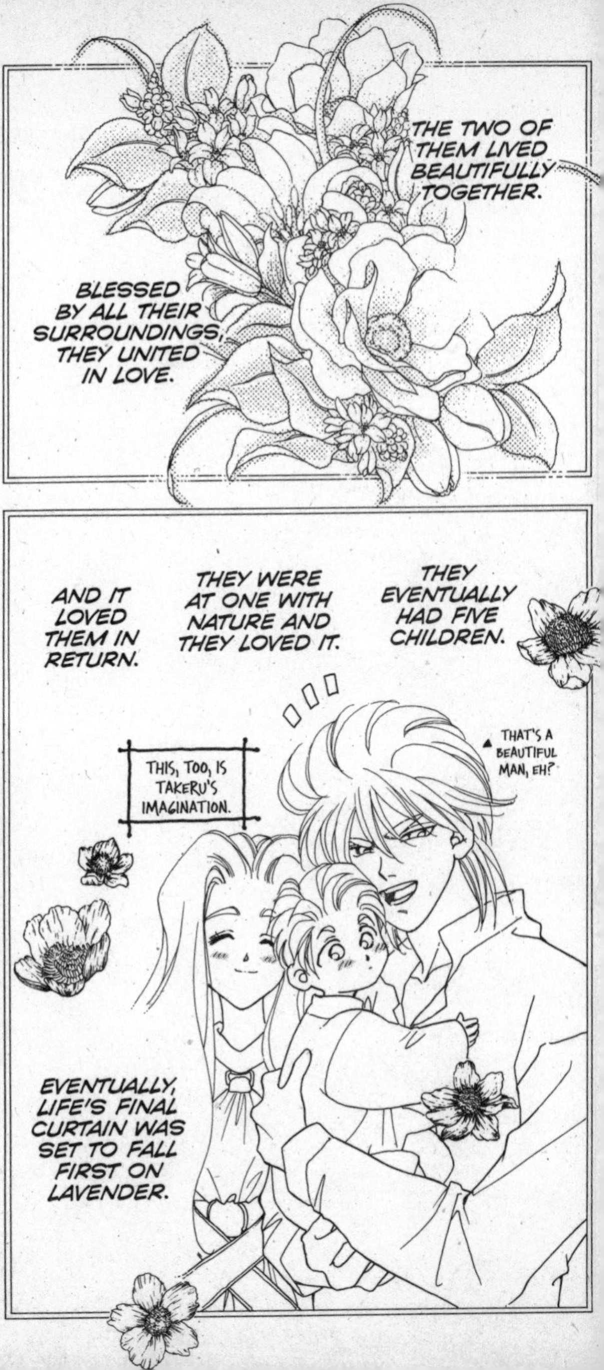
THE TWO OF THEM LIVED BEAUTIFULLY TOGETHER.
BLESSED BY ALL THEIR SURROUNDINGS, THEY UNITED IN LOVE.
THEY EVENTUALLY HAD FIVE CHILDREN.
THEY WERE AT ONE WITH NATURE AND THEY LOVED IT.
AND IT LOVED THEM IN RETURN.
THAT'S A BEAUTIFUL MAN, EH?
THIS, TOO, IS TAKERU'S IMAGINATION.
EVENTUALLY, LIFE'S FINAL CURTAIN WAS SET TO FALL FIRST ON LAVENDER.

Sidebar No. 7

Zephyr's really cute, isn't he? So cute I even showed him to my robot. That game provided me enough inspiration for all the shojo manga I'll ever need to write. I'll definitely play it again! There simply must be some other paths to take through the story...

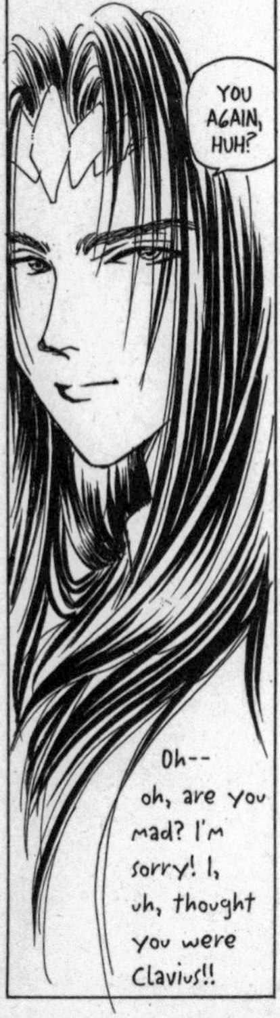
YOU AGAIN, HUH?
Oh--oh, are you mad? I'm sorry! I, uh, thought you were Clavius!!

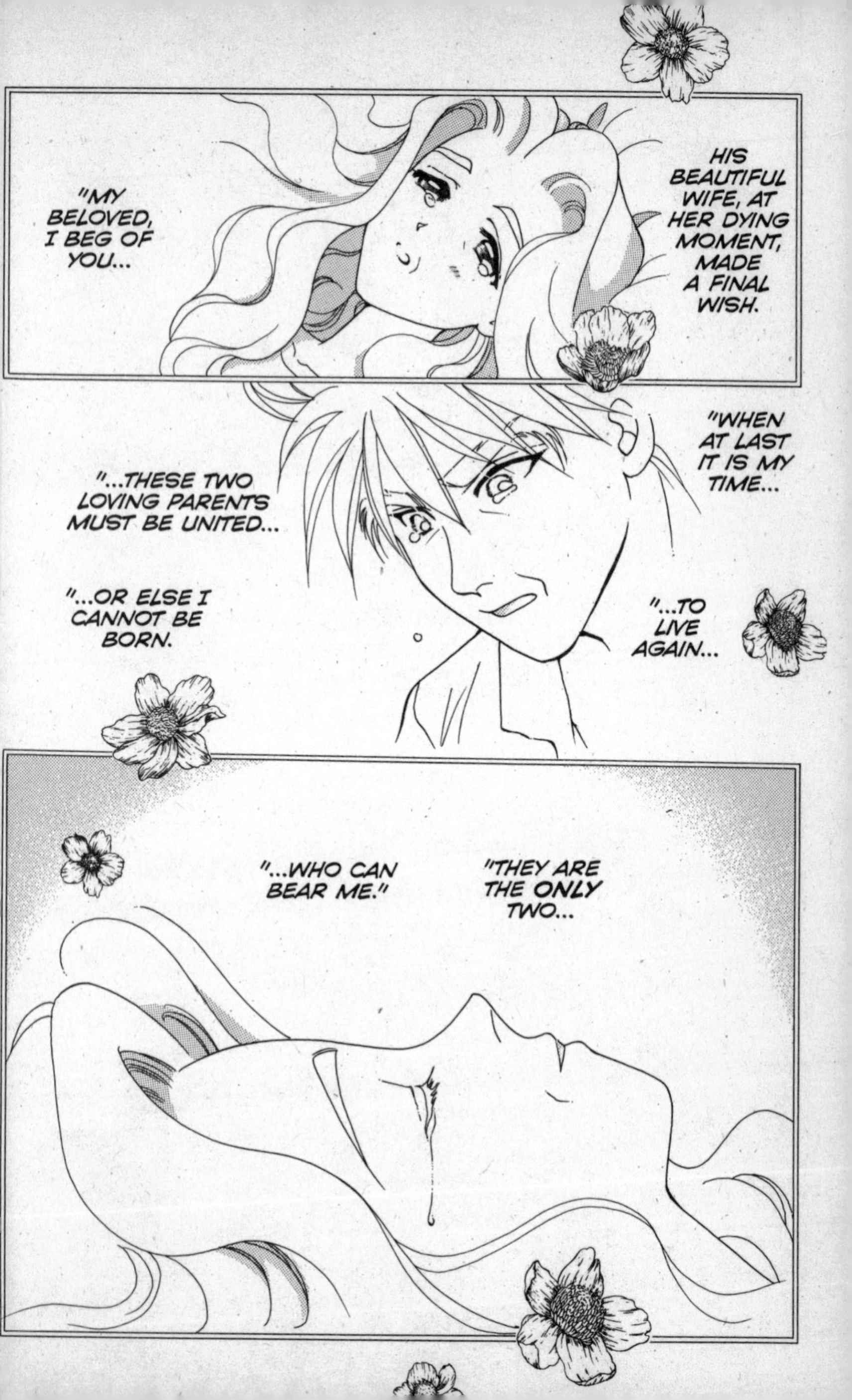
HIS BEAUTIFUL WIFE, AT HER DYING MOMENT, MADE A FINAL WISH.
"MY BELOVED, I BEG OF YOU...
"WHEN AT LAST IT IS MY TIME...
"...TO LIVE AGAIN...
"...THESE TWO LOVING PARENTS MUST BE UNITED...
"...OR ELSE I CANNOT BE BORN.
"THEY ARE THE ONLY TWO...
"...WHO CAN BEAR ME."

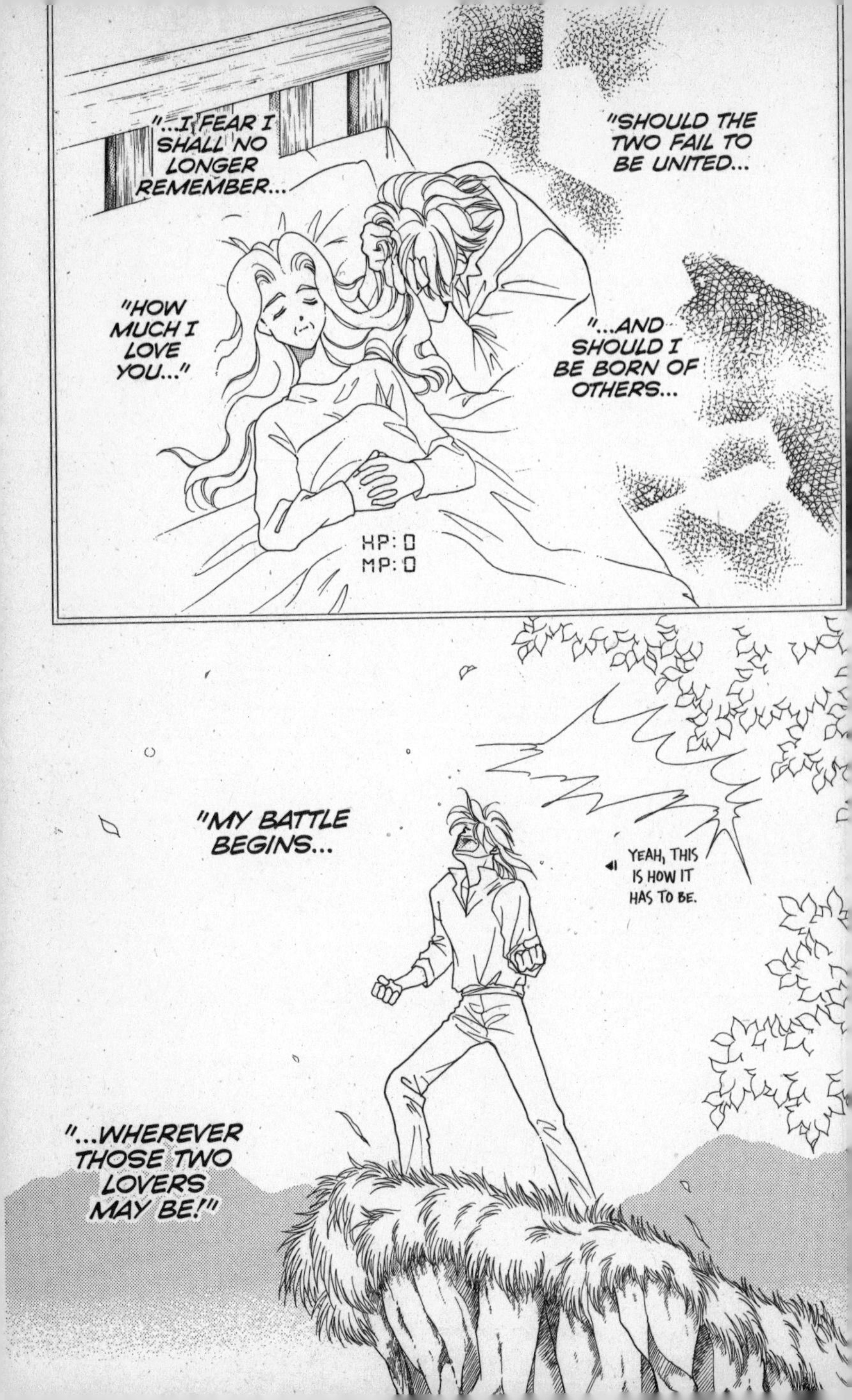
"SHOULD THE TWO FAIL TO BE UNITED...
"...AND SHOULD I BE BORN OF OTHERS...
"...I FEAR I SHALL NO LONGER REMEMBER...
"HOW MUCH I LOVE YOU..."
HP: 0
MP: 0
YEAH, THIS IS HOW IT HAS TO BE.
"MY BATTLE BEGINS...
"...WHEREVER THOSE TWO LOVERS MAY BE!"

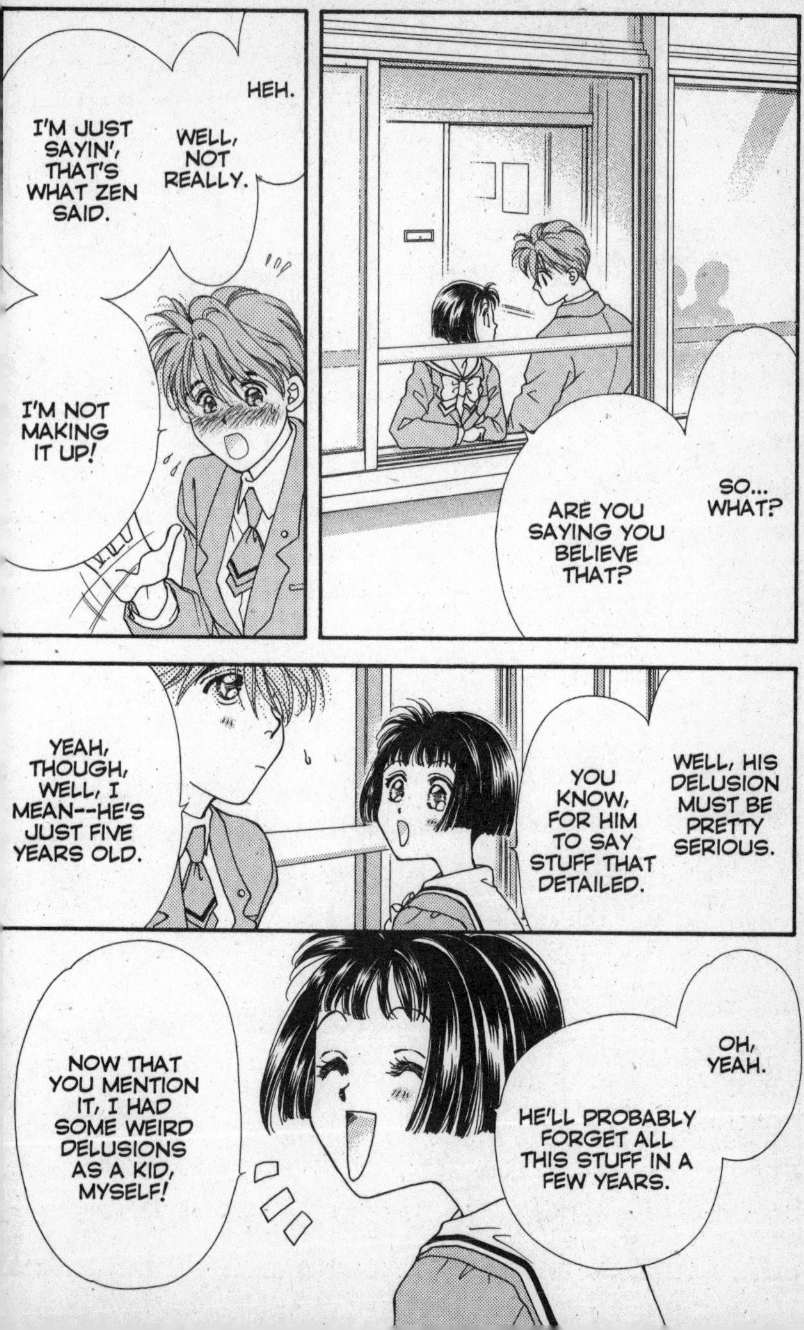
SO... WHAT?
ARE YOU SAYING YOU BELIEVE THAT?
HEH.
WELL, NOT REALLY.
I'M JUST SAYIN', THAT'S WHAT ZEN SAID.
I'M NOT MAKING IT UP!
WELL, HIS DELUSION MUST BE PRETTY SERIOUS.
YOU KNOW, FOR HIM TO SAY STUFF THAT DETAILED.
YEAH, THOUGH, WELL, I MEAN--HE'S JUST FIVE YEARS OLD.
OH, YEAH.
HE'LL PROBABLY FORGET ALL THIS STUFF IN A FEW YEARS.
NOW THAT YOU MENTION IT, I HAD SOME WEIRD DELUSIONS AS A KID, MYSELF!

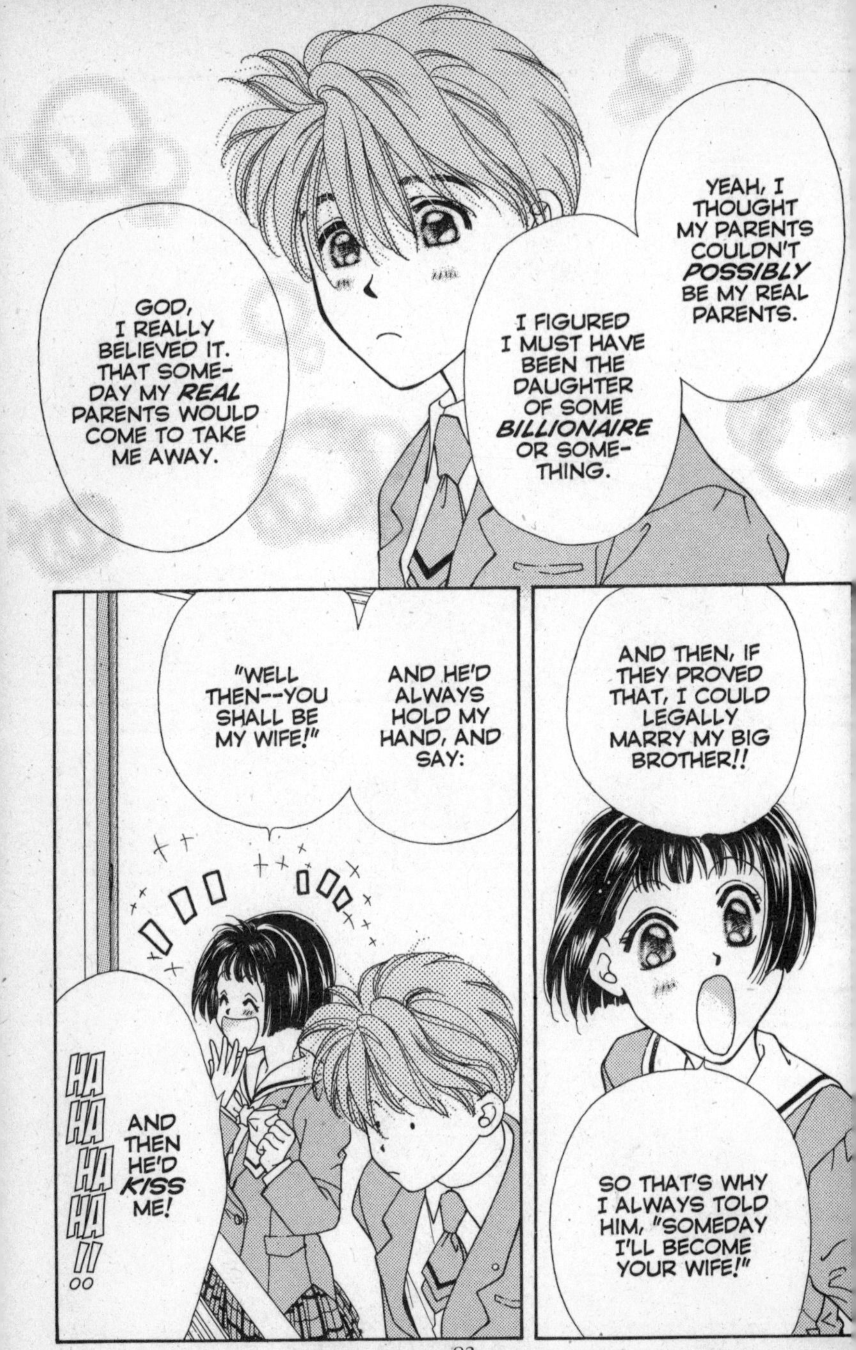
YEAH, I THOUGHT MY PARENTS COULDN'T *POSSIBLY* BE MY REAL PARENTS.
I FIGURED I MUST HAVE BEEN THE DAUGHTER OF SOME *BILLIONAIRE* OR SOME-THING.
GOD, I REALLY BELIEVED IT. THAT SOME-DAY MY *REAL* PARENTS WOULD COME TO TAKE ME AWAY.
AND THEN, IF THEY PROVED THAT, I COULD LEGALLY MARRY MY BIG BROTHER!!
SO THAT'S WHY I ALWAYS TOLD HIM, "SOMEDAY I'LL BECOME YOUR WIFE!"
AND HE'D ALWAYS HOLD MY HAND, AND SAY:
"WELL THEN--YOU SHALL BE MY WIFE!"
AND THEN HE'D *KISS* ME!
HA HA HA HA!!

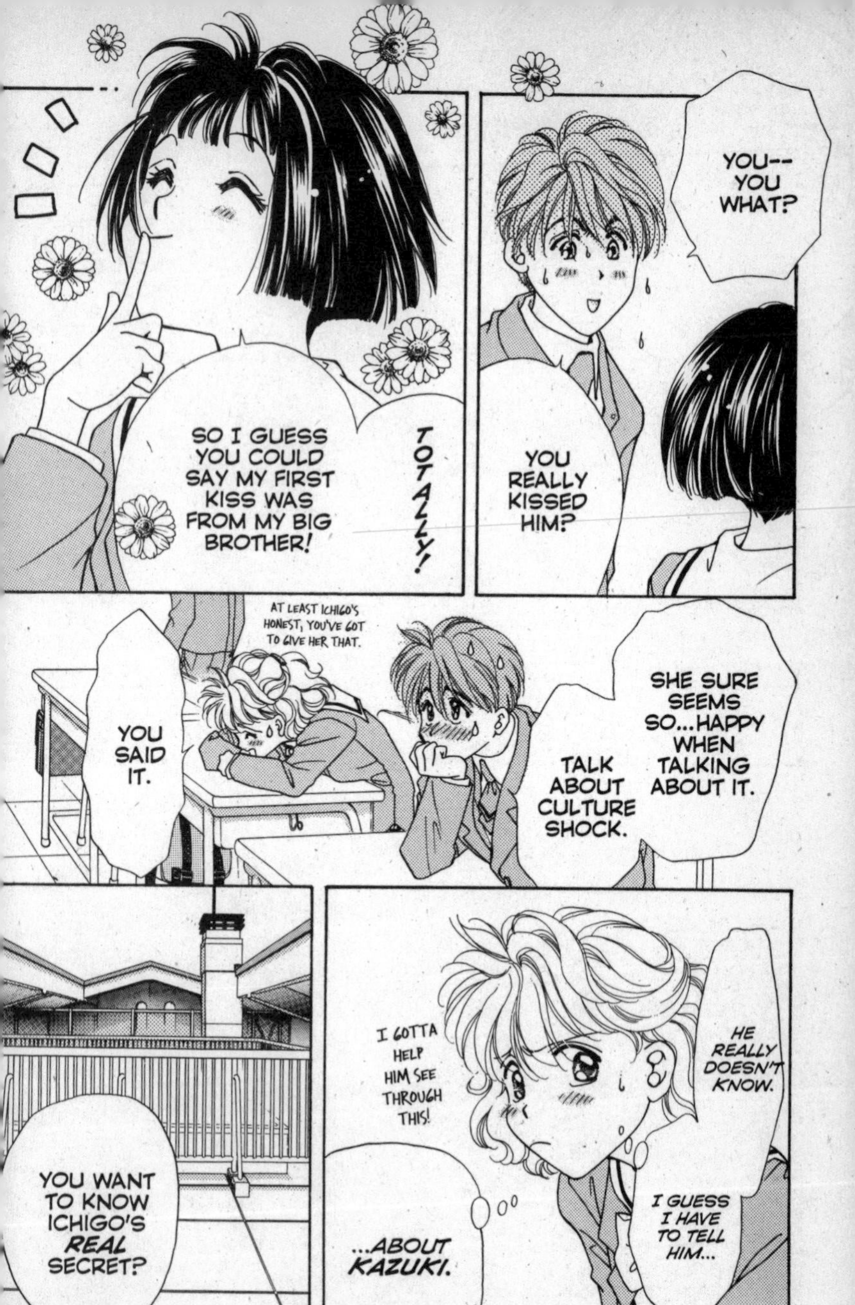
YOU-- YOU WHAT?
YOU REALLY KISSED HIM?
SO I GUESS YOU COULD SAY MY FIRST KISS WAS FROM MY BIG BROTHER!
TOTALLY!
SHE SURE SEEMS SO...HAPPY WHEN TALKING ABOUT IT.
TALK ABOUT CULTURE SHOCK.
AT LEAST ICHIGO'S HONEST, YOU'VE GOT TO GIVE HER THAT.
YOU SAID IT.
HE REALLY DOESN'T KNOW.
I GUESS I HAVE TO TELL HIM...
I GOTTA HELP HIM SEE THROUGH THIS!
...ABOUT KAZUKI.
YOU WANT TO KNOW ICHIGO'S REAL SECRET?

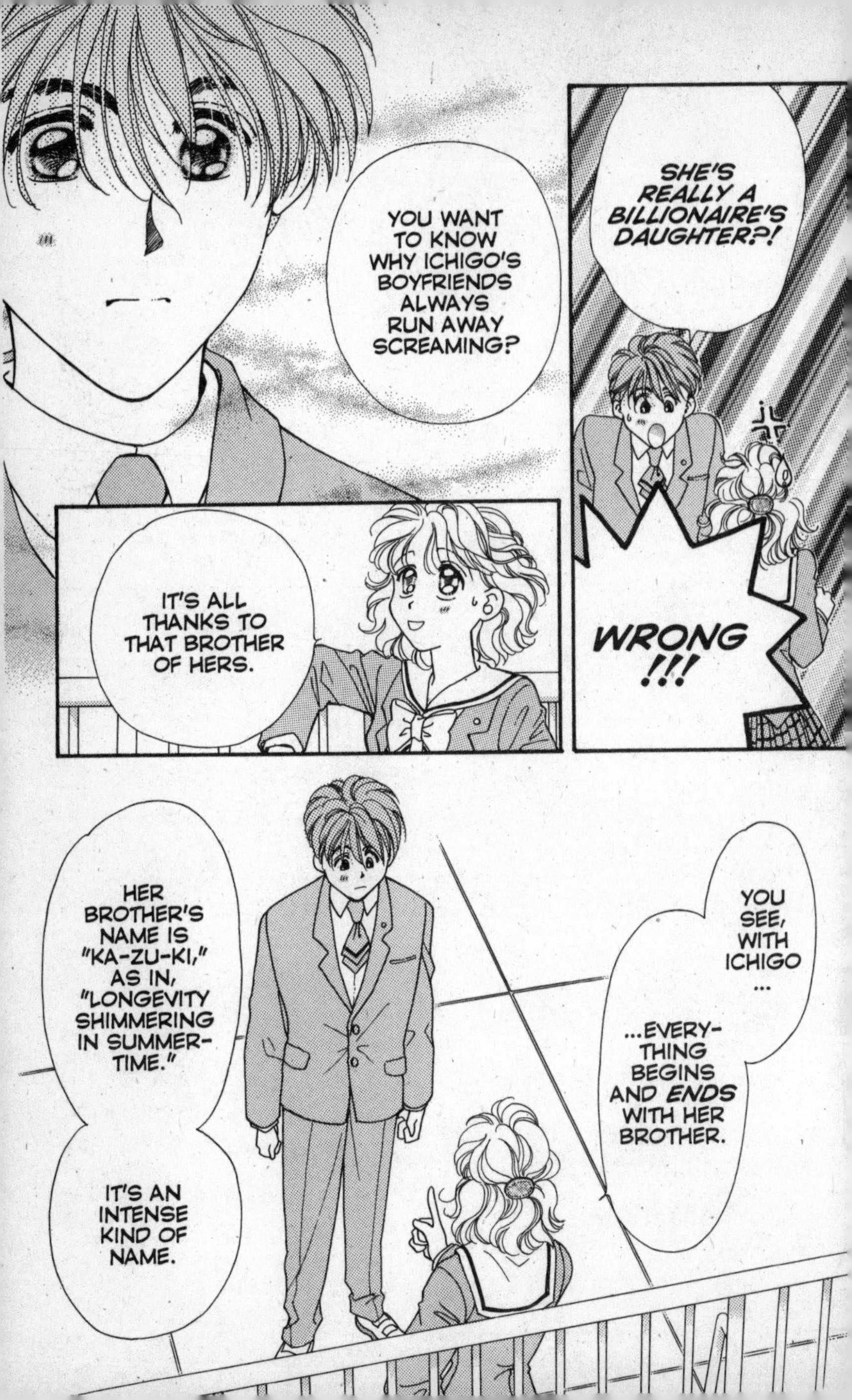
SHE'S REALLY A BILLIONAIRE'S DAUGHTER?!
WRONG !!!
YOU WANT TO KNOW WHY ICHIGO'S BOYFRIENDS ALWAYS RUN AWAY SCREAMING?
IT'S ALL THANKS TO THAT BROTHER OF HERS.
YOU SEE, WITH ICHIGO ...
...EVERY-THING BEGINS AND *ENDS* WITH HER BROTHER.
HER BROTHER'S NAME IS "KA-ZU-KI," AS IN, "LONGEVITY SHIMMERING IN SUMMER-TIME."
IT'S AN INTENSE KIND OF NAME.

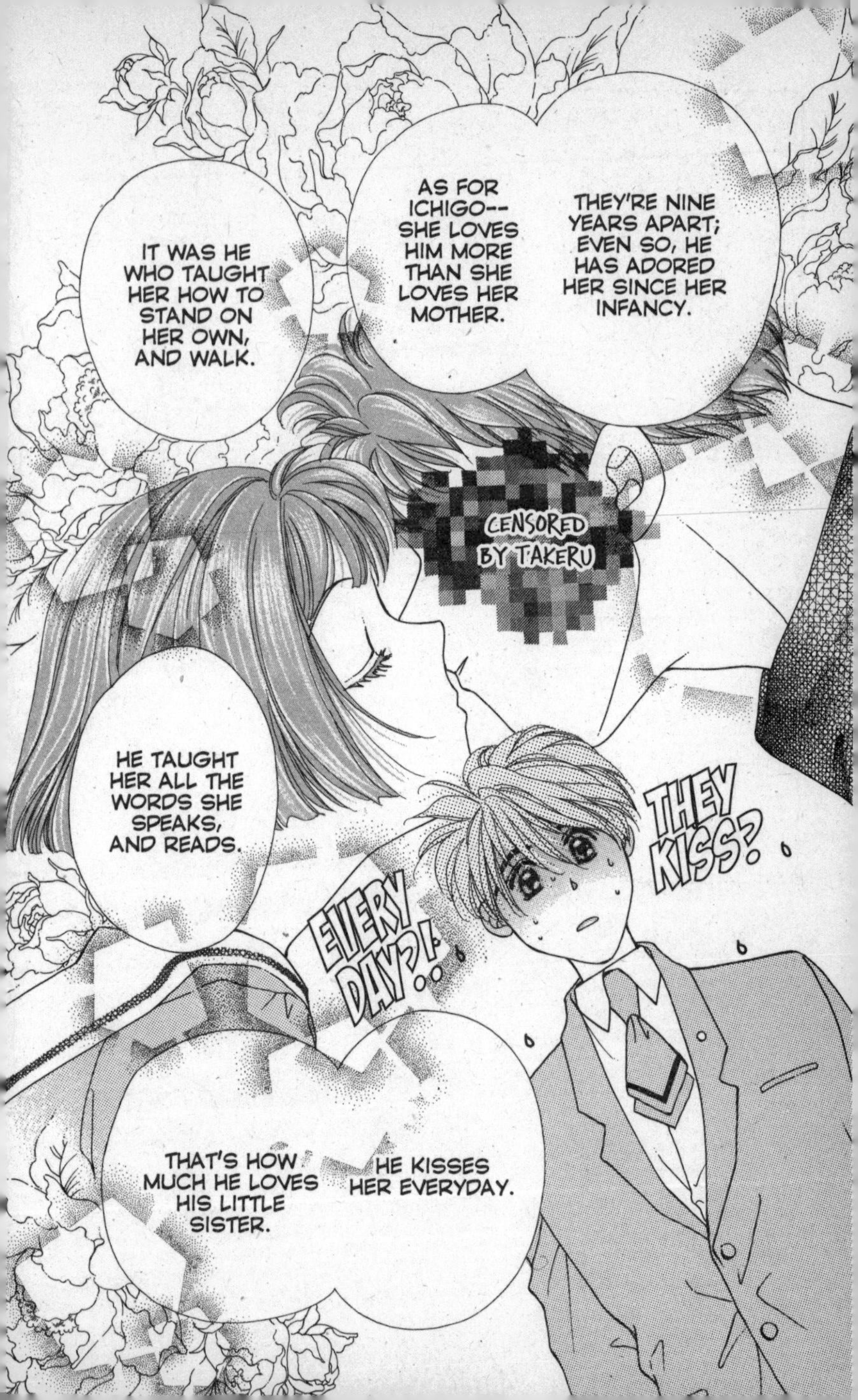
THEY'RE NINE YEARS APART; EVEN SO, HE HAS ADORED HER SINCE HER INFANCY.
AS FOR ICHIGO-- SHE LOVES HIM MORE THAN SHE LOVES HER MOTHER.
IT WAS HE WHO TAUGHT HER HOW TO STAND ON HER OWN, AND WALK.
CENSORED BY TAKERU
HE TAUGHT HER ALL THE WORDS SHE SPEAKS, AND READS.
HE KISSES HER EVERYDAY.
THAT'S HOW MUCH HE LOVES HIS LITTLE SISTER.
THEY KISS?
EVERY DAY?!

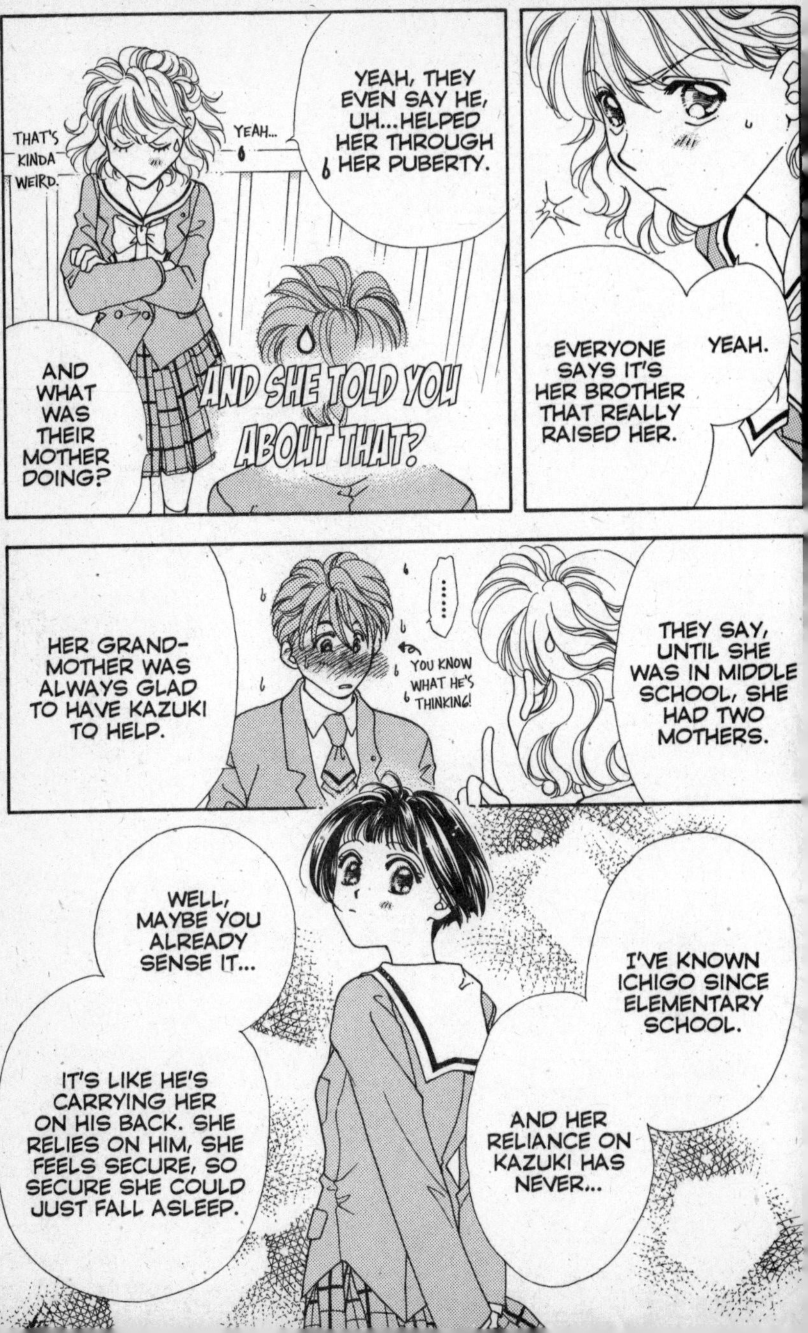
YEAH.
EVERYONE SAYS IT'S HER BROTHER THAT REALLY RAISED HER.
YEAH, THEY EVEN SAY HE, UH...HELPED HER THROUGH HER PUBERTY.
YEAH...
THAT'S KINDA WEIRD.
AND SHE TOLD YOU ABOUT THAT?
AND WHAT WAS THEIR MOTHER DOING?
THEY SAY, UNTIL SHE WAS IN MIDDLE SCHOOL, SHE HAD TWO MOTHERS.
......
YOU KNOW WHAT HE'S THINKING!
HER GRAND-MOTHER WAS ALWAYS GLAD TO HAVE KAZUKI TO HELP.
I'VE KNOWN ICHIGO SINCE ELEMENTARY SCHOOL.
WELL, MAYBE YOU ALREADY SENSE IT...
AND HER RELIANCE ON KAZUKI HAS NEVER...
IT'S LIKE HE'S CARRYING HER ON HIS BACK. SHE RELIES ON HIM, SHE FEELS SECURE, SO SECURE SHE COULD JUST FALL ASLEEP.

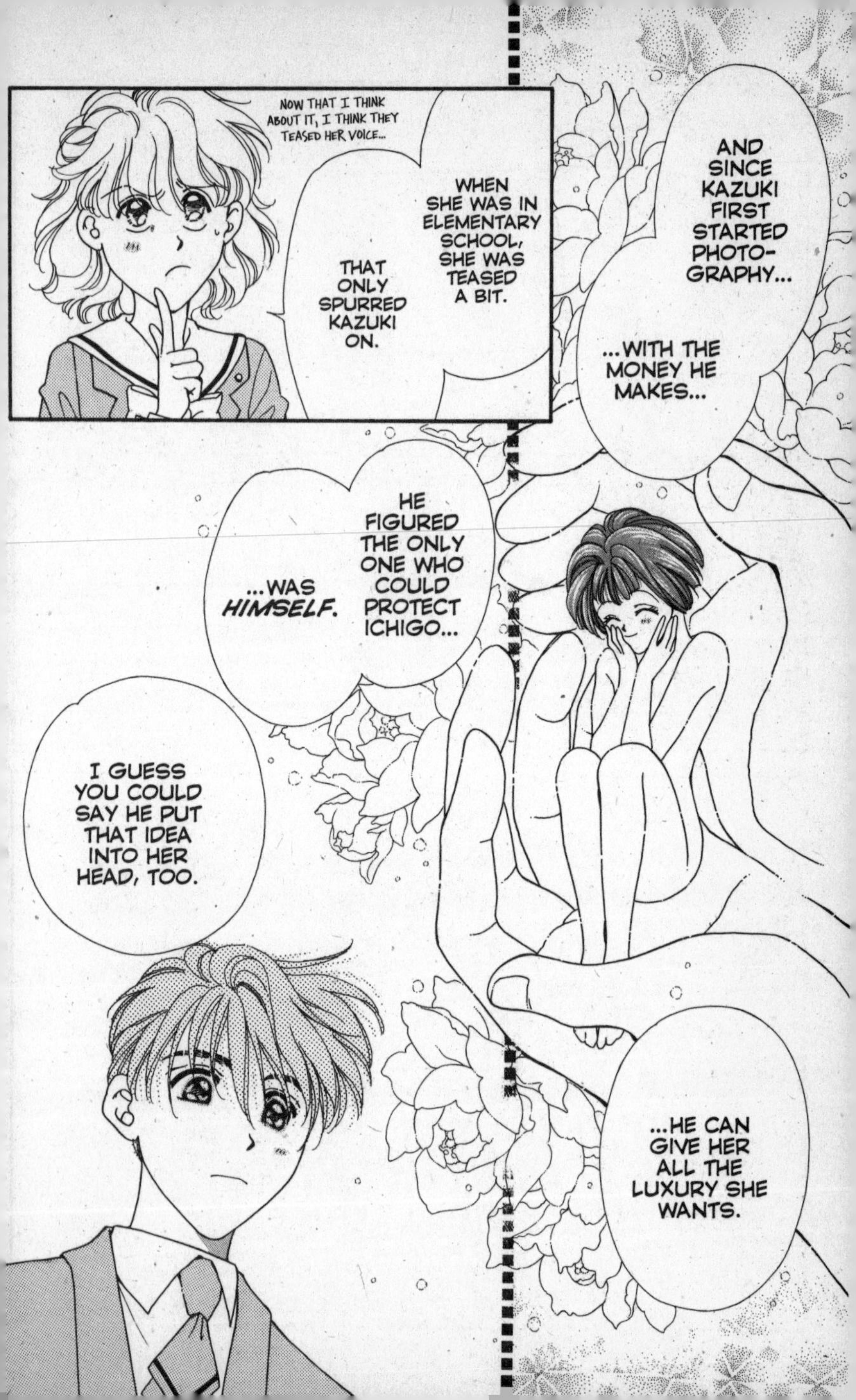
WHEN SHE WAS IN ELEMENTARY SCHOOL, SHE WAS TEASED A BIT.
THAT ONLY SPURRED KAZUKI ON.
NOW THAT I THINK ABOUT IT, I THINK THEY TEASED HER VOICE...
HE FIGURED THE ONLY ONE WHO COULD PROTECT ICHIGO...
...WAS *HIMSELF*.
AND SINCE KAZUKI FIRST STARTED PHOTO-GRAPHY...
...WITH THE MONEY HE MAKES...
...HE CAN GIVE HER ALL THE LUXURY SHE WANTS.
I GUESS YOU COULD SAY HE PUT THAT IDEA INTO HER HEAD, TOO.

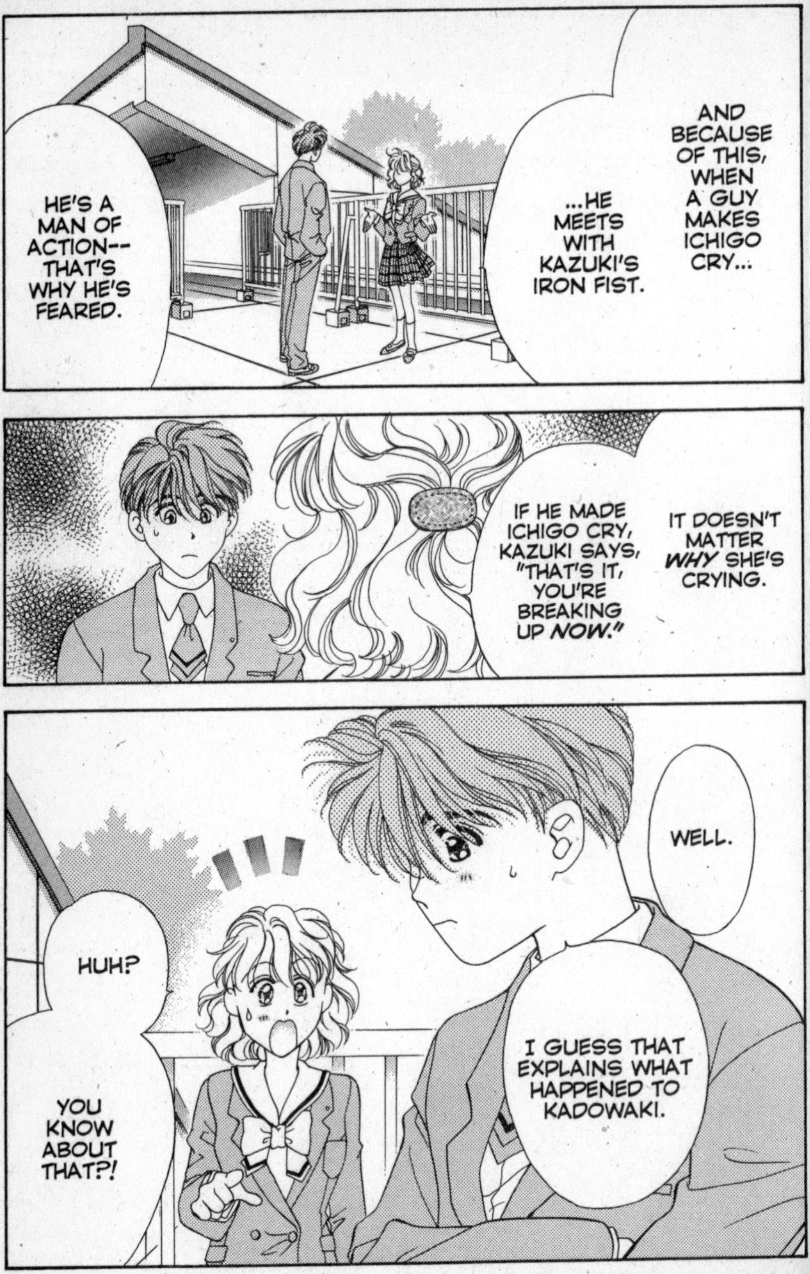
AND BECAUSE OF THIS, WHEN A GUY MAKES ICHIGO CRY...
...HE MEETS WITH KAZUKI'S IRON FIST.
HE'S A MAN OF ACTION--THAT'S WHY HE'S FEARED.
IT DOESN'T MATTER *WHY* SHE'S CRYING.
IF HE MADE ICHIGO CRY, KAZUKI SAYS, "THAT'S IT, YOU'RE BREAKING UP *NOW*."
WELL.
I GUESS THAT EXPLAINS WHAT HAPPENED TO KADOWAKI.
HUH?
YOU KNOW ABOUT THAT?!

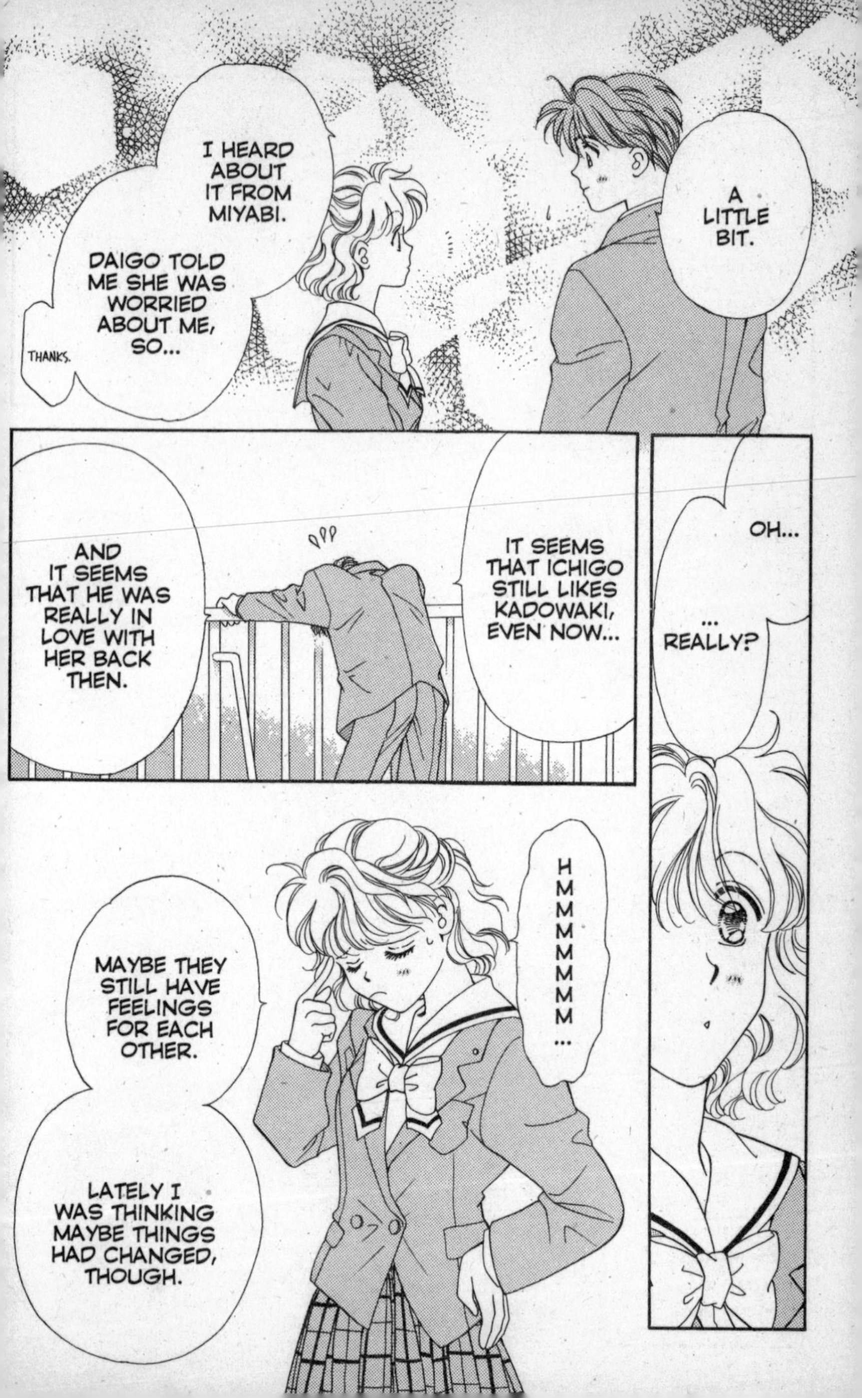
A LITTLE BIT.
I HEARD ABOUT IT FROM MIYABI.
DAIGO TOLD ME SHE WAS WORRIED ABOUT ME, SO...
THANKS.
OH...
... REALLY?
IT SEEMS THAT ICHIGO STILL LIKES KADOWAKI, EVEN NOW...
AND IT SEEMS THAT HE WAS REALLY IN LOVE WITH HER BACK THEN.
HMMMMMMM...
MAYBE THEY STILL HAVE FEELINGS FOR EACH OTHER.
LATELY I WAS THINKING MAYBE THINGS HAD CHANGED, THOUGH.

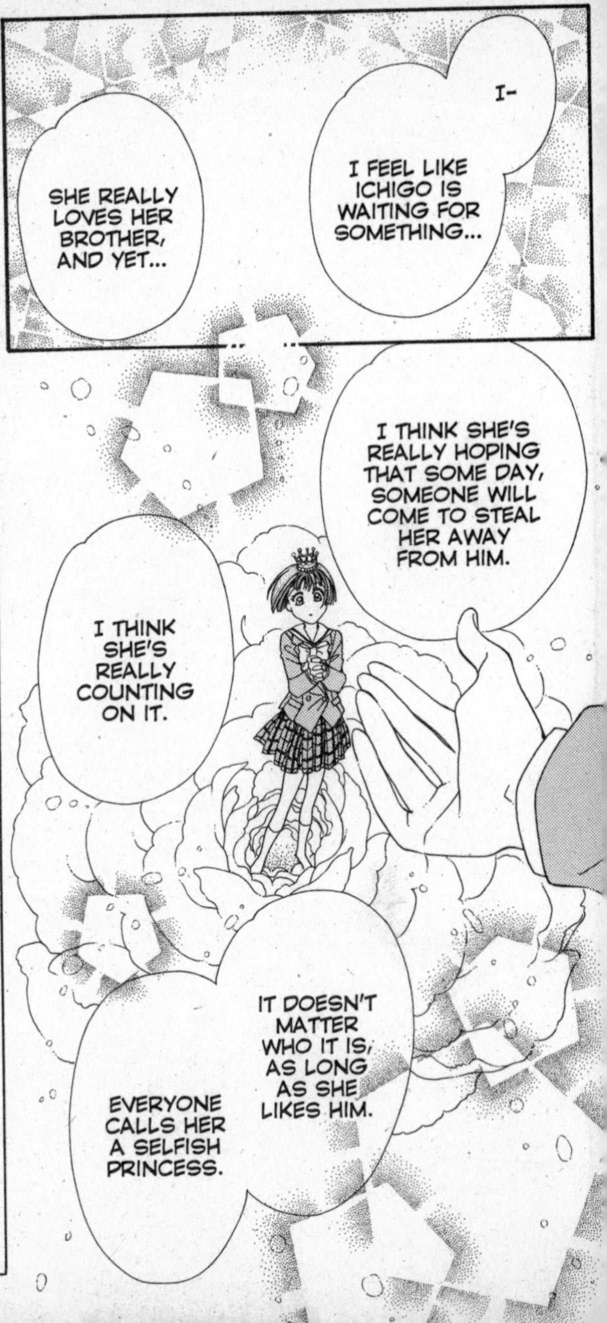
I-
I FEEL LIKE ICHIGO IS WAITING FOR SOMETHING...
SHE REALLY LOVES HER BROTHER, AND YET...
....
I THINK SHE'S REALLY HOPING THAT SOME DAY, SOMEONE WILL COME TO STEAL HER AWAY FROM HIM.
I THINK SHE'S REALLY COUNTING ON IT.
IT DOESN'T MATTER WHO IT IS, AS LONG AS SHE LIKES HIM.
EVERYONE CALLS HER A SELFISH PRINCESS.

Sidebar No. 8

When you think about it, there really aren't enough games for girls, like this one. It'd be really great if there were, though, wouldn't it? Why don't they make a girly version of something like "Torneko's Mysterious Dungeon?" Don't you think that'd be kind of interesting? You open a treasure box, and out pops a really hot guy? That'd be... Really fun... I think I lost my train of thought... Ahhhh! I just thought of one--"Valkyrie's Adventure," for Famicom. (Kind of a stupid title.) I played that one a long time ago. That one was kinda for girls. In the beginning they made you put in your zodiac sign and everything. Ahh, thinking about it again gets me all choked up.

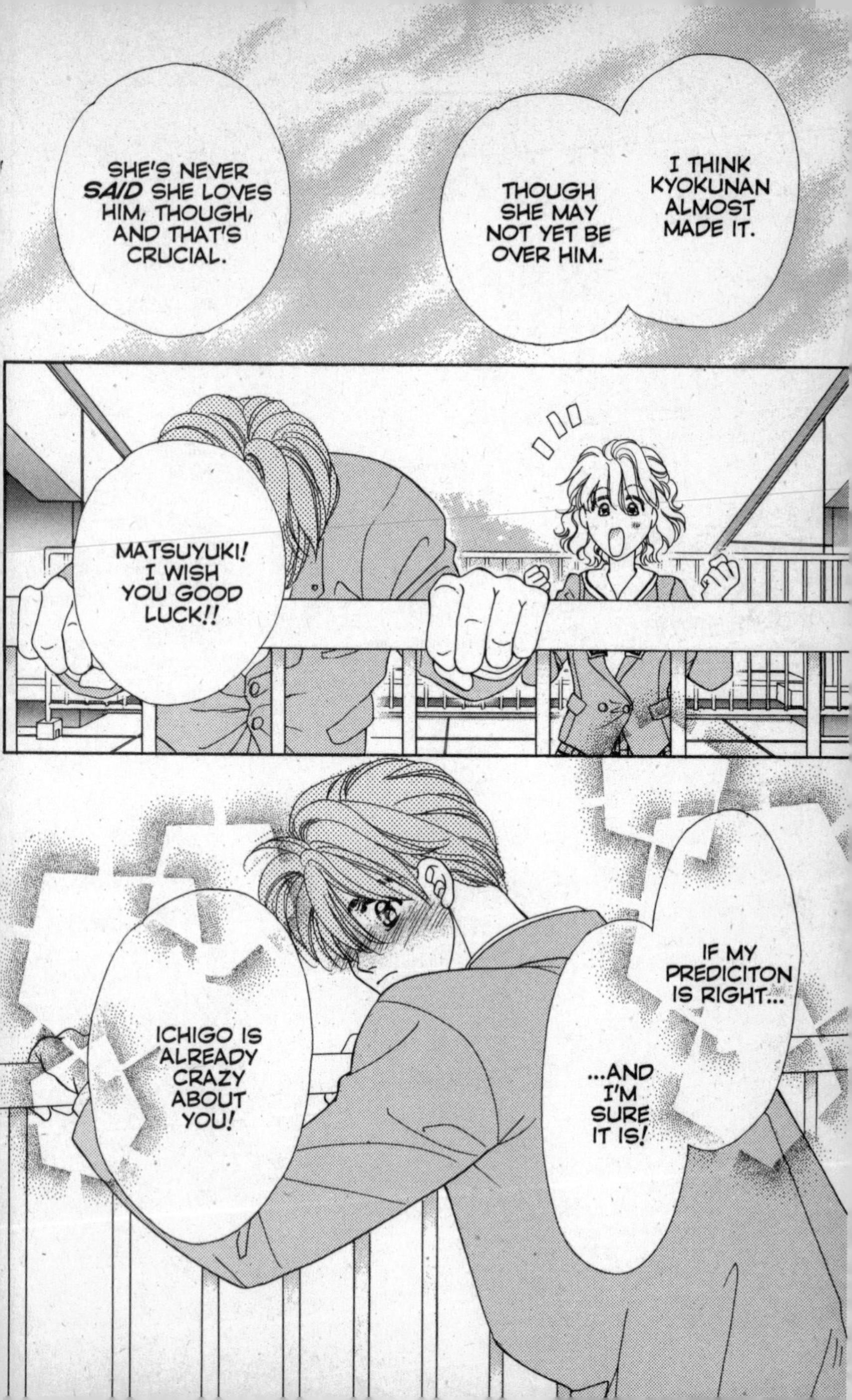
I THINK KYOKUNAN ALMOST MADE IT.
THOUGH SHE MAY NOT YET BE OVER HIM.
SHE'S NEVER *SAID* SHE LOVES HIM, THOUGH, AND THAT'S CRUCIAL.
MATSUYUKI! I WISH YOU GOOD LUCK!!
IF MY PREDICITON IS RIGHT...
...AND I'M SURE IT IS!
ICHIGO IS ALREADY CRAZY ABOUT YOU!

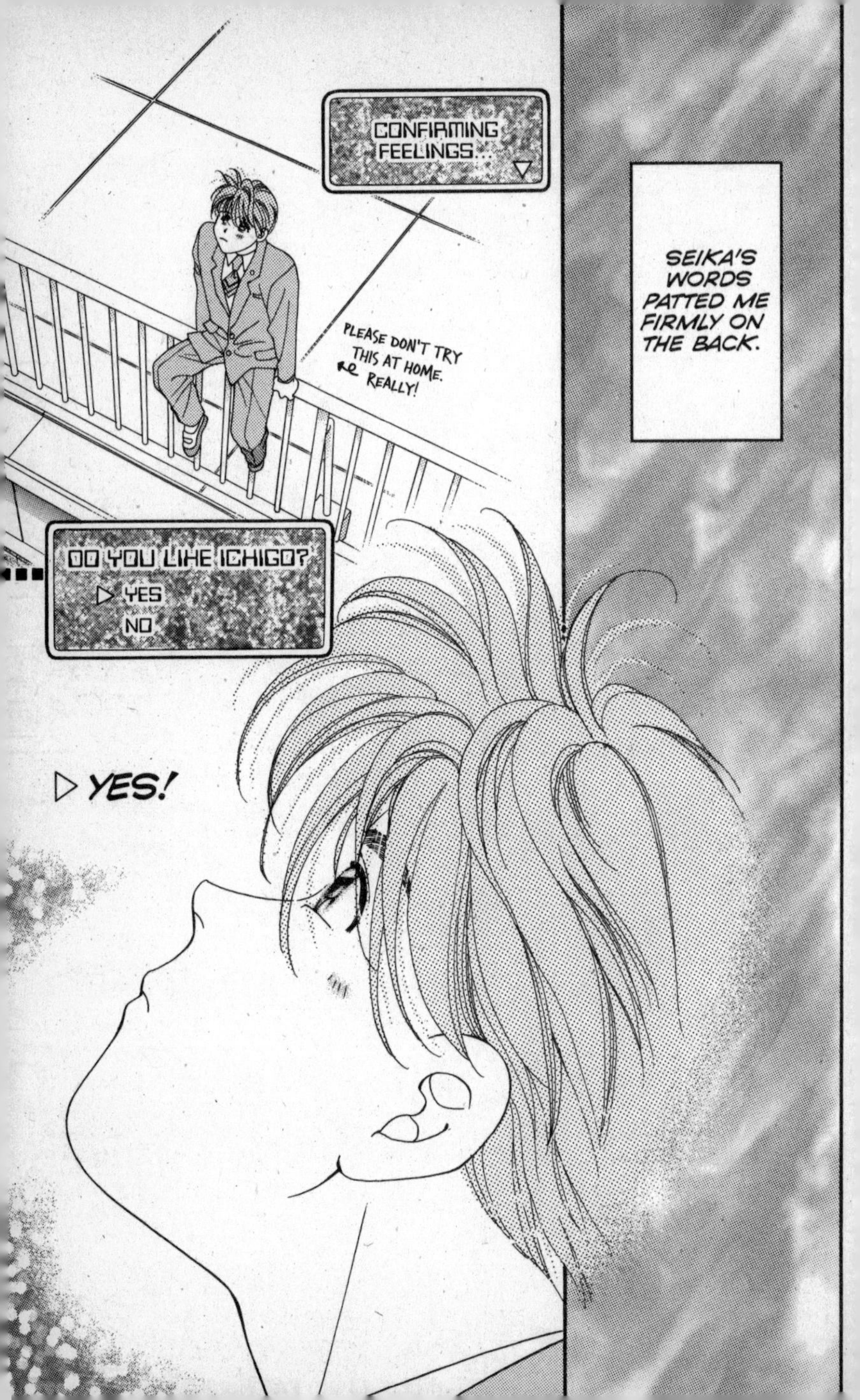
SEIKA'S WORDS PATTED ME FIRMLY ON THE BACK.
CONFIRMING FEELINGS... ▽
PLEASE DON'T TRY THIS AT HOME. REALLY!
DO YOU LIKE ICHIGO?
▷ YES
NO
▷ YES!

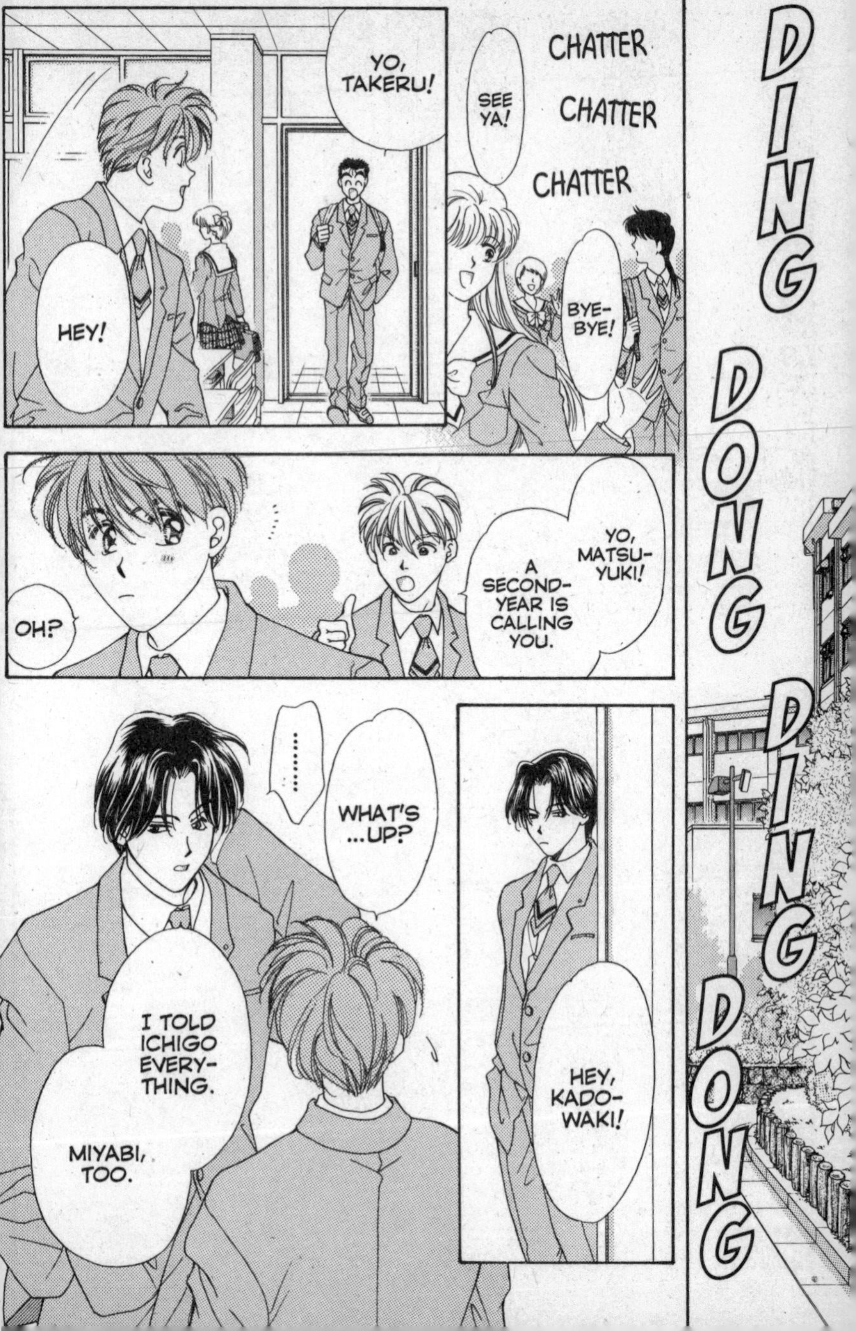
DING DONG DING DONG
CHATTER CHATTER CHATTER
SEE YA!
YO, TAKERU!
BYE-BYE!
HEY!
YO, MATSU-YUKI! A SECOND-YEAR IS CALLING YOU.
OH?
HEY, KADO-WAKI!
......
WHAT'S ...UP?
I TOLD ICHIGO EVERY-THING.
MIYABI, TOO.

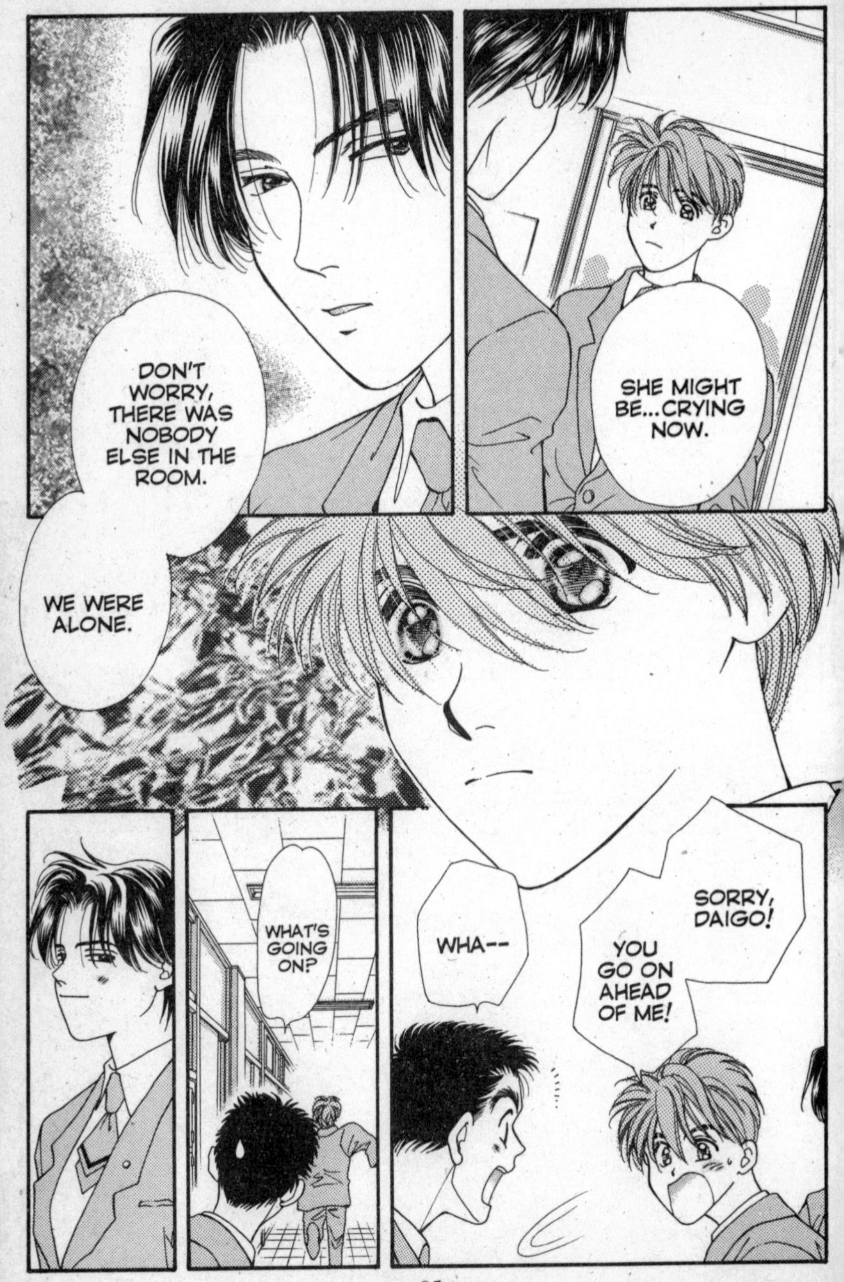
SHE MIGHT BE...CRYING NOW.
DON'T WORRY, THERE WAS NOBODY ELSE IN THE ROOM.
WE WERE ALONE.
SORRY, DAIGO!
YOU GO ON AHEAD OF ME!
WHA--
WHAT'S GOING ON?

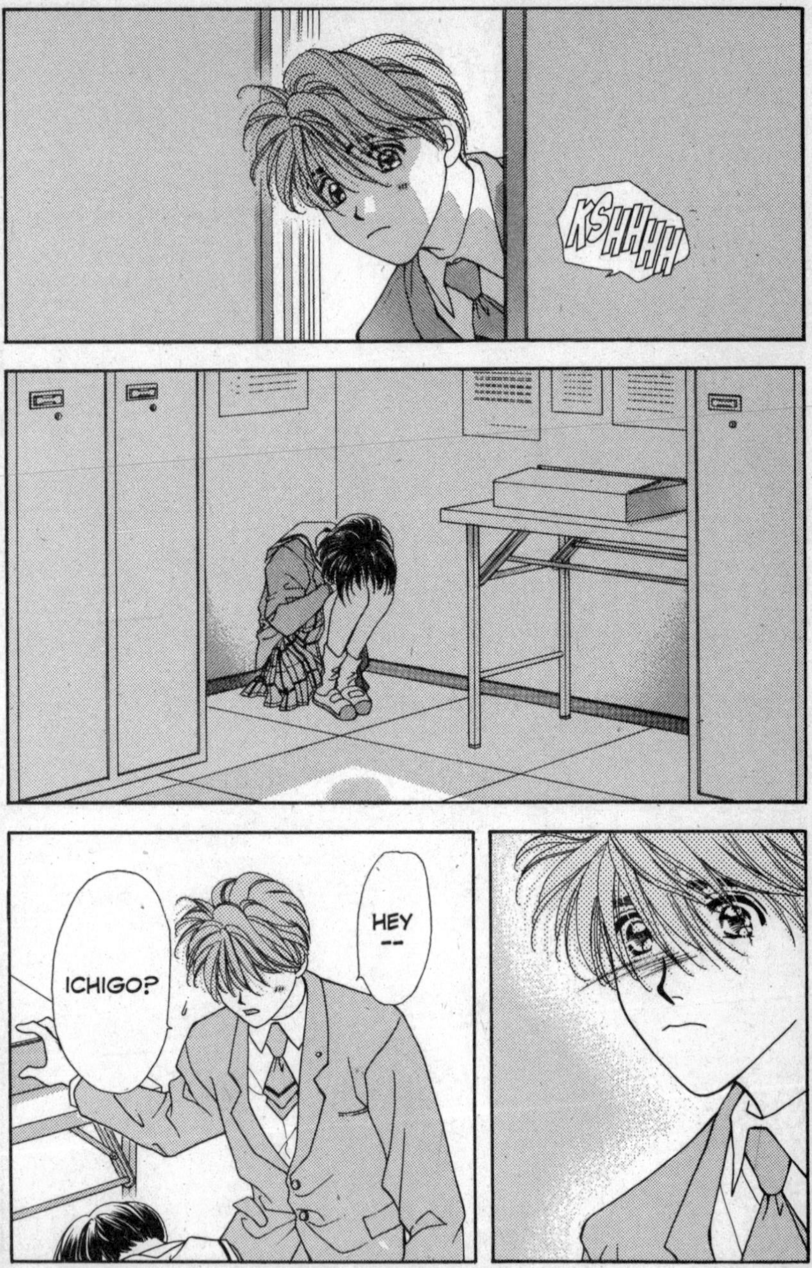
KSHHHH
HEY --
ICHIGO?

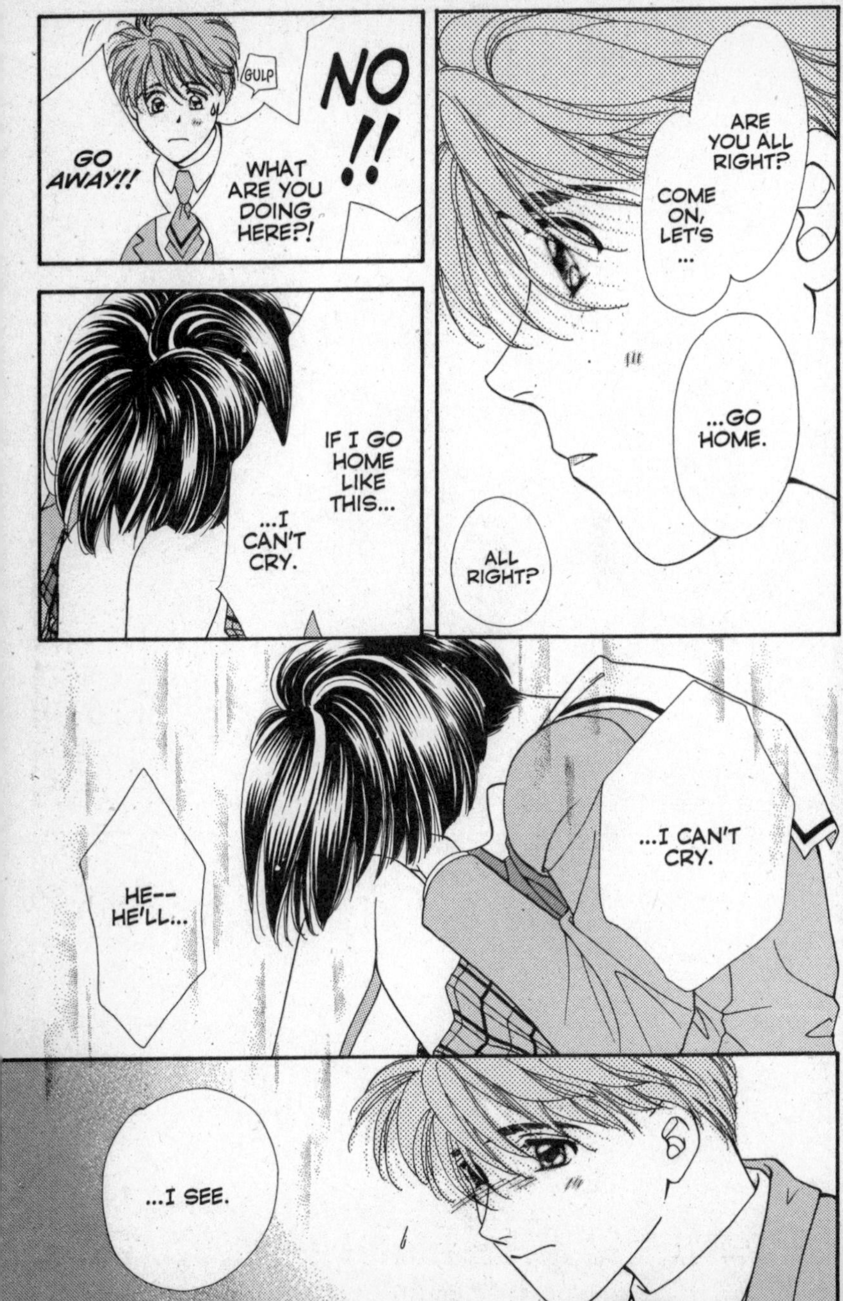
ARE YOU ALL RIGHT?
COME ON, LET'S ...
...GO HOME.
ALL RIGHT?
NO!!
GULP
WHAT ARE YOU DOING HERE?!
GO AWAY!!
IF I GO HOME LIKE THIS...
...I CAN'T CRY.
...I CAN'T CRY.
HE-- HE'LL...
...I SEE.

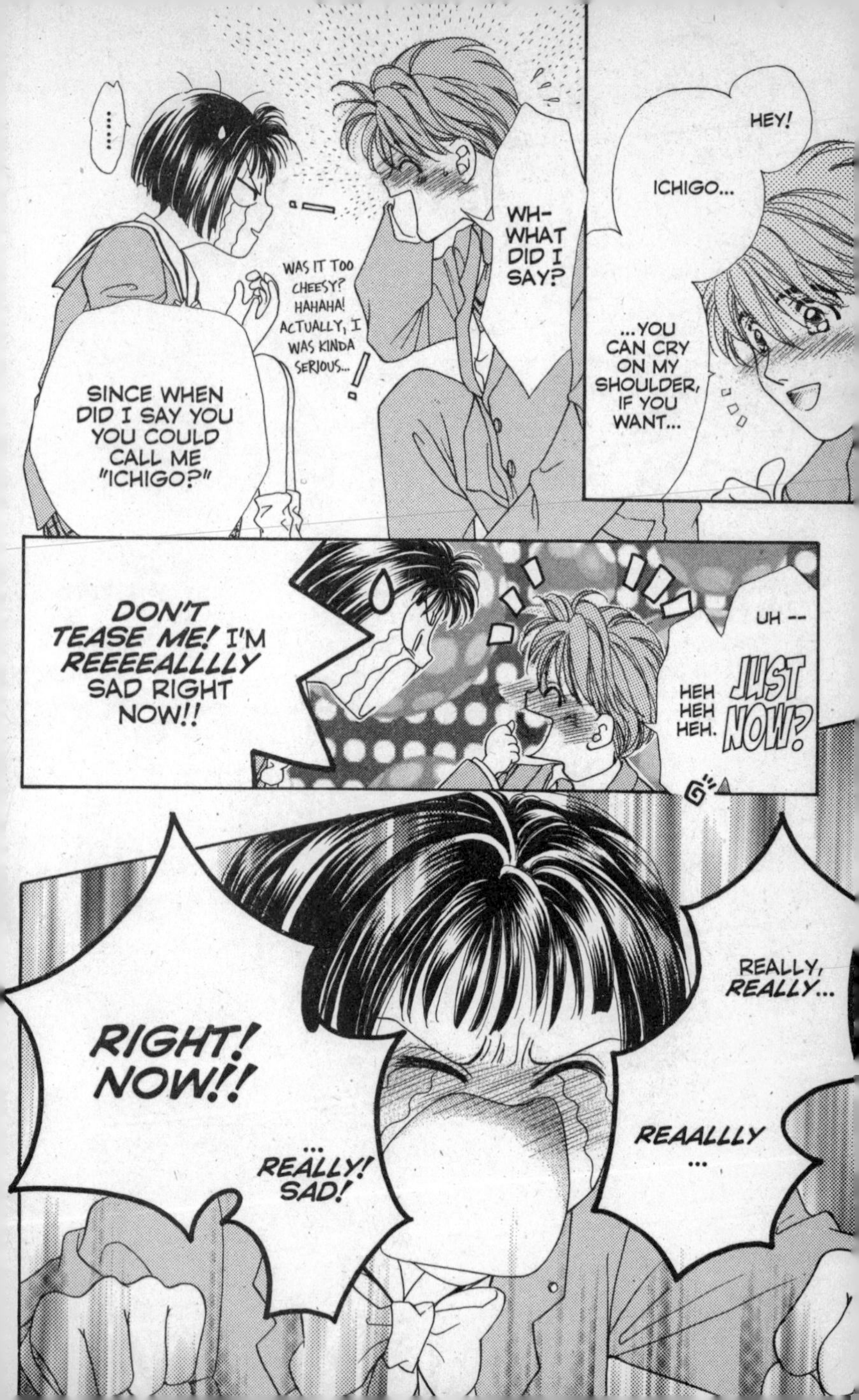
HEY!
ICHIGO...
...YOU CAN CRY ON MY SHOULDER, IF YOU WANT...
WH-WHAT DID I SAY?
WAS IT TOO CHEESY? HAHAHA! ACTUALLY, I WAS KINDA SERIOUS...
......
SINCE WHEN DID I SAY YOU YOU COULD CALL ME "ICHIGO?"
UH --
JUST NOW?
HEH HEH HEH.
DON'T TEASE ME! I'M REEEEALLLLLY SAD RIGHT NOW!!
REALLY, REALLY...
REAALLLY ...
... REALLY! SAD!
RIGHT! NOW!!

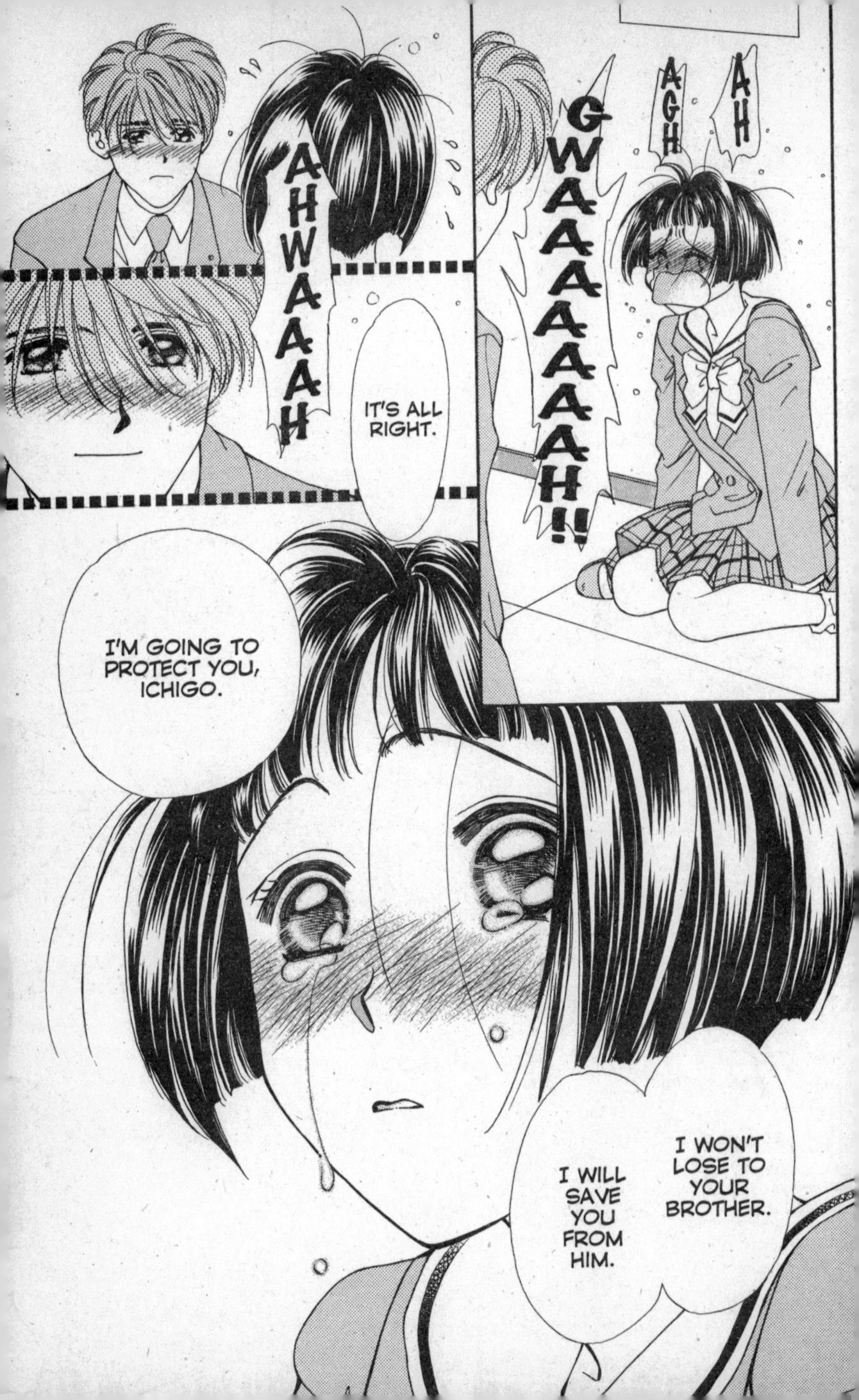
AH
AGH
GWAAAAAAAH!!
AHWAAAH
IT'S ALL RIGHT.
I'M GOING TO PROTECT YOU, ICHIGO.
I WON'T LOSE TO YOUR BROTHER.
I WILL SAVE YOU FROM HIM.

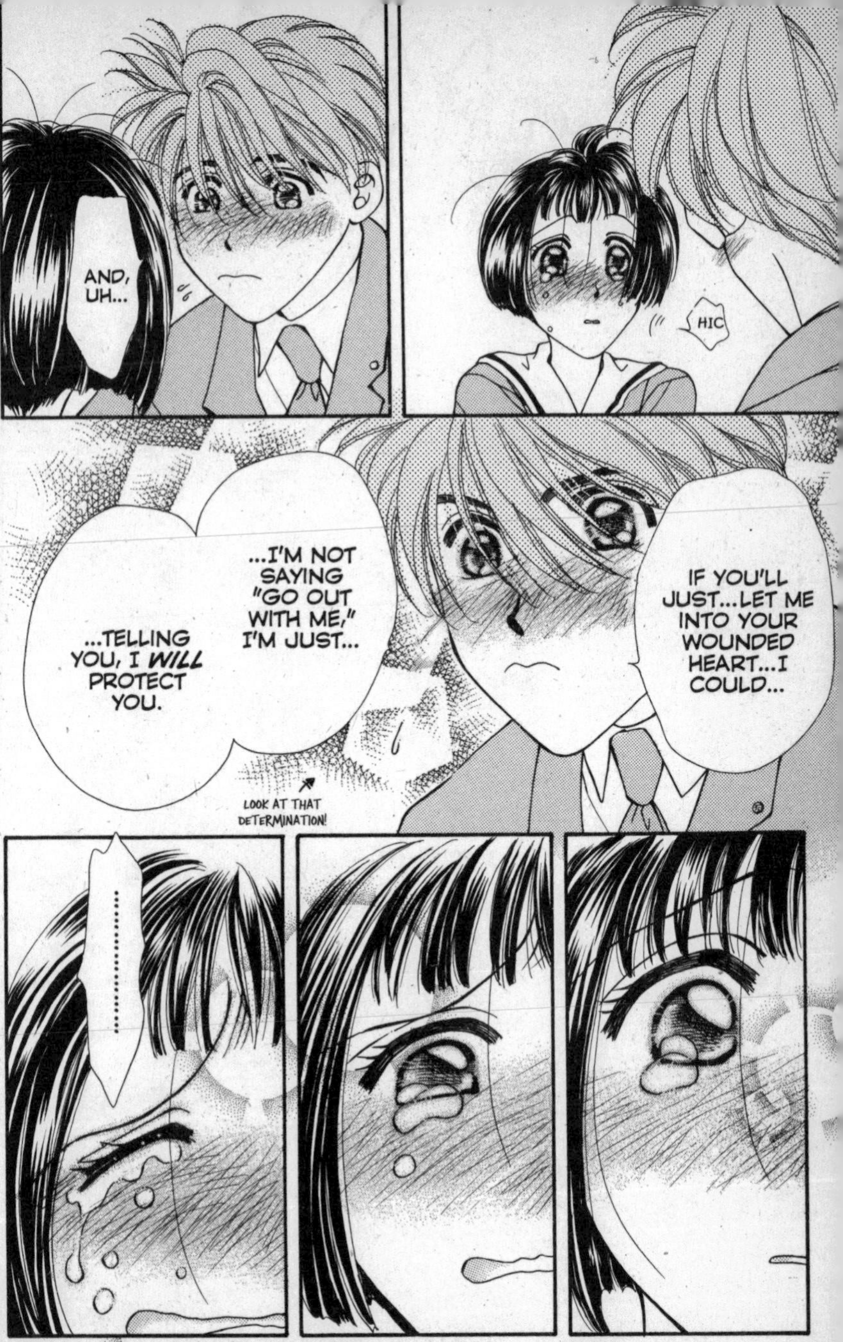
HIC
AND, UH...
IF YOU'LL JUST...LET ME INTO YOUR WOUNDED HEART...I COULD...
...I'M NOT SAYING "GO OUT WITH ME," I'M JUST...
...TELLING YOU, I *WILL* PROTECT YOU.
LOOK AT THAT DETERMINATION!
......

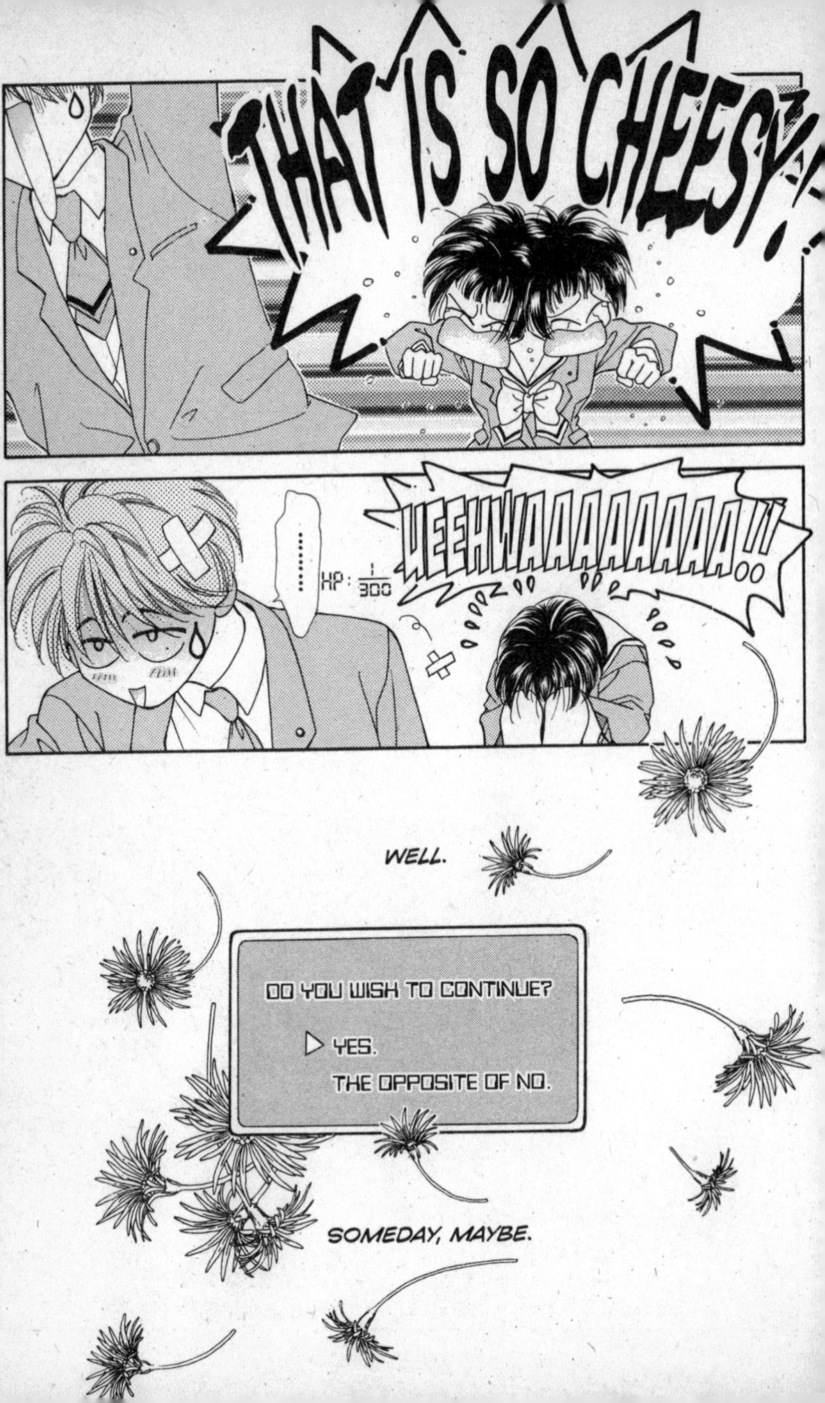

THAT IS SO CHEESY!!
WEEHWAAAAAAAA!!
HP: 1/300
......
WELL.
DO YOU WISH TO CONTINUE?
▷ YES.
THE OPPOSITE OF NO.
SOMEDAY, MAYBE.

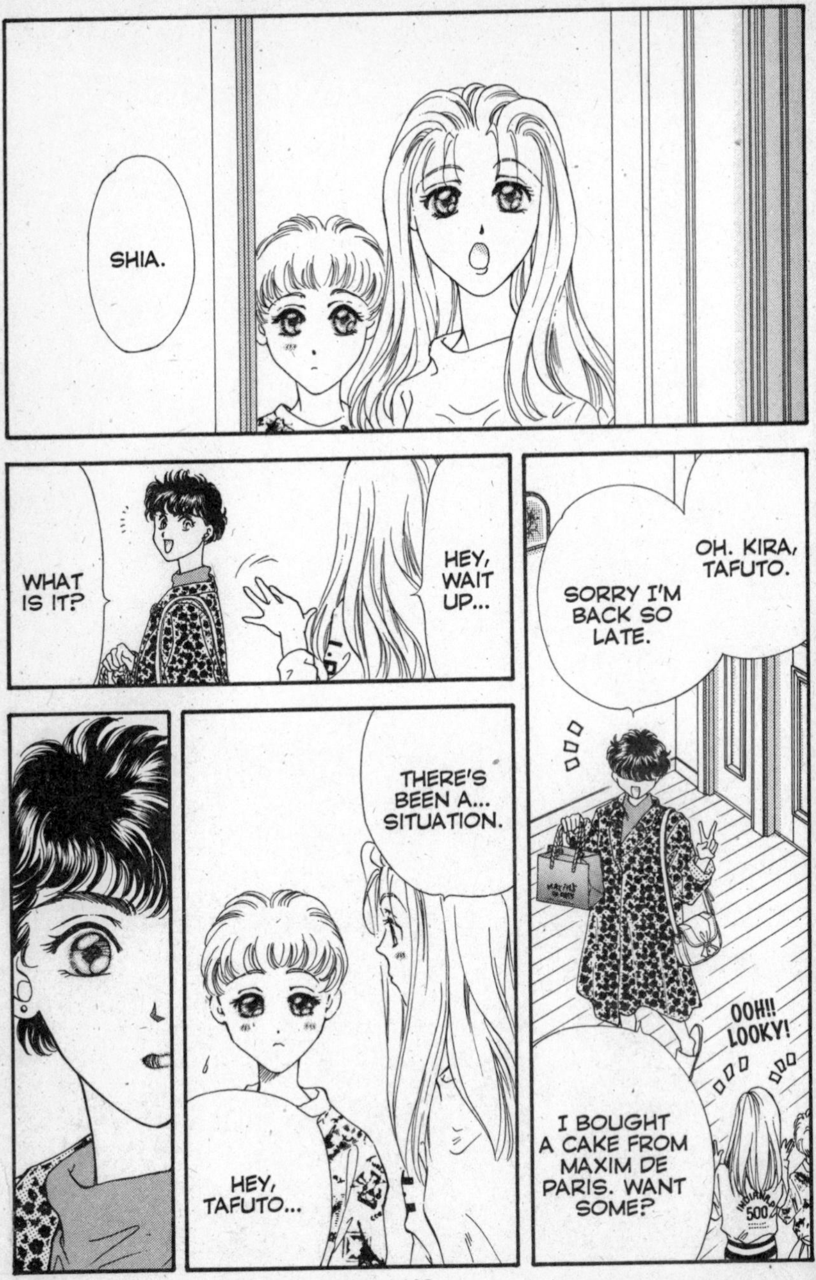
SHIA.
OH. KIRA, TAFUTO.
SORRY I'M BACK SO LATE.
OOH!! LOOKY!
I BOUGHT A CAKE FROM MAXIM DE PARIS. WANT SOME?
HEY, WAIT UP...
WHAT IS IT?
THERE'S BEEN A... SITUATION.
HEY, TAFUTO...

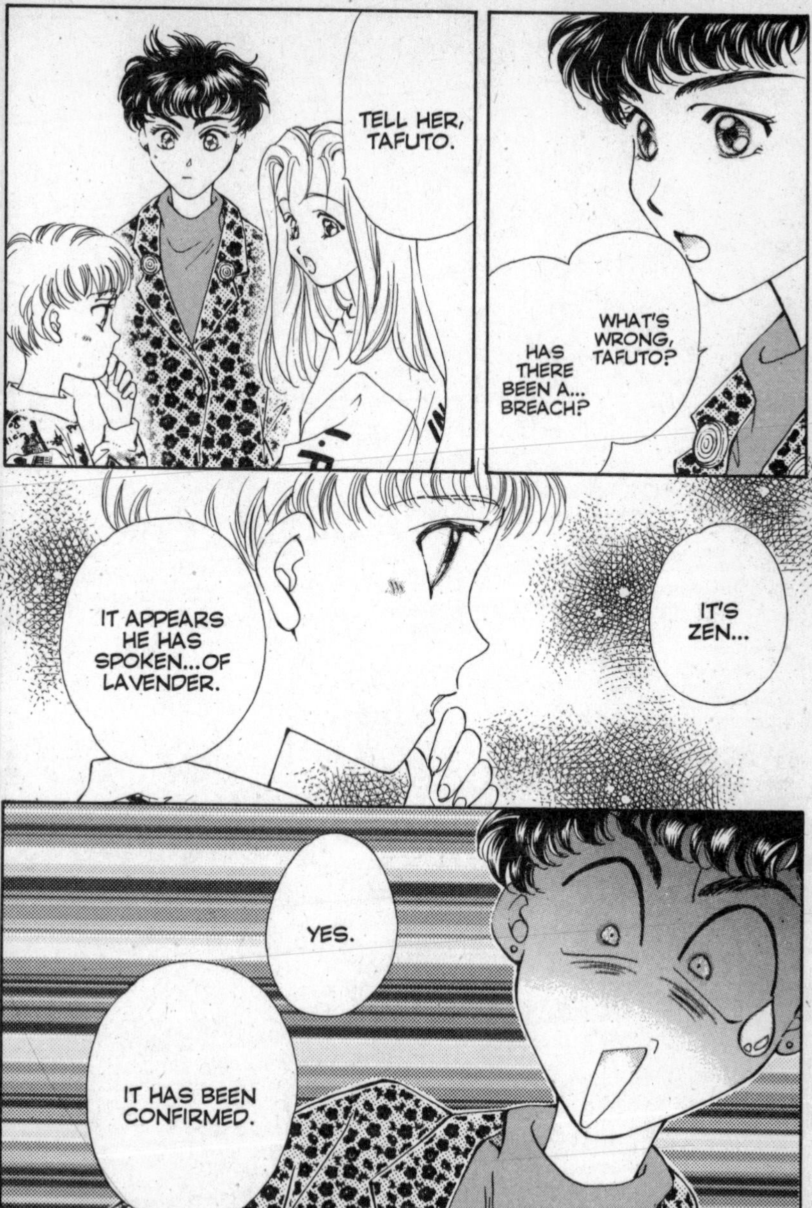
WHAT'S WRONG, TAFUTO?
HAS THERE BEEN A... BREACH?
TELL HER, TAFUTO.
IT'S ZEN...
IT APPEARS HE HAS SPOKEN...OF LAVENDER.
YES.
IT HAS BEEN CONFIRMED.

Sidebar No. 9

Sooo...what happened between the publications of volume two and volume three...let's see. Oh yeah. There was a fire in my apartment building. I looked out the window of the room I use to draw, and there was a fire just raging out there. While waiting for the fire truck to come, I kept thinking, why didn't I notice it sooner? People were going crazy at the time. I had to get out my three cats, the manga I was drawing at the time, and some important documents. I had a big pile of stuff outside. And then they put the fire out. This was the third time I've seen a fire like that. I hope there's no episode four. Fires suck! Anyway, no one was injured in the fire, so I guess everything turned out okay.

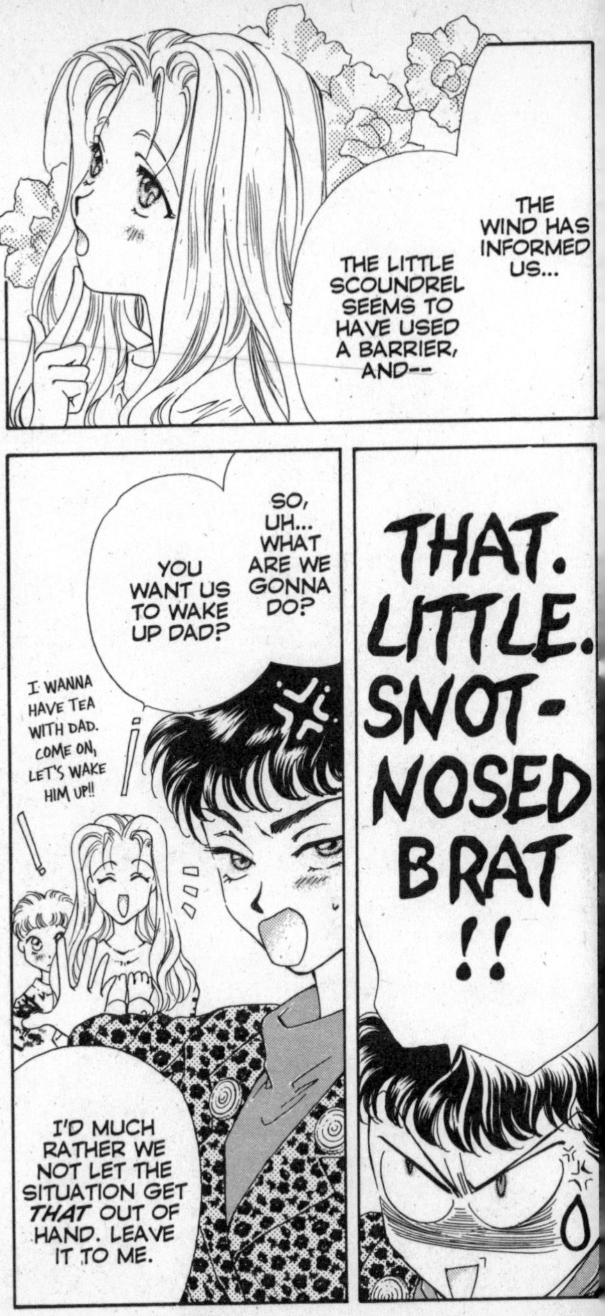
THE WIND HAS INFORMED US...
THE LITTLE SCOUNDREL SEEMS TO HAVE USED A BARRIER, AND--
THAT. LITTLE. SNOT-NOSED BRAT!!
SO, UH... WHAT ARE WE GONNA DO?
YOU WANT US TO WAKE UP DAD?
I WANNA HAVE TEA WITH DAD. COME ON, LET'S WAKE HIM UP!!
I'D MUCH RATHER WE NOT LET THE SITUATION GET *THAT* OUT OF HAND. LEAVE IT TO ME.

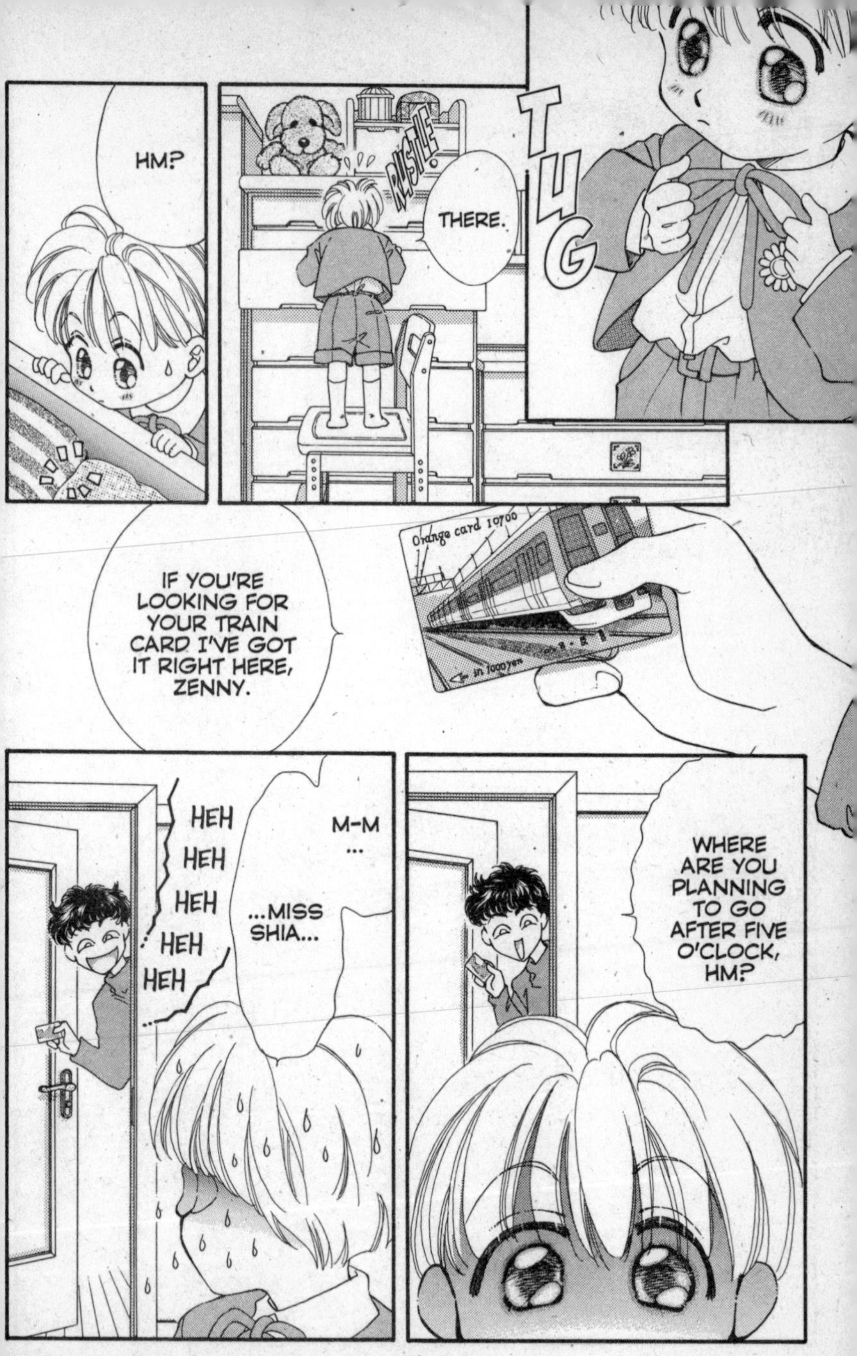
TUG
RUSTLE
THERE.
HM?
Orange card 10700
IF YOU'RE LOOKING FOR YOUR TRAIN CARD I'VE GOT IT RIGHT HERE, ZENNY.
WHERE ARE YOU PLANNING TO GO AFTER FIVE O'CLOCK, HM?
M-M ...
...MISS SHIA...
HEH HEH HEH HEH HEH

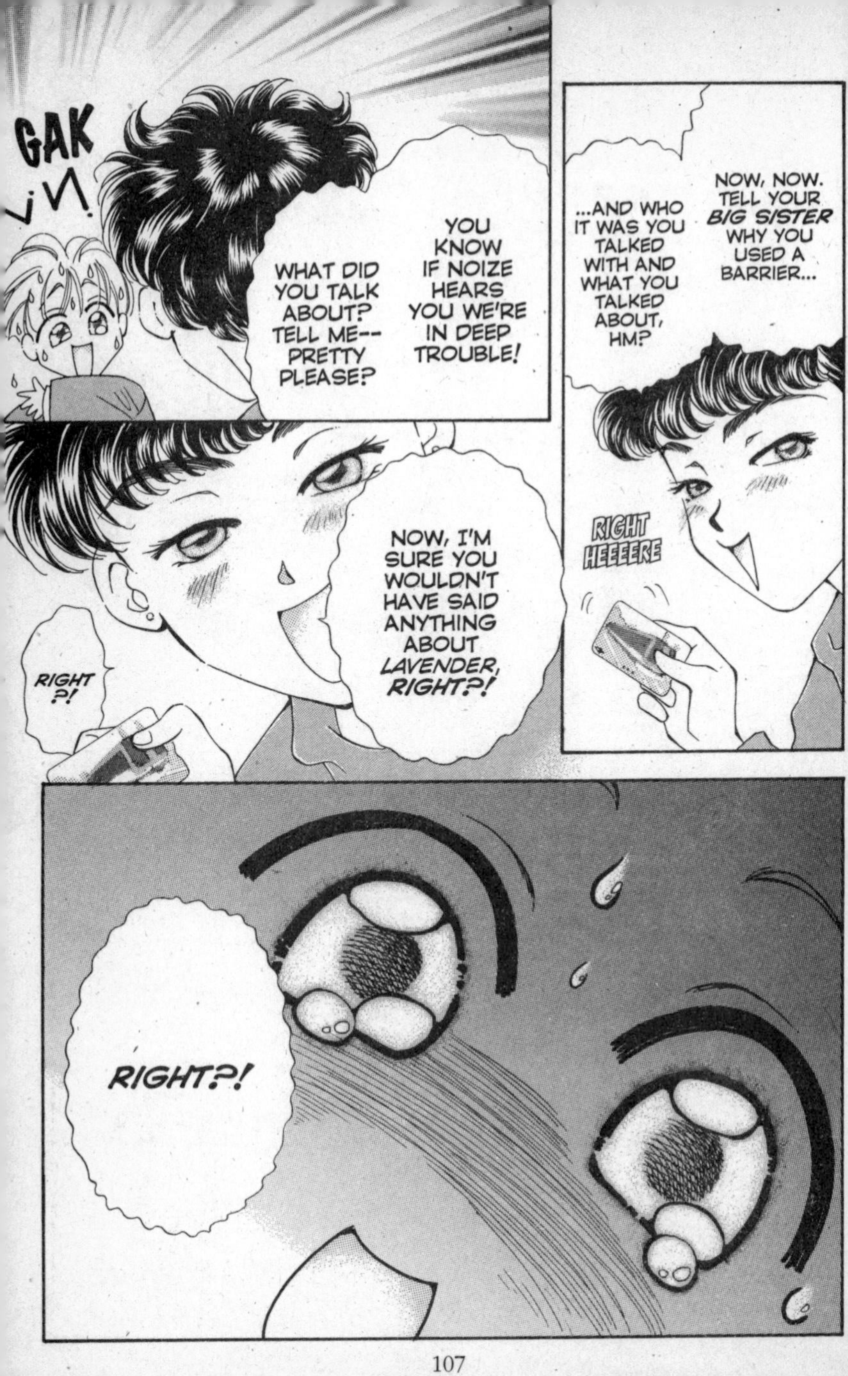
NOW, NOW. TELL YOUR *BIG SISTER* WHY YOU USED A BARRIER...
...AND WHO IT WAS YOU TALKED WITH AND WHAT YOU TALKED ABOUT, HM?
RIGHT HEEEERE
YOU KNOW IF NOIZE HEARS YOU WE'RE IN DEEP TROUBLE!
WHAT DID YOU TALK ABOUT? TELL ME-- PRETTY PLEASE?
GAK
NOW, I'M SURE YOU WOULDN'T HAVE SAID ANYTHING ABOUT *LAVENDER, RIGHT?!*
RIGHT ?!
RIGHT?!

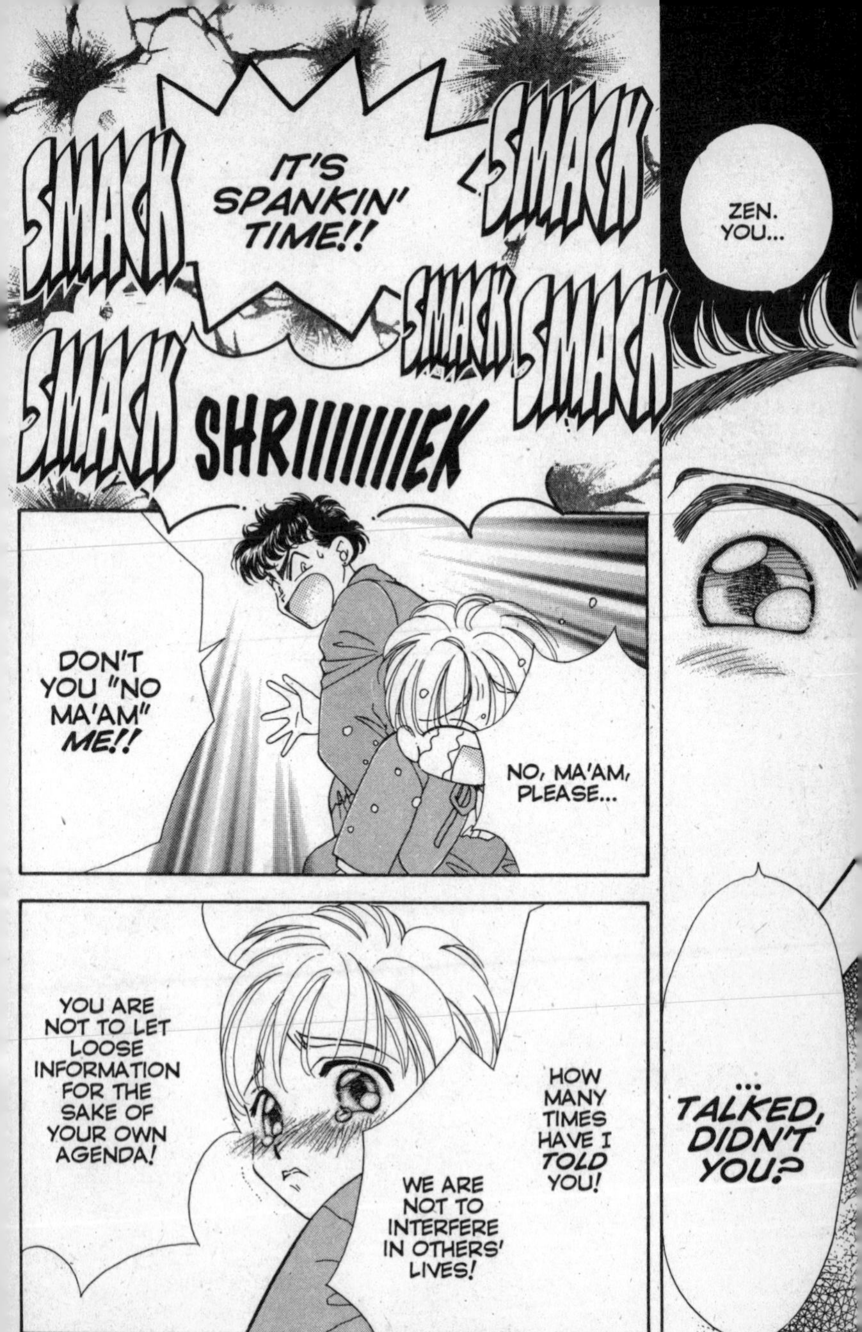
ZEN. YOU...
... TALKED, DIDN'T YOU?
SMACK
SMACK
SMACK
IT'S SPANKIN' TIME!!
SMACK
SHRIIIIIIIEK
SMACK
NO, MA'AM, PLEASE...
DON'T YOU "NO MA'AM" ME!!
HOW MANY TIMES HAVE I TOLD YOU!
WE ARE NOT TO INTERFERE IN OTHERS' LIVES!
YOU ARE NOT TO LET LOOSE INFORMATION FOR THE SAKE OF YOUR OWN AGENDA!

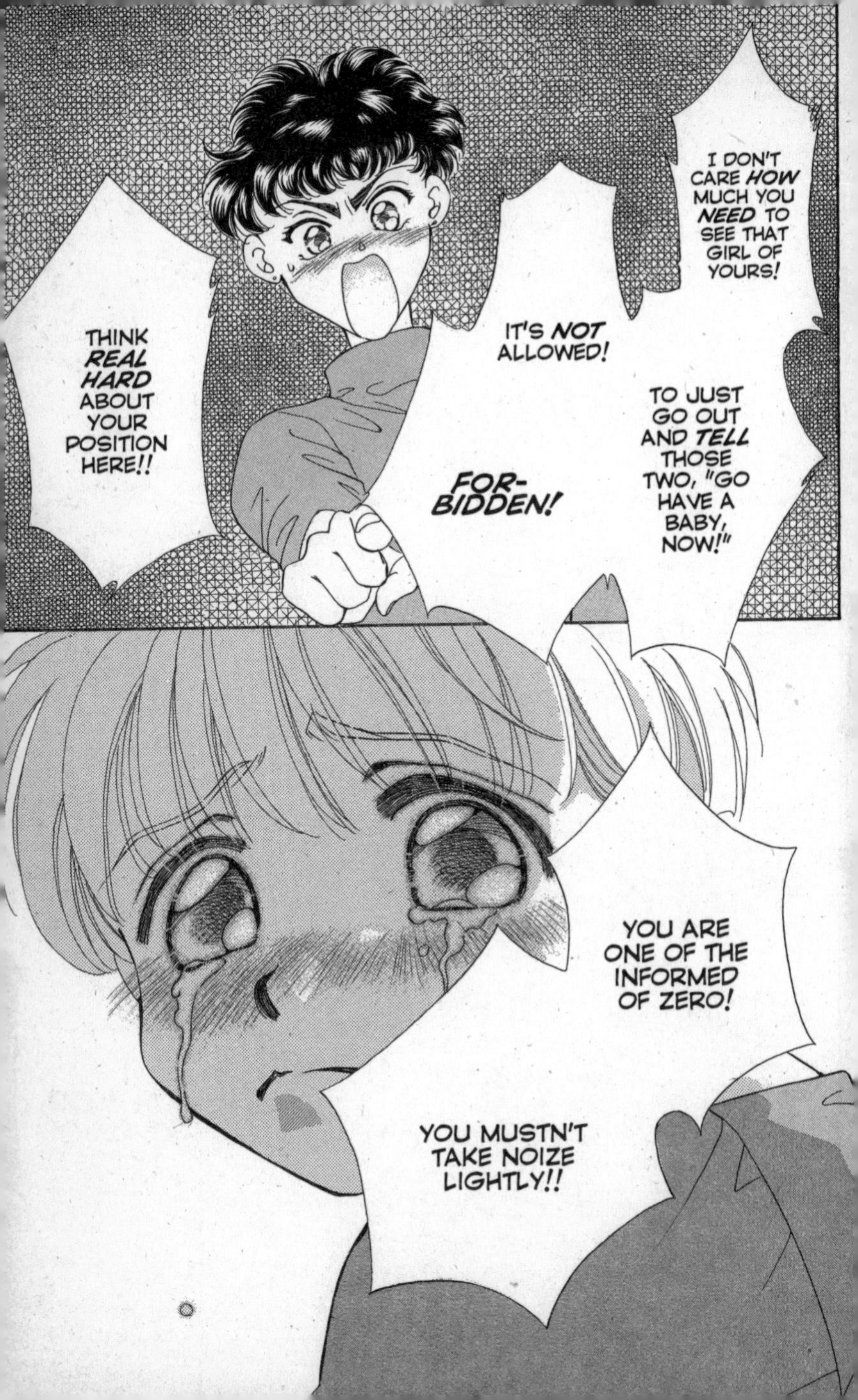
I DON'T CARE *HOW* MUCH YOU *NEED* TO SEE THAT GIRL OF YOURS!
TO JUST GO OUT AND *TELL* THOSE TWO, "GO HAVE A BABY, NOW!"
IT'S *NOT* ALLOWED!
FOR-BIDDEN!
THINK *REAL HARD* ABOUT YOUR POSITION HERE!!
YOU ARE ONE OF THE INFORMED OF ZERO!
YOU MUSTN'T TAKE NOIZE LIGHTLY!!

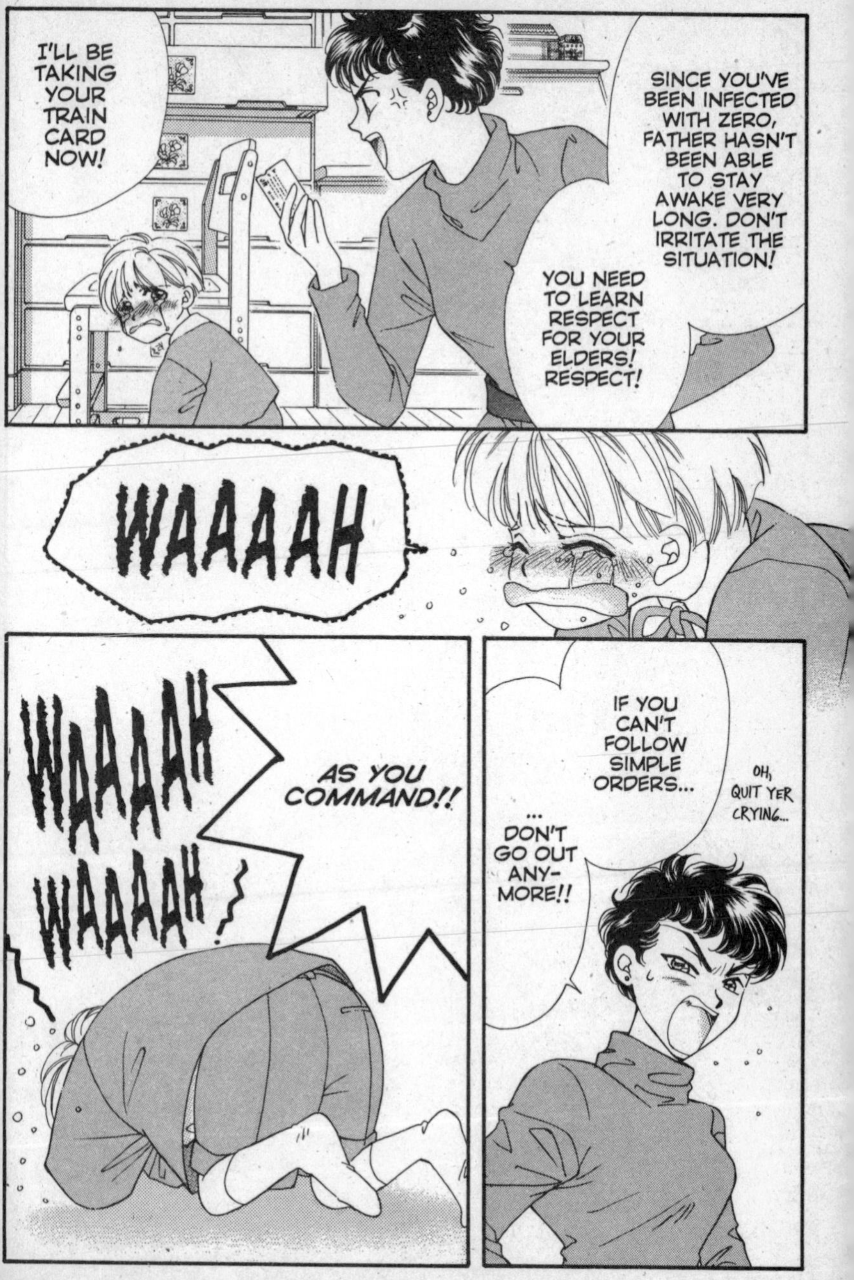
SINCE YOU'VE BEEN INFECTED WITH ZERO, FATHER HASN'T BEEN ABLE TO STAY AWAKE VERY LONG. DON'T IRRITATE THE SITUATION!
YOU NEED TO LEARN RESPECT FOR YOUR ELDERS! RESPECT!
I'LL BE TAKING YOUR TRAIN CARD NOW!
WAAAAH
OH, QUIT YER CRYING...
IF YOU CAN'T FOLLOW SIMPLE ORDERS...
... DON'T GO OUT ANY-MORE!!
AS YOU COMMAND!!
WAAAAH
WAAAAH

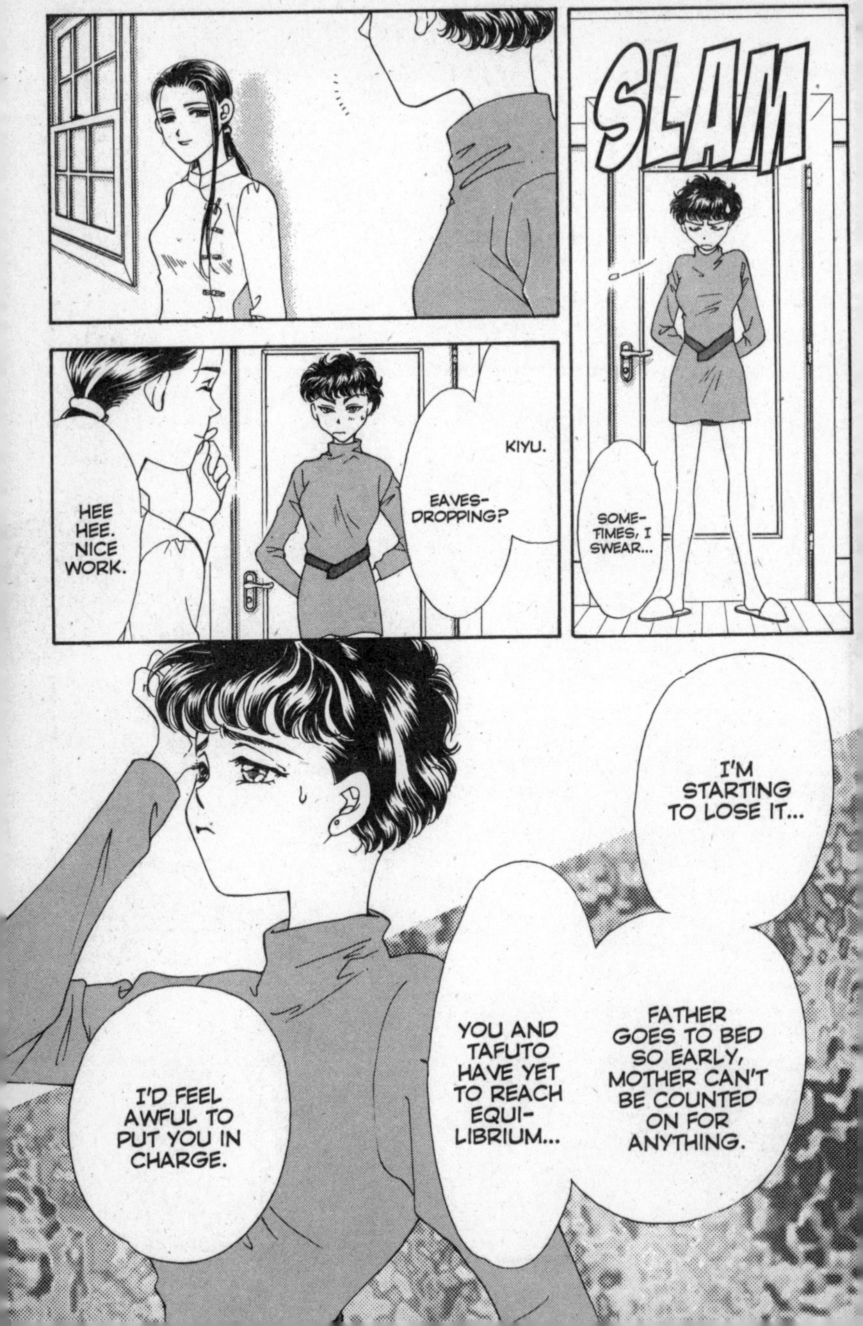
SLAM
SOMETIMES, I SWEAR...
KIYU.
EAVESDROPPING?
HEE HEE. NICE WORK.
I'M STARTING TO LOSE IT...
FATHER GOES TO BED SO EARLY, MOTHER CAN'T BE COUNTED ON FOR ANYTHING.
YOU AND TAFUTO HAVE YET TO REACH EQUILIBRIUM...
I'D FEEL AWFUL TO PUT YOU IN CHARGE.

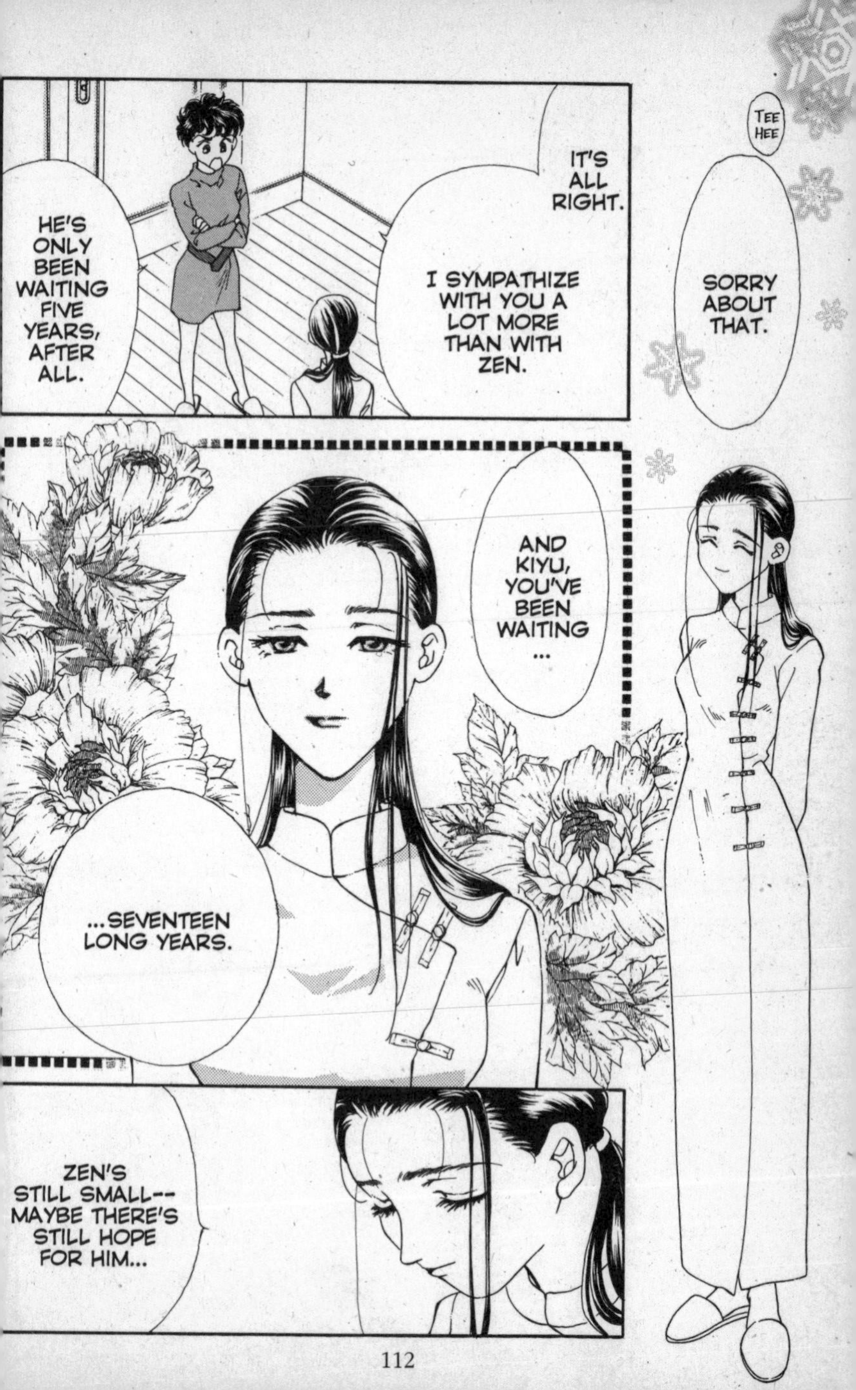

TEE HEE
SORRY ABOUT THAT.
IT'S ALL RIGHT.
I SYMPATHIZE WITH YOU A LOT MORE THAN WITH ZEN.
HE'S ONLY BEEN WAITING FIVE YEARS, AFTER ALL.
AND KIYU, YOU'VE BEEN WAITING ...
...SEVENTEEN LONG YEARS.
ZEN'S STILL SMALL-- MAYBE THERE'S STILL HOPE FOR HIM...

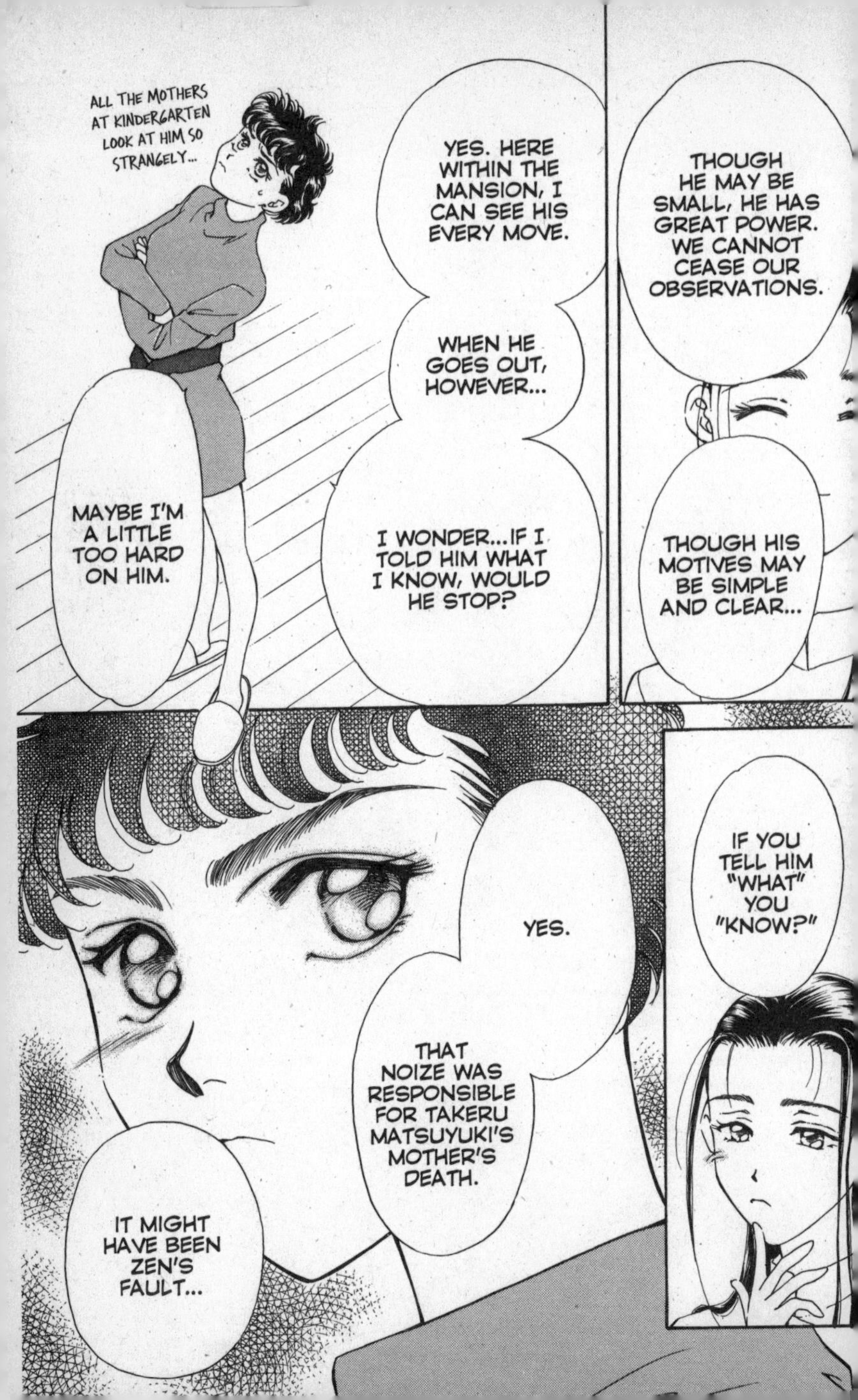
THOUGH HE MAY BE SMALL, HE HAS GREAT POWER. WE CANNOT CEASE OUR OBSERVATIONS.
THOUGH HIS MOTIVES MAY BE SIMPLE AND CLEAR...
YES. HERE WITHIN THE MANSION, I CAN SEE HIS EVERY MOVE.
WHEN HE GOES OUT, HOWEVER...
I WONDER...IF I TOLD HIM WHAT I KNOW, WOULD HE STOP?
ALL THE MOTHERS AT KINDERGARTEN LOOK AT HIM SO STRANGELY...
MAYBE I'M A LITTLE TOO HARD ON HIM.
IF YOU TELL HIM "WHAT" YOU "KNOW?"
YES.
THAT NOIZE WAS RESPONSIBLE FOR TAKERU MATSUYUKI'S MOTHER'S DEATH.
IT MIGHT HAVE BEEN ZEN'S FAULT...

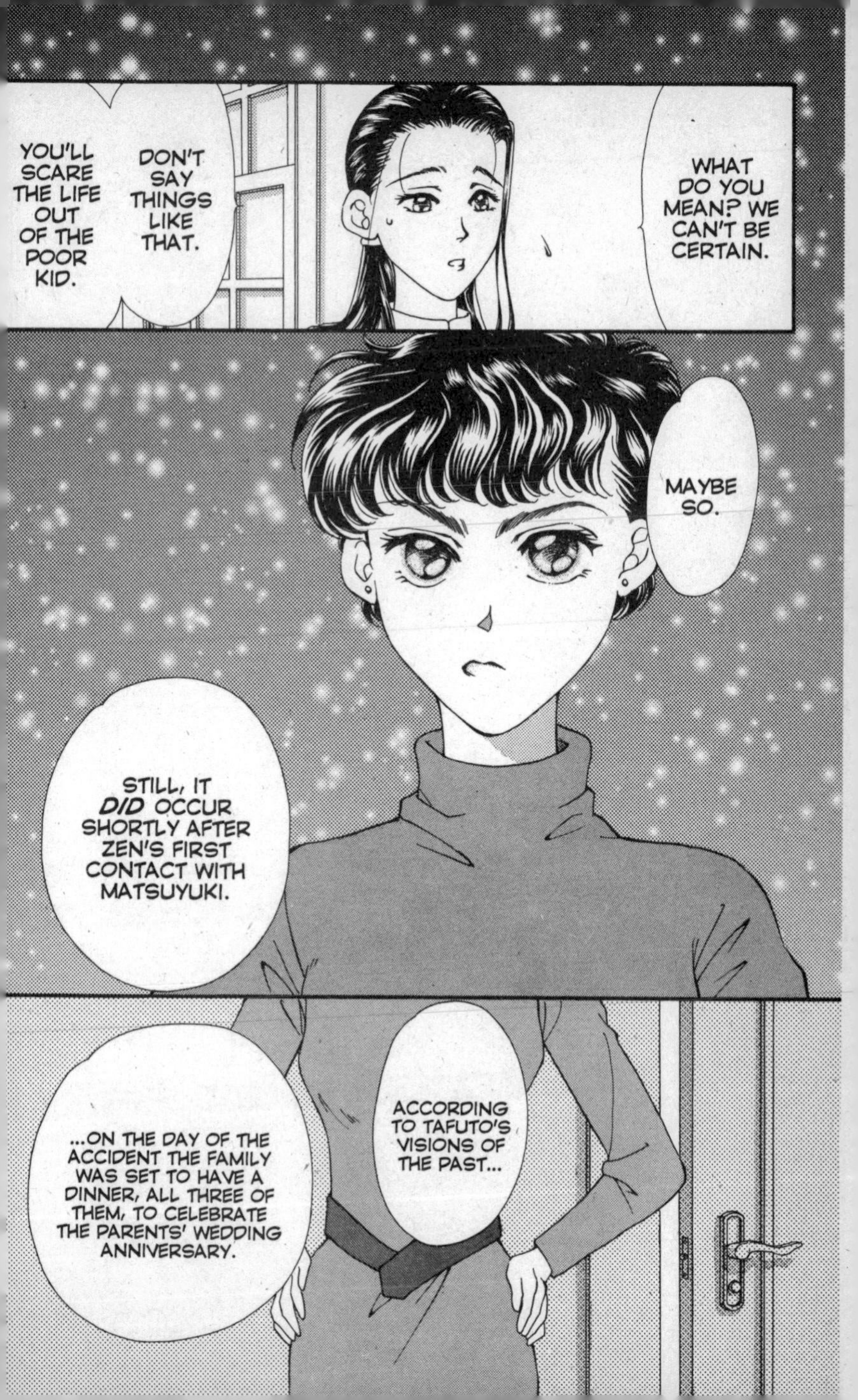
WHAT DO YOU MEAN? WE CAN'T BE CERTAIN.
DON'T SAY THINGS LIKE THAT.
YOU'LL SCARE THE LIFE OUT OF THE POOR KID.
MAYBE SO.
STILL, IT *DID* OCCUR SHORTLY AFTER ZEN'S FIRST CONTACT WITH MATSUYUKI.
ACCORDING TO TAFUTO'S VISIONS OF THE PAST...
...ON THE DAY OF THE ACCIDENT THE FAMILY WAS SET TO HAVE A DINNER, ALL THREE OF THEM, TO CELEBRATE THE PARENTS' WEDDING ANNIVERSARY.

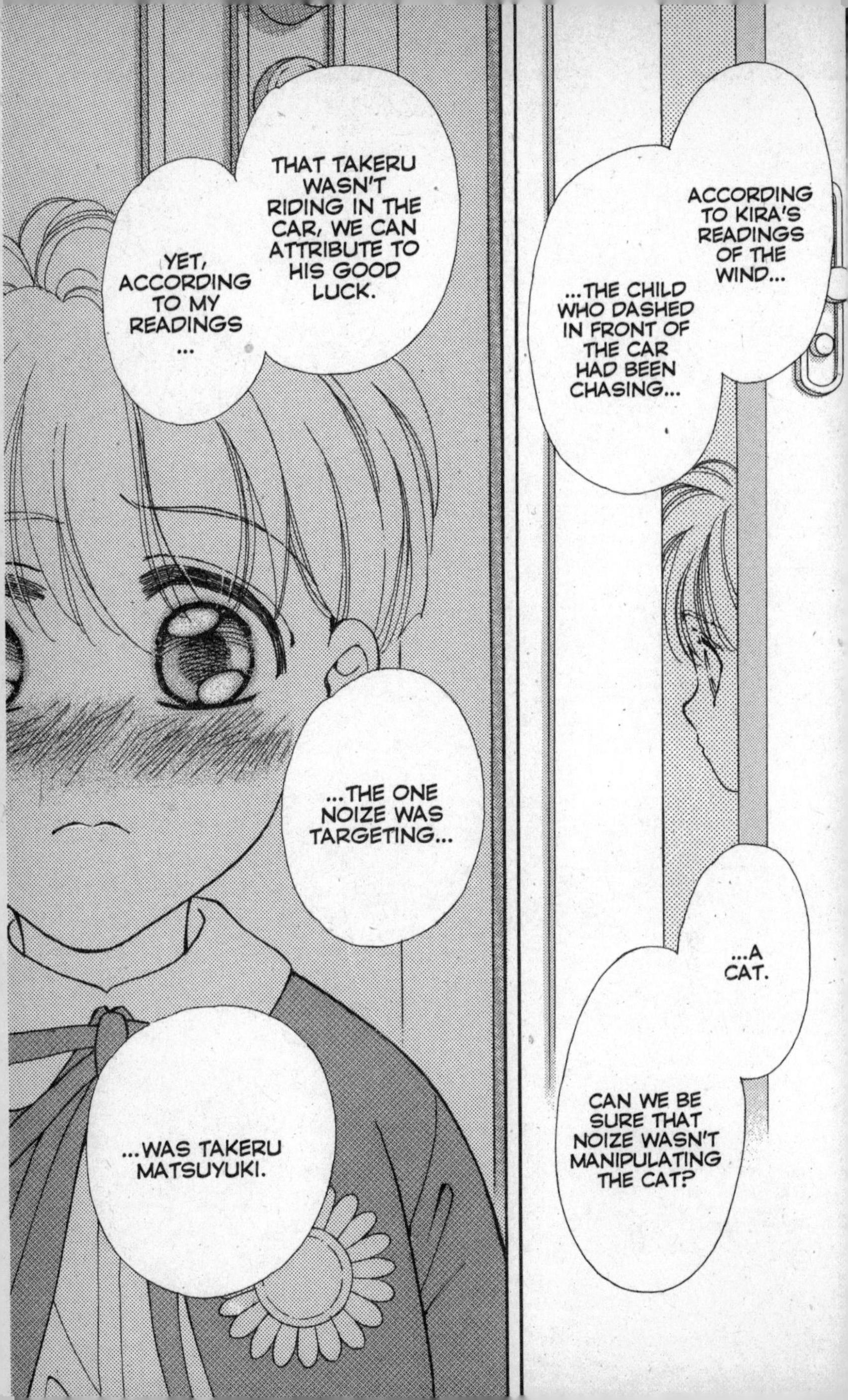
ACCORDING TO KIRA'S READINGS OF THE WIND...
...THE CHILD WHO DASHED IN FRONT OF THE CAR HAD BEEN CHASING...
...A CAT.
CAN WE BE SURE THAT NOIZE WASN'T MANIPULATING THE CAT?
THAT TAKERU WASN'T RIDING IN THE CAR, WE CAN ATTRIBUTE TO HIS GOOD LUCK.
YET, ACCORDING TO MY READINGS...
...THE ONE NOIZE WAS TARGETING...
...WAS TAKERU MATSUYUKI.

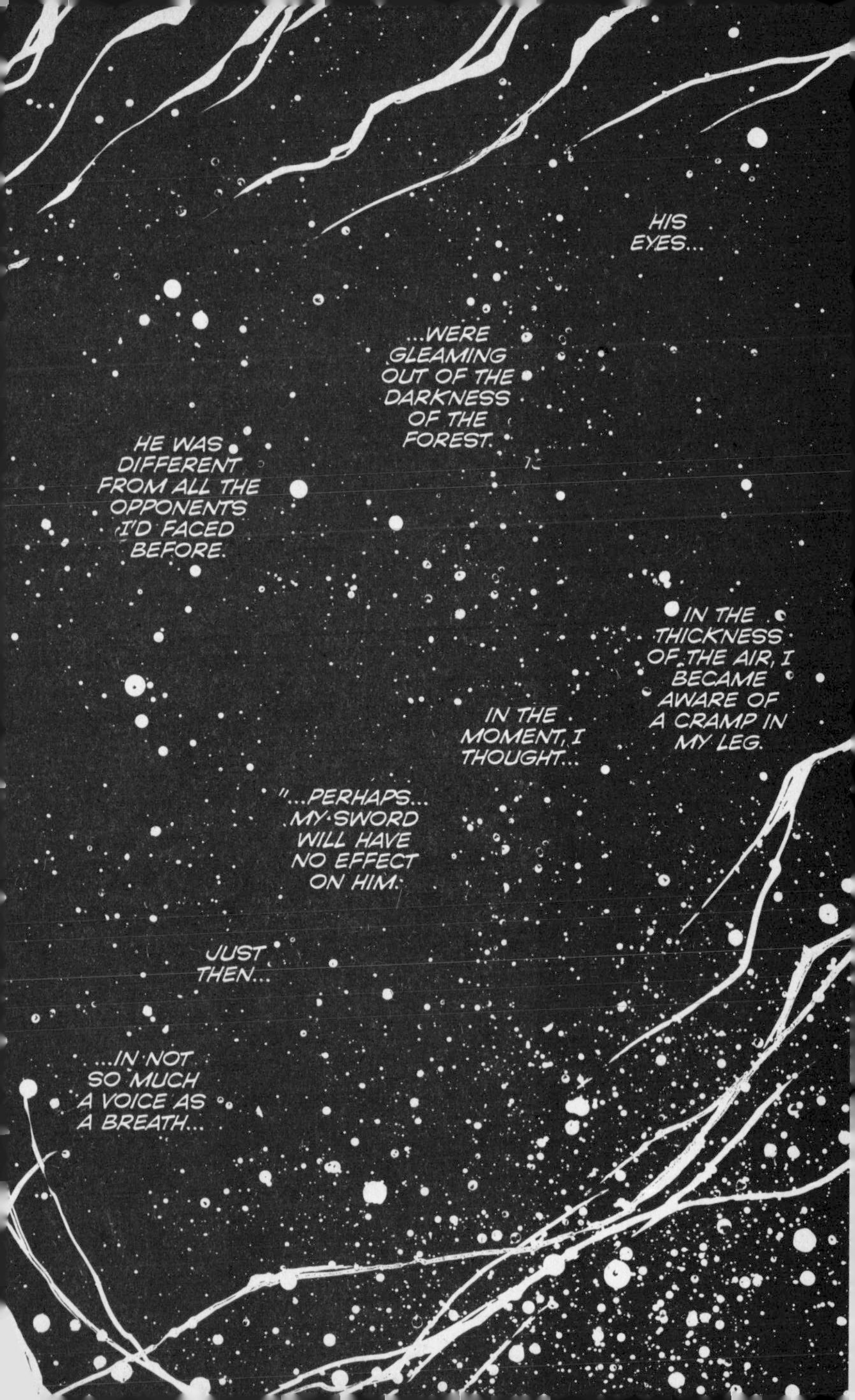
HIS EYES...
...WERE GLEAMING OUT OF THE DARKNESS OF THE FOREST.
HE WAS DIFFERENT FROM ALL THE OPPONENTS I'D FACED BEFORE.
IN THE THICKNESS OF THE AIR, I BECAME AWARE OF A CRAMP IN MY LEG.
IN THE MOMENT, I THOUGHT...
"...PERHAPS... MY SWORD WILL HAVE NO EFFECT ON HIM.
JUST THEN...
...IN NOT SO MUCH A VOICE AS A BREATH...

Sidebar No. 10

Now that I think about it, isn't it odd for one person to witness so many fires in her lifetime? I've moved about three times, though everywhere I seem to go, some strange incident occurs, spurring me to move again, forever seeking peace and quiet. Perhaps I summon these incidents with my dormant psychic powers? Once, a car accident happened right in front of me while I was waiting to cross the street, and my mom said, "It happened because you were standing there." Thanks a lot, mom! And sometimes, even more...well, maybe that's not fit to write about here.

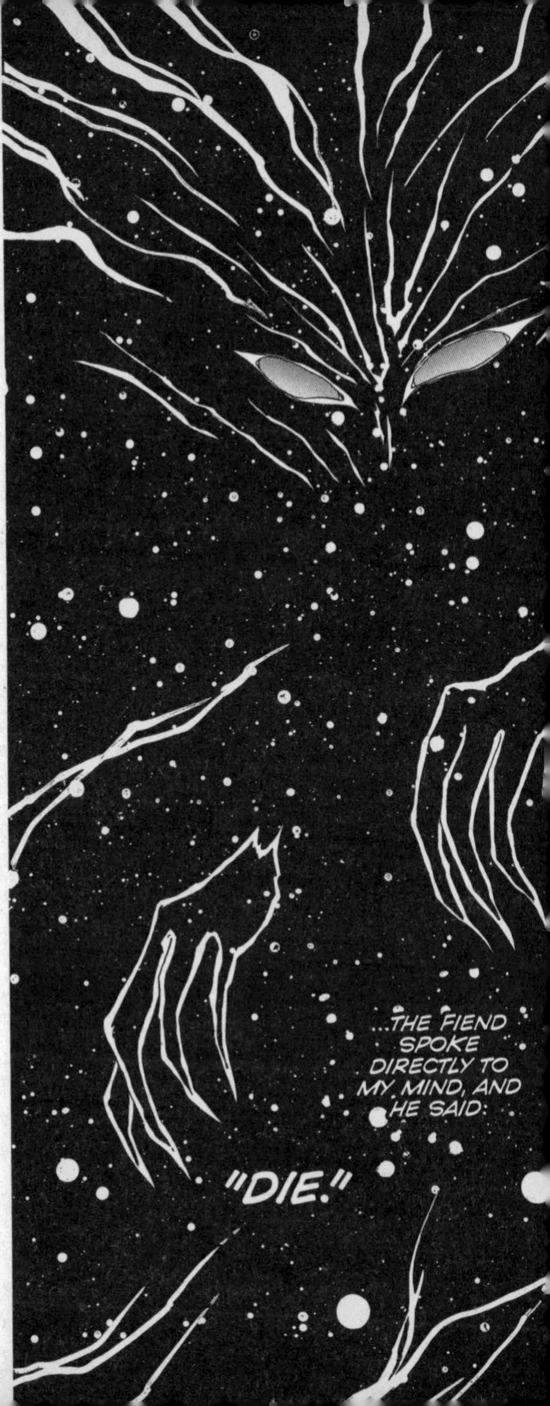
...THE FIEND SPOKE DIRECTLY TO MY MIND, AND HE SAID:
"DIE."

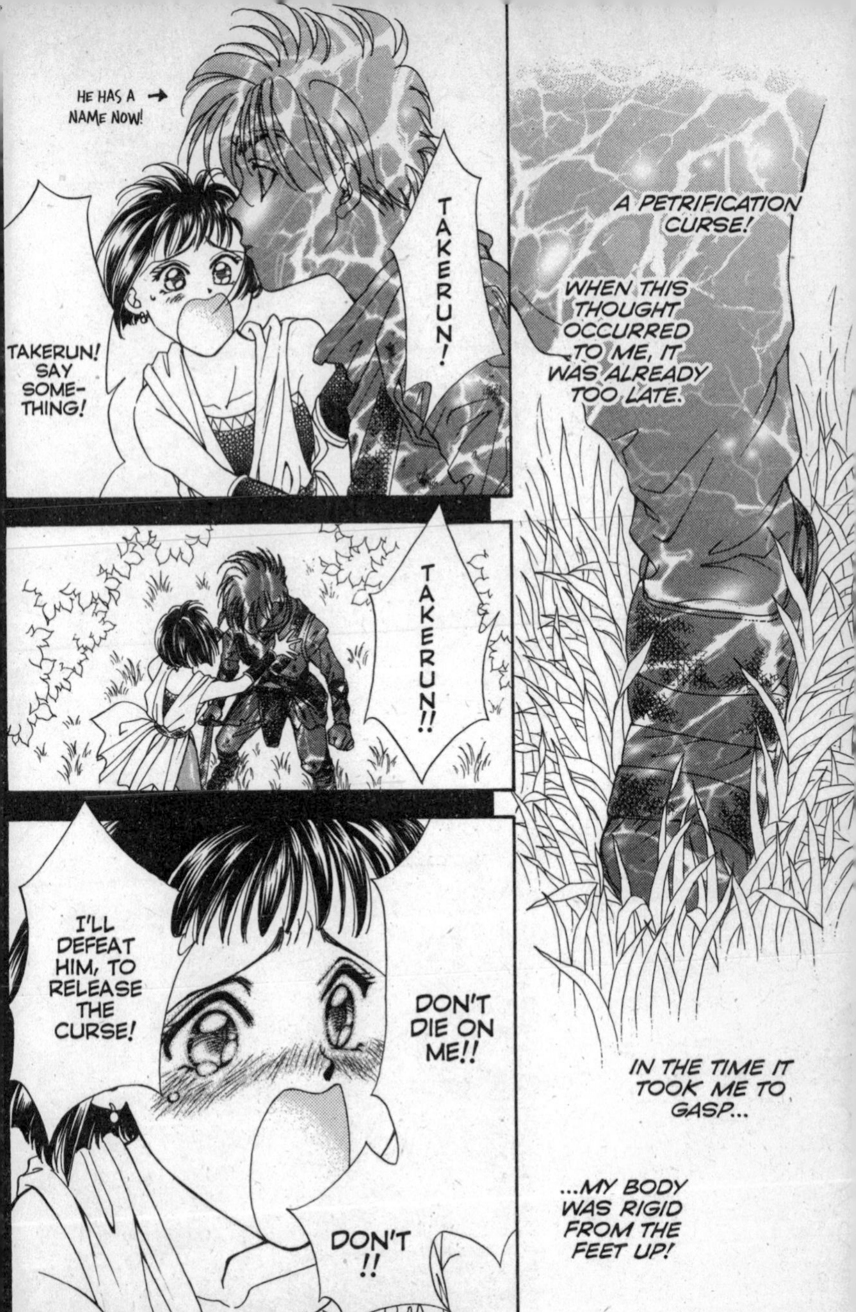
A PETRIFICATION CURSE!
WHEN THIS THOUGHT OCCURRED TO ME, IT WAS ALREADY TOO LATE.
IN THE TIME IT TOOK ME TO GASP...
...MY BODY WAS RIGID FROM THE FEET UP!
TAKERUN!
HE HAS A NAME NOW!
TAKERUN! SAY SOME-THING!
TAKERUN!!
DON'T DIE ON ME!!
I'LL DEFEAT HIM, TO RELEASE THE CURSE!
DON'T !!

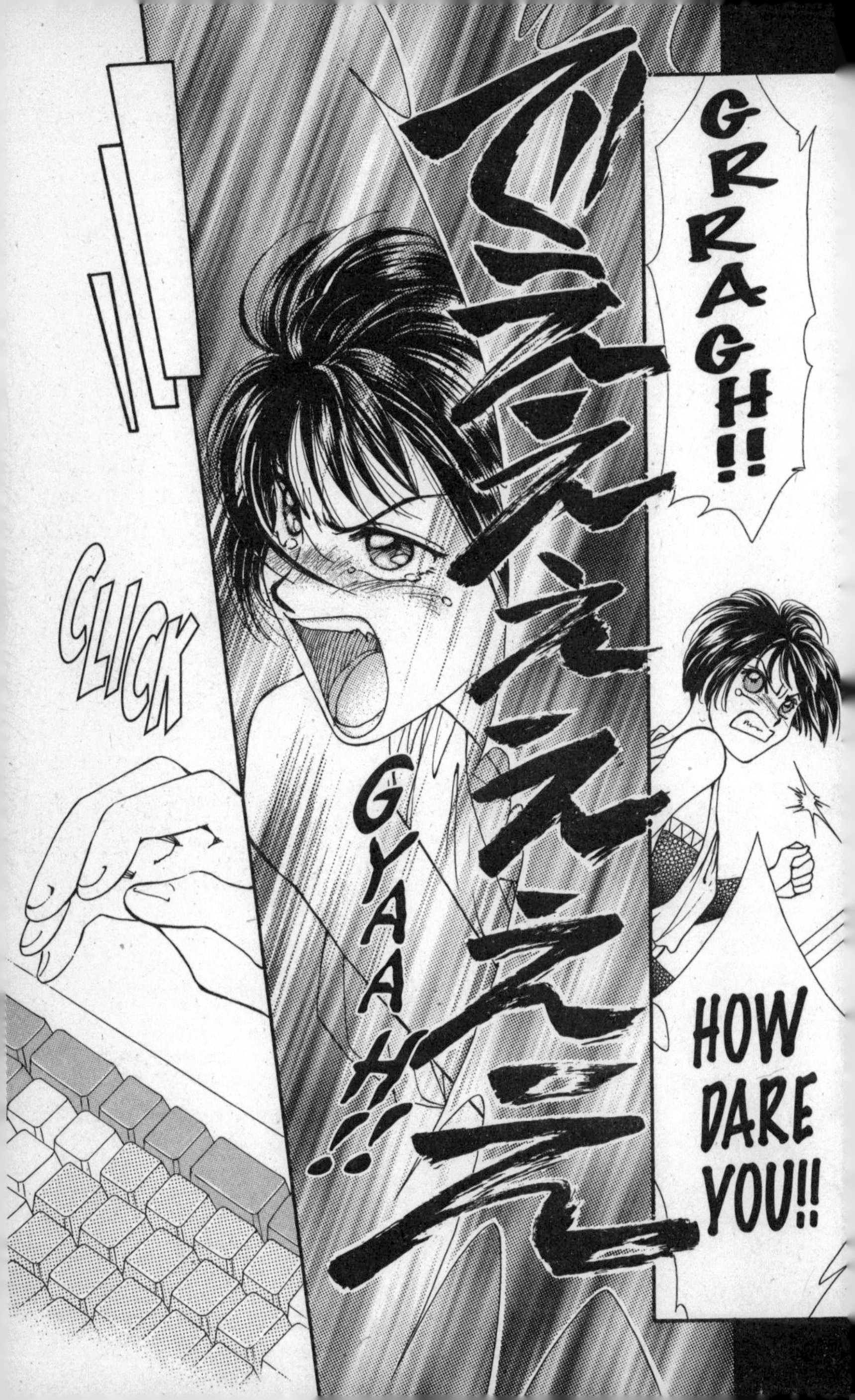
GRRAGH!!
HOW DARE YOU!!
GYAAH!!
CLICK

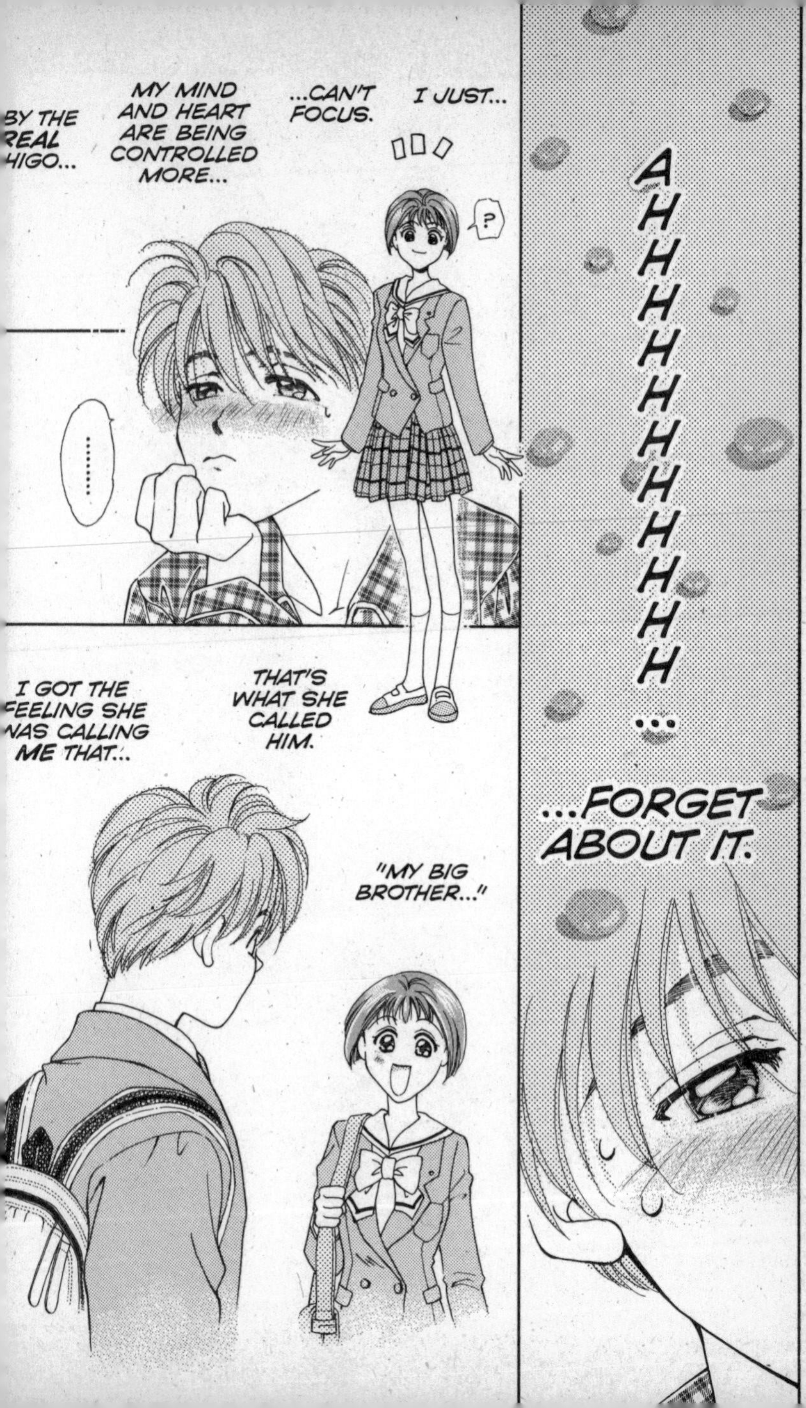
AHHHHHHHHHHHHH...
...FORGET ABOUT IT.
I JUST...
...CAN'T FOCUS.
MY MIND AND HEART ARE BEING CONTROLLED MORE...
BY THE REAL HIGO...
?
......
THAT'S WHAT SHE CALLED HIM.
I GOT THE FEELING SHE WAS CALLING ME THAT...
"MY BIG BROTHER..."

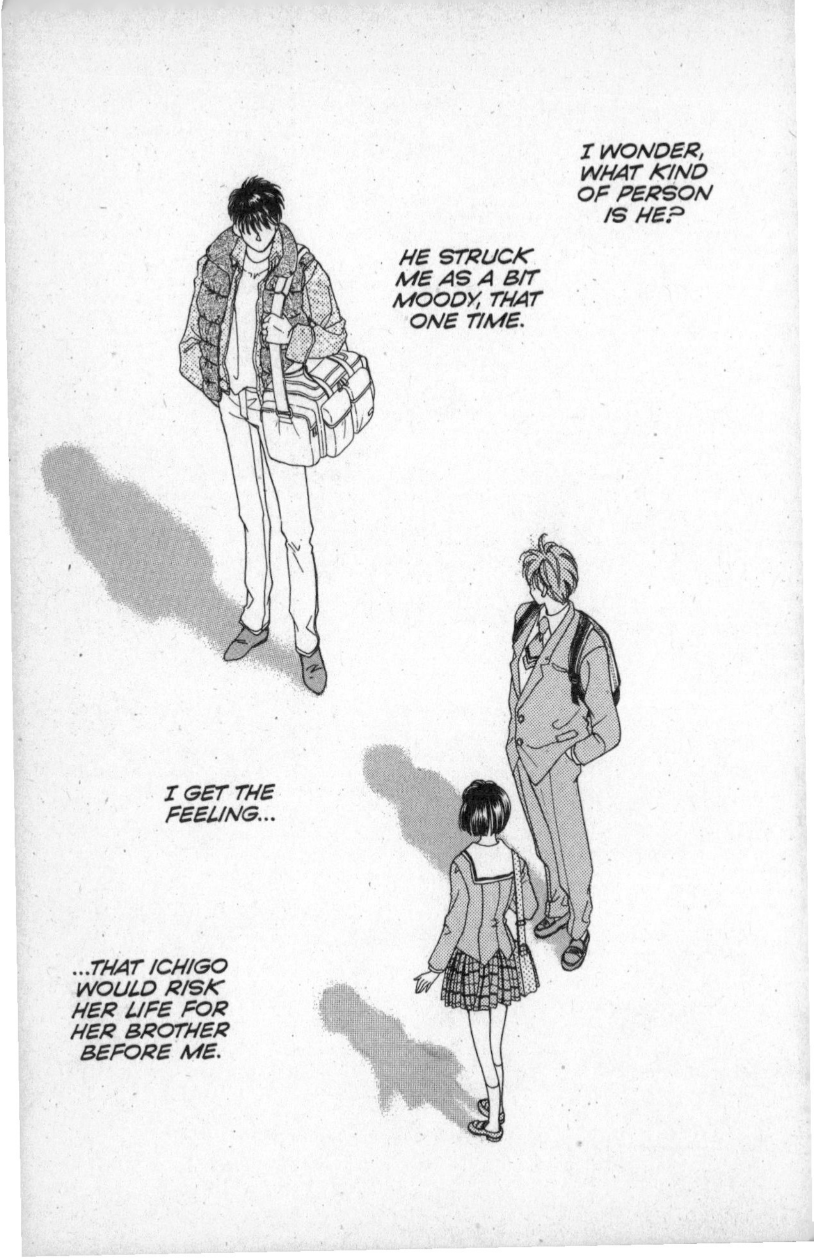
I WONDER, WHAT KIND OF PERSON IS HE?
HE STRUCK ME AS A BIT MOODY, THAT ONE TIME.
I GET THE FEELING...
...THAT ICHIGO WOULD RISK HER LIFE FOR HER BROTHER BEFORE ME.

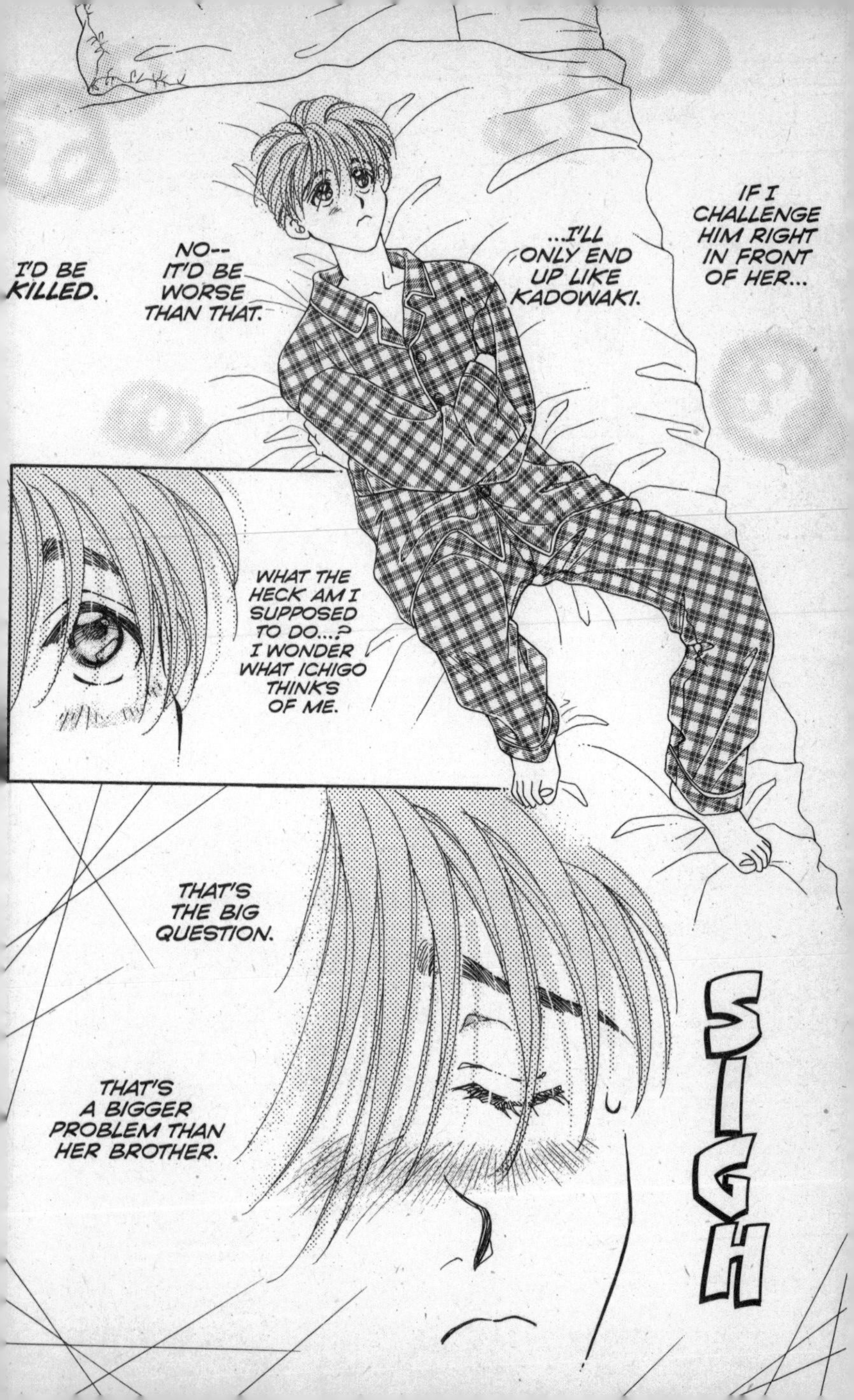
IF I CHALLENGE HIM RIGHT IN FRONT OF HER...
...I'LL ONLY END UP LIKE KADOWAKI.
I'D BE **KILLED**.
NO-- IT'D BE WORSE THAN THAT.
WHAT THE HECK AM I SUPPOSED TO DO...? I WONDER WHAT ICHIGO THINKS OF ME.
THAT'S THE BIG QUESTION.
THAT'S A BIGGER PROBLEM THAN HER BROTHER.
SIGH

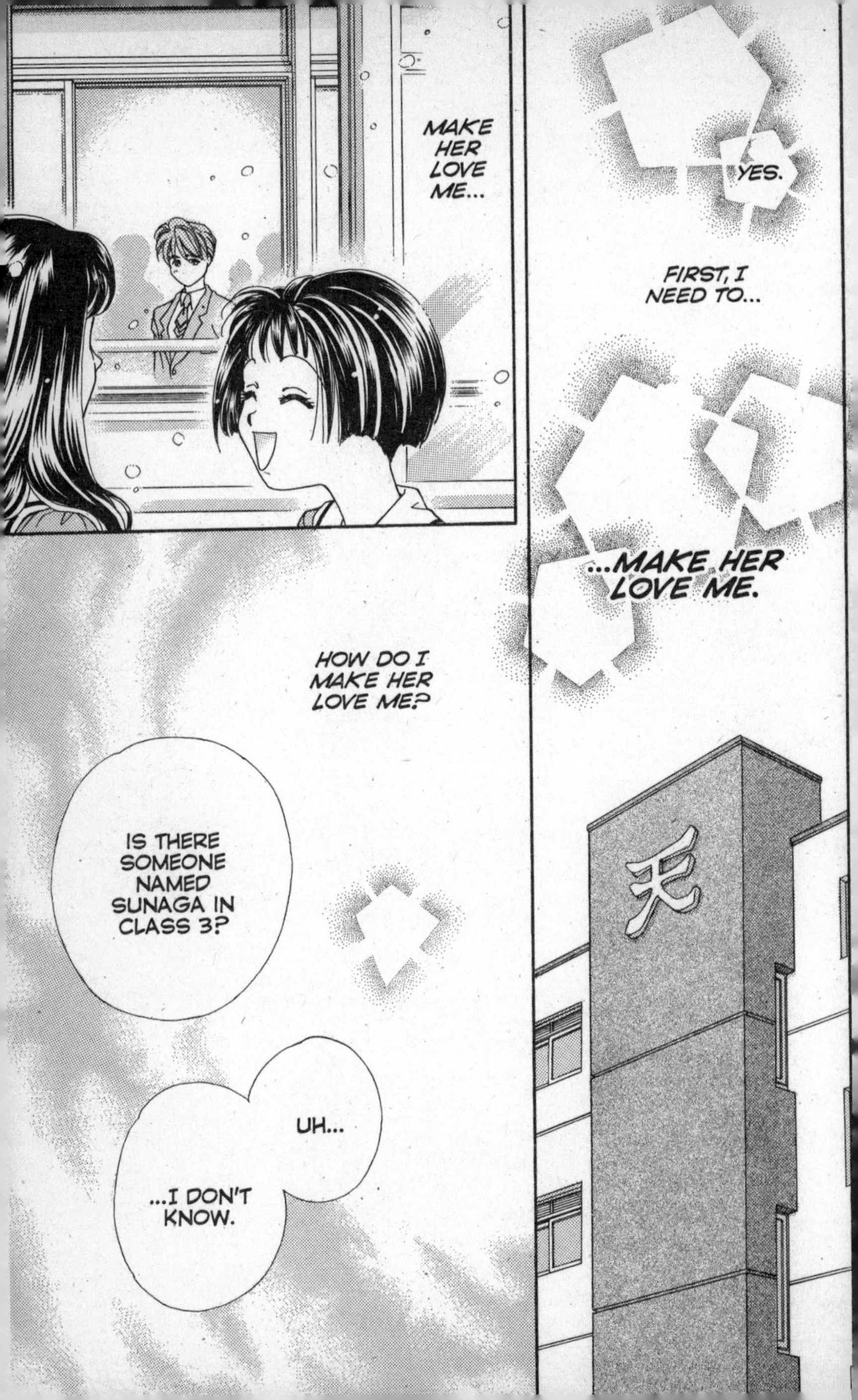
YES.
FIRST, I NEED TO...
...MAKE HER LOVE ME.
天
MAKE HER LOVE ME...
HOW DO I MAKE HER LOVE ME?
IS THERE SOMEONE NAMED SUNAGA IN CLASS 3?
UH...
...I DON'T KNOW.

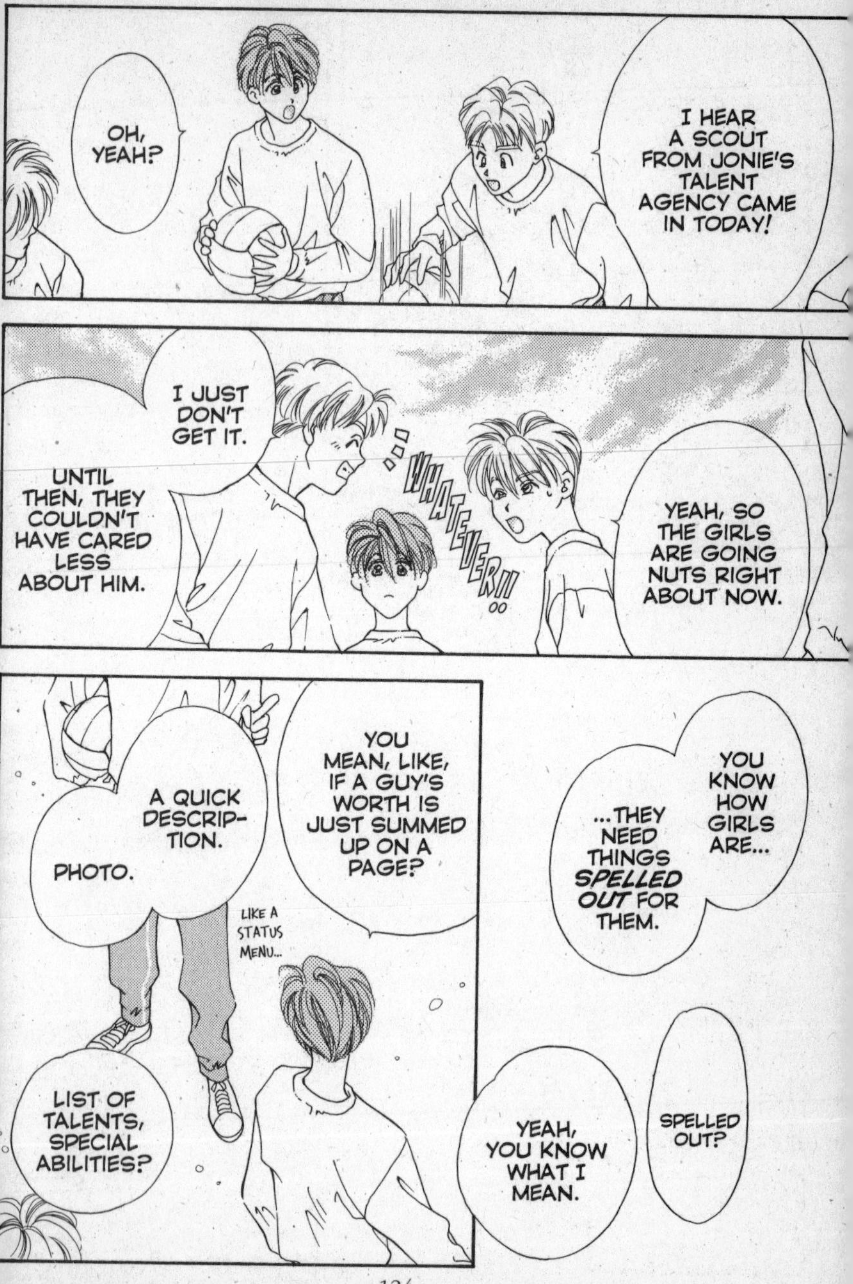
I HEAR A SCOUT FROM JONIE'S TALENT AGENCY CAME IN TODAY!
OH, YEAH?
YEAH, SO THE GIRLS ARE GOING NUTS RIGHT ABOUT NOW.
WHATEVER!!
I JUST DON'T GET IT.
UNTIL THEN, THEY COULDN'T HAVE CARED LESS ABOUT HIM.
YOU KNOW HOW GIRLS ARE...
...THEY NEED THINGS *SPELLED OUT* FOR THEM.
SPELLED OUT?
YEAH, YOU KNOW WHAT I MEAN.
YOU MEAN, LIKE, IF A GUY'S WORTH IS JUST SUMMED UP ON A PAGE?
A QUICK DESCRIP-TION.
PHOTO.
LIKE A STATUS MENU...
LIST OF TALENTS, SPECIAL ABILITIES?

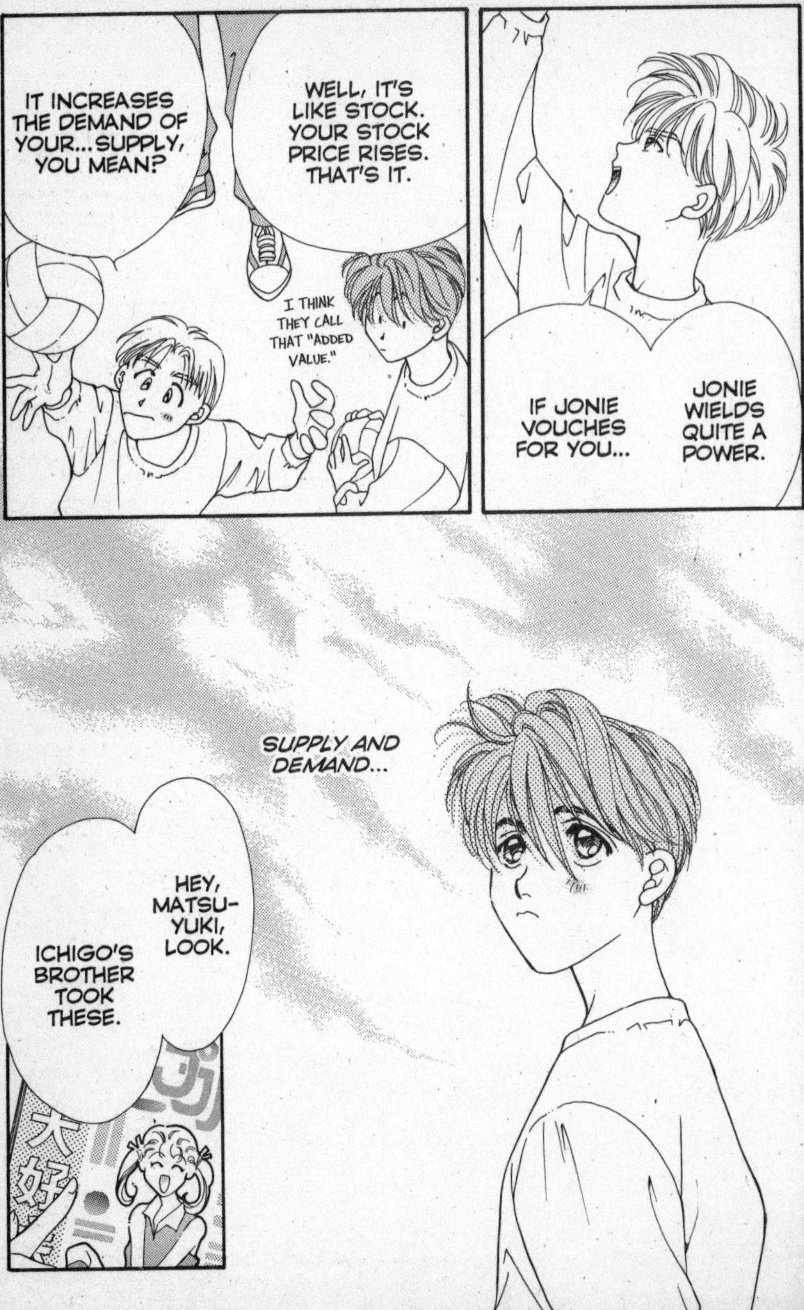
JONIE WIELDS QUITE A POWER.
IF JONIE VOUCHES FOR YOU...
WELL, IT'S LIKE STOCK. YOUR STOCK PRICE RISES. THAT'S IT.
IT INCREASES THE DEMAND OF YOUR...SUPPLY, YOU MEAN?
I THINK THEY CALL THAT "ADDED VALUE."
SUPPLY AND DEMAND...
HEY, MATSU-YUKI, LOOK.
ICHIGO'S BROTHER TOOK THESE.

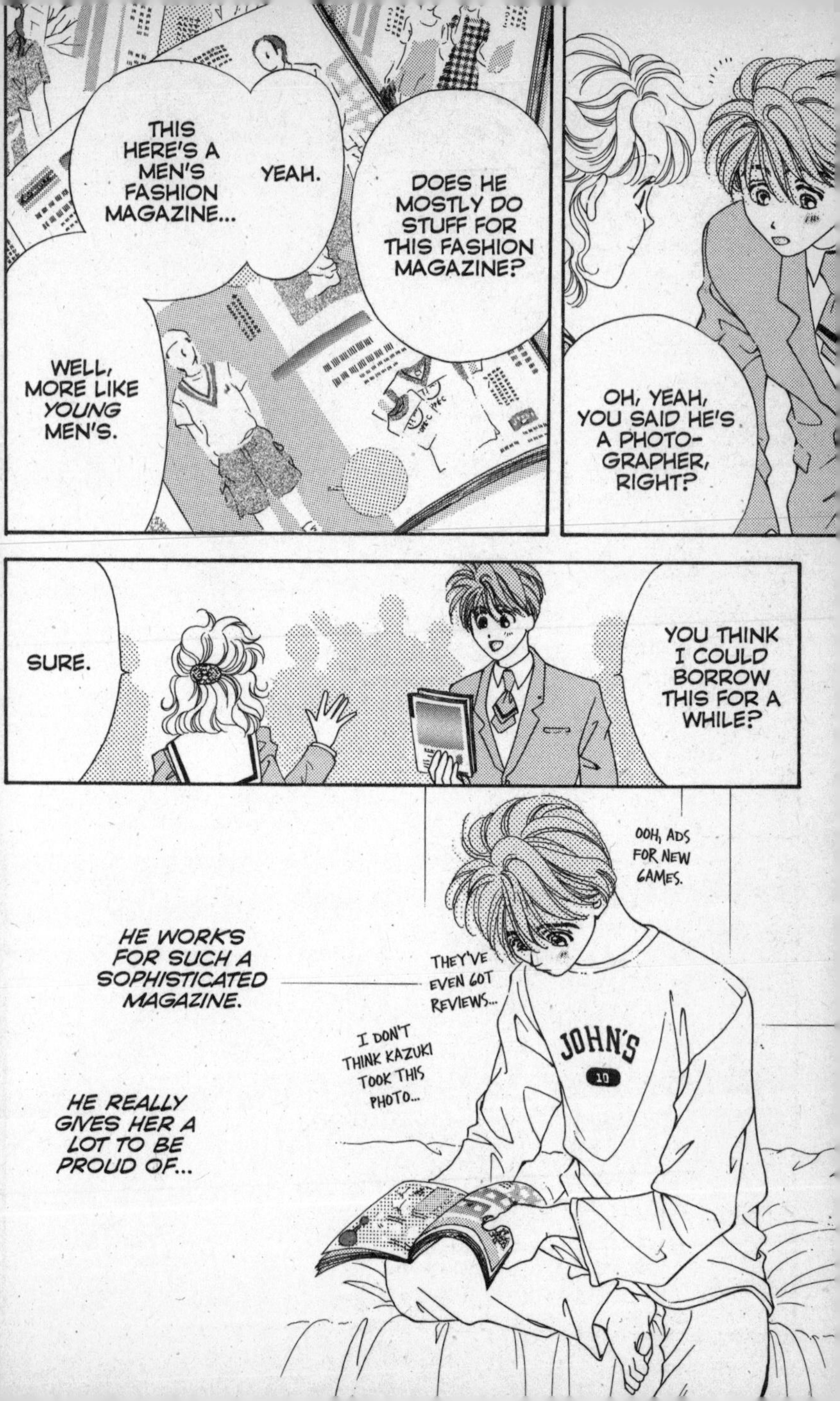
OH, YEAH, YOU SAID HE'S A PHOTO-GRAPHER, RIGHT?
DOES HE MOSTLY DO STUFF FOR THIS FASHION MAGAZINE?
YEAH.
THIS HERE'S A MEN'S FASHION MAGAZINE...
WELL, MORE LIKE *YOUNG* MEN'S.
YOU THINK I COULD BORROW THIS FOR A WHILE?
SURE.
OOH, ADS FOR NEW GAMES.
THEY'VE EVEN GOT REVIEWS...
HE WORKS FOR SUCH A SOPHISTICATED MAGAZINE.
I DON'T THINK KAZUKI TOOK THIS PHOTO...
HE REALLY GIVES HER A LOT TO BE PROUD OF...
JOHN'S
10

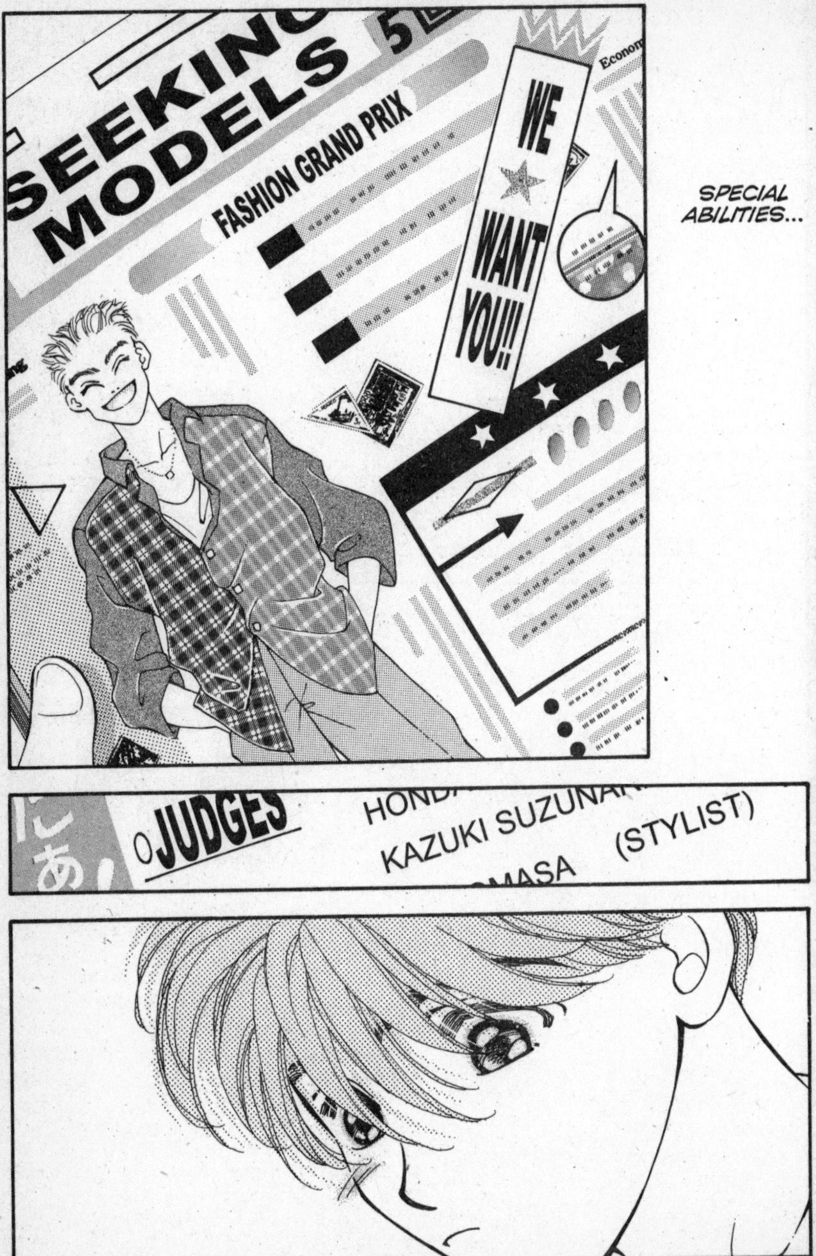
SPECIAL ABILITIES...
SEEKIN
MODELS
FASHION GRAND PRIX
WE ★ WANT YOU!!
JUDGES
HOND
KAZUKI SUZUNA
MASA (STYLIST)

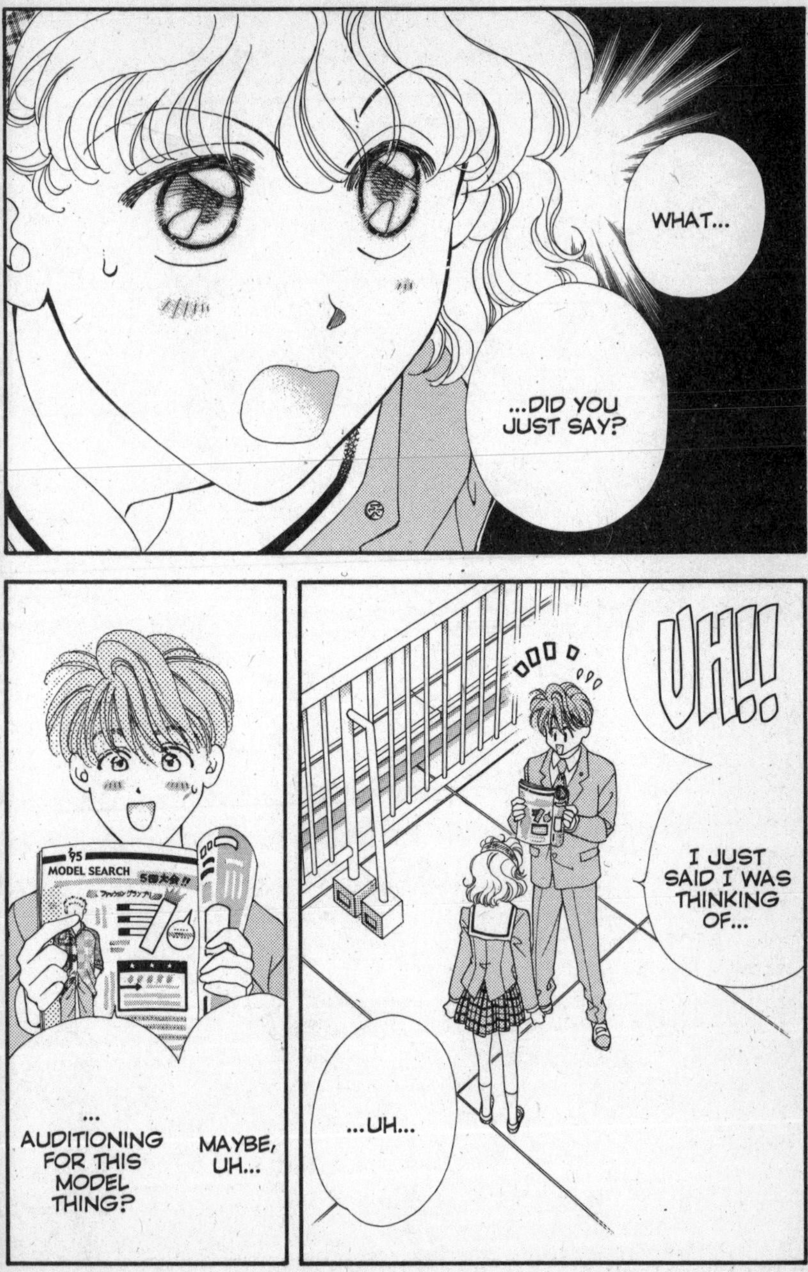
WHAT...
...DID YOU JUST SAY?
UH!!
I JUST SAID I WAS THINKING OF...
...UH...
MODEL SEARCH
MAYBE, UH...
... AUDITIONING FOR THIS MODEL THING?

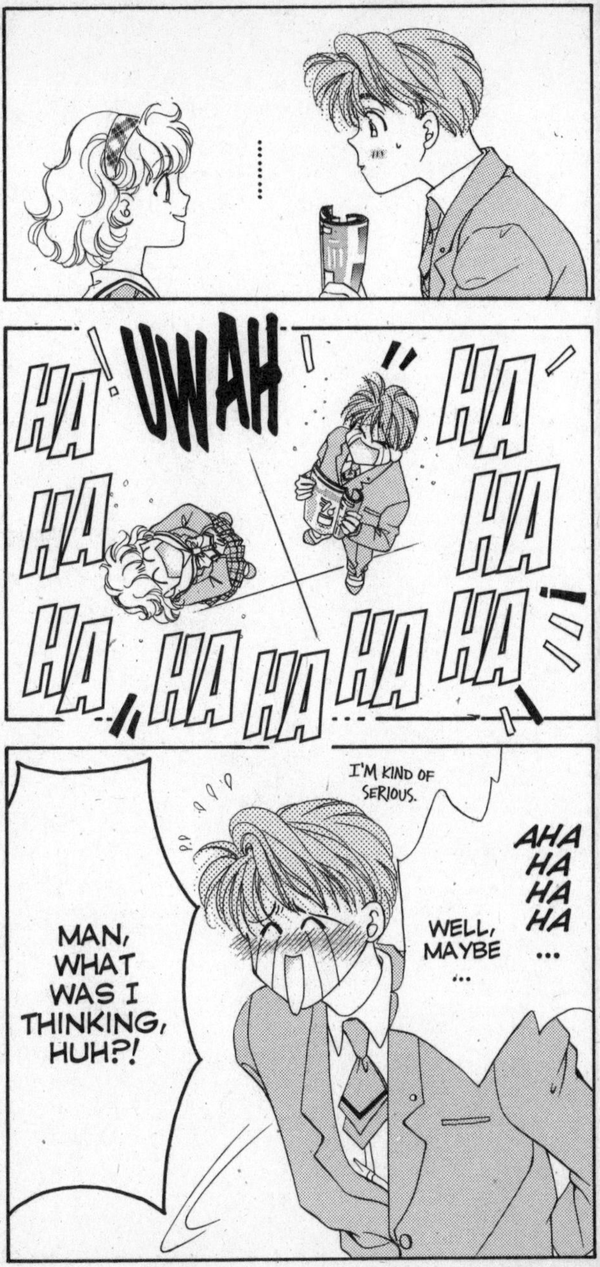
......
UWAH
HA HA HA HA HA HA HA HA HA HA
AHA HA HA HA ...
I'M KIND OF SERIOUS.
WELL, MAYBE ...
MAN, WHAT WAS I THINKING, HUH?!

Sidebar No. 11

So anyway, about, uh, this comic right here, "Tower of the Future." It's just now nearing the climax of "LEVEL 2." I think. I've already got all the names in place; now it's time to start preparing for LEVEL 3. I keep thinking, "I want to get my hair cut like Ichigo!" It's so tempting to just go to the hairdresser's and say, "Cut it all off!" And short hair is getting so popular now. Ahh. I'll just keep it how it is. It's easiest that way, I guess. Maybe I should just let it grow, keep cutting my bangs myself. Hmmm...

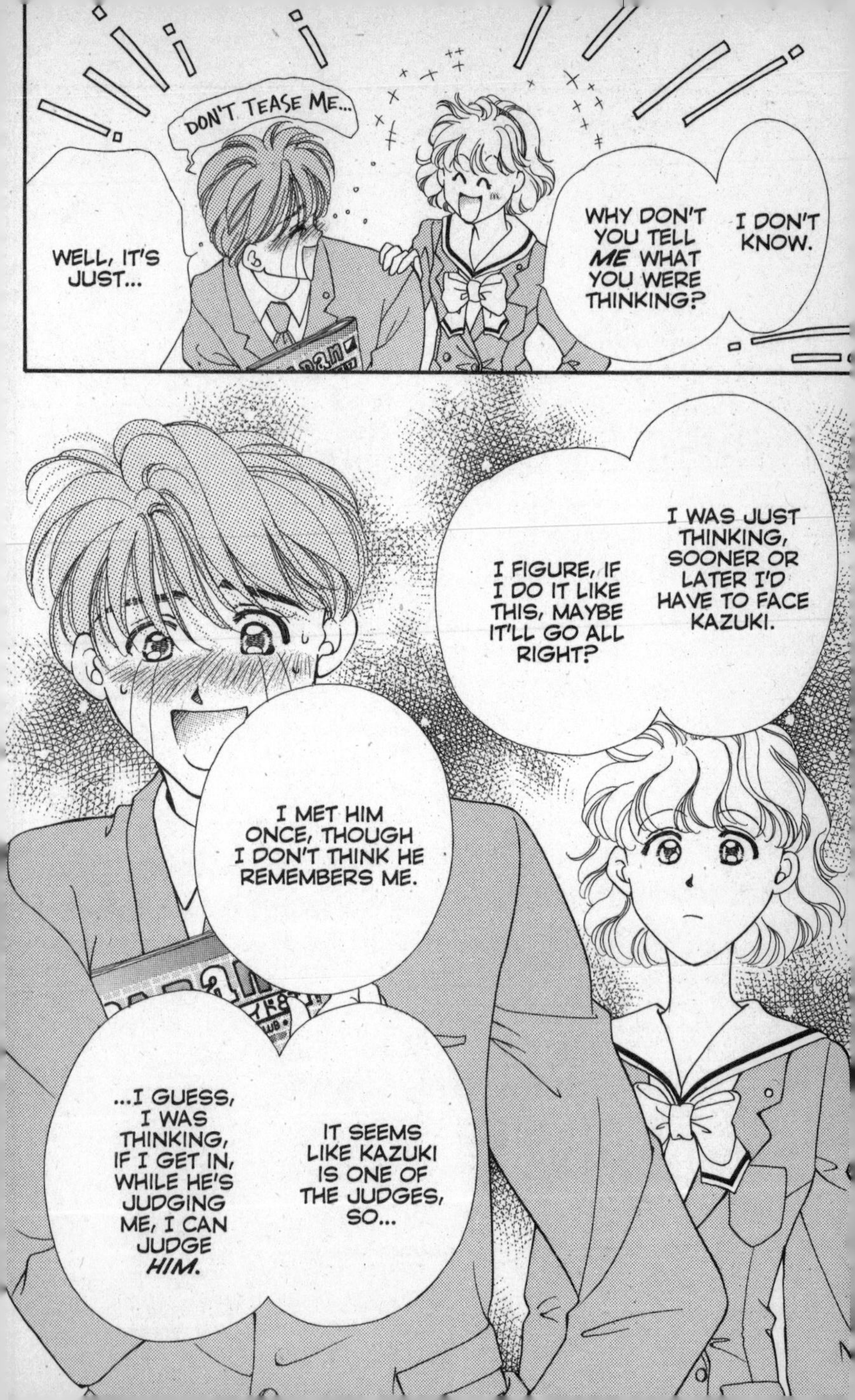
I DON'T KNOW.
WHY DON'T YOU TELL *ME* WHAT YOU WERE THINKING?
DON'T TEASE ME...
WELL, IT'S JUST...
I WAS JUST THINKING, SOONER OR LATER I'D HAVE TO FACE KAZUKI.
I FIGURE, IF I DO IT LIKE THIS, MAYBE IT'LL GO ALL RIGHT?
I MET HIM ONCE, THOUGH I DON'T THINK HE REMEMBERS ME.
IT SEEMS LIKE KAZUKI IS ONE OF THE JUDGES, SO...
...I GUESS, I WAS THINKING, IF I GET IN, WHILE HE'S JUDGING ME, I CAN JUDGE *HIM*.

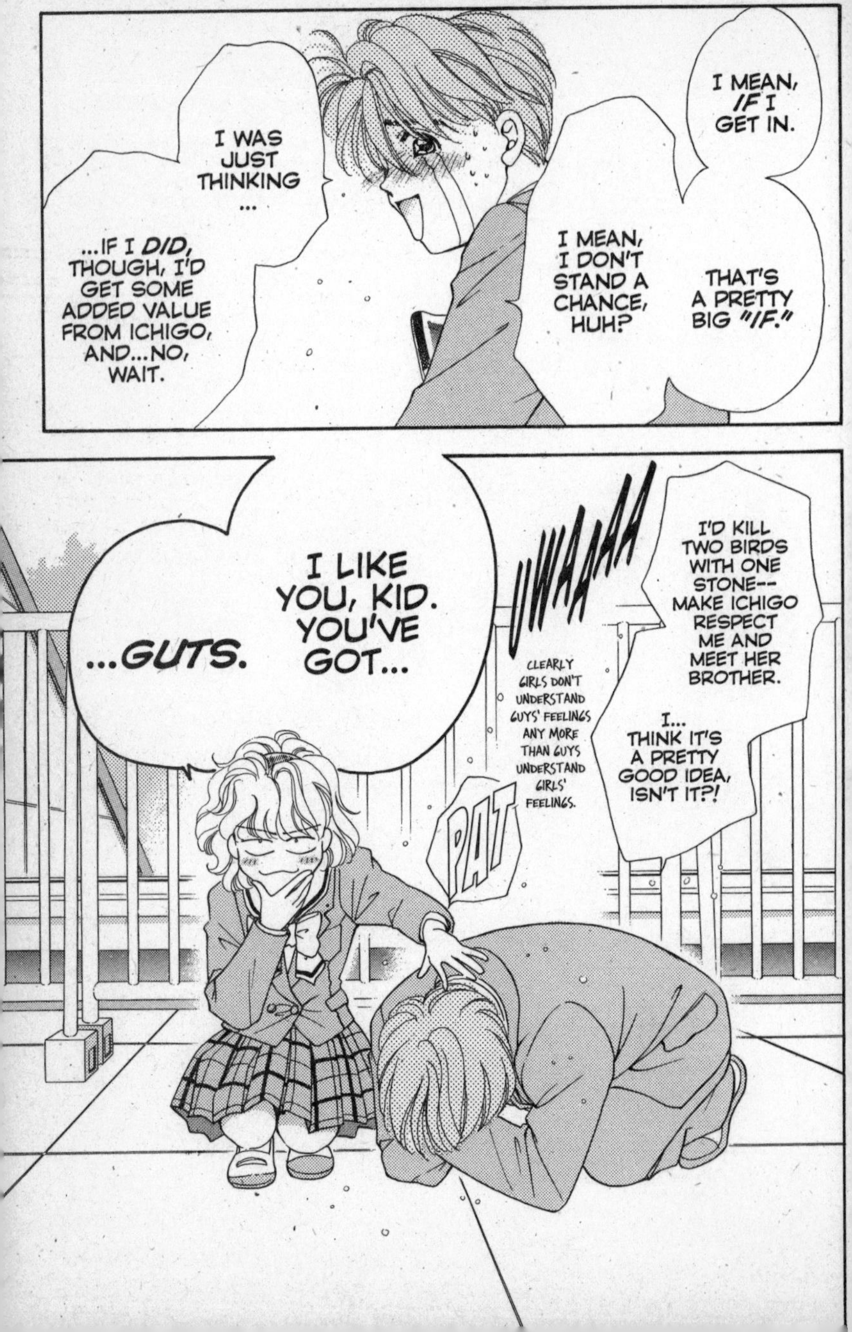
I MEAN, *IF* I GET IN.
THAT'S A PRETTY BIG *"IF."*
I MEAN, I DON'T STAND A CHANCE, HUH?
I WAS JUST THINKING ...
...IF I *DID*, THOUGH, I'D GET SOME ADDED VALUE FROM ICHIGO, AND...NO, WAIT.
I'D KILL TWO BIRDS WITH ONE STONE-- MAKE ICHIGO RESPECT ME AND MEET HER BROTHER.
I... THINK IT'S A PRETTY GOOD IDEA, ISN'T IT?!
UWAAAA
CLEARLY GIRLS DON'T UNDERSTAND GUYS' FEELINGS ANY MORE THAN GUYS UNDERSTAND GIRLS' FEELINGS.
I LIKE YOU, KID. YOU'VE GOT...
...GUTS.
PAT

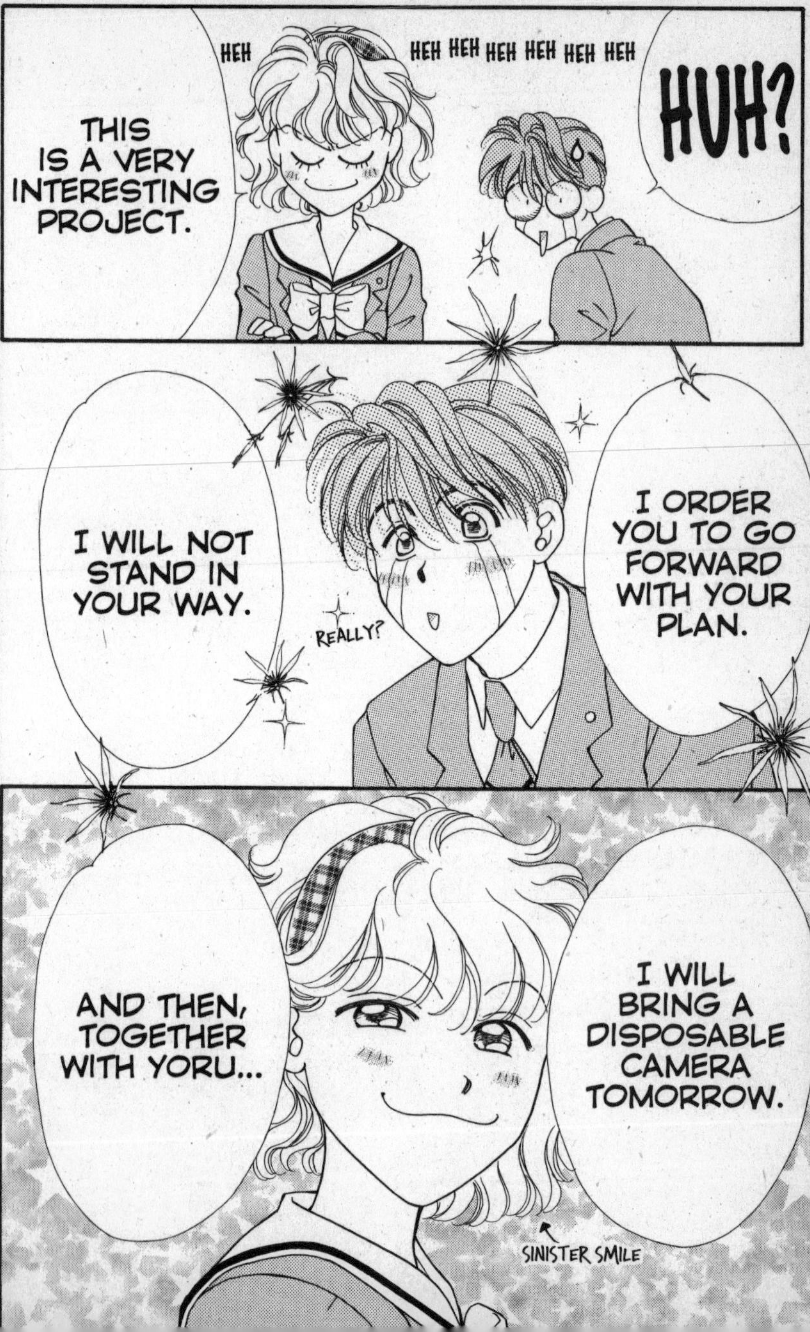
HUH?
HEH HEH HEH HEH HEH HEH
HEH
THIS IS A VERY INTERESTING PROJECT.
I ORDER YOU TO GO FORWARD WITH YOUR PLAN.
REALLY?
I WILL NOT STAND IN YOUR WAY.
I WILL BRING A DISPOSABLE CAMERA TOMORROW.
SINISTER SMILE
AND THEN, TOGETHER WITH YORU...

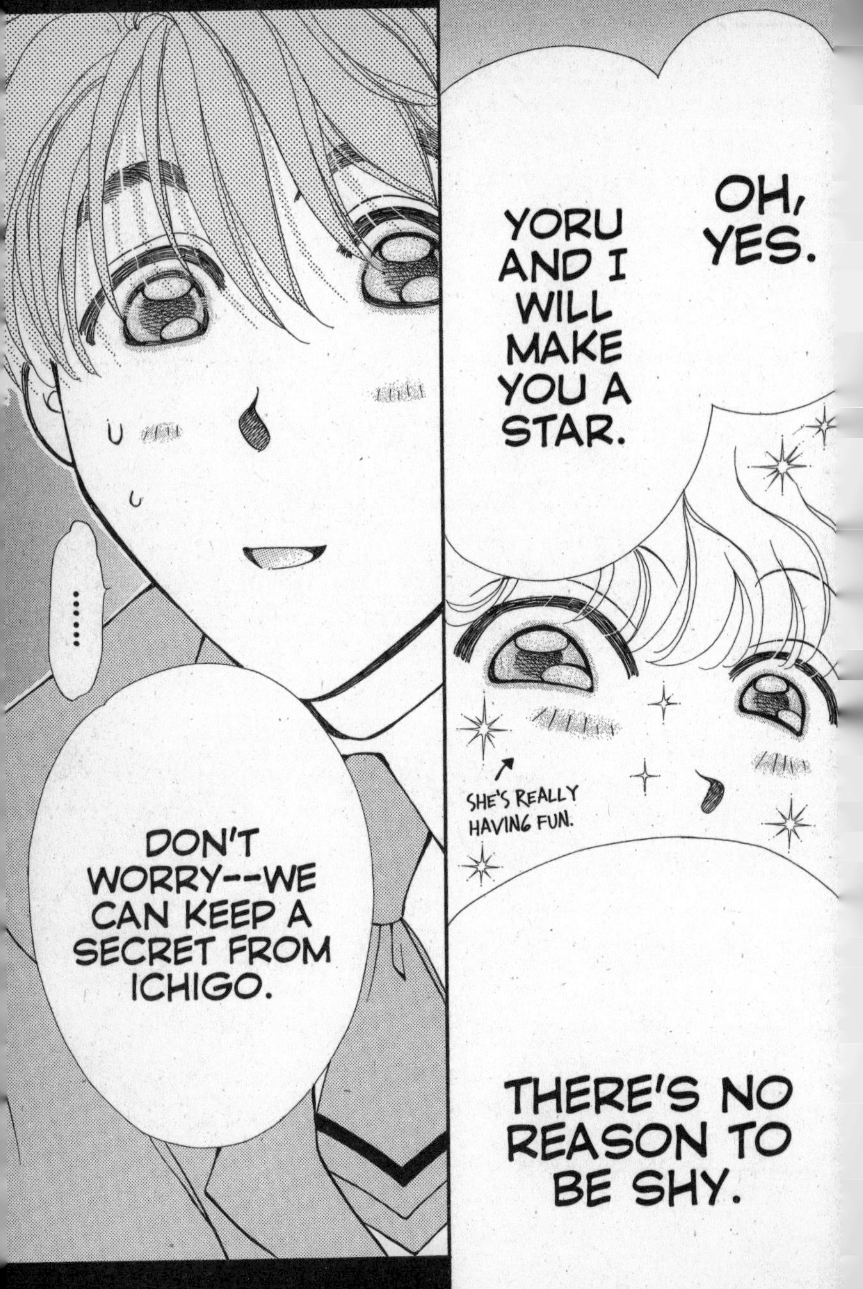
OH, YES.
YORU AND I WILL MAKE YOU A STAR.
SHE'S REALLY HAVING FUN.
THERE'S NO REASON TO BE SHY.
......
DON'T WORRY--WE CAN KEEP A SECRET FROM ICHIGO.

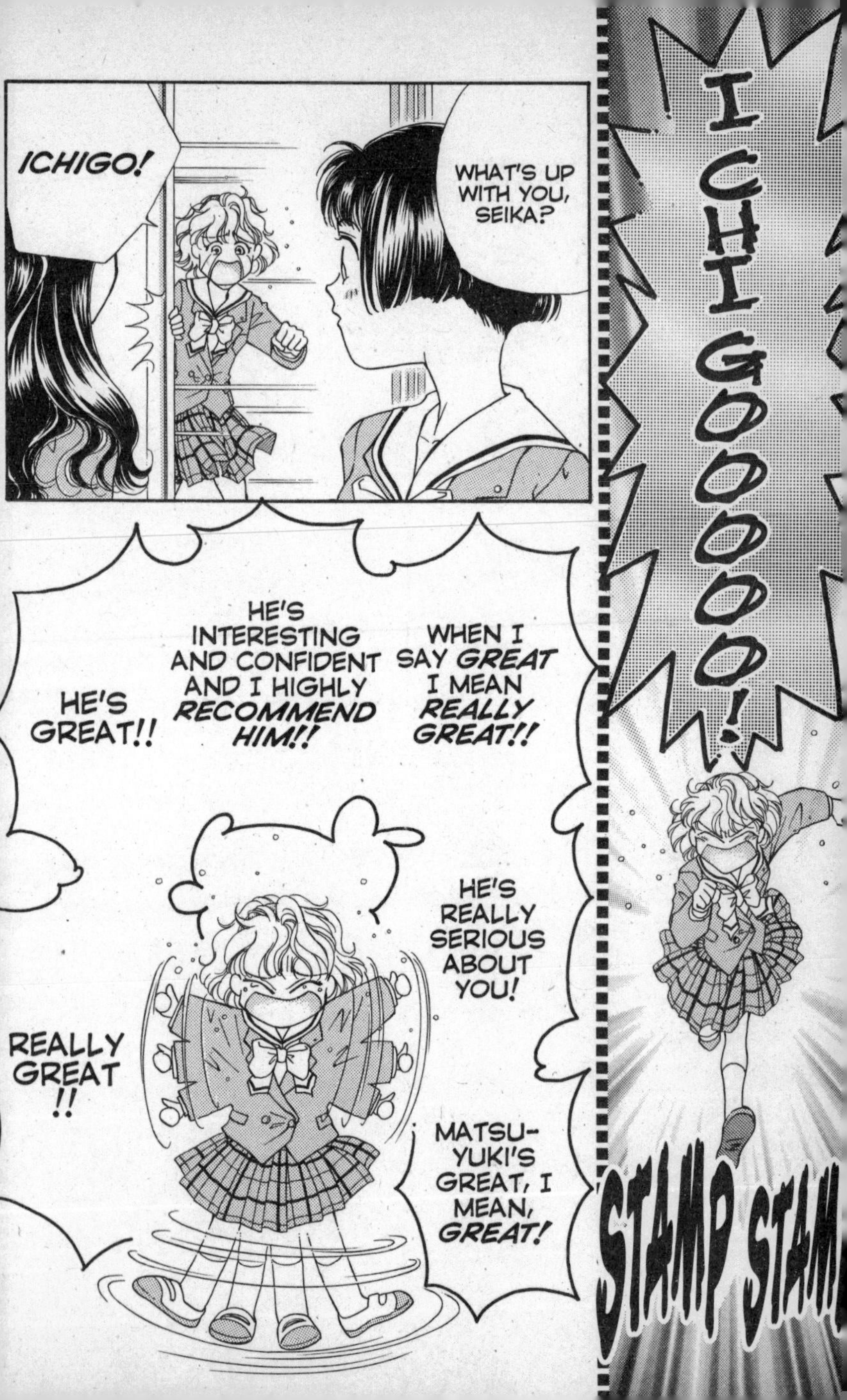
ICHIGOOOOOO!
STAMP STAM
WHAT'S UP WITH YOU, SEIKA?
ICHIGO!
WHEN I SAY *GREAT* I MEAN *REALLY GREAT!!*
HE'S INTERESTING AND CONFIDENT AND I HIGHLY *RECOMMEND HIM!!*
HE'S GREAT!!
HE'S REALLY SERIOUS ABOUT YOU!
MATSU-YUKI'S GREAT, I MEAN, *GREAT!*
REALLY GREAT !!

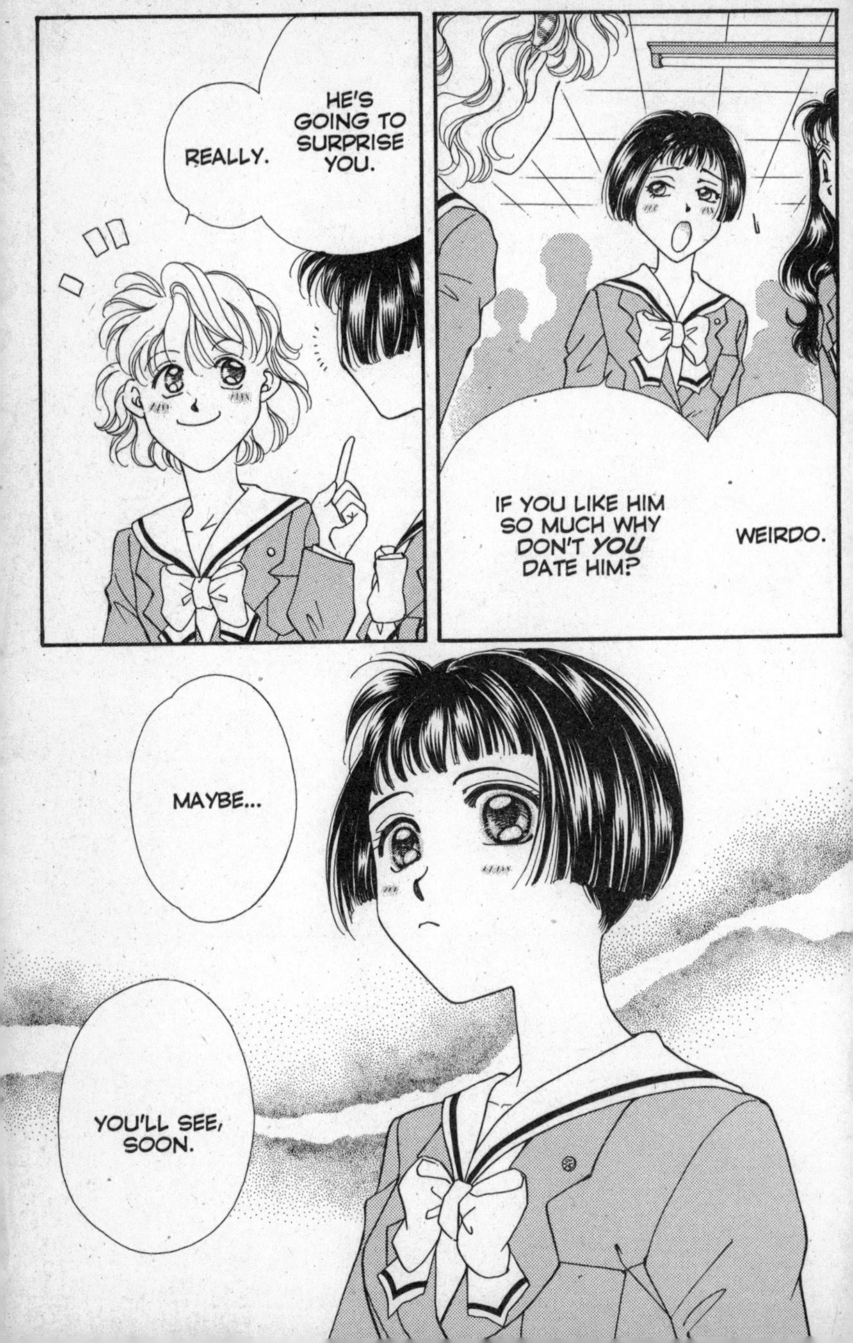
IF YOU LIKE HIM SO MUCH WHY DON'T *YOU* DATE HIM?
WEIRDO.
HE'S GOING TO SURPRISE YOU.
REALLY.
MAYBE...
YOU'LL SEE, SOON.

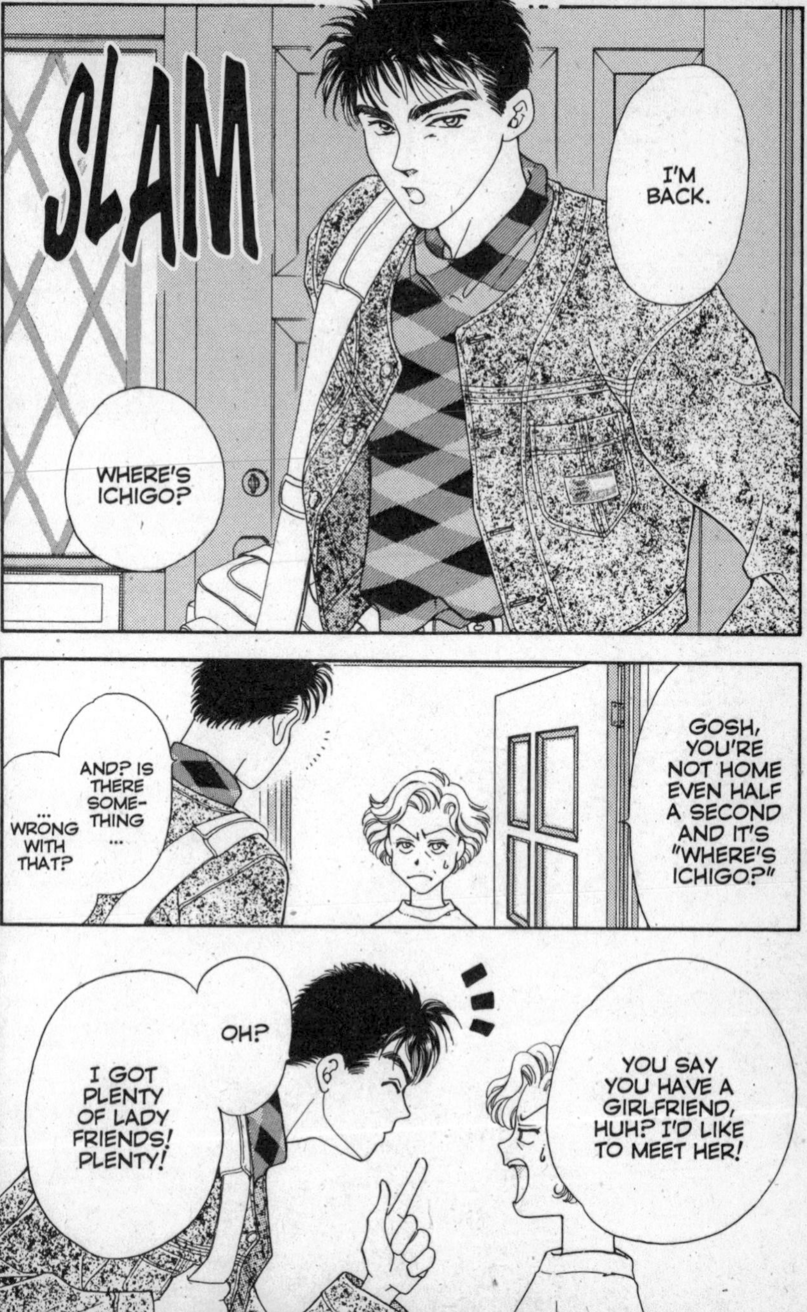
I'M BACK.
SLAM
WHERE'S ICHIGO?
GOSH, YOU'RE NOT HOME EVEN HALF A SECOND AND IT'S "WHERE'S ICHIGO?"
AND? IS THERE SOME-THING ... WRONG WITH THAT?
YOU SAY YOU HAVE A GIRLFRIEND, HUH? I'D LIKE TO MEET HER!
OH?
I GOT PLENTY OF LADY FRIENDS! PLENTY!

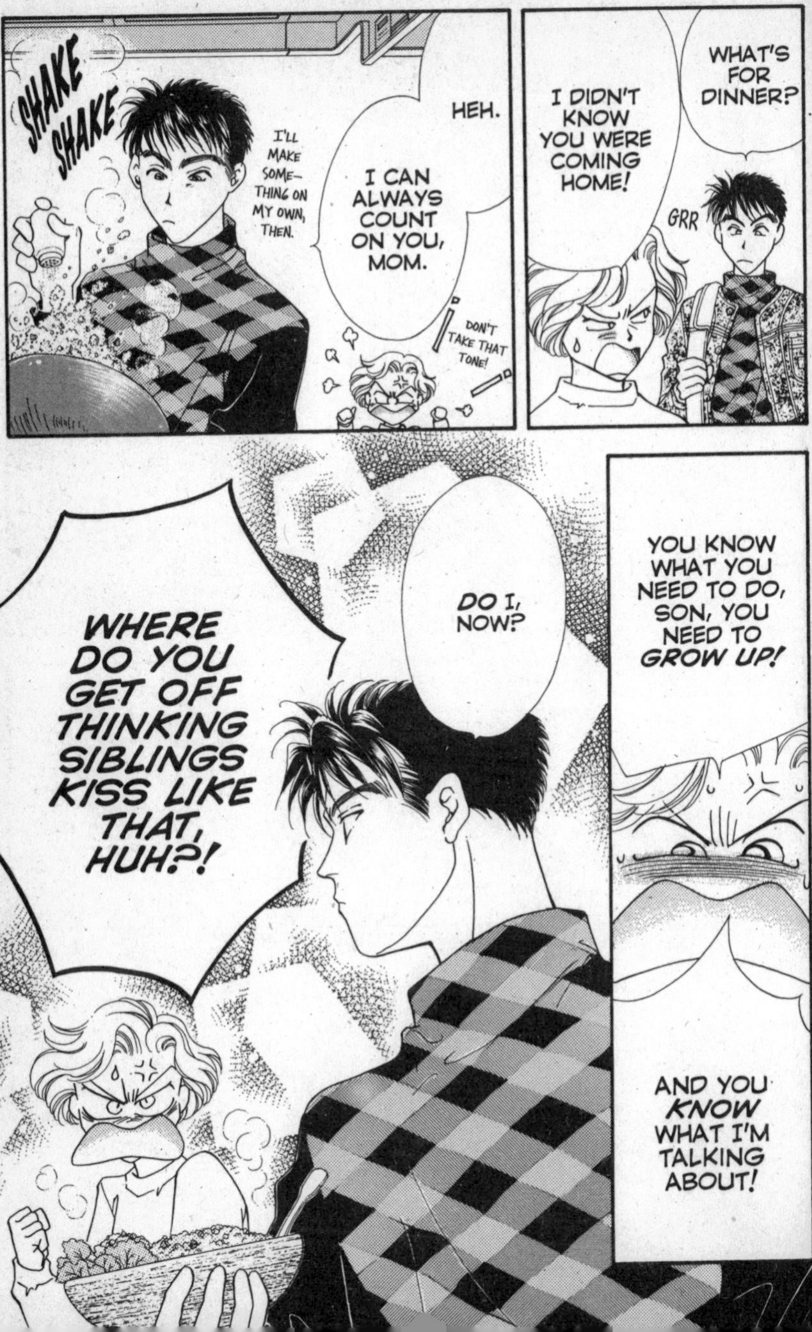

WHAT'S FOR DINNER?
I DIDN'T KNOW YOU WERE COMING HOME!
GRR
HEH.
I CAN ALWAYS COUNT ON YOU, MOM.
DON'T TAKE THAT TONE!
I'LL MAKE SOME-THING ON MY OWN, THEN.
SHAKE SHAKE
YOU KNOW WHAT YOU NEED TO DO, SON, YOU NEED TO *GROW UP!*
AND YOU *KNOW* WHAT I'M TALKING ABOUT!
DO I, NOW?
WHERE DO YOU GET OFF THINKING SIBLINGS KISS LIKE THAT, HUH?!

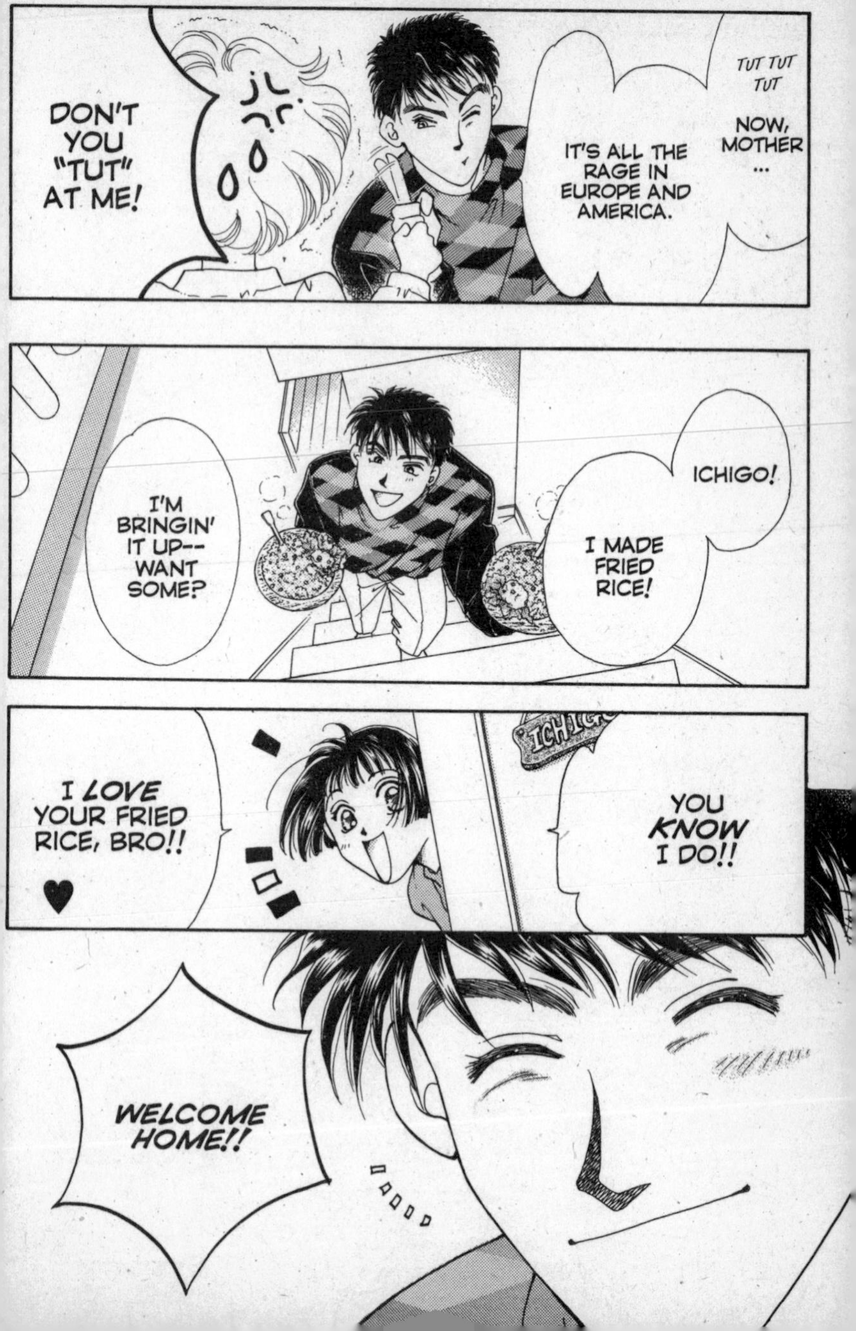
TUT TUT TUT
NOW, MOTHER ...
IT'S ALL THE RAGE IN EUROPE AND AMERICA.
DON'T YOU "TUT" AT ME!
ICHIGO!
I MADE FRIED RICE!
I'M BRINGIN' IT UP-- WANT SOME?
YOU KNOW I DO!!
I LOVE YOUR FRIED RICE, BRO!! ♥
WELCOME HOME!!

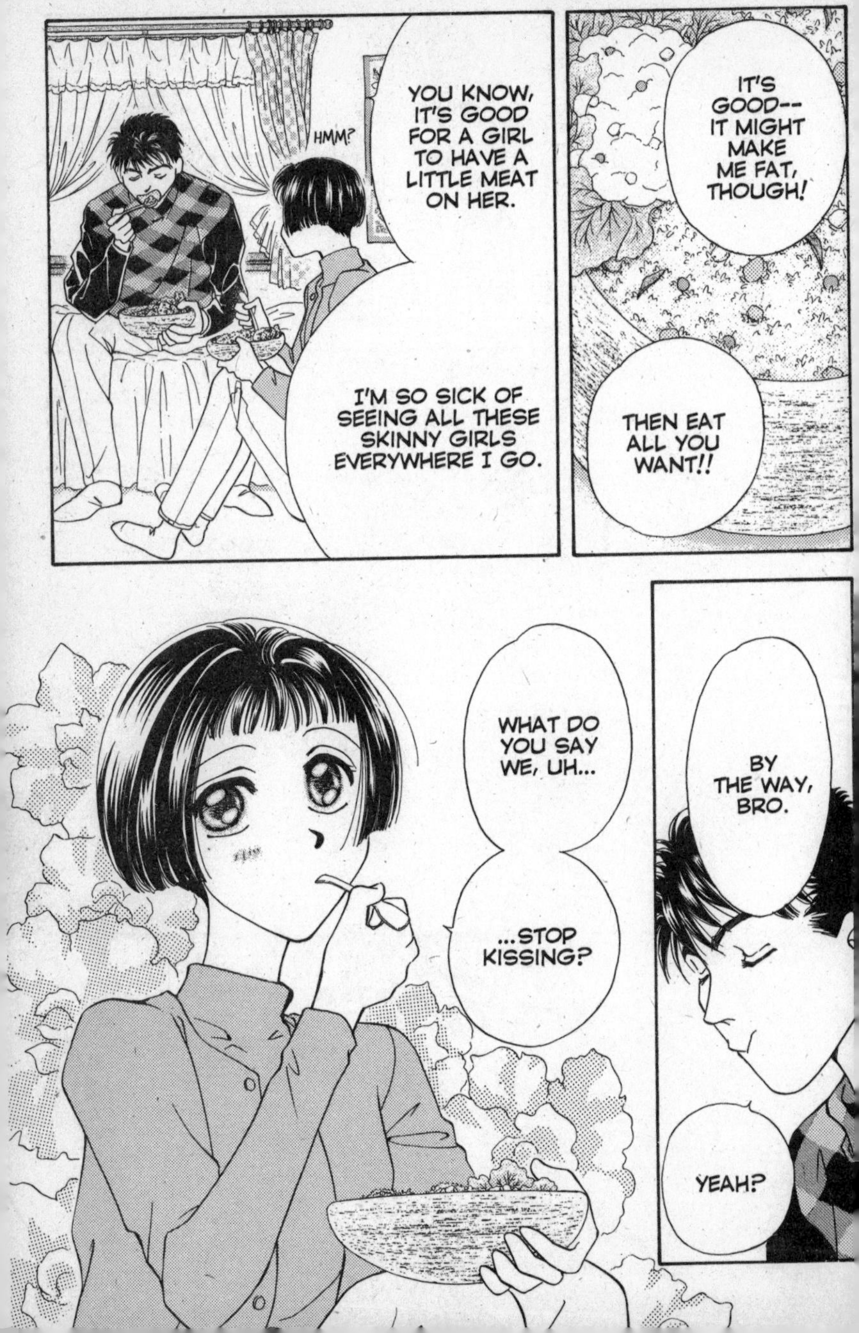
IT'S GOOD-- IT MIGHT MAKE ME FAT, THOUGH!
THEN EAT ALL YOU WANT!!
YOU KNOW, IT'S GOOD FOR A GIRL TO HAVE A LITTLE MEAT ON HER.
HMM?
I'M SO SICK OF SEEING ALL THESE SKINNY GIRLS EVERYWHERE I GO.
BY THE WAY, BRO.
YEAH?
WHAT DO YOU SAY WE, UH...
...STOP KISSING?

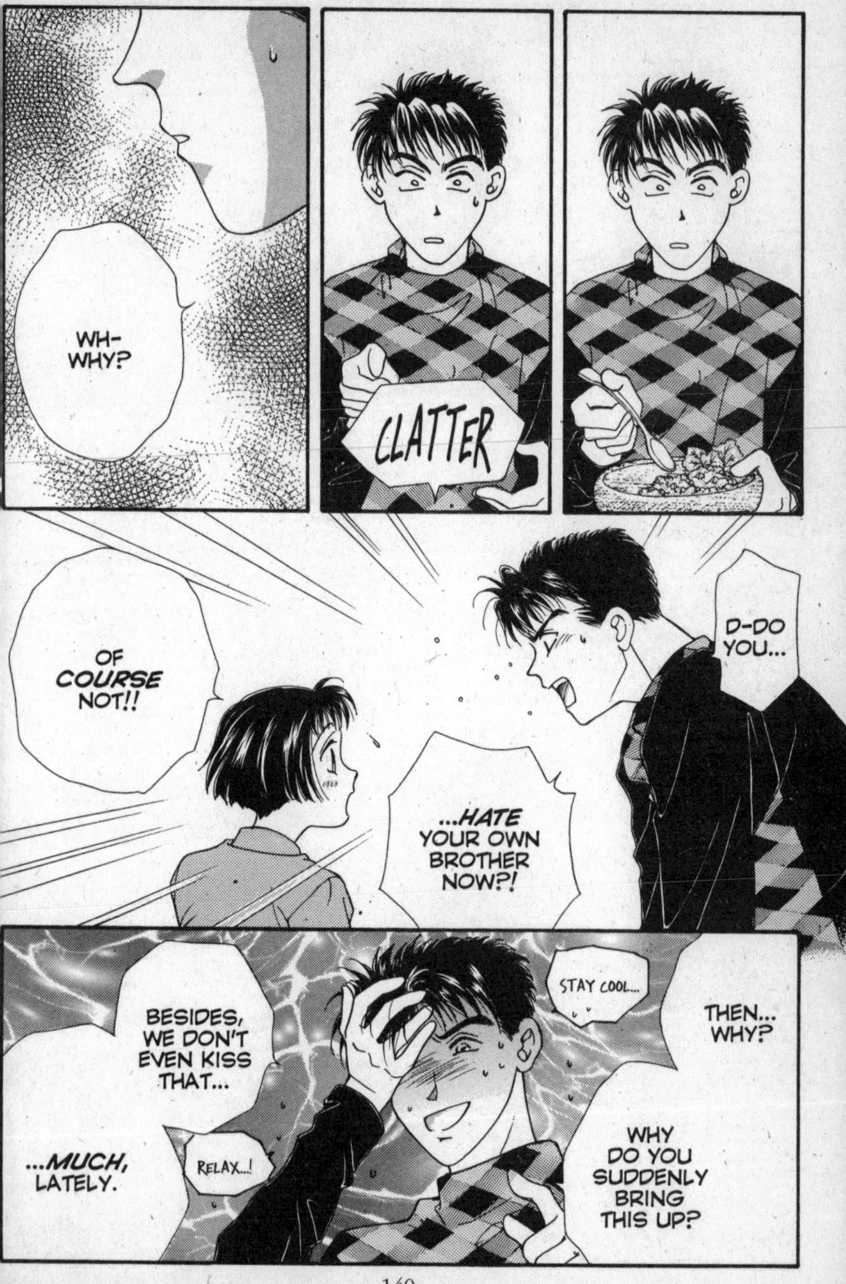
CLATTER
WH- WHY?
D-DO YOU...
...HATE YOUR OWN BROTHER NOW?!
OF COURSE NOT!!
THEN... WHY?
WHY DO YOU SUDDENLY BRING THIS UP?
STAY COOL...
BESIDES, WE DON'T EVEN KISS THAT...
RELAX...!
...MUCH, LATELY.

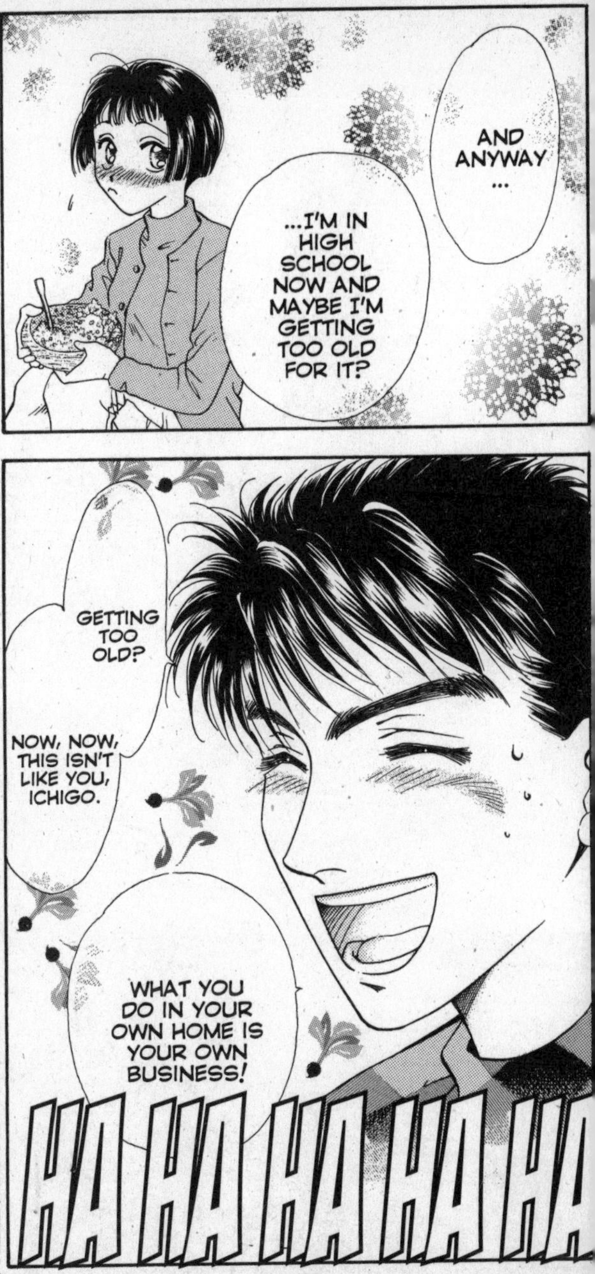
AND ANYWAY ...
...I'M IN HIGH SCHOOL NOW AND MAYBE I'M GETTING TOO OLD FOR IT?
GETTING TOO OLD?
NOW, NOW, THIS ISN'T LIKE YOU, ICHIGO.
WHAT YOU DO IN YOUR OWN HOME IS YOUR OWN BUSINESS!
HA HA HA HA HA HA
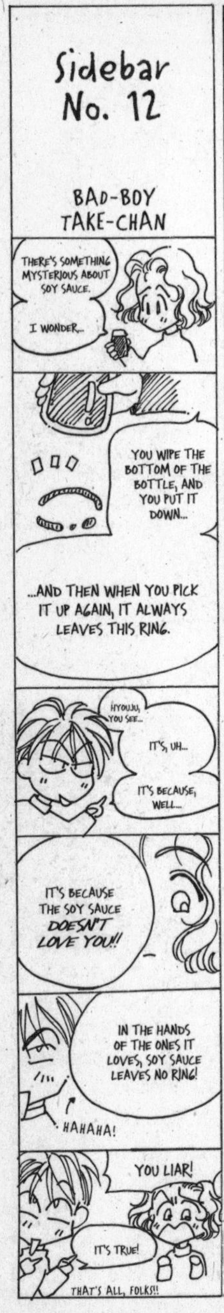
Sidebar No. 12
BAD-BOY TAKE-CHAN
THERE'S SOMETHING MYSTERIOUS ABOUT SOY SAUCE.
I WONDER...
YOU WIPE THE BOTTOM OF THE BOTTLE, AND YOU PUT IT DOWN...
...AND THEN WHEN YOU PICK IT UP AGAIN, IT ALWAYS LEAVES THIS RING.
HYOUJU, YOU SEE...
IT'S, UH...
IT'S BECAUSE, WELL...
IT'S BECAUSE THE SOY SAUCE DOESN'T LOVE YOU!!
IN THE HANDS OF THE ONES IT LOVES, SOY SAUCE LEAVES NO RING!
HAHAHA!
YOU LIAR!
IT'S TRUE!
THAT'S ALL, FOLKS!!

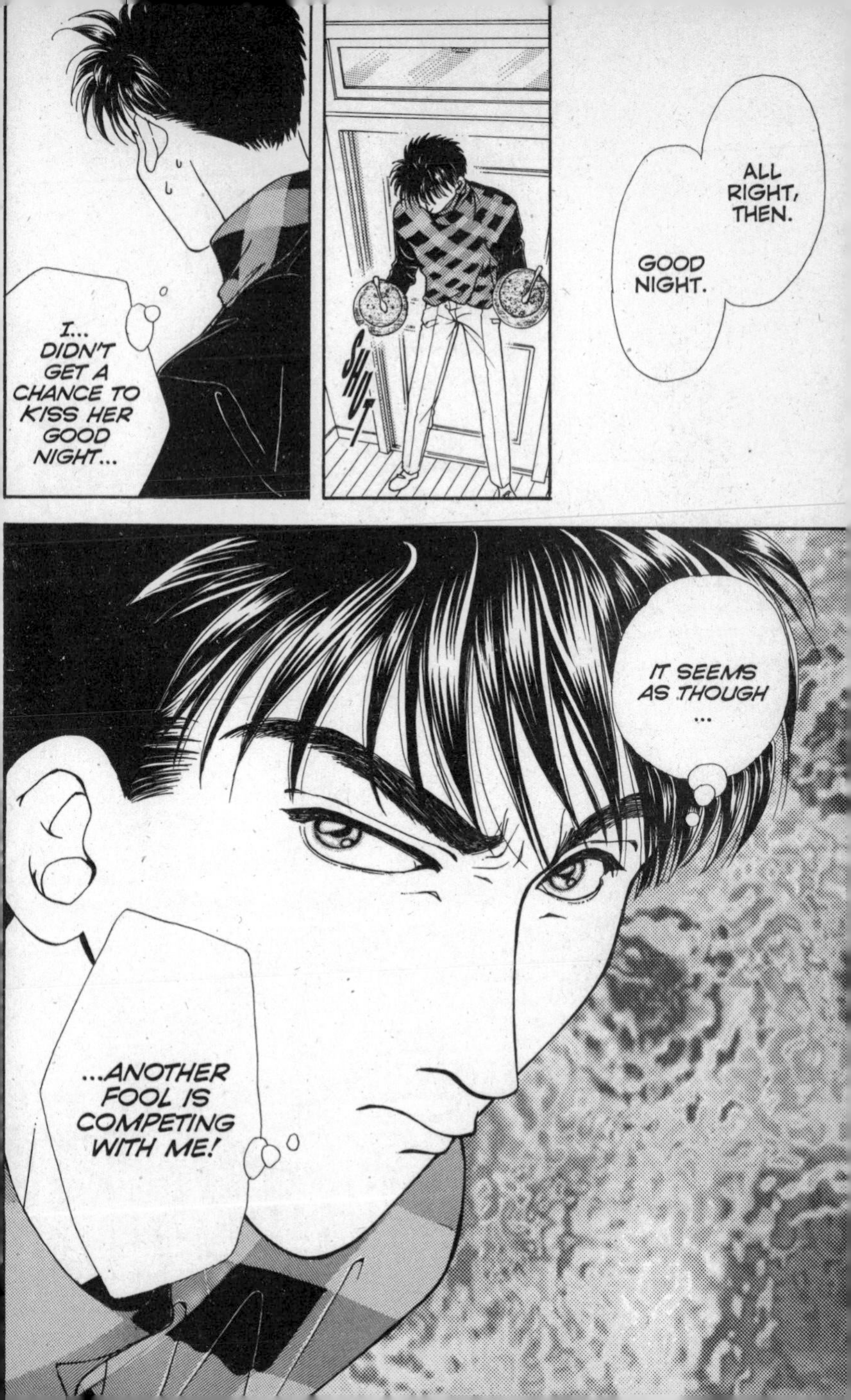

ALL RIGHT, THEN.
GOOD NIGHT.
SHUT
I... DIDN'T GET A CHANCE TO KISS HER GOOD NIGHT...
IT SEEMS AS THOUGH ...
...ANOTHER FOOL IS COMPETING WITH ME!

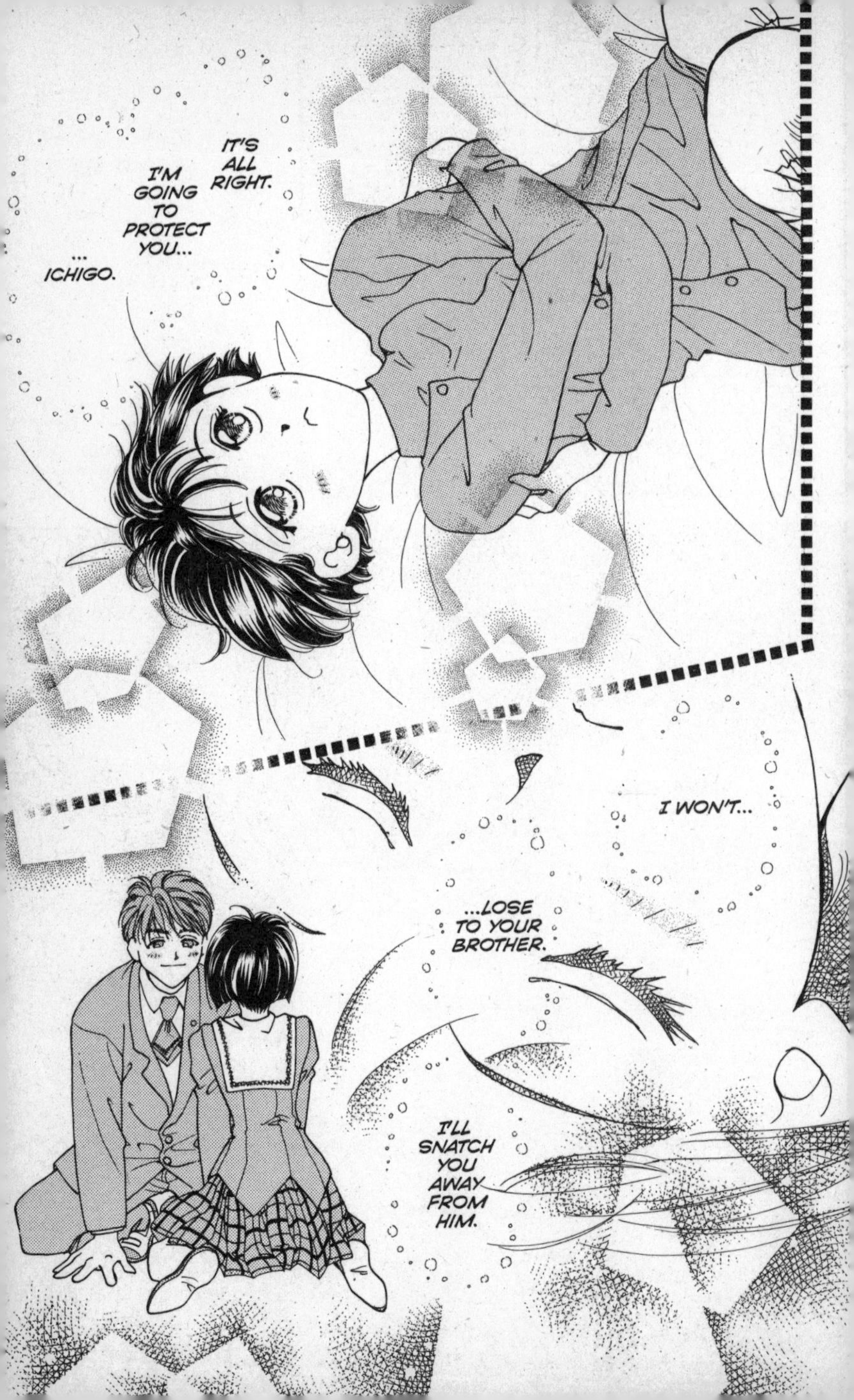
IT'S ALL RIGHT.
I'M GOING TO PROTECT YOU...
...ICHIGO.
I WON'T...
...LOSE TO YOUR BROTHER.
I'LL SNATCH YOU AWAY FROM HIM.

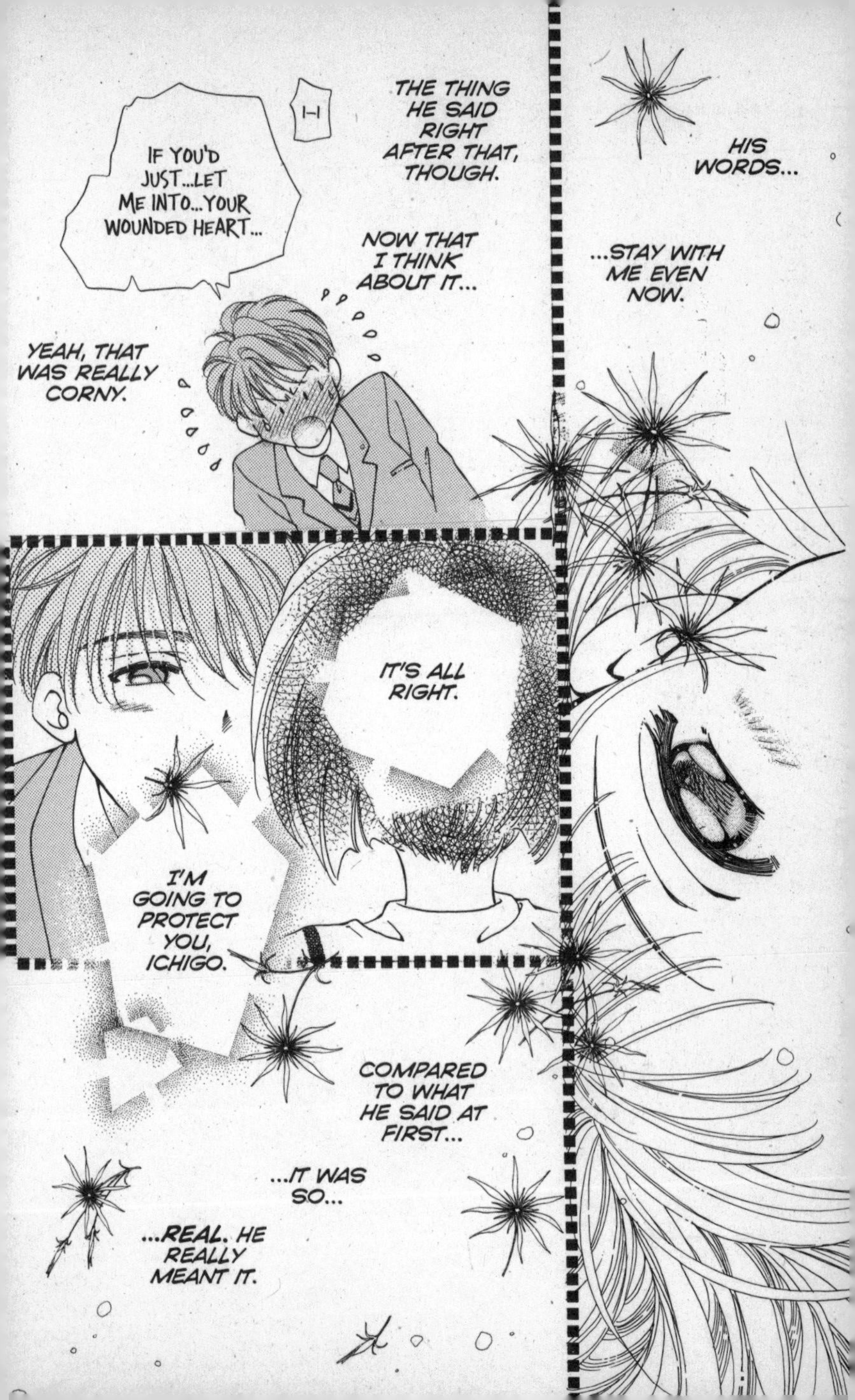
HIS WORDS...
...STAY WITH ME EVEN NOW.
THE THING HE SAID RIGHT AFTER THAT, THOUGH.
I-I
IF YOU'D JUST...LET ME INTO...YOUR WOUNDED HEART...
NOW THAT I THINK ABOUT IT...
YEAH, THAT WAS REALLY CORNY.
IT'S ALL RIGHT.
I'M GOING TO PROTECT YOU, ICHIGO.
COMPARED TO WHAT HE SAID AT FIRST...
...IT WAS SO...
...REAL. HE REALLY MEANT IT.

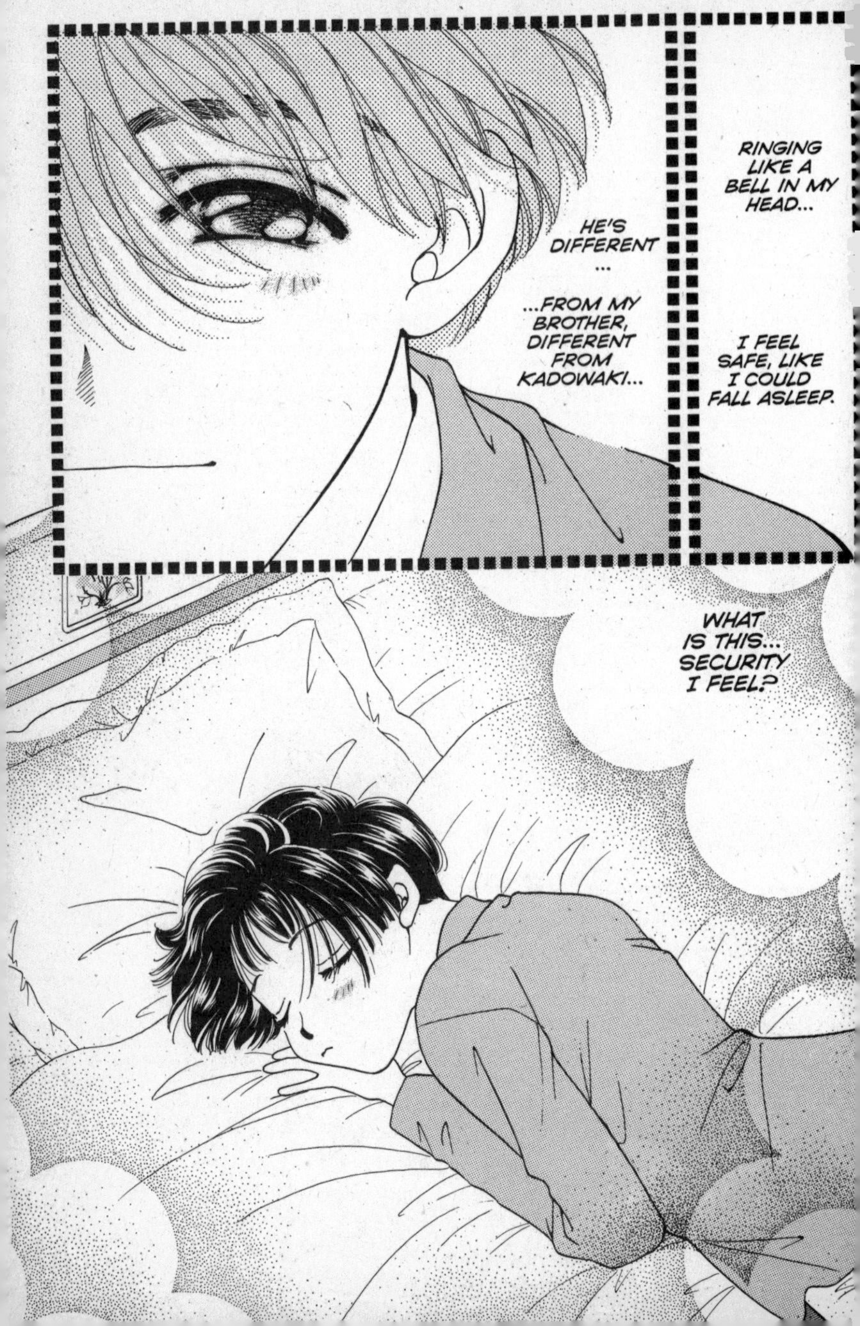
RINGING LIKE A BELL IN MY HEAD...
I FEEL SAFE, LIKE I COULD FALL ASLEEP.
HE'S DIFFERENT ...
...FROM MY BROTHER, DIFFERENT FROM KADOWAKI...
WHAT IS THIS... SECURITY I FEEL?

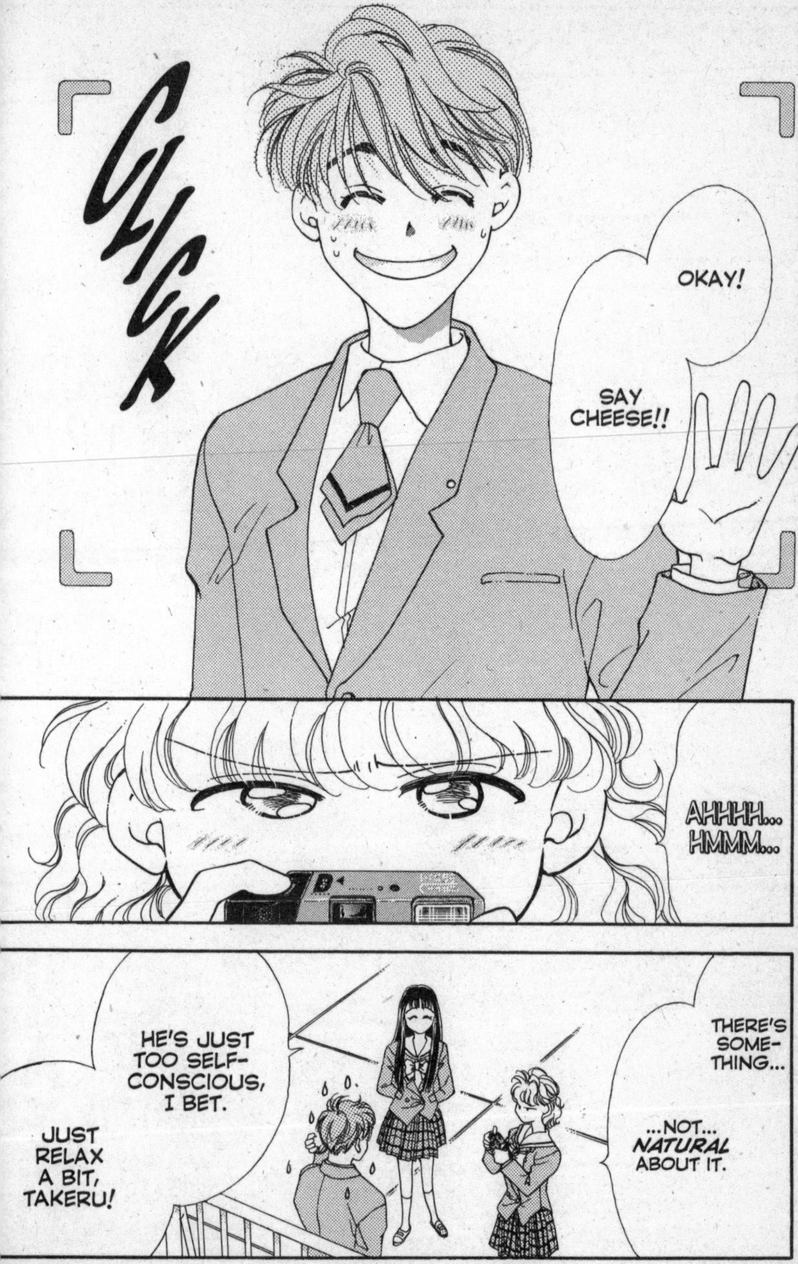
OKAY!
SAY CHEESE!!
CLICK
AHHHH... HMMM...
THERE'S SOME-THING...
...NOT... *NATURAL* ABOUT IT.
HE'S JUST TOO SELF-CONSCIOUS, I BET.
JUST RELAX A BIT, TAKERU!

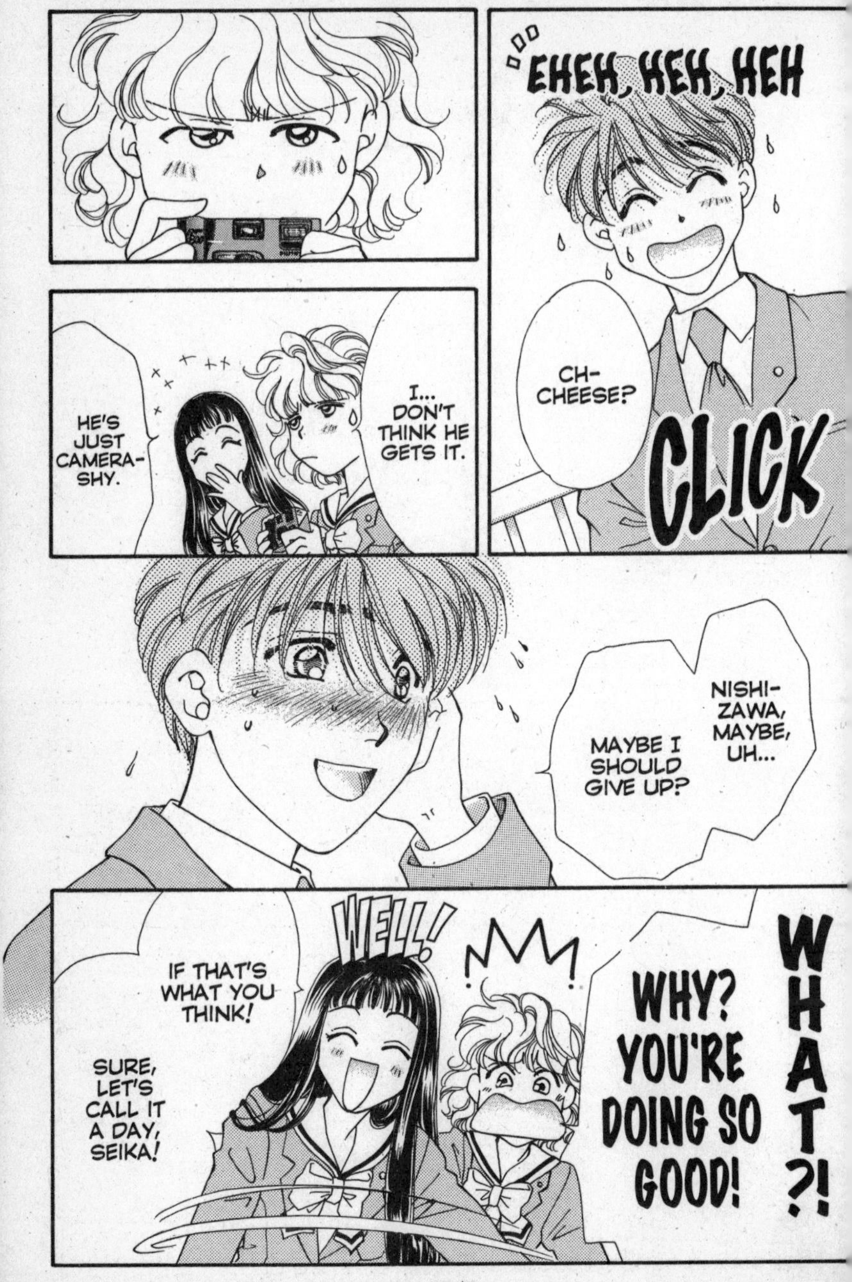
EHEH, HEH, HEH
CH-CHEESE?
CLICK
I... DON'T THINK HE GETS IT.
HE'S JUST CAMERA-SHY.
NISHI-ZAWA, MAYBE, UH...
MAYBE I SHOULD GIVE UP?
WHAT?!
WHY? YOU'RE DOING SO GOOD!
WELL!
IF THAT'S WHAT YOU THINK!
SURE, LET'S CALL IT A DAY, SEIKA!

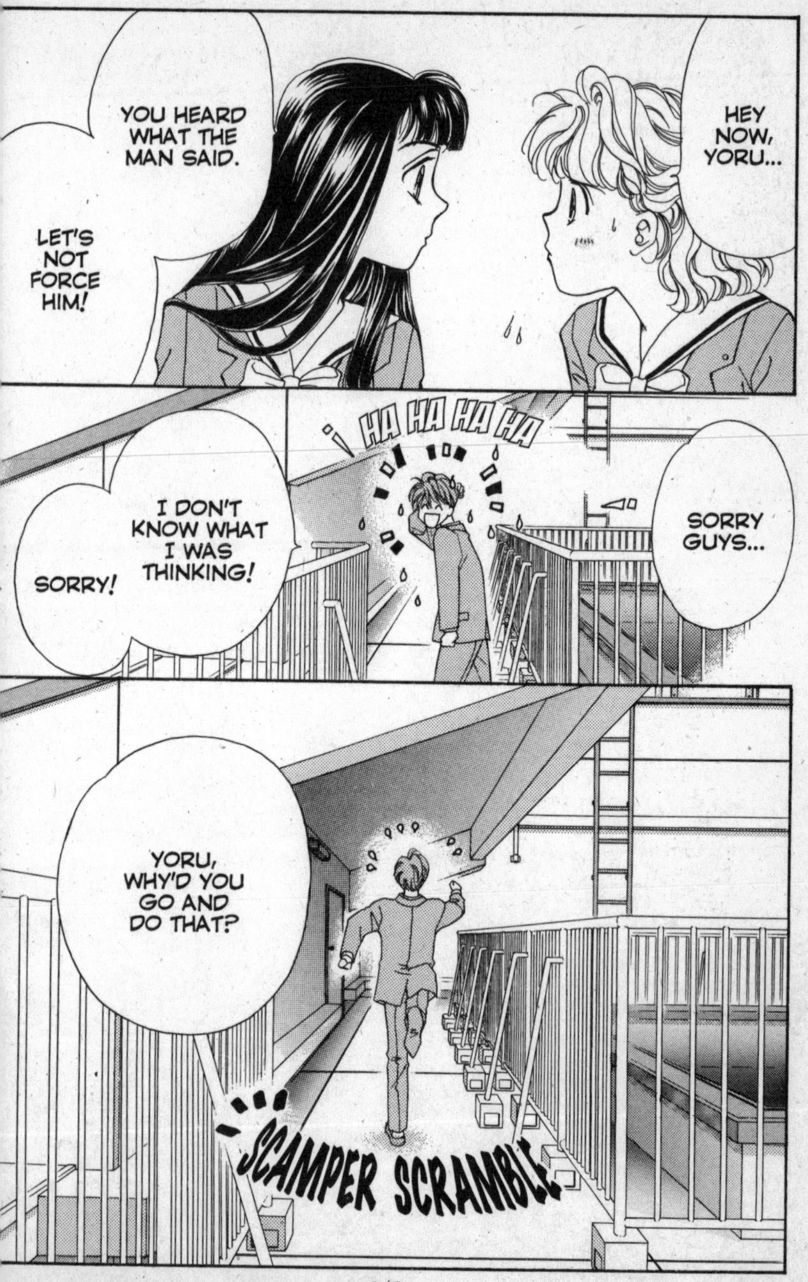
HEY NOW, YORU...
YOU HEARD WHAT THE MAN SAID.
LET'S NOT FORCE HIM!
SORRY GUYS...
HA HA HA HA
I DON'T KNOW WHAT I WAS THINKING!
SORRY!
YORU, WHY'D YOU GO AND DO THAT?
SCAMPER SCRAMBLE

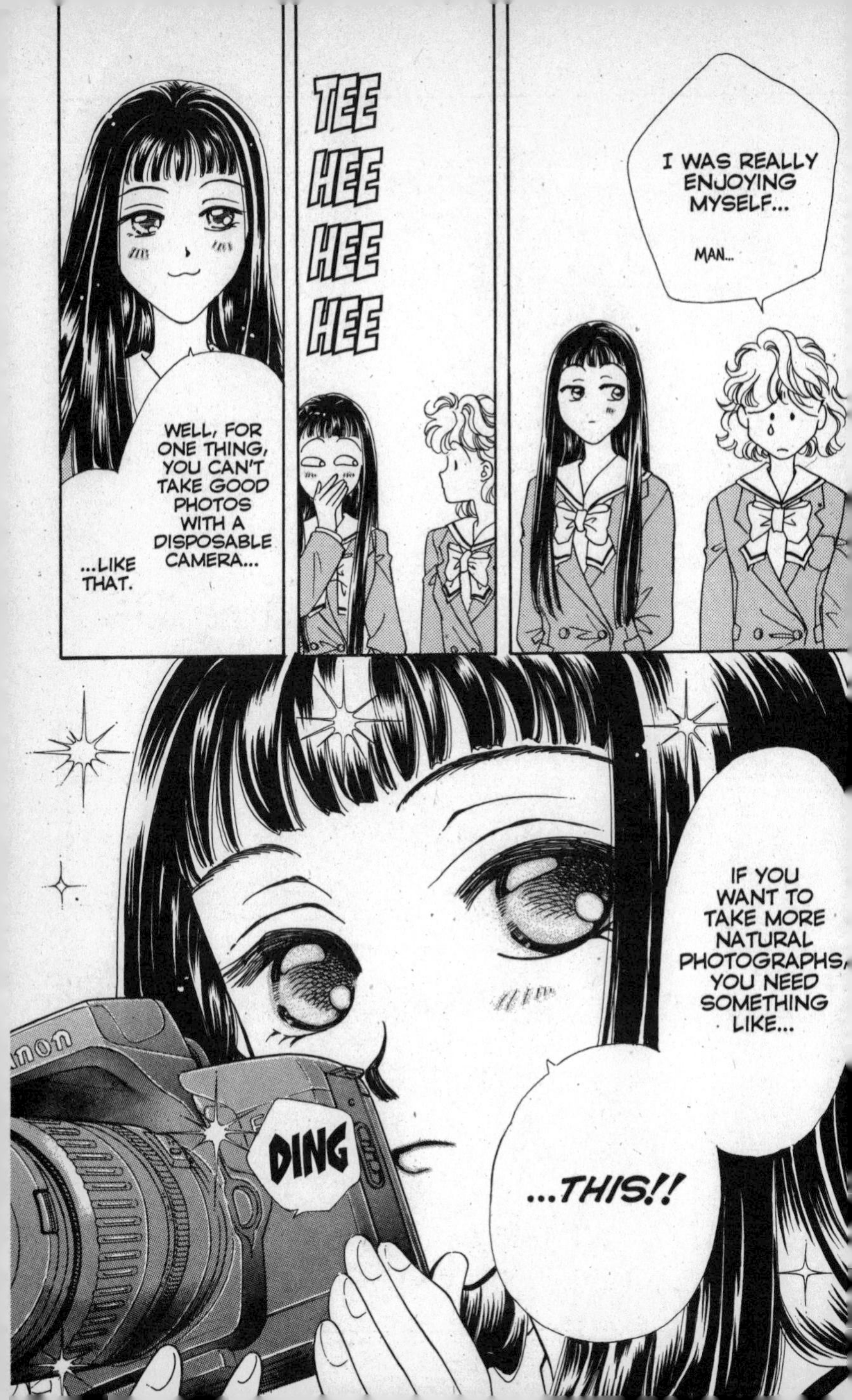
I WAS REALLY ENJOYING MYSELF...
MAN...
TEE HEE HEE HEE
WELL, FOR ONE THING, YOU CAN'T TAKE GOOD PHOTOS WITH A DISPOSABLE CAMERA...
...LIKE THAT.
IF YOU WANT TO TAKE MORE NATURAL PHOTOGRAPHS, YOU NEED SOMETHING LIKE...
...THIS!!
DING

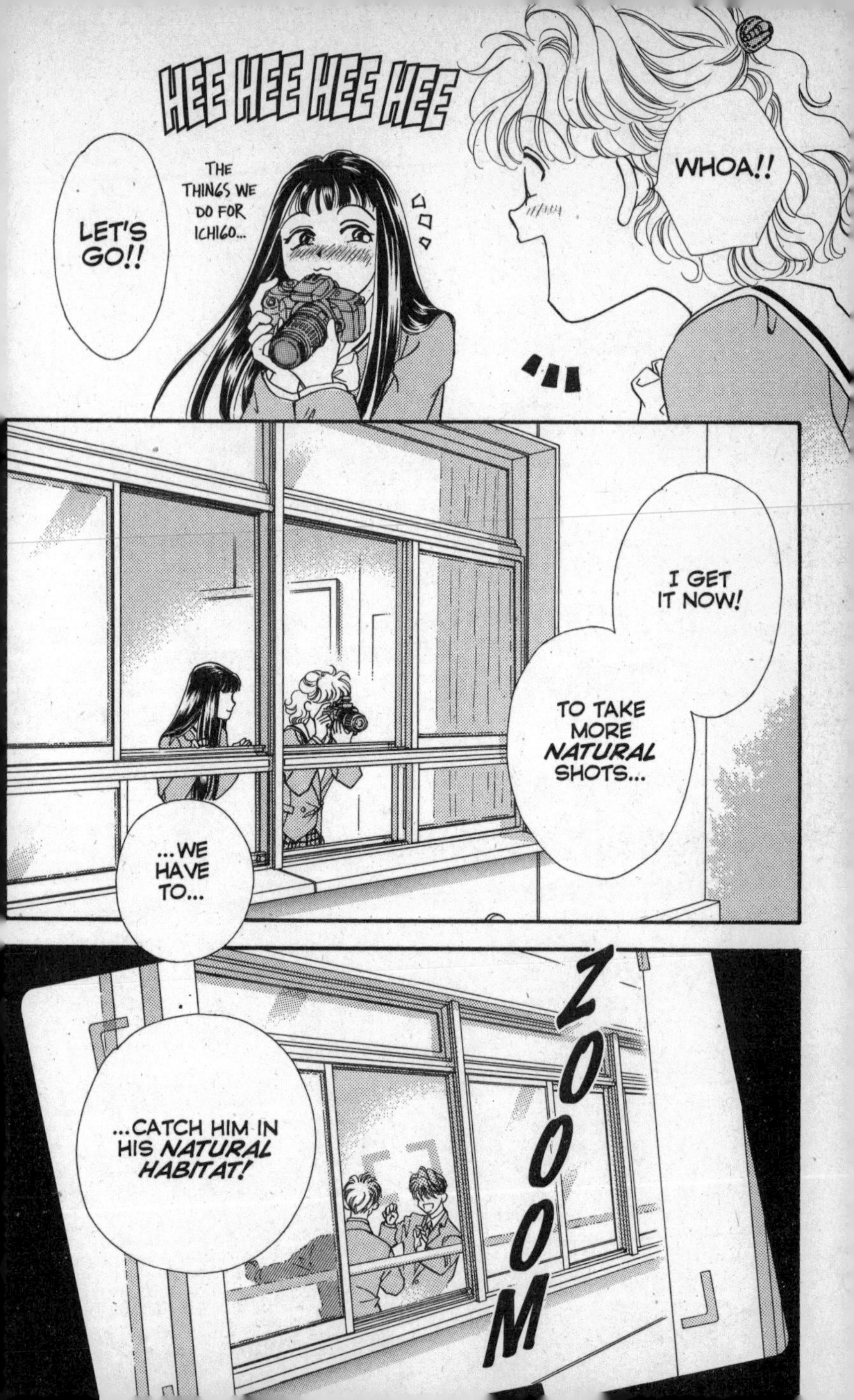
WHOA!!
HEE HEE HEE HEE
THE THINGS WE DO FOR ICHIGO...
LET'S GO!!
I GET IT NOW!
TO TAKE MORE *NATURAL* SHOTS...
...WE HAVE TO...
...CATCH HIM IN HIS *NATURAL HABITAT!*
ZOOOOM

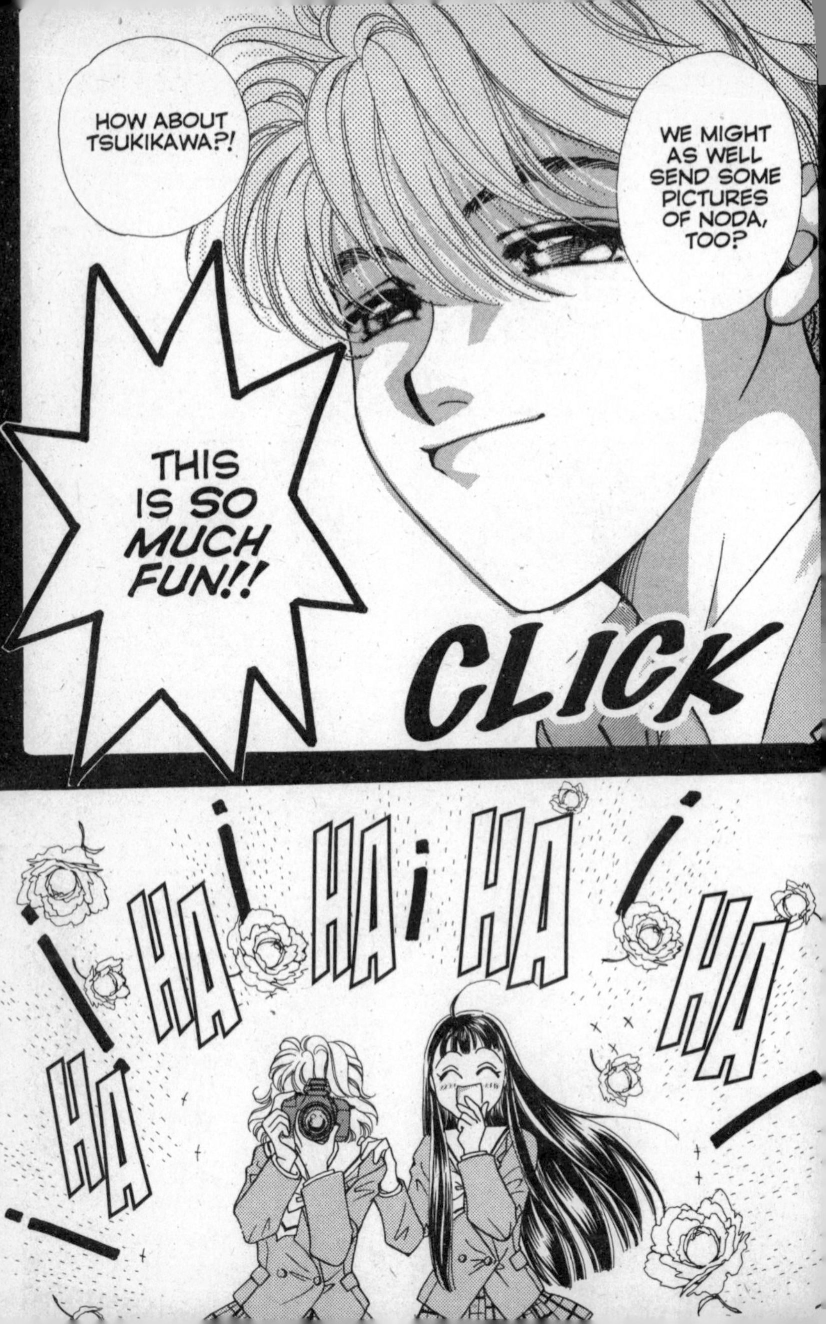
WE MIGHT AS WELL SEND SOME PICTURES OF NODA, TOO?
HOW ABOUT TSUKIKAWA?!
THIS IS SO *MUCH* FUN!!
CLICK
HA! HA! HA! HA! HA!

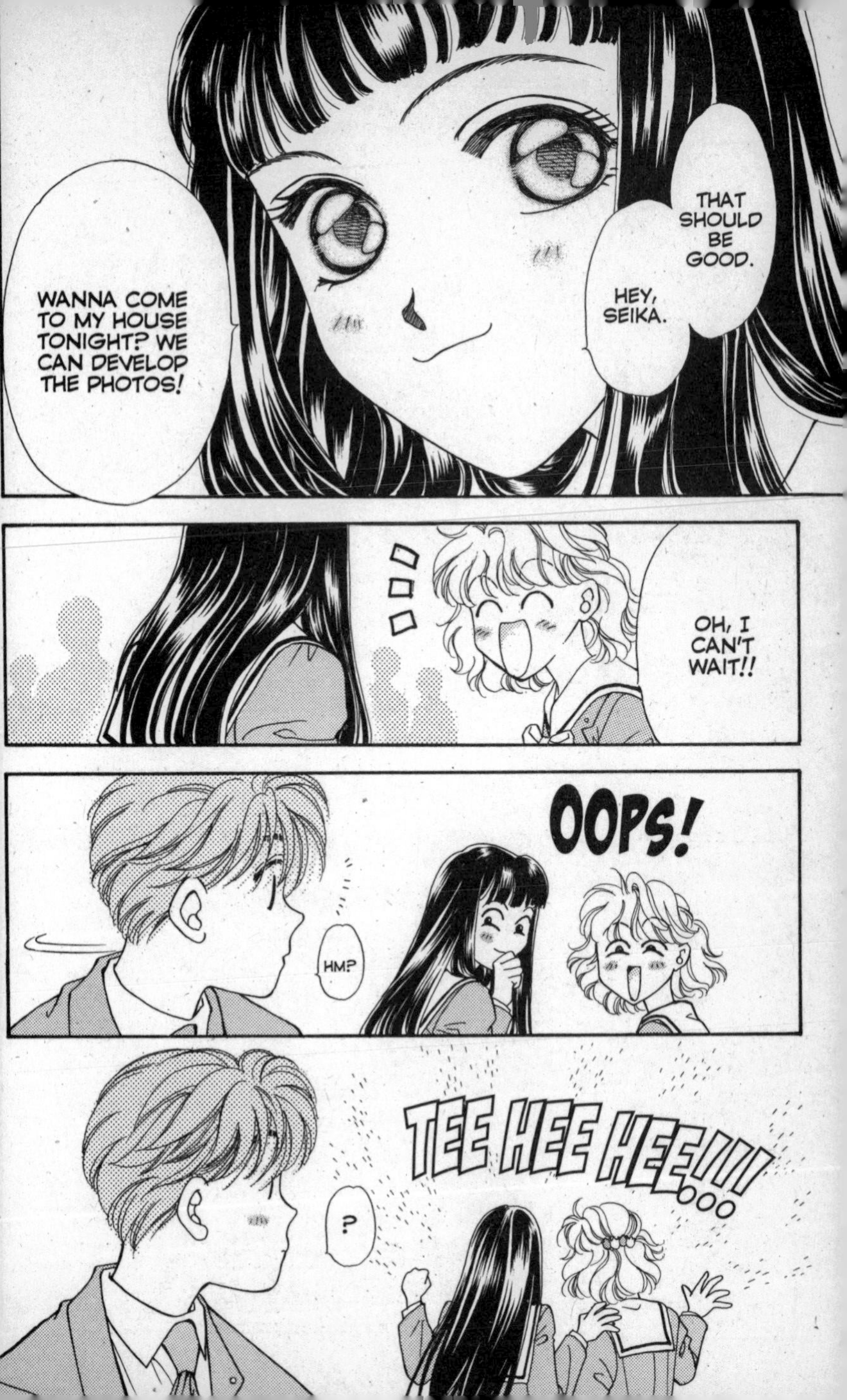
THAT SHOULD BE GOOD.
HEY, SEIKA.
WANNA COME TO MY HOUSE TONIGHT? WE CAN DEVELOP THE PHOTOS!
OH, I CAN'T WAIT!!
OOPS!
HM?
TEE HEE HEE!!!
?

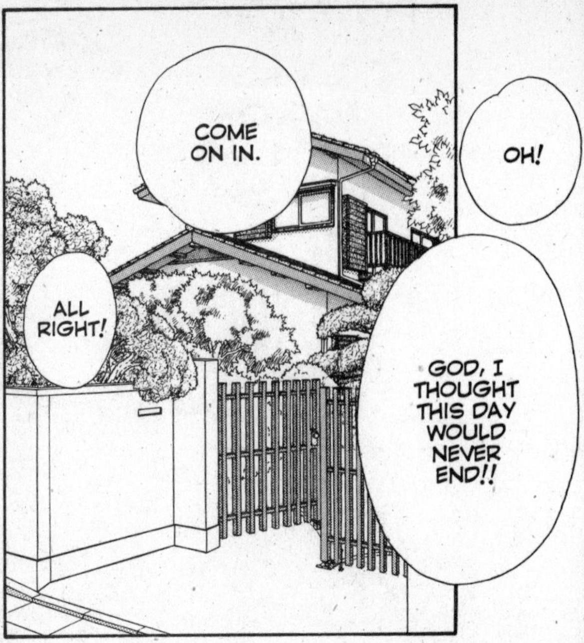
OH!
GOD, I THOUGHT THIS DAY WOULD NEVER END!!
COME ON IN.
ALL RIGHT!

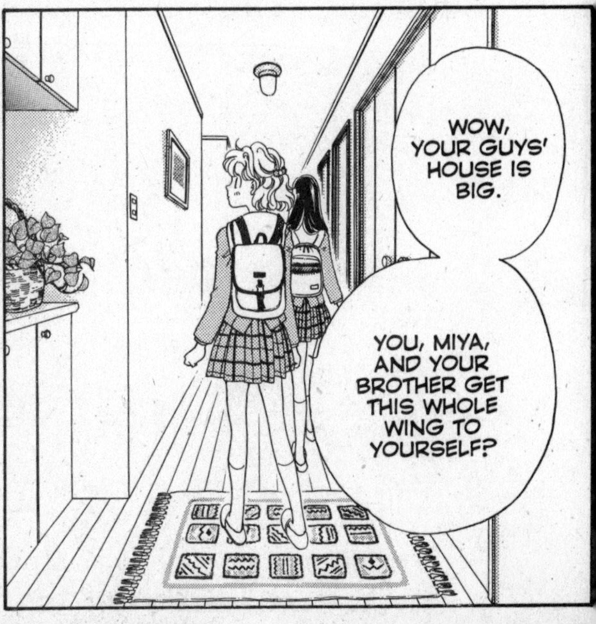
WOW, YOUR GUYS' HOUSE IS BIG.
YOU, MIYA, AND YOUR BROTHER GET THIS WHOLE WING TO YOURSELF?

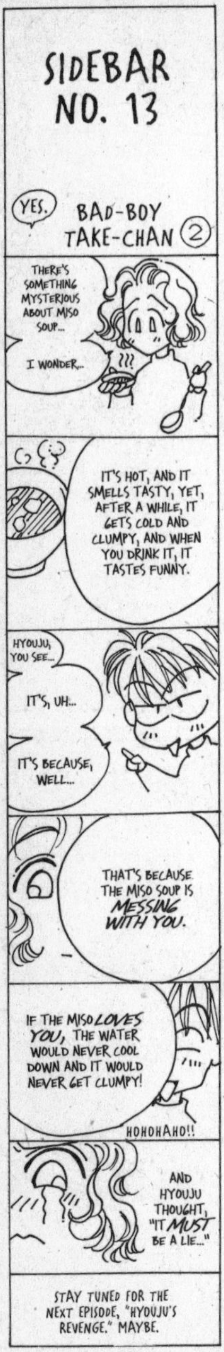
SIDEBAR NO. 13
YES.
BAD-BOY TAKE-CHAN ②
THERE'S SOMETHING MYSTERIOUS ABOUT MISO SOUP...
I WONDER...
???
IT'S HOT, AND IT SMELLS TASTY, YET, AFTER A WHILE, IT GETS COLD AND CLUMPY, AND WHEN YOU DRINK IT, IT TASTES FUNNY.
HYOUJU, YOU SEE...
IT'S, UH...
IT'S BECAUSE, WELL...
THAT'S BECAUSE THE MISO SOUP IS *MESSING WITH YOU.*
IF THE MISO *LOVES YOU,* THE WATER WOULD NEVER COOL DOWN AND IT WOULD NEVER GET CLUMPY!
HOHOHAHO!!
AND HYOUJU THOUGHT, "IT *MUST* BE A LIE..."
STAY TUNED FOR THE NEXT EPISODE, "HYOUJU'S REVENGE." MAYBE.

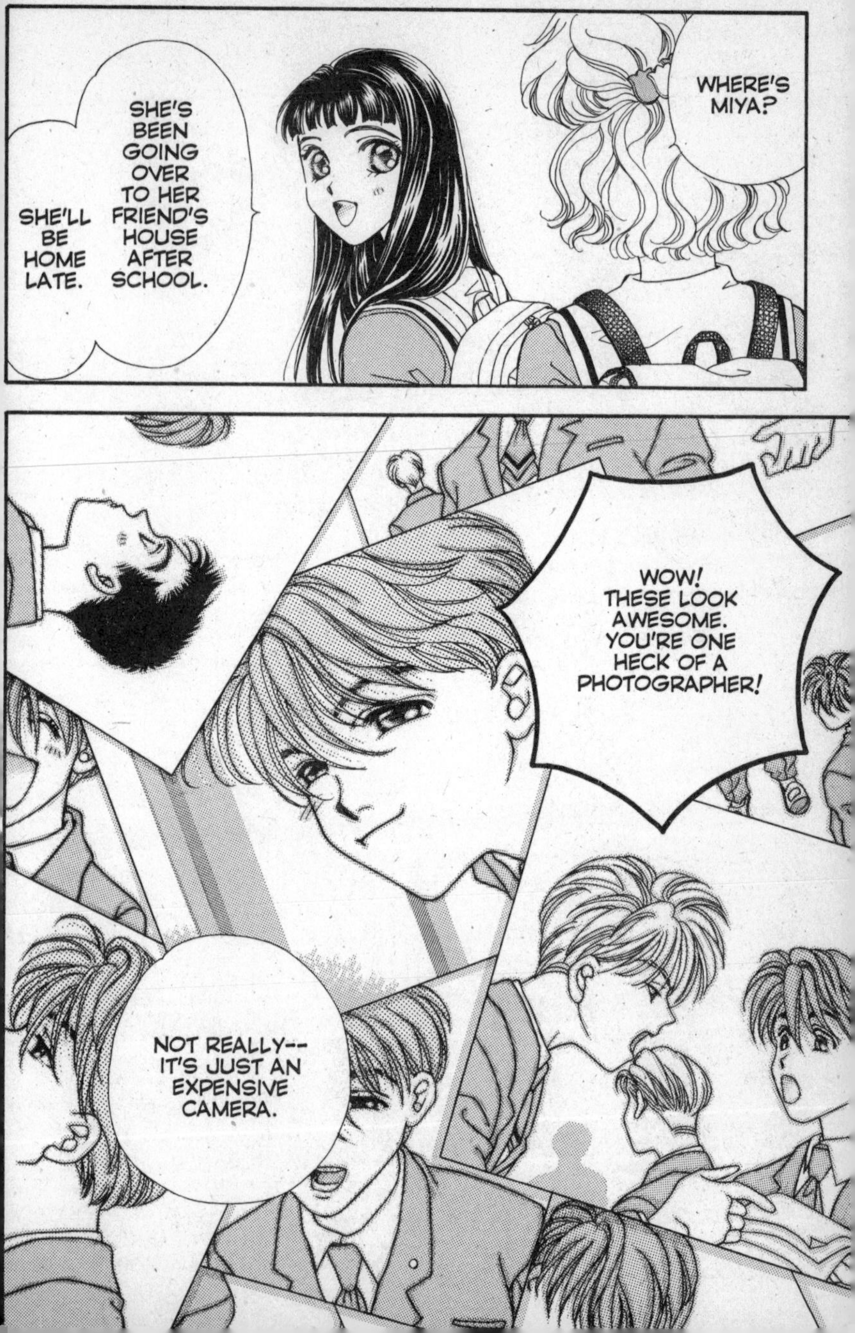
WHERE'S MIYA?
SHE'S BEEN GOING OVER TO HER FRIEND'S HOUSE AFTER SCHOOL.
SHE'LL BE HOME LATE.
WOW! THESE LOOK AWESOME. YOU'RE ONE HECK OF A PHOTOGRAPHER!
NOT REALLY--IT'S JUST AN EXPENSIVE CAMERA.

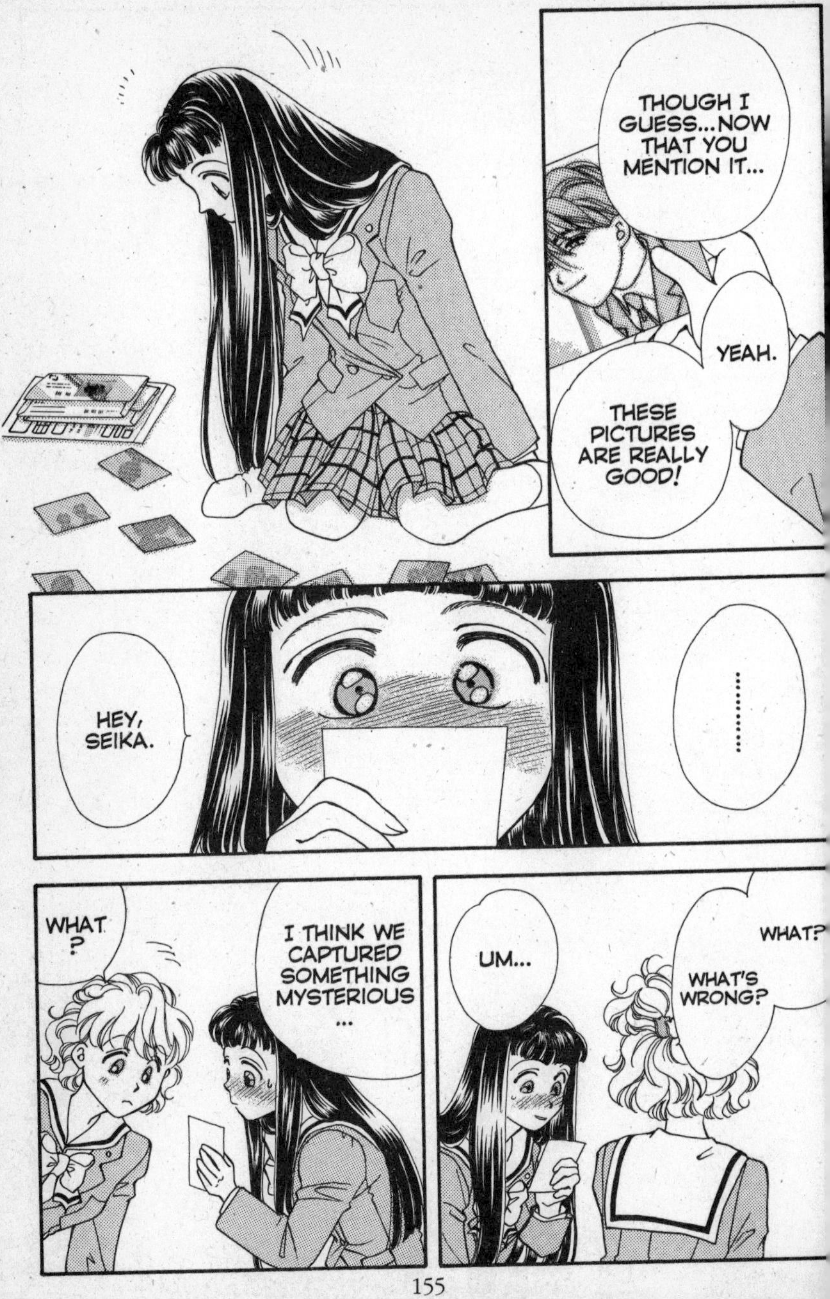
THOUGH I GUESS...NOW THAT YOU MENTION IT...
YEAH.
THESE PICTURES ARE REALLY GOOD!
....
HEY, SEIKA.
WHAT?
WHAT'S WRONG?
UM...
I THINK WE CAPTURED SOMETHING MYSTERIOUS...
WHAT?

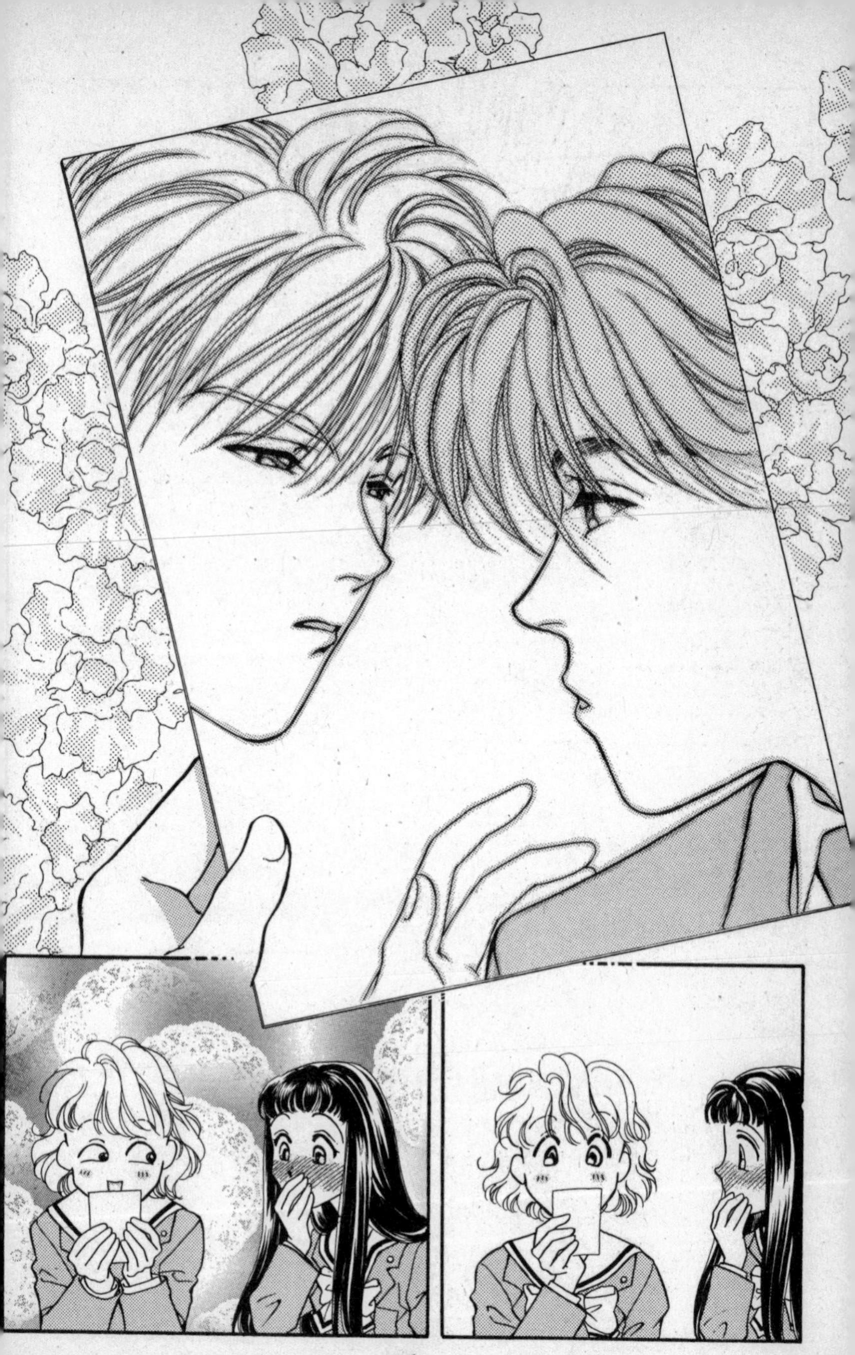

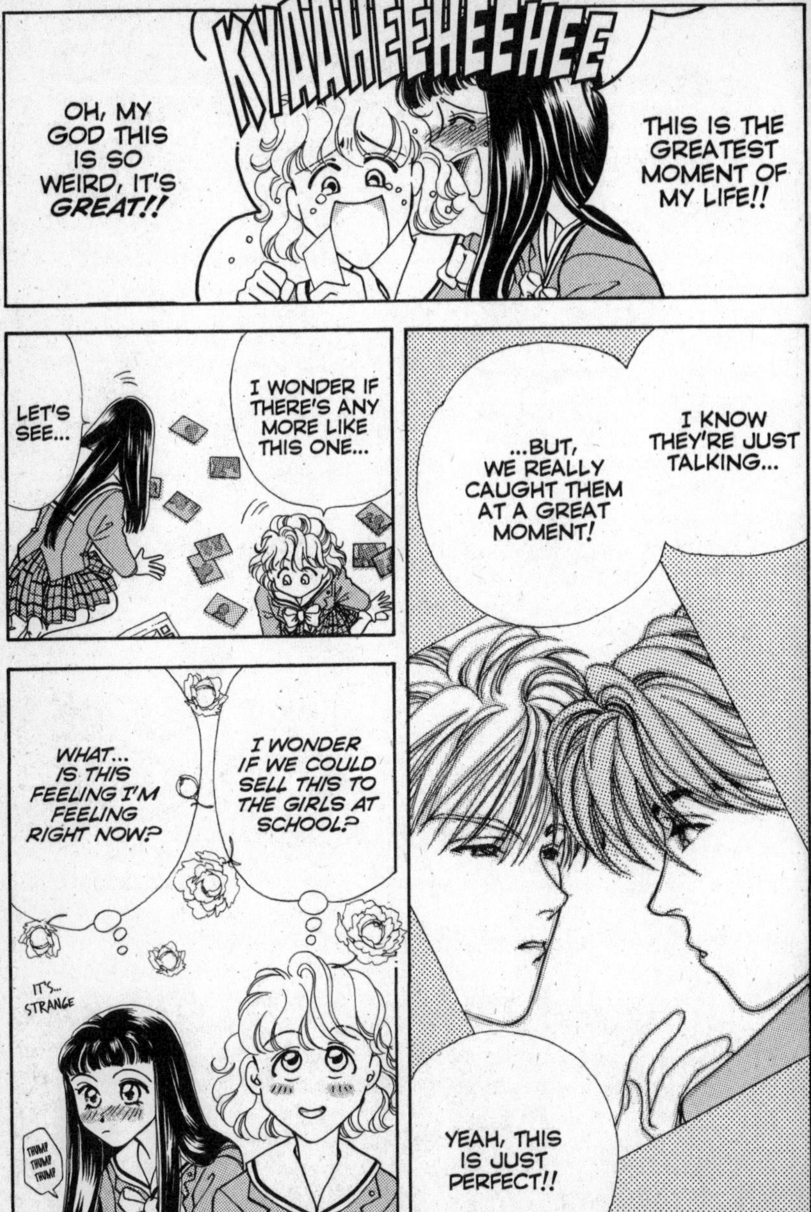
KYAAHEEHEEHEE
THIS IS THE GREATEST MOMENT OF MY LIFE!!
OH, MY GOD THIS IS SO WEIRD, IT'S *GREAT!!*
I KNOW THEY'RE JUST TALKING...
...BUT, WE REALLY CAUGHT THEM AT A GREAT MOMENT!
YEAH, THIS IS JUST PERFECT!!
I WONDER IF THERE'S ANY MORE LIKE THIS ONE...
LET'S SEE...
I WONDER IF WE COULD SELL THIS TO THE GIRLS AT SCHOOL?
WHAT... IS THIS FEELING I'M FEELING RIGHT NOW?
IT'S... STRANGE
THUMP THUMP THUMP

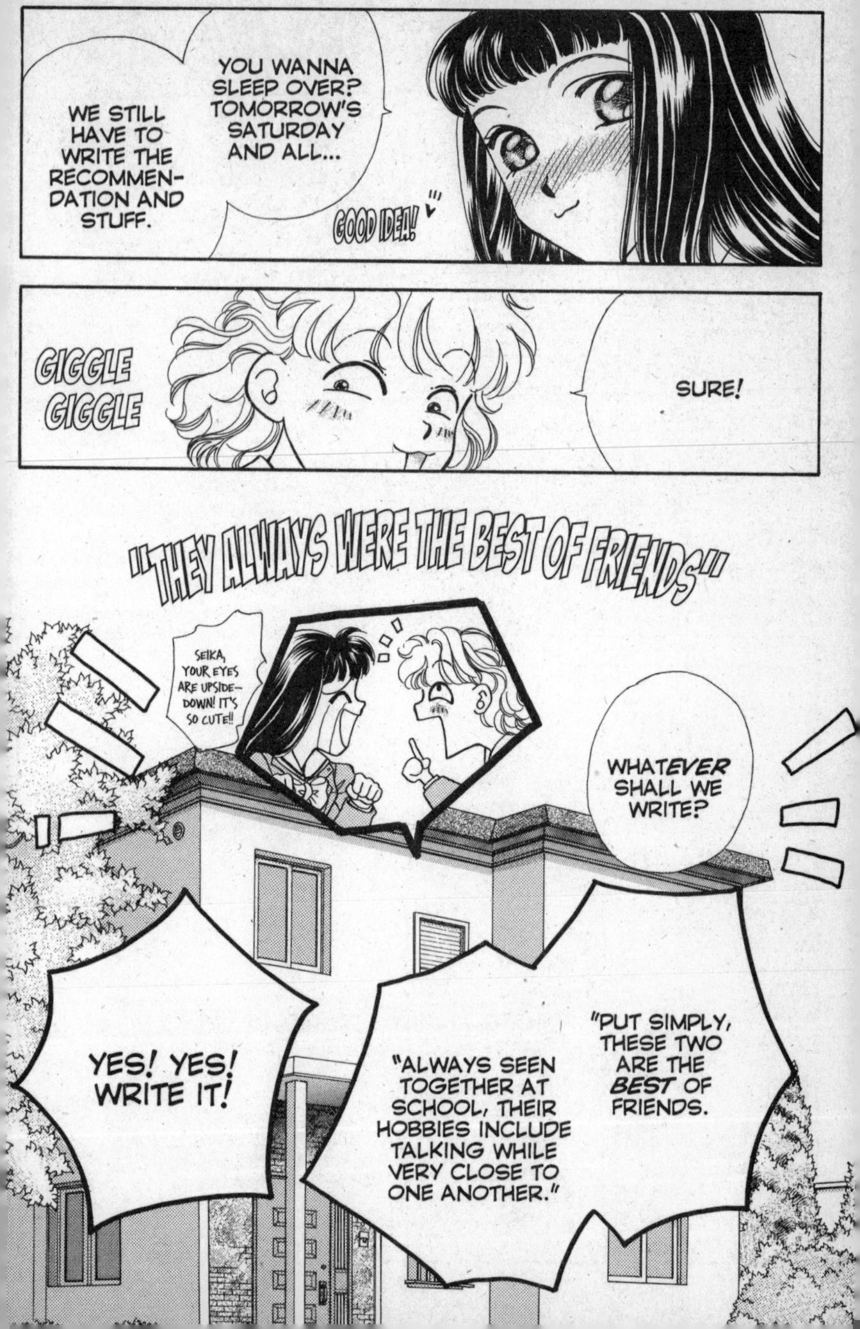
YOU WANNA SLEEP OVER? TOMORROW'S SATURDAY AND ALL...
WE STILL HAVE TO WRITE THE RECOMMEN-DATION AND STUFF.
GOOD IDEA!
SURE!
GIGGLE GIGGLE
"THEY ALWAYS WERE THE BEST OF FRIENDS"
WHATEVER SHALL WE WRITE?
SEIKA, YOUR EYES ARE UPSIDE-DOWN! IT'S SO CUTE!!
"PUT SIMPLY, THESE TWO ARE THE BEST OF FRIENDS.
"ALWAYS SEEN TOGETHER AT SCHOOL, THEIR HOBBIES INCLUDE TALKING WHILE VERY CLOSE TO ONE ANOTHER."
YES! YES! WRITE IT!

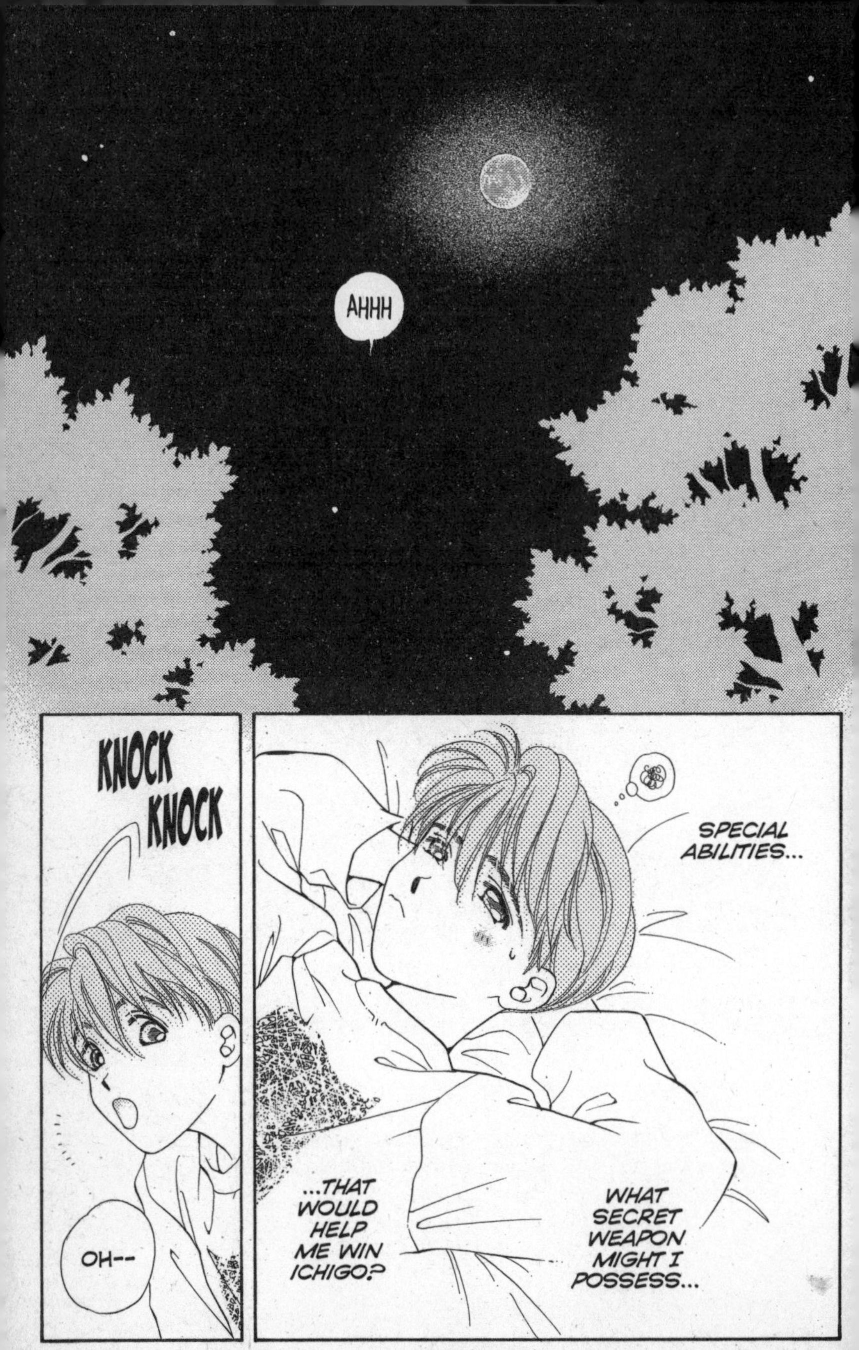
AHHH
SPECIAL ABILITIES...
WHAT SECRET WEAPON MIGHT I POSSESS...
...THAT WOULD HELP ME WIN ICHIGO?
KNOCK KNOCK
OH--

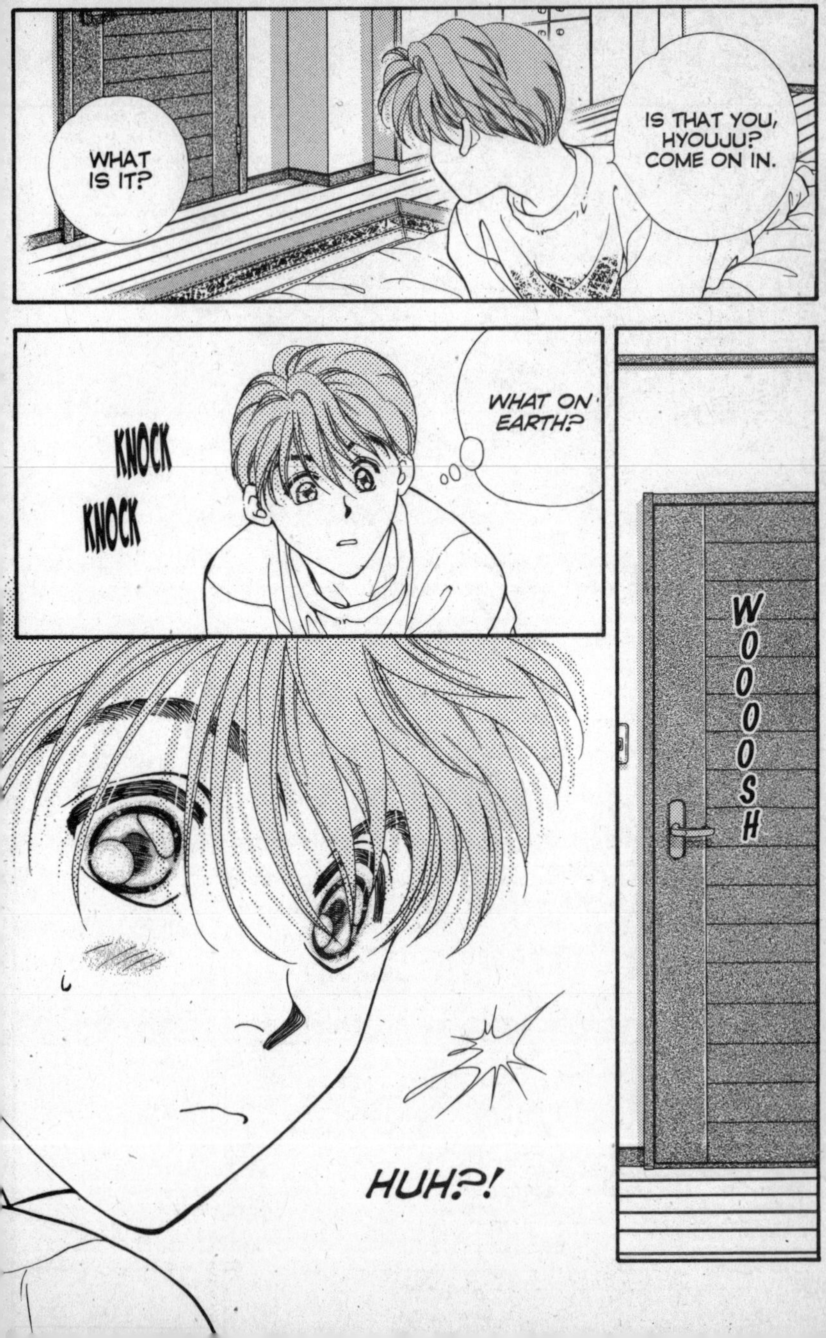
IS THAT YOU, HYOUJU? COME ON IN.
WHAT IS IT?
WOOOOOSH
WHAT ON EARTH?
KNOCK KNOCK
HUH?!

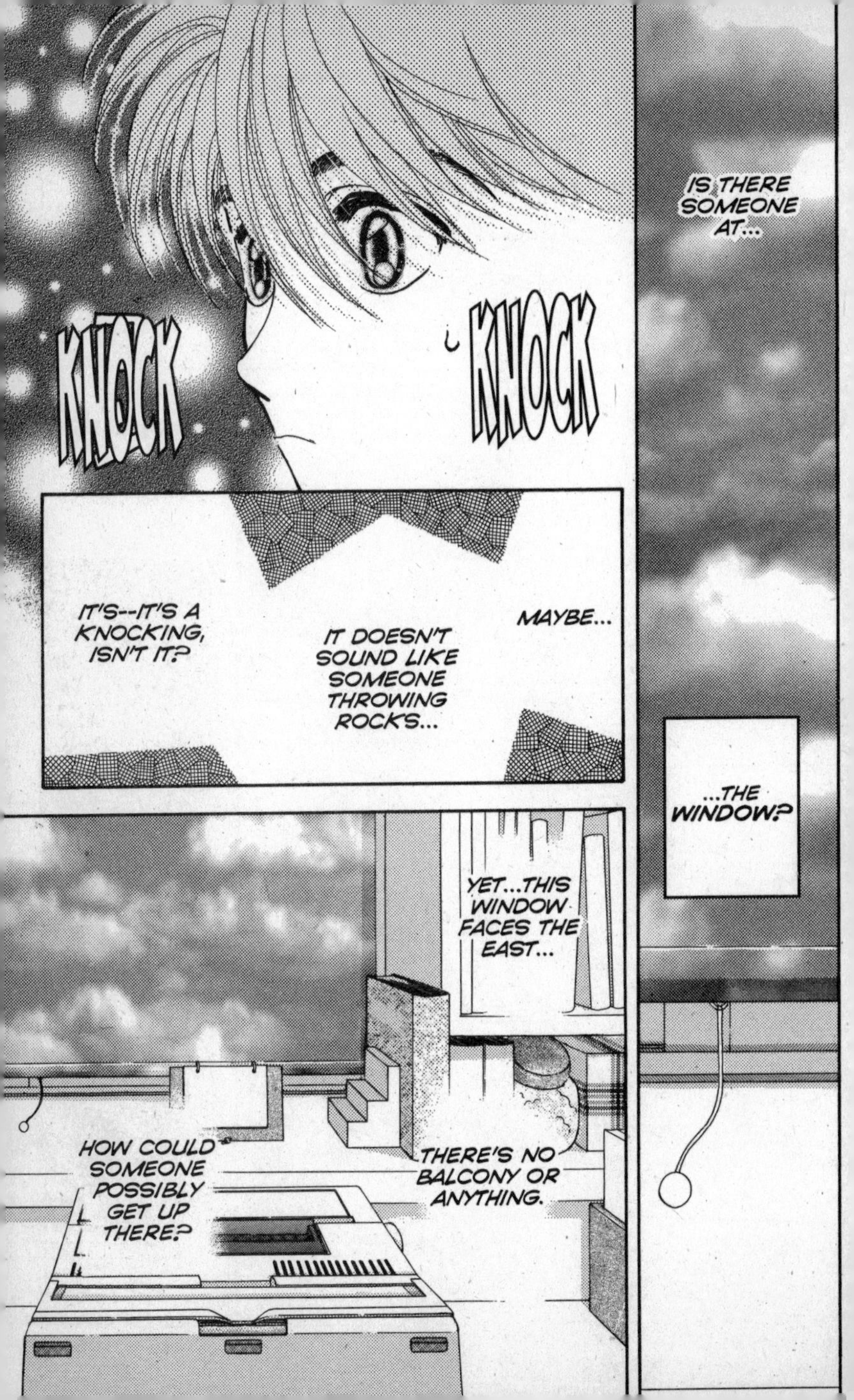
IS THERE SOMEONE AT...
...THE WINDOW?
KNOCK
KNOCK
MAYBE...
IT DOESN'T SOUND LIKE SOMEONE THROWING ROCKS...
IT'S--IT'S A KNOCKING, ISN'T IT?
YET...THIS WINDOW FACES THE EAST...
THERE'S NO BALCONY OR ANYTHING.
HOW COULD SOMEONE POSSIBLY GET UP THERE?

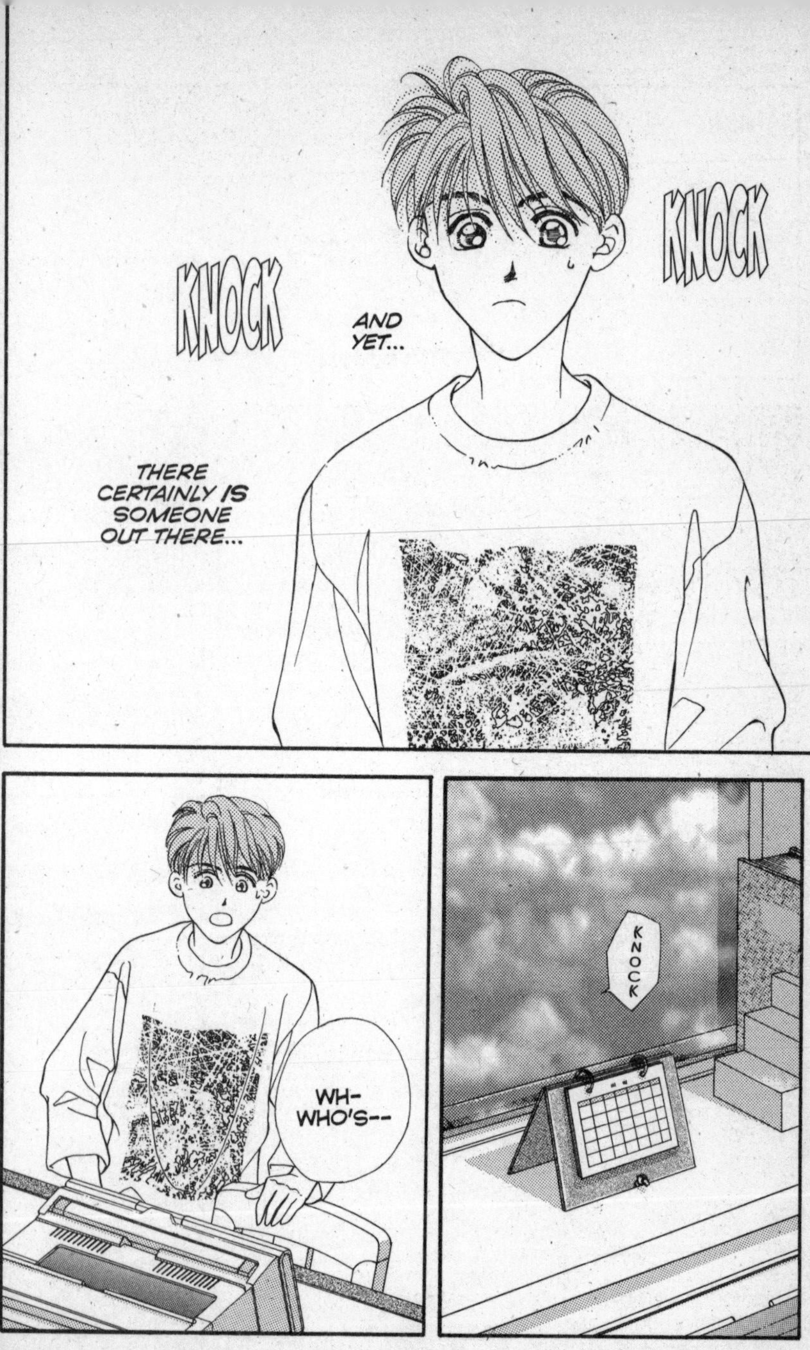
KNOCK
AND YET...
KNOCK
THERE CERTAINLY IS SOMEONE OUT THERE...
KNOCK
WH- WHO'S--

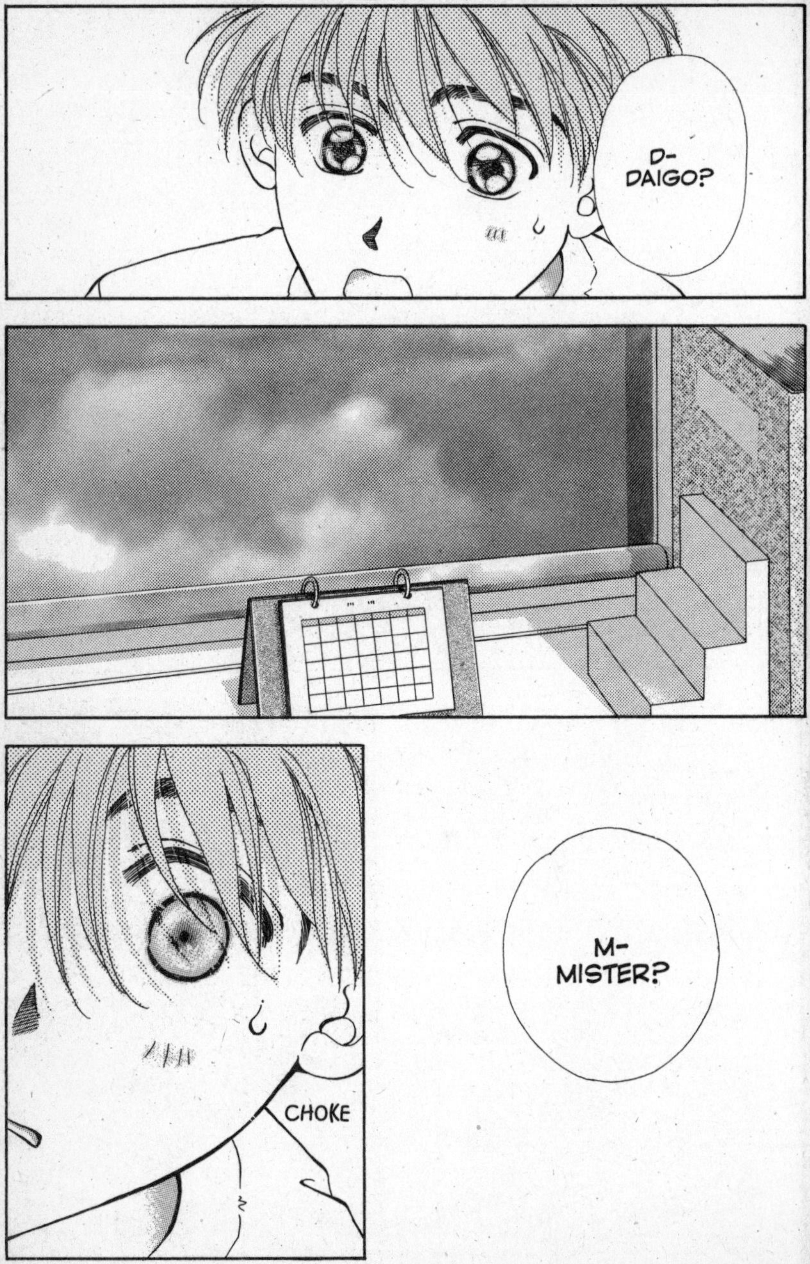
D-
DAIGO?
M-
MISTER?
CHOKE

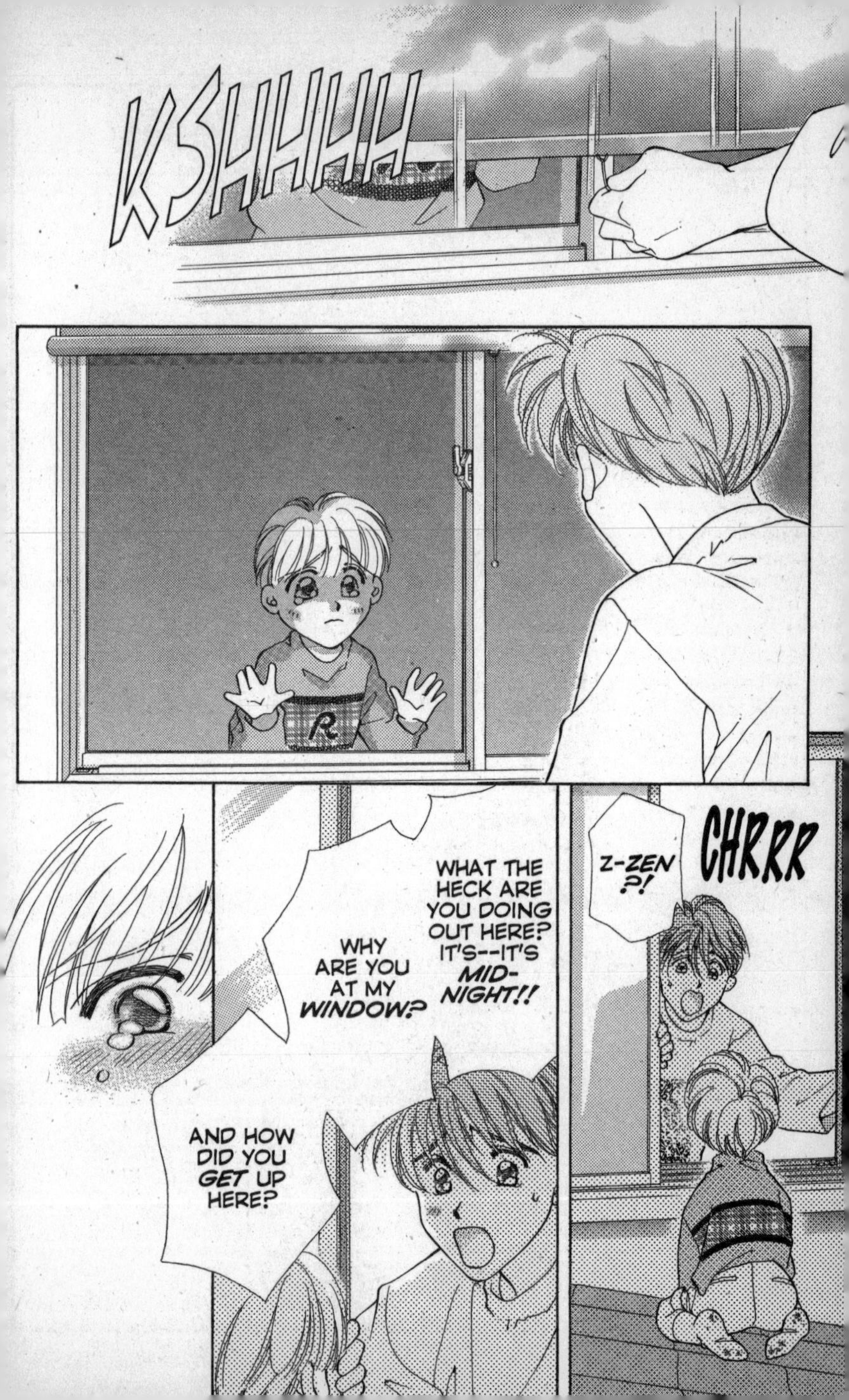
KSHHHHH
CHRRR
Z-ZEN?!
WHAT THE HECK ARE YOU DOING OUT HERE? IT'S--IT'S *MID-NIGHT!!*
WHY ARE YOU AT MY *WINDOW?*
AND HOW DID YOU *GET* UP HERE?

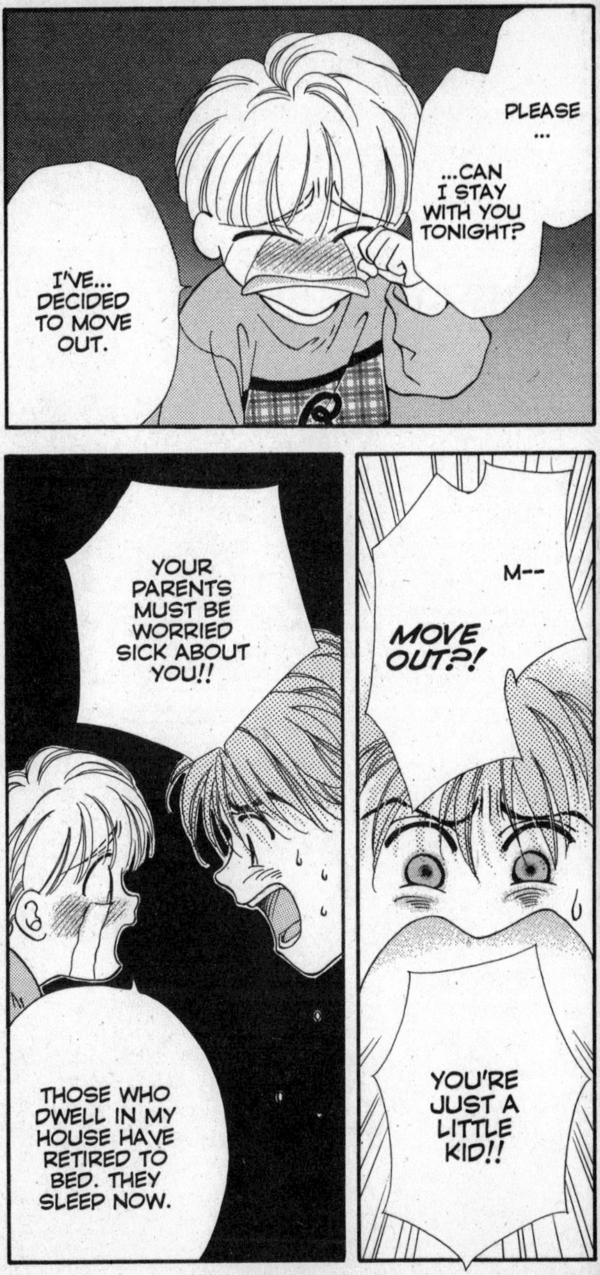
PLEASE ...
...CAN I STAY WITH YOU TONIGHT?
I'VE... DECIDED TO MOVE OUT.
M--
MOVE OUT?!
YOU'RE JUST A LITTLE KID!!
YOUR PARENTS MUST BE WORRIED SICK ABOUT YOU!!
THOSE WHO DWELL IN MY HOUSE HAVE RETIRED TO BED. THEY SLEEP NOW.

Sidebar No. 14

So yeah, I bought a PlayStation. Even though the Nintendo 64 is coming out soon. I bought the system and Tokimeki Memorial, and I don't really know why. It seems so...annoying. Frustrating. And I haven't even started Dragon Quest VI yet!! I think I'll wait until it gets a little cheaper before I buy it. Ahhhhh, I can't wait. Anyway, I keep buying stuff like this, and my apartment is getting smaller and smaller. You see, my apartment is also my office, so if I have too many personal things around, it starts to get in the way of my work. Hm! Anyway, everyone, keep reaching for the stars and keep your feet planted on the ground, and please, by all means, be well! I will see you soon!!

(And if you have any game recommendations, let me know!!)

1995. 12. 30.

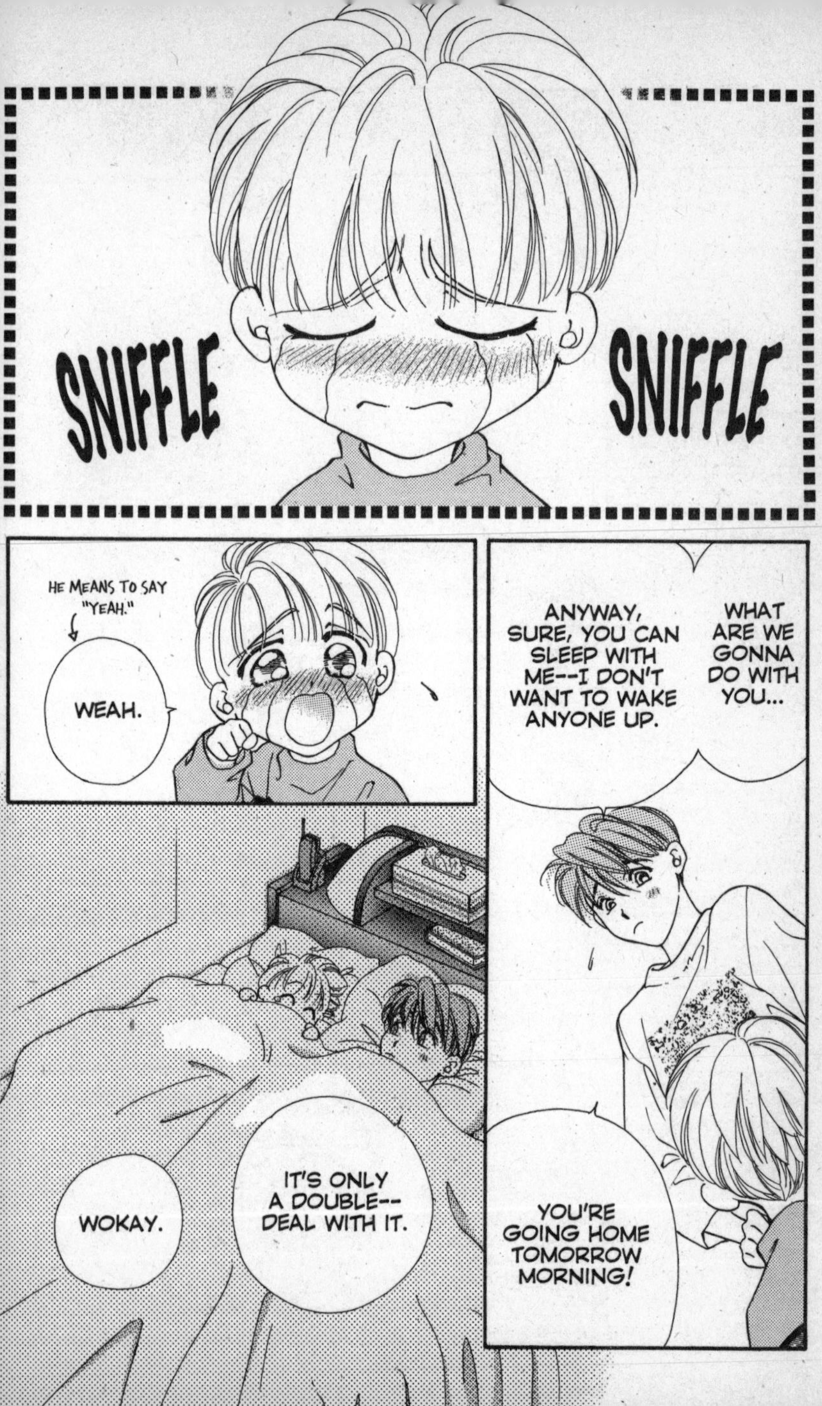
SNIFFLE
SNIFFLE
WHAT ARE WE GONNA DO WITH YOU...
ANYWAY, SURE, YOU CAN SLEEP WITH ME--I DON'T WANT TO WAKE ANYONE UP.
YOU'RE GOING HOME TOMORROW MORNING!
HE MEANS TO SAY "YEAH."
WEAH.
IT'S ONLY A DOUBLE--DEAL WITH IT.
WOKAY.

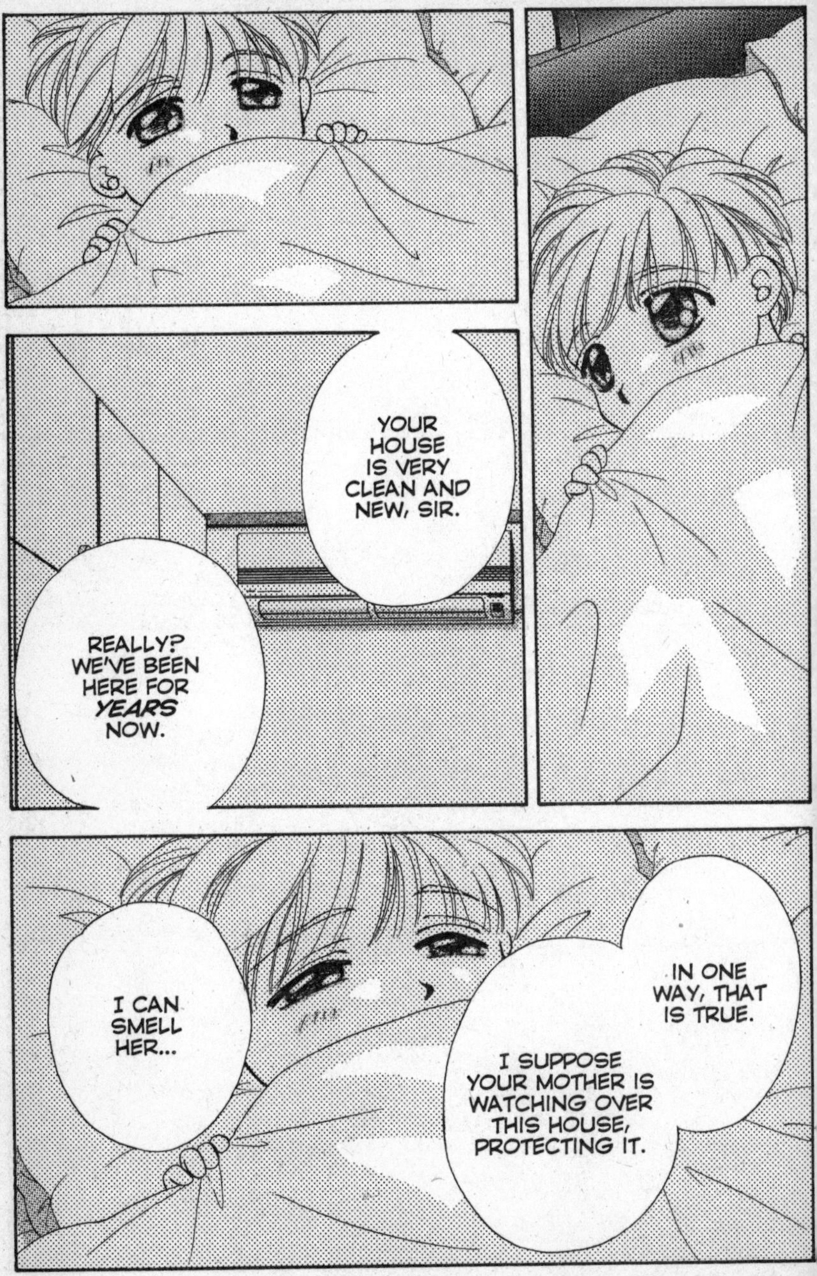
YOUR HOUSE IS VERY CLEAN AND NEW, SIR.
REALLY? WE'VE BEEN HERE FOR *YEARS* NOW.
IN ONE WAY, THAT IS TRUE.
I SUPPOSE YOUR MOTHER IS WATCHING OVER THIS HOUSE, PROTECTING IT.
I CAN SMELL HER...

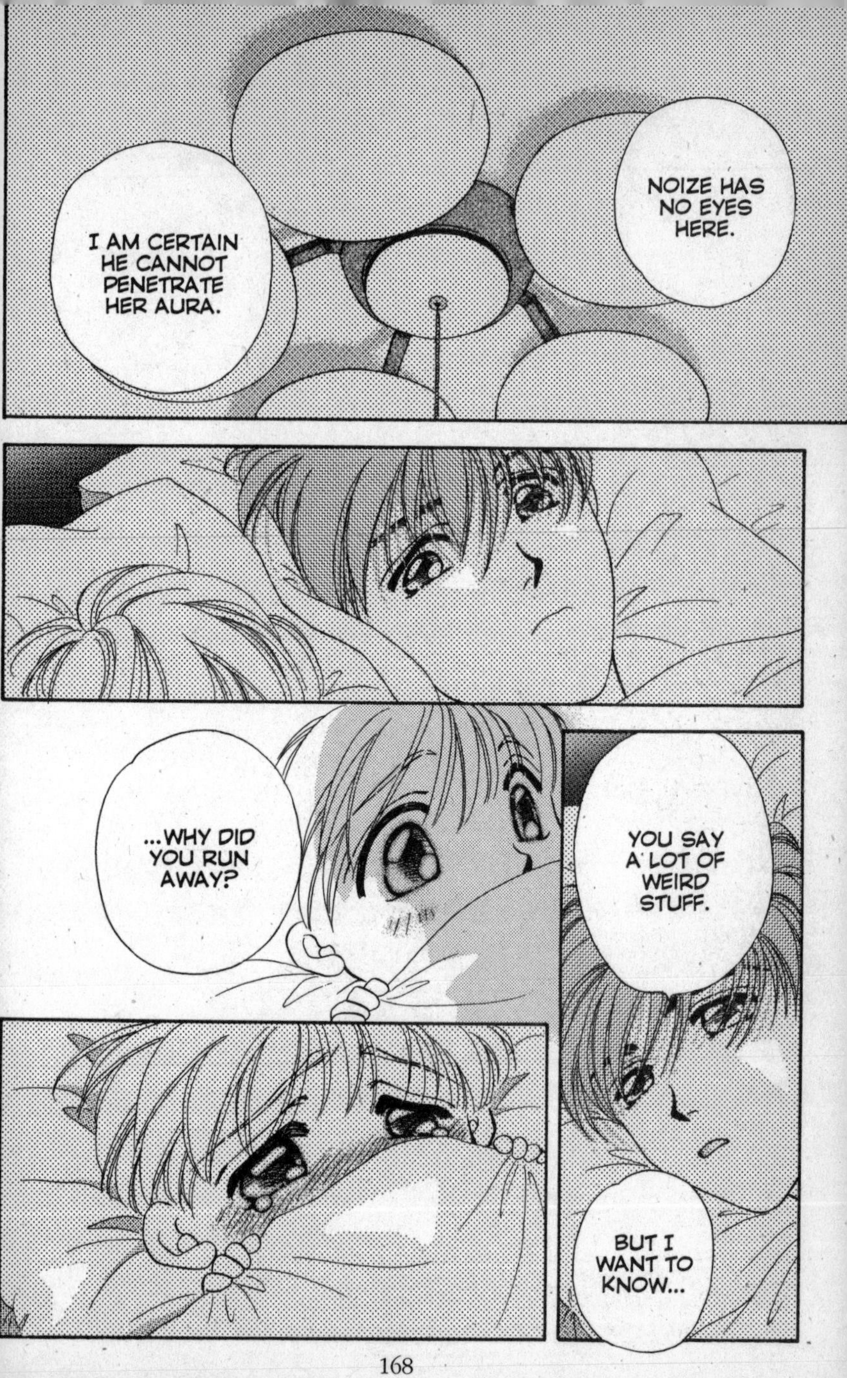
NOIZE HAS NO EYES HERE.
I AM CERTAIN HE CANNOT PENETRATE HER AURA.
YOU SAY A LOT OF WEIRD STUFF.
BUT I WANT TO KNOW...
...WHY DID YOU RUN AWAY?

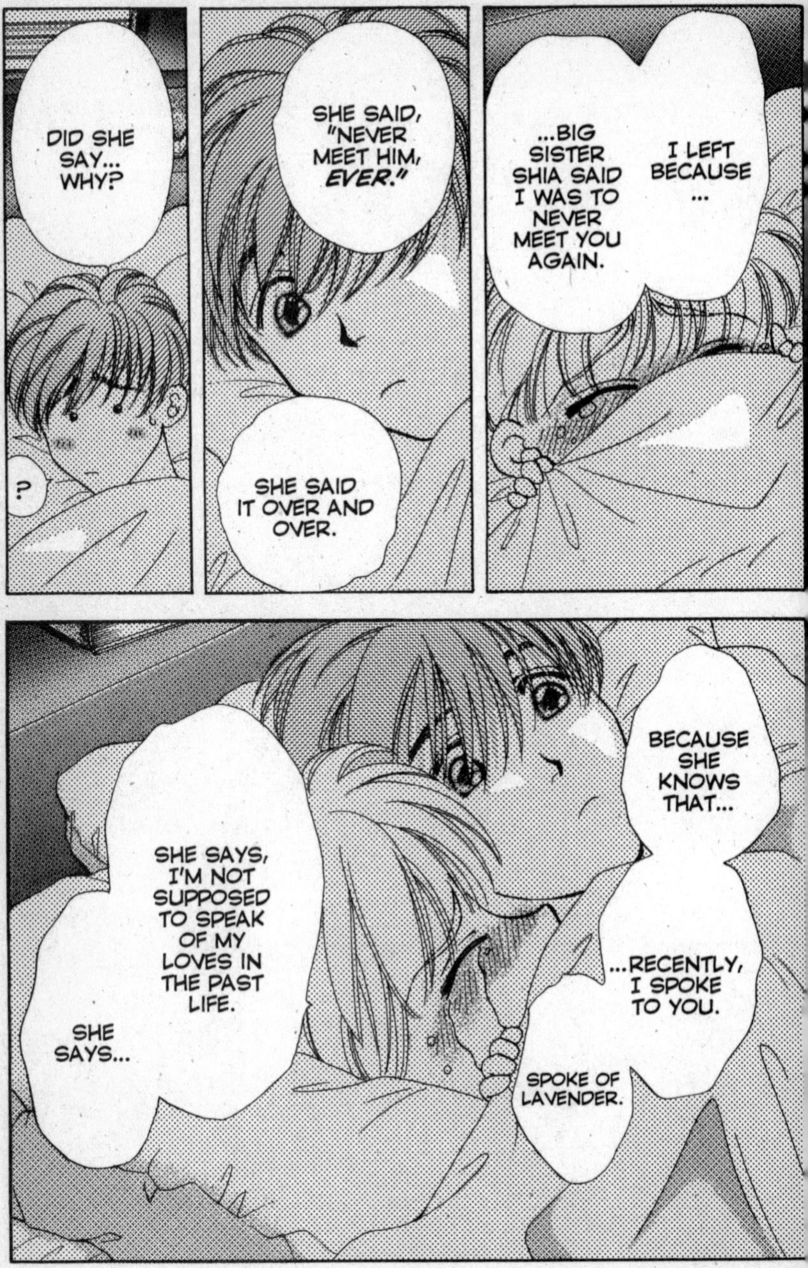
I LEFT BECAUSE ...
...BIG SISTER SHIA SAID I WAS TO NEVER MEET YOU AGAIN.
SHE SAID, "NEVER MEET HIM, *EVER.*"
SHE SAID IT OVER AND OVER.
DID SHE SAY... WHY?
?
BECAUSE SHE KNOWS THAT...
...RECENTLY, I SPOKE TO YOU.
SPOKE OF LAVENDER.
SHE SAYS, I'M NOT SUPPOSED TO SPEAK OF MY LOVES IN THE PAST LIFE.
SHE SAYS...

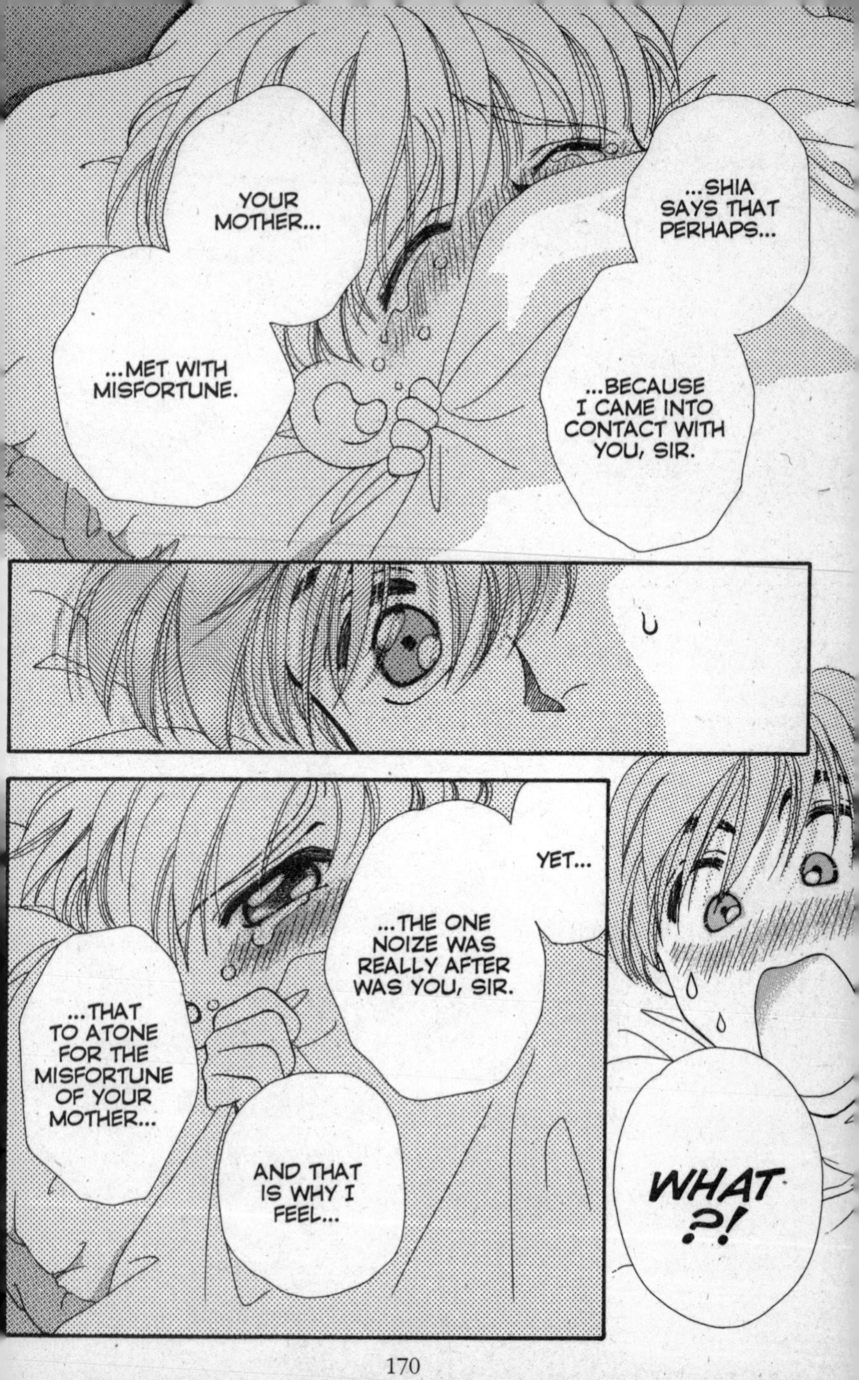
...SHIA SAYS THAT PERHAPS...
...BECAUSE I CAME INTO CONTACT WITH YOU, SIR.
YOUR MOTHER...
...MET WITH MISFORTUNE.
YET...
...THE ONE NOIZE WAS REALLY AFTER WAS YOU, SIR.
AND THAT IS WHY I FEEL...
...THAT TO ATONE FOR THE MISFORTUNE OF YOUR MOTHER...
WHAT?!

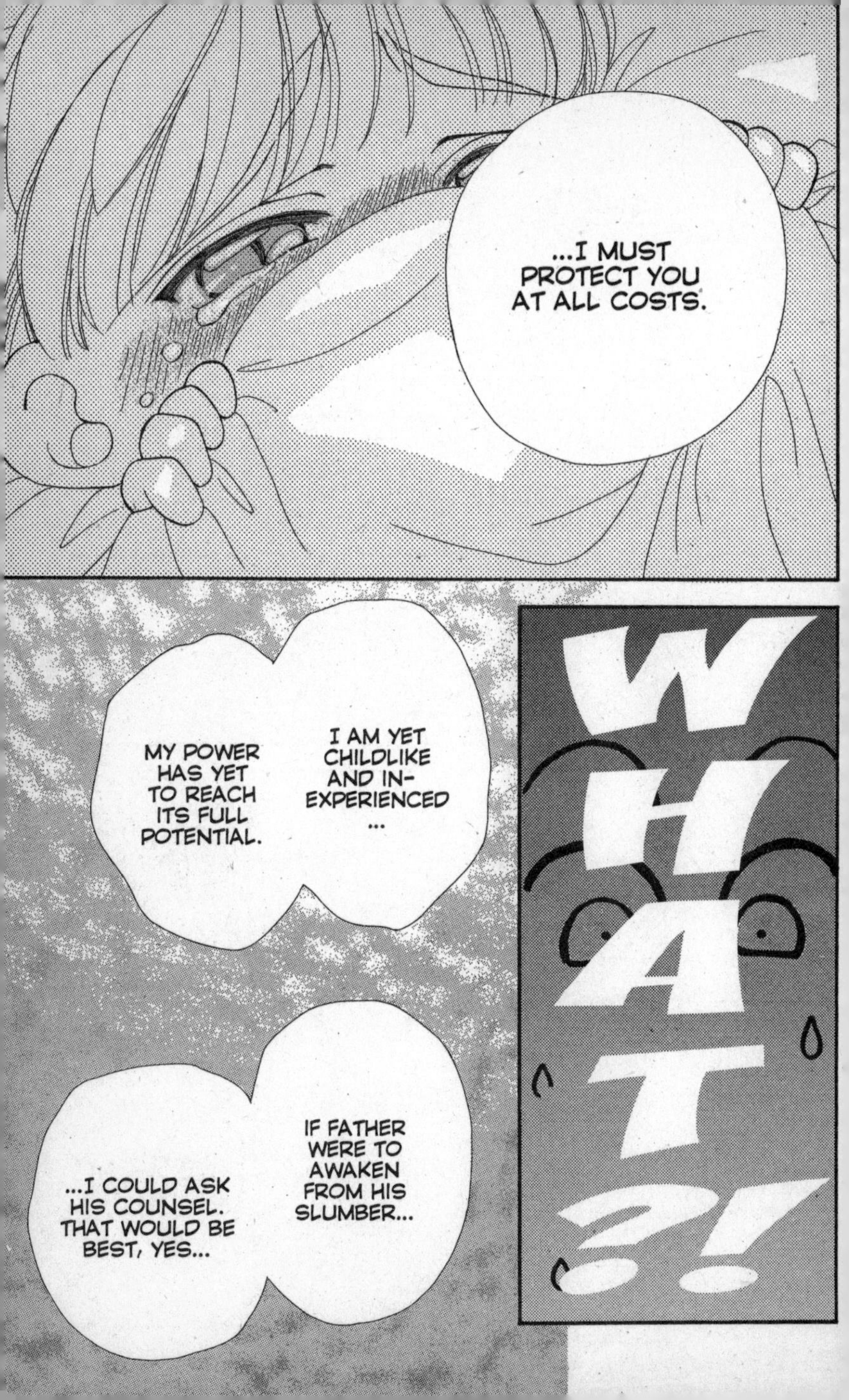
...I MUST PROTECT YOU AT ALL COSTS.
WHAT?!
I AM YET CHILDLIKE AND IN-EXPERIENCED ...
MY POWER HAS YET TO REACH ITS FULL POTENTIAL.
IF FATHER WERE TO AWAKEN FROM HIS SLUMBER...
...I COULD ASK HIS COUNSEL. THAT WOULD BE BEST, YES...

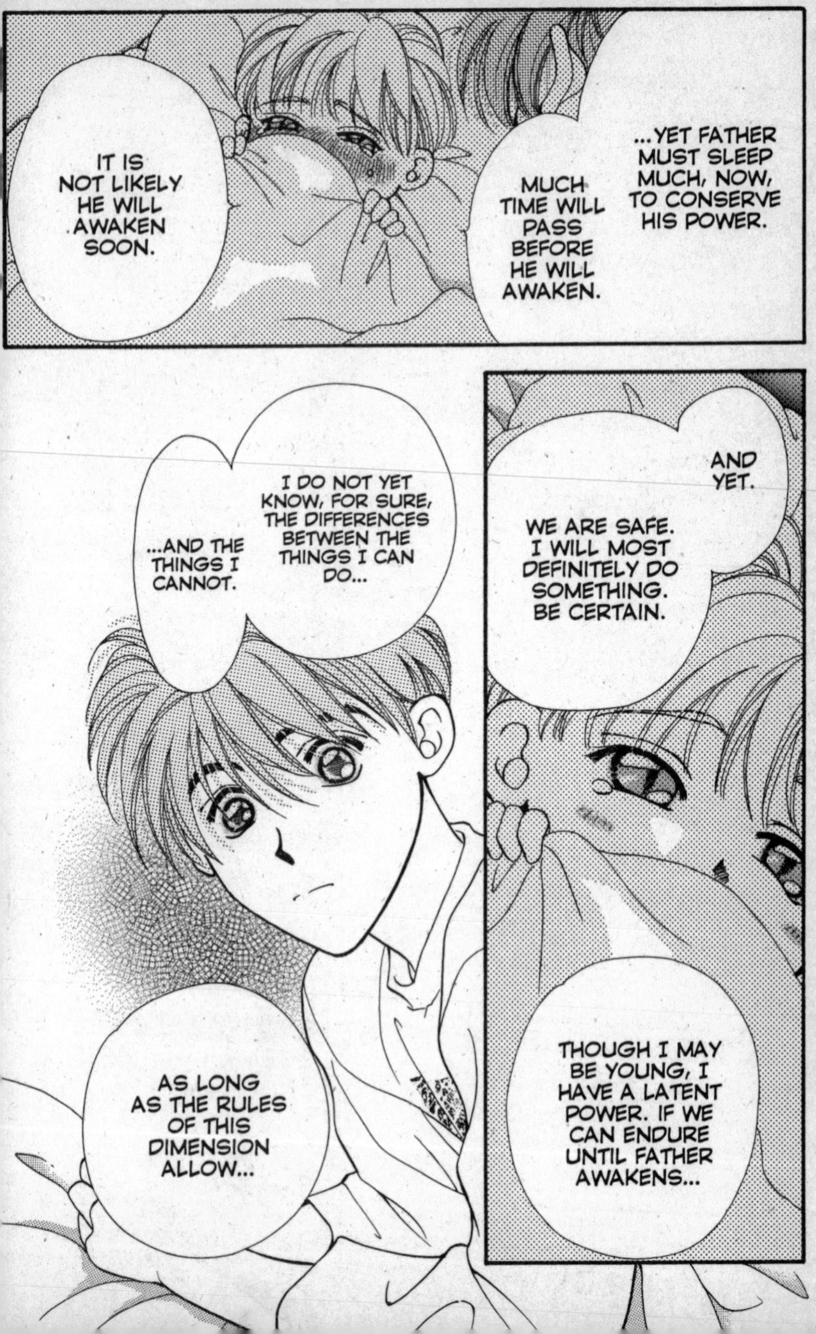
...YET FATHER MUST SLEEP MUCH, NOW, TO CONSERVE HIS POWER.
MUCH TIME WILL PASS BEFORE HE WILL AWAKEN.
IT IS NOT LIKELY HE WILL AWAKEN SOON.
AND YET.
WE ARE SAFE. I WILL MOST DEFINITELY DO SOMETHING. BE CERTAIN.
THOUGH I MAY BE YOUNG, I HAVE A LATENT POWER. IF WE CAN ENDURE UNTIL FATHER AWAKENS...
I DO NOT YET KNOW, FOR SURE, THE DIFFERENCES BETWEEN THE THINGS I CAN DO...
...AND THE THINGS I CANNOT.
AS LONG AS THE RULES OF THIS DIMENSION ALLOW...

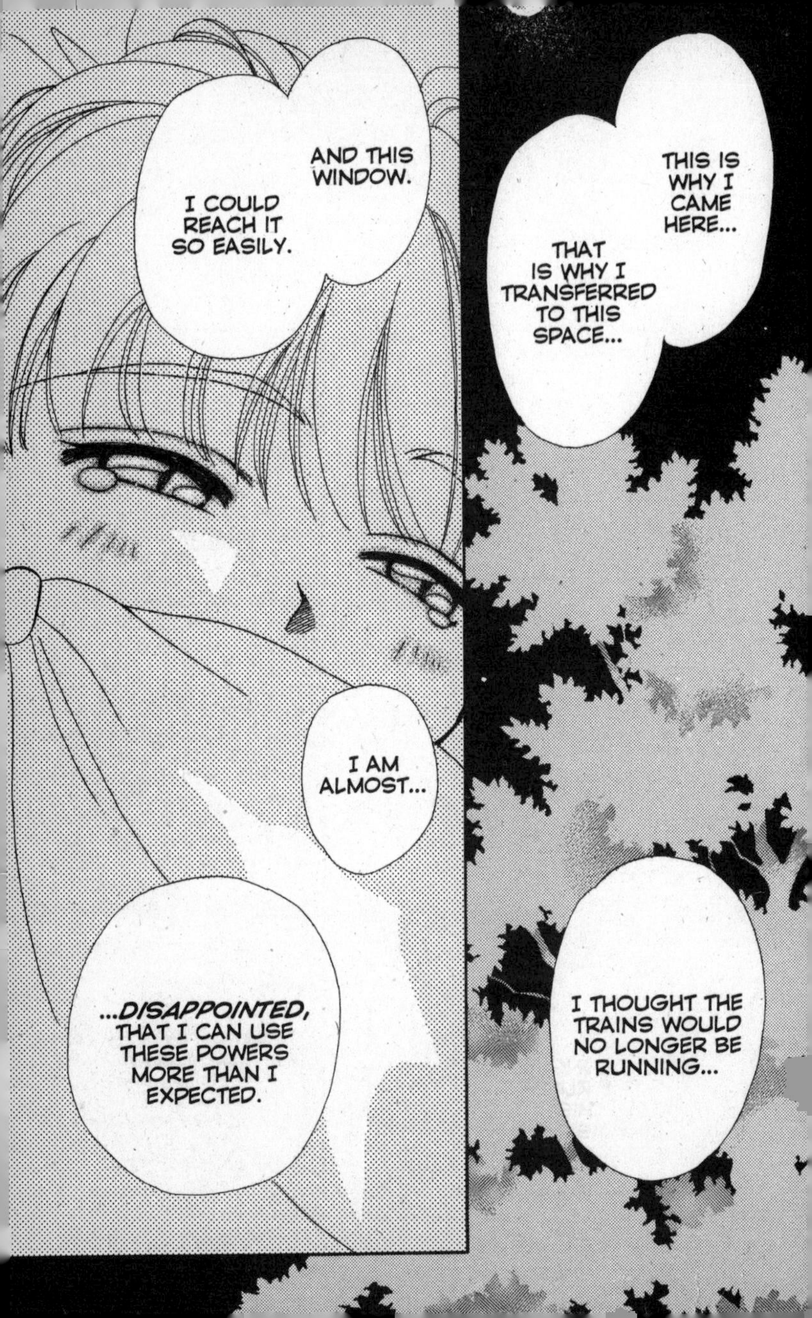
THIS IS WHY I CAME HERE...
THAT IS WHY I TRANSFERRED TO THIS SPACE...
I THOUGHT THE TRAINS WOULD NO LONGER BE RUNNING...
AND THIS WINDOW.
I COULD REACH IT SO EASILY.
I AM ALMOST...
...*DISAPPOINTED,* THAT I CAN USE THESE POWERS MORE THAN I EXPECTED.

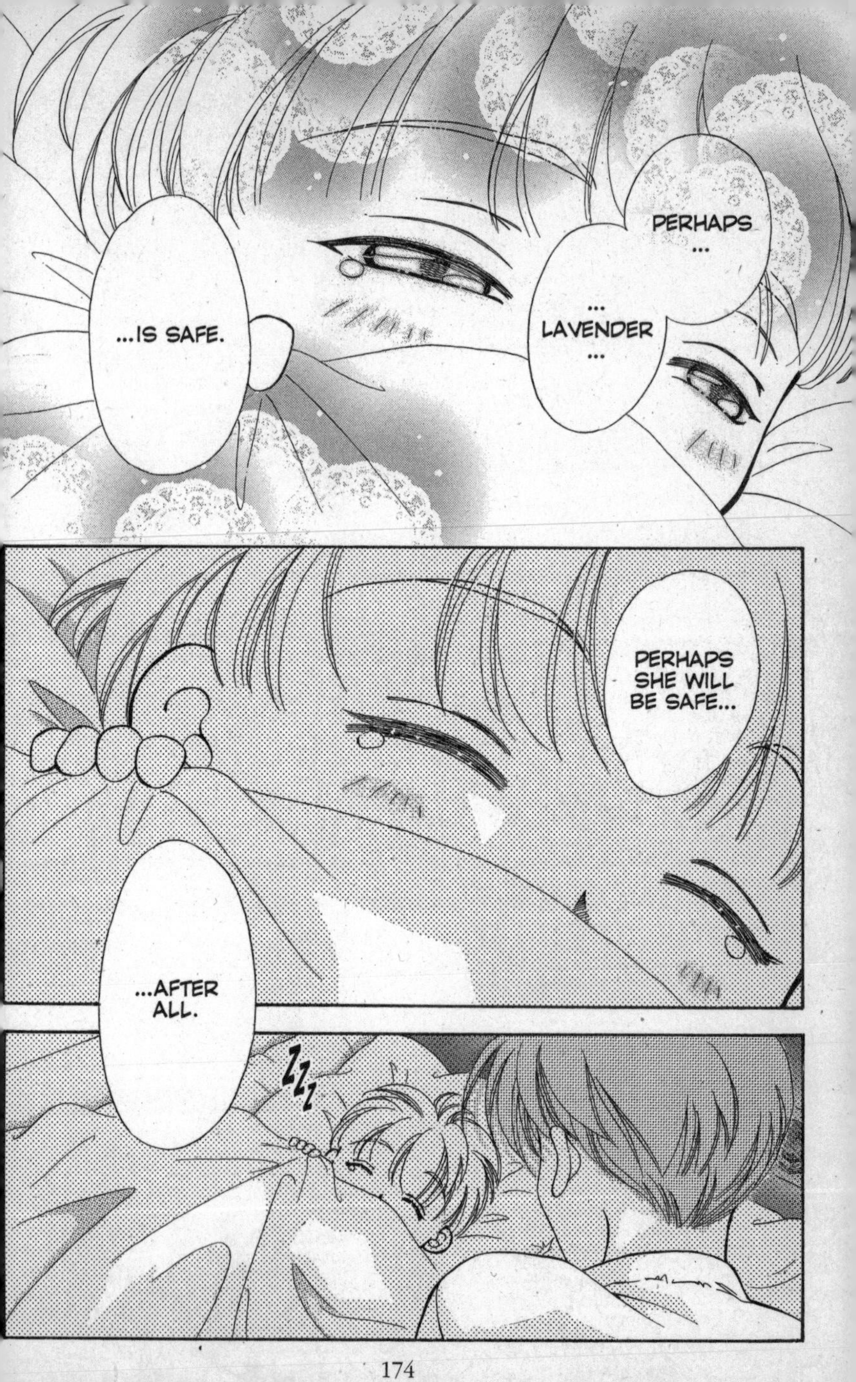
PERHAPS ...
... LAVENDER ...
...IS SAFE.
PERHAPS SHE WILL BE SAFE...
...AFTER ALL.
ZZZ

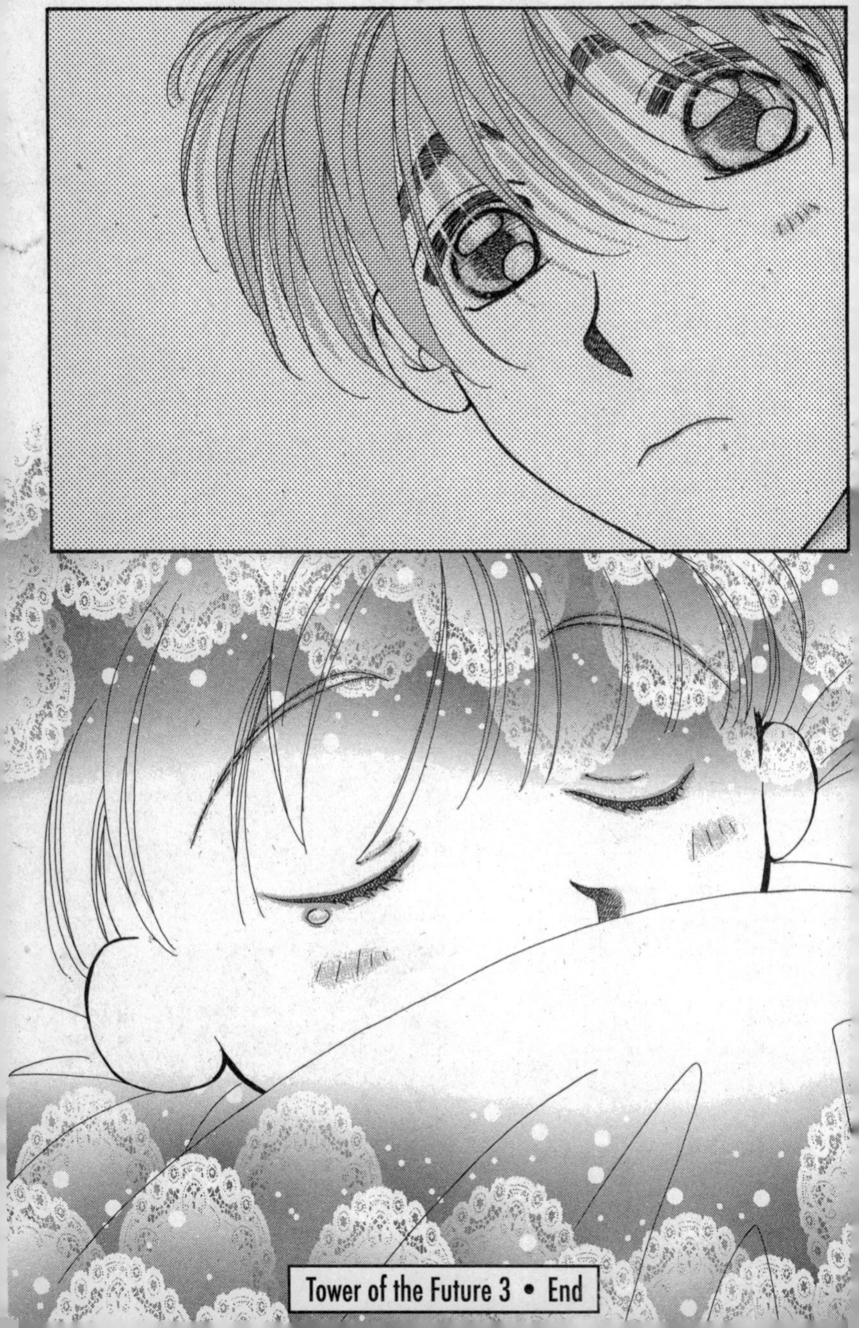
Tower of the Future 3 • End

FLIP IT!!

All the pages in this book were created—and are printed here—in Japanese RIGHT-to-LEFT format. No artwork has been reversed or altered, so you can read the stories the way the creators meant for them to be read.

RIGHT TO LEFT?!

Traditional Japanese manga starts at the upper right-hand corner, and moves right-to-left as it goes down the page. Follow this guide for an easy understanding.

MIRAI NO UTENA Volume 3 by Saki Hiwatari © 1994 Saki Hiwatari All Rights reserved. First published in Japan in 2003 by HAKUSENSHA, INC.

POWER OF THE FUTURE Volume 3 published by WildStorm Productions, an imprint of DC Comics, 888 Prospect St. #240, La Jolla, CA 92037. English Translation © 2006. All Rights Reserved. English translation rights in U.S.A. and Canada arranged by HAKUSENSHA, INC. through Tuttle-Mori Agency, Inc., Tokyo. The stories, characters, and incidents mentioned in this magazine are entirely fictional. Printed on recyclable paper. WildStorm does not read or accept unsolicited submissions of ideas, stories or artwork. Printed in Canada.

 DC Comics, a Warner Bros. Entertainment Company.

Tim Rogers – Translation and adaptation

Cameron Bennett – Lettering

Larry Berry – Design

Jim Chadwick– Editor

ISBN: 1-4012-0816-9
ISBN-13: 978-1-4012-0816-5

190320